Reading Sex in the Eighteenth Century

D1593163

Karen Harvey explores the construction of sexual difference and gender identity in eighteenth-century England. Using erotic texts and their illustrations,
and rooting this evidence firmly in historical context, Harvey provides a thoroughgoing critique of the orthodoxy of recent work on sexual difference in
the history of the body. She argues that eighteenth-century English erotic culture combined a distinctive mode of writing and reading in which the form of
refinement was applied to the matter of sex. Erotic culture was male-centred
and it was in this environment, Harvey argues, that men could enjoy both
the bawdy, raucous, libidinous elements of the eighteenth century and the
refined politeness for which the period is also renowned. This book makes
a significant contribution to the history of masculinity and advocates a new
approach to change in gender history, one capable of capturing the processes
of negotiation and contestation integral to cultural change.

KAREN HARVEY is a Lecturer in Cultural History at the University of
Sheffield. She is the editor of *The Kiss in History* (2004).

A HRB

Arts + Humanities

Research Board

Cambridge Social and Cultural Histories

Series Editors:

Margot C. Finn, *University of Warwick*
Colin Jones, *University of Warwick*
Keith Wrightson, *Yale University*

New cultural histories have recently expanded the parameters (and enriched the methodologies) of social history. Cambridge Social and Cultural Histories recognizes the plurality of current approaches to social and cultural history as distinctive points of entry into a common explanatory project. Open to innovative and interdisciplinary work, regardless of its chronological or geographical location, the series encompasses a broad range of histories of social relationships and of the cultures that inform them and lend them meaning. Historical anthropology, historical sociology, comparative history, gender history and historicist literary studies – among other subjects – all fall within the remit of Cambridge Social and Cultural Histories.

Titles in the series:
1 Margot C. Finn *The Character of Credit: Personal Debt in English Culture, 1740–1914*
   ISBN 0 521 82342 0
2 M. J. D. Roberts *Making English Morals: Volunteer Association and Moral Reform in England, 1787–1886*
   ISBN 0 521 83389 2
3 Karen Harvey *Reading Sex in the Eighteenth Century: Bodies and Gender in English Erotic Culture*
   ISBN 0 521 82235 1

Reading Sex in the Eighteenth Century

Bodies and Gender in English Erotic Culture

Karen Harvey

University of Sheffield

CAMBRIDGE
UNIVERSITY PRESS

CAMBRIDGE UNIVERSITY PRESS
Cambridge, New York, Melbourne, Madrid, Cape Town, Singapore, São Paulo

Cambridge University Press
The Edinburgh Building, Cambridge CB2 8RU, UK

Published in the United States of America by Cambridge University Press, New York

www.cambridge.org
Information on this title: www.cambridge.org/9780521822350

First published 2004
This digitally printed version 2008

A catalogue record for this publication is available from the British Library

Library of Congress Cataloguing in Publication data
Harvey, Karen, 1971 –
Reading sex in the eighteenth century : bodies and gender in English erotic culture /
Karen Harvey.
    p.   cm. – (Cambridge social and cultural histories; 3)
Includes bibliographical references and index.
ISBN 0 521 82235 1
1. English literature – 18th century – History and criticism.   2. Erotic literature,
English – History and criticism.   3. Gender identity in literature.   4. Body, Human,
in literature.   5. Sex in literature.   I. Title.   II. Series.
PR448.E75H37   2004
820.09´3538´09033 – dc22   2004045743

ISBN 978-0-521-82235-0 hardback
ISBN 978-0-521-05572-7 paperback

Contents

List of illustrations   *page* vi
Acknowledgements   viii

Introduction   1

1   Contexts   35

2   Sexual difference   78

3   Female bodies   102

4   Male bodies   124

5   Space   146

6   Movement   175

7   Pleasure   199

Conclusion   222

Bibliography   226
Index   256

Illustrations

1 Pandora's Box. Frontispiece to *A New Description of Merryland*,
7th edn. (1741). By permission of the British Library.   *page* 14

2 *The Dog* (1784). Inserted in *A Voyage to Lethe* (1741) BL:
Cup.1001.c.4. By permission of the British Library.   15

3 Masturbation in the kitchen. Inserted in *A Voyage to Lethe* (1741)
BL: Cup.1001.c.4. By permission of the British Library.   17

4 *Entwine. The Myrtle of Venus with Bacchus's Vine*. Frontispiece to
The Bacchanalian Magazine (1793). By permission of the British
Library.   53

5 Richard Cosway, *Group of Connoisseurs* (1771–5). By permission
of Towneley Hall Art Gallery and Museum, Burnley.   69

6 William Hogarth, *A Midnight Modern Conversation* (c. 1732). By
permission of Yale Center for British Art.   70

7 James Worsdale, *The Limerick Hell-Fire Club* (c. 1736). By
permission of the National Gallery of Ireland.   72

8 *The Jolly Bacchanals*. In *The Bacchanalian Magazine* (1793). By
permission of the British Library.   73

9 A female body as grotto. Frontispiece to *Little Merlin's Cave*
(1737). By permission of the British Library.   92

10 Female genitals as grotto and the male genitals as tree. *Arbor
Vitae: or, the Natural History of the Tree of Life* (For E. Hill, 1741).
By permission of the British Library.   92

11 *The Torpedo or I am not what I seem*. Title page of *The Electrical
Eel; or Gymnotus Electricus: and, The Torpedo*
(c. 1774). By permission of the British Library.   107

12 *Propagation by the Bud; and by the Branch*. In *Great News from
Hell* (1760). By permission of the British Library.   115

13 The great upright torch thistle. Richard Bradley's *History of
Succulent Plants* (1716). By permission of the British Library.   135

14 *The Peeper, or a stolen View of Lady C's Premises*. Inserted in *A
Voyage to Lethe* (1741) BL: Cup.1001.c.4. By permission of the
British Library.   153

15 Timante enters Araminta's bed-chamber. Frontispiece to *The Surprize* (1739). By permission of the British Library. 154

16 *The Three Gracelesses*. Inserted in *A Voyage to Lethe* (1741) BL: Cup.1001.c.4. By permission of the British Library. 155

17 Woman and child in suggestive scene. Inserted in *A Voyage to Lethe* (1741) BL: Cup.1001.c.4. By permission of the British Library. 160

18 Armchair scene by the fire. Inserted in *A Voyage to Lethe* (1741) BL: Cup.1001.c.4. By permission of the British Library. 161

19 Sofa scene I. Inserted in *A Voyage to Lethe* (1741) BL: Cup.1001.c.4. By permission of the British Library. 163

20 Sofa scene II. Inserted in *A Voyage to Lethe* (1741) BL: Cup.1001.c.4. By permission of the British Library. 164

21 *The Priest-ridden Washerwoman*. In *The Bacchanalian Magazine* (1793). By permission of the British Library. 168

22 J. Wake, *The Sailor's Adventure to the Streights of Merryland Or, An Evening View on Ludgate Hill*, engraved by John June (1749). By permission of Guildhall Library, Corporation of London. 169

23 A female torso and reproductive organs. Francis Mauriceau's *The Diseases of Women with Child* (1736). By permission of the British Library. 182

24 *A Map or Chart of the Road of Love*. Inserted in *A Voyage to Lethe* (1741) BL: Cup.1001.c.4. By permission of the British Library. 183

25 *A Fine Subject on the Carpet*. Inserted in *A Voyage to Lethe* (1741) BL: Cup.1001.c.4. By permission of the British Library. 189

26 Sexual violence. Frontispiece of *Kick Him Jenny* (1737). By permission of the British Library. 194

27 The wedding night. From title page of *Kick Him Nan* (1734). By permission of the British Library. 195

Acknowledgements

Encounters with four women have shaped this book. Ann Hughes introduced me to women's history as an undergraduate, and supervised my first piece of work on the body. Lyndal Roper had a formative impact during my postgraduate studies and beyond; throughout she has been extremely generous with her time and thoughts. Pene Corfield provided a warm yet steadying hand during my PhD, and posed some vital questions that have made this work what it is. My greatest debt is to Amanda Vickery, who lit up the eighteenth century for me and was critical in my decision to undertake a PhD. As a supervisor she was ever the enthusiast; since then she has been a dear friend.

I am also grateful to several people who have read earlier versions of this work. As my PhD examiners, the late Roy Porter and Mark Jenner asked provocative questions – both big and small – and forced me to think more broadly and more carefully about the book. James Raven gave suggestions on chapter one far too numerous to mention. In various forms, this work was also read by Mike Braddick, Sandra Cavallo, Justin Champion, Michèle Cohen, Lyndal Roper, Eve Setch, Nick Stargardt, David Stevenson and Nick Webb. I am also very grateful for the extremely valuable reports of the two anonymous readers for Cambridge University Press.

Several people have made significant comments or given important references. These include Francesca Berry, Arthur Burns, Anna Clark, Seth Denbo, Charlotte Grant, A. D. Harvey, Clare Haynes, Judith Hawley, Martin Lengwiler, Anthony Milton, John Mullan, Miles Ogborn, John Sainsbury, Nick Webb and Helen Weinstein. Academic audiences too numerous to mention have listened and commented.

I have also benefited from discussions with a number of friends and colleagues, including Sarah Barry, Helen Berry, Hera Cook, Brian Cowan, Seth Denbo, Jonathan Durrant, Tanya Evans, Tim Hitchcock, Eve Setch, Bob Shoemaker, Richard Tacey, Sarah Toulalan, David Turner and Susan Whyman.

The research for this book was funded by several awards from the British Academy. The Royal Historical Society provided additional support. I would like to thank staff at the British Library, Sheffield University Library Special

Collections, Chetham's Library in Manchester, the William Andrews Clark Memorial Library, UCLA, and The Huntington Library in California.

I am grateful to all the staff at Cambridge University Press, and particularly to Elizabeth Howard. Caroline Howlett performed a careful job on the copy-editing, though all errors remain my own.

An earlier version of chapter two was published as 'The Substance of Sexual Difference: Change and Persistence in Eighteenth-Century Representations of the Body', *Gender and History* 14 (2002), pp. 202–23, reproduced courtesy of Blackwell Publishing. Sections of chapter four appeared in '"The Majesty of the Masculine Form": Multiplicity and Male Bodies in Eighteenth-Century Erotica', in Tim Hitchcock and Michèle Cohen (eds.), *English Masculinities, 1660–1800* (Harlow: Longman, 1999), pp. 193–214, and are reproduced courtesy of Pearson Educational. Some of the material which appears in chapter five was discussed in 'Gender, Space and Modernity in Eighteenth-Century England: A Place Called Sex', *History Workshop Journal* 51 (2001), pp. 158–79, and is reproduced by permission of Oxford University Press. Sections of chapter six are also discussed in 'Spaces of Erotic Delight', in Miles Ogborn and Charles W. J. Withers (eds.), *Georgian Geographies: Space, Place and Landscape in the Eighteenth Century* (Manchester: Manchester University Press, 2004), reproduced by permission of Manchester University Press.

The book was written and rewritten during posts in the Department of History at the University of Manchester, and at the AHRB Centre for the Study of the Domestic Interior (based at the Royal College of Art, the Victoria and Albert Museum, and Royal Holloway). I am very appreciative of the support given by Hannah Barker at Manchester and by Jeremy Aynsley, John Styles and Amanda Vickery at the CSDI. The race to the finish was enabled by the Department of History at the University of Sheffield and particularly to the generosity of Professor Edmund King.

But there are more personal debts to acknowledge. Nick Webb saw this project take shape as a PhD thesis. He gave loving companionship and intellectual support throughout, and sustained me through the process.

My parents have never flinched either at the cost of putting their daughter through years of education or at the topics she has chosen to study. For their loving and laissez-faire support I will always be extremely grateful.

Lastly, I would like to thank Mike Braddick. He has been a true helpmeet throughout the writing of this book, generous with his thoughts and his time, and patiently picking up the slack when my job as historian has encroached on my responsibilities as wife and as mother to Cora. In thanks for his love and support, this book is for him.

Introduction

> Politeness was primarily about the social control of the individual at a time of intense enthusiasm for individual rights and responsibilities.[1]

> Amongst the affluent and leisured, sexuality thawed out. The libido was liberated and erotic gratification was dissociated from sin and shame.[2]

The 'identity' of eighteenth century England has provoked much debate, with discussion often turning on the relative vibrancy of features displaying 'modernity' or the lingering aspects of an 'ancien regime'.[3] The polite vision of Langford and the Enlightened, liberated world seen by Porter share an emphasis on the eighteenth century looking forward. Yet these are contrasting pictures: on the one hand, we see a time of control and restraint; on the other, a time of freedom and licence. The allure and distinctiveness of eighteenth-century erotic culture – centring on erotic texts and images and comprising particular modes of cultural practice – was its ambiguous relationship to both aspects of eighteenth-century England. Erotic culture promised sexual gratification of a kind, but unbridled pleasure flew in the face of eighteenth-century restraint. The tone of eighteenth-century erotic culture, therefore, was not one of reckless sexual frenzy. Instead, producers of erotic material rendered depictions of sex and bodies hazy, and cloaks of metaphor and suspended denouements forged a decorous distance between reader and text. This stylistic temperance was accompanied by embargoes placed on the type of liaison in which characters

---

[1] Paul Langford, *A Polite and Commercial People: England, 1727–1783* (Oxford: Oxford University Press, 1989), p. 5.

[2] Roy Porter, *English Society in the Eighteenth Century* (Harmondsworth: Penguin, 1982), p. 278.

[3] J. C. D. Clark, *English Society, 1688–1832: Ideology, Social Structure and Political Practice during the Ancien Regime* (Cambridge: Cambridge University Press, 1985). The second edition is published as *English Society, 1660–1832* (Cambridge: Cambridge University Press, 2000). For accounts emphasizing the 'modern' aspects of this society, see, for example, N. McKendrick, J. Brewer and J. H. Plumb, *The Birth of a Consumer Society: The Commercialisation of Eighteenth-Century England* (London: Europa, 1982) and Miles Ogborn, *Spaces of Modernity: London's Geographies, 1680–1780* (New York: Guilford Press, 1998). Anthony Fletcher sets up a similar contrast between politeness and sexual freedom in the eighteenth century in *Gender, Sex and Subordination in England 1500–1800* (New Haven: Yale University Press, 1995), pp. 339–46. His interpretation of this is significantly different from my own. I engage with this issue in chapter one.

1

engaged: kindly depiction was reserved for potentially reproductive sexual acts. The liberated libido was constrained by consistently demarcated desire. Wily though some of their measures may have been, the producers and consumers of erotic material prided themselves on their resistance to naked, unabashed voluptuousness. The pleasures of eighteenth-century erotic culture certainly indulged the libido, but they also championed individual self-control. At the heart of erotic culture were the many hundred English erotic books and their illustrations, and the saturation of this material with depictions of the female form is testament to the fascination men had with women's bodies. The pleasures of erotic culture were those of 'Merryland', an imaginary place which promised the delights of sex and female bodies.[4] These depictions carried complex ideas about women and femininity, and in particular about sexual difference. The core of this book explores these understandings of sexual difference in erotic texts and images. But this is framed by placing erotic material in a context, by considering the social and cultural conditions of reading erotica.[5] In analysing both representations of sexual difference and the reading of sex, this book seeks to explore meaning in context.

In adopting this approach, I want to build on a brand of cultural history that focuses on meaning and culture. Cultural history is often defined by its object of study, and it is true that cultural history is distinguished from art history, literary history and intellectual history in part by a relatively broad and coherent definition of 'culture' inspired by anthropologists.[6] Perhaps the most influential definition is that of the anthropologist Clifford Geertz, for whom culture was 'an historically transmitted pattern of meanings embodied in symbols'.[7] In this tradition, cultural history is most readily defined as 'a history of representation', juxtaposed against a social history interested in experience.[8] As Catherine Belsey puts it, '[s]ocial history gives priority to describing practices, while cultural history records meanings'.[9] However, I contend that the social and cultural context of meaning is critical to our comprehension of meaning, and this book focuses on both the discursive and the material aspects of erotic

---

[4] See chapter five for a discussion of the term 'Merryland' and its significance.

[5] I use the term 'erotica' as a singular noun throughout this book. Although the *OED* records only the plural noun, this seems to be out of step with common usage.

[6] Peter Burke, 'Overture: The New History, its Past and its Future', in Peter Burke (ed.), *New Perspectives on Historical Writing* (Cambridge: Polity Press, 1991), p. 2; Robert Darnton, 'Intellectual and Cultural History', in Michael Kammen (ed.), *The Past Before US: Contemporary Historical Writing in the United States* (Ithaca, N.Y.: Cornell University Press, 1980), p. 347.

[7] Clifford Geertz, 'Religion as a Cultural System', in his *The Interpretation of Cultures: Selected Essays* (1973; London: Fontana, 1993), p. 89.

[8] Catherine Belsey, 'Reading Cultural History', in Tamsin Spargo (ed.), *Reading the Past: Literature and History* (Basingstoke: Palgrave, 2000), p. 106. See also Lynn Hunt, 'Introduction: History, Culture, and Text', in Lynn Hunt (ed.), *The New Cultural History* (Berkeley: University of California Press, 1989), p. 19.

[9] Belsey, 'Reading Cultural History', p. 107.

culture. There are important literary and textual contexts for erotica that are explored here, but there is a social and cultural context of reading that can be reconstructed, and which roots a cultural history of meaning in an experiential world. The later chapters of this book consider the representations of male and female bodies in erotic material, but chapter one presents the context of a gendered model of reading. Sex and gender differences were constructed both in erotic texts and through the reading of erotic texts.

The material, social and spatial contexts of this material are crucial; the broader cultural contexts of the ideas which circulated within erotic culture are also key. We should not view erotica as a marginal or underside feature of the eighteenth century; it was not fenced off from the rest of eighteenth-century culture, but was shaped by and reflected a number of contemporary developments: economic and social (agricultural innovation, enclosure, the acquisition of colonies), cultural (the expansion of the public sphere, the growth of the reading public, the Enlightenment and cosmopolitanism), literary (the lapse of pre-publication censorship in 1695, Grub Street plagiarism and the rise of the novel) and scientific (overseas exploration and the emergence of new bodies of knowledge such as botany). For example, depictions of sex and sexual relations were shaped by geographical knowledge and its modes of expression, as discussed in chapter six. But while these authors drew on modes of geographical knowledge, they also satirized them. In their deployment of geographical modes, those involved in erotic culture played with notions of truth and knowledge, blurring the distinction between empirical knowledge and imaginary knowledge, even calling into question the ideological underpinnings of the Enlightenment.

The degree to which erotic authors were engaged in this lively cultural exchange is striking. Historians have discussed 'shared cultures' for some time, but the cultural processes of selection, exchange, translation and reiteration are rarely explored.[10] In this study, it will emerge that erotic books did not simply transport previously formed ideas into an erotic context. Instead, erotic authors selected ideas about gender and bodies in a strategic way, and these ideas were transformed in the transplantation to erotica. This was very clear in erotic discussions of sexual difference. In their attempts to convey both sexual equivalence and male superiority, erotic authors found existing scientific and medical theories wanting; they therefore combined aspects of apparently conflicting theories in their discussions of how male and female bodies worked, forging a distinct vision of sexual difference. Erotic authors performed many such acts

[10] Quote from Ludmilla Jordanova, 'Introduction', in her *Languages of Nature: Critical Essays on Science and Literature* (London: Free Association Books, 1986), p. 17. A rare example of work on processes of cultural exchange is Robert Darnton's study of the clandestine books of revolutionary France. See his *The Forbidden Best-Sellers of Pre-Revolutionary France* (New York: Norton, 1995), especially pp. 181–97.

of selective borrowing from several eighteenth-century fiction and non-fiction genres. Indeed, one of the distinctive features of erotica was its absorbency and reflexivity with regard to other genres and contemporary events. This genre was fully embedded in eighteenth-century culture and can therefore tell us much about England between 1700 and 1800.

Gender history

As much of the point of erotica was (and is) sex and desire, this material is particularly useful for thinking about eighteenth-century understandings of bodies and gender. Indeed, eighteenth-century erotic material was a genre very much concerned with gender and bodies at a time when gender relations and ideas about sexual difference allegedly underwent considerable change. In the dominant narrative of pre-twentieth-century women's history, the eighteenth century is a pivotal moment. This narrative might be usefully separated into three distinct but interlinked strands, concerning female gender roles, female sexuality, and understandings of bodies.[11] Women's historians have long been arguing that a new middle-class female character appeared on the cultural scene in the eighteenth century. She was a chaste and modest wifely figure, firmly ensconced in a privatized nuclear family.[12] The apogee of a new domesticity, this woman was in part the product of industrial development. Building on well-established narratives of economic history, historians have argued that middle-class women were increasingly associated with home, and pushed out of the world of paid work.[13] Changes in female gender roles are apparently mirrored in changes in early-modern female sexuality. The key moment was the eighteenth century, when the desiring, appetitive early-modern woman was replaced by her prudish, passive and constrained nineteenth-century successor. Affectionate but asexual, this less lusty woman was a counterpart to the newly domesticated middle-class woman in the home.[14]

[11] See Karen Harvey, 'The Century of Sex? Gender, Bodies and Sexuality in the Long Eighteenth Century', *The Historical Journal* 45 (2002), pp. 899–916.
[12] Margaret George, 'From "Goodwife" to "Mistress": The Transformation of the Female in Bourgeois Culture', *Science and Society* 37 (1973); Nancy Armstrong, *Desire and Domestic Fiction: A Political History of the Novel* (Oxford: Oxford University Press, 1987).
[13] The classic accounts are Alice Clark, *Working Life of Women in the Seventeenth Century* (1919; London: Routledge, 1992) and Ivy Pinchbeck, *Women Workers and the Industrial Revolution, 1750–1850* (1930; London: Virago, 1981). For more recent refinements, see Leonore Davidoff and Catherine Hall, *Family Fortunes: Men and Women of the English Middle Class, 1780–1850* (London: Routledge, 1987) and Bridget Hill, *Women, Work and Sexual Politics in the Eighteenth Century* (1989; Montreal: McGill-Queen's University Press, 1994). For a critical account of this work, see Amanda Vickery, 'Golden Age to Separate Spheres? A Review of the Categories and Chronology of English Women's History', *The Historical Journal* 36 (1993), pp. 383–414.
[14] Angus McLaren, 'The Pleasures of Procreation: Traditional and Biomedical Theories of Conception', in W. F. Bynum and Roy Porter (eds.), *William Hunter and the Eighteenth-Century*

Older stories of change about female gender roles and sexuality have been reinvigorated by recent work on the history of the body and sexual difference. The key statement is by Thomas Laqueur in his *Making Sex: Body and Gender from the Greeks to Freud* (1990), described as 'perhaps the most influential work of medical history published in the last two decades'.[15] Laqueur argued that 'in or about the late eighteenth century' there occurred a shift in the way that human bodies were understood.[16] Using elite scientific and medical texts, Laqueur suggested that prior to the eighteenth century men and women were placed on a vertical, hierarchical axis, in which their bodies were seen as two comparable variants of one kind whose bodies were structurally the same. Sexual difference was understood through a 'one-sex' model. After the eighteenth century, Laqueur argued, a 'two-sex' model achieved hegemony. Women and men were arranged horizontally: anatomical differences were stressed, and their bodies were seen as qualitatively distinct. Modern and opposite sexes were thus born in the eighteenth century. In many accounts, this argument about sexual difference is melded with narratives of gender roles and sexual desire:

In the 1700s and before, women were assumed to resemble men. Even their bodies – though of course less perfect – were thought to resemble men's. Hence, women were assumed to be sensual and strong, to be nearly as independent after marriage as before. By 1788 this female being who had been defined chiefly as a lesser man had been redefined as a separate and oppositional being, by 'nature' chaste and domestic.[17]

Work on women's gender roles, sexuality and, most recently, the body has been compressed to produce a deep and broad narrative of women's history in which the eighteenth century is key, and this narrative suggests a vision

Medical World (Cambridge: Cambridge University Press, 1985), p. 340. See also Carolyn Merchant, *The Death of Nature: Women, Ecology, and the Scientific Revolution* (London: Wildwood House, 1982); Luisa Accati, 'The Spirit of Fornication: Virtue of the Soul and Virtue of the Body in Friuli, 1600–1800', in E. Muir and G. Ruggiero (eds.), *Sex and Gender in Historical Perspective* (Baltimore: Johns Hopkins University Press, 1990); Kimberly Crouch, 'The Public Life of Actresses: Prostitutes or Ladies?', in Hannah Barker and Elaine Chalus (eds.), *Gender in Eighteenth-Century England: Roles, Representations and Responsibilities* (Harlow: Longman, 1997), pp. 58–78; Ruth Perry, 'Colonising the Breast: Sexuality and Maternity in Eighteenth-Century England', in J. C. Fout (ed.), *Forbidden History: The State, Society, and the Regulation of Sexuality in Modern Europe* (Chicago: University of Chicago Press, 1992); Londa Schiebinger, 'Skeletons in the Closet: The First Illustrations of the Female Skeleton in Eighteenth-Century Anatomy', in C. Gallagher and T. Laqueur (eds.), *The Making of the Modern Body: Sexuality and Society in the Nineteenth Century* (Berkeley: University of California Press, 1987); Londa Schiebinger, 'Gender and Natural History', in N. Jardine, J. A. Secord and E. C. Spary (eds.), *Cultures of Natural History* (Cambridge: Cambridge University Press, 1996), p. 163.
[15] Mark S. R. Jenner and Bertrand O. Taithe, 'The Historiographical Body', in R. Cooter and J. Pickstone (eds.), *Medicine in the Twentieth Century* (Amsterdam: Harwood Academic, 2000), p. 191.
[16] Thomas Laqueur, *Making Sex: Body and Gender from the Greeks to Freud* (Cambridge, Mass.: Harvard University Press, 1990), p. 5.
[17] Janice Farrar Thaddeus, 'Mary Delany, Model to the Age', in Beth Fowkes Tobin (ed.), *History, Gender and Eighteenth-Century Literature* (Athens: University of Georgia Press, 1994), p. 113.

not simply of changing roles or ideals, but of increased rigidity and closure in the nature of those ideals. As this has variously been described, image-makers were 'defining male/female relations with new exactness', 'greater definitional rigour was imposed on gender roles', and women suffered 'the long march of the empires of gender over the entirety of the person'.[18] Individuals were increasingly saturated with gender.

Making Sex has been crucial for historians of gender, not simply offering fresh ways to think about bodies and sexual difference, but for many enabling us to think about them. The groundbreaking nature of the book is reflected in the incorporation of Laqueur's central thesis – that there was a massive change in the way bodies were understood to differ from one another – into many recent works of women's and gender history.[19] Given the dominance of these ideas in accounts of the eighteenth century, we need to ask how widespread and how widely felt were these changes. In part, this book is a lengthy engagement with Laqueur's argument; I want to assess the extent to which understandings of bodies and sexual difference in erotic culture can be understood through the one-sex to two-sex vision of change. In so doing, I will engage with what I see as a series of limitations with the dominant narrative of women's history.

The first problem is with the conceptualization of change. The allure of the dominant narrative is in part its compelling fusion of older economic and political histories with newer fields of inquiry. This serves the important function of resisting the marginalization of the histories of women, gender and bodies. Certainly Laqueur's book is positioned against a backdrop of a number of economic, social and cultural developments, ranging from the rise of Evangelicalism and factories to the French Revolution and the birth of classes. The driving force behind changing understandings of bodies, however, was political. In order to bolster political theorists' use of the language of natural rights, bodies were redefined as opposite sexes: power could only be formally granted to one group (men) and withheld from another (women) if those groups were distinct and incommensurable.[20] '[N]atural rights could be countered only by

---

[18] George, 'From "Goodwife" to "Mistress"', p. 159; Tim Hitchcock, 'Redefining Sex in Eighteenth-Century England', *History Workshop Journal* 41 (1996), p. 77; Denise Riley, '*Am I That Name?*': *Feminism and the Category of 'Women' in History* (London: Macmillan, 1988), p. 14.

[19] See, for example, Kathleen Brown, ' "Changed . . . into the Fashion of a Man": The Politics of Sexual Difference in a Seventeenth-Century Anglo-American Settlement', *Journal of the History of Sexuality* 6 (1995), p. 173; Fletcher, *Gender, Sex and Subordination*, pp. 291, 402, 407; Hitchcock, 'Redefining Sex'; Michael McKeon, 'Historicizing Patriarchy: The Emergence of Gender Difference in England, 1660–1760', *Eighteenth-Century Studies* 28 (1995), pp. 300–1; Robert B. Shoemaker, *Gender in English Society, 1650–1850: The Emergence of Separate Spheres?* (Harlow: Longman, 1998), pp. 31–5, 85, 313–14; Randolph Trumbach, *Sex and the Gender Revolution. Volume I: Heterosexuality and the Third Gender in Enlightenment London* (Chicago: University of Chicago Press, 1998), pp. 1–11. For a more detailed discussion of the place of the body in work on gender, see the discussion in chapter two. This work is discussed at greater length in Harvey, 'Century of Sex?'.

[20] Laqueur, *Making Sex*, pp. 194–207.

proof of natural inequalities.'[21] Political theory was legitimized by science and medicine.

There are problems in applying older narratives of change to new areas, though, and the fastening of the history of the body to a political narrative has provoked criticism. Discussed more fully in chapter two, these critiques all suggest that the linear chronology of Laqueur is flawed. Similarly, erotic discussions of sexual difference cannot be encapsulated in period-specific models. There was considerable endurance in discussions of sexual difference, combined with short-term shifts in language. Moreover, discussions of female and male seemed subject to distinct forces for change. Representation of female bodies, discussed in chapter three, reveals a considerable degree of persistence; in contrast, as chapter four argues, discussions of male bodies displayed a sharper degree of historical specificity. Clearly, models of change established in one arena cannot necessarily be transplanted into another. But much gender history deals poorly with change, and this arises in part from its roots in cultural history, a field which is strongest in its analysis of the synchronic rather than the diachronic. As Peter Burke said of the culturally inflected 'new history', it has been united, not by a 'narrative of events', but by the 'analysis of structures'.[22] But there are ways in which change in culture can be studied without recourse to the established narratives of economic and political development. First, indebted to the Annales school and historians of mentalities, cultural historians combine change and persistence, exploring how 'new structures may be superimposed upon old ones'.[23] Second, often emerging from work on transmission and reception, cultural historians can expose change by exploring conflict and difference within cultures, and by analysing how these processes generate new positions.[24] This book combines these approaches to change and transformation. It does not seek to replace a story of linear change with one of stasis and continuity; rather, it shows that eighteenth-century understandings of bodies combined the old and the new and that the integration of the new involved debate and the production of new understandings.

In transplanting one narrative of change to another area we are essentially interpreting one body of evidence through the conclusions drawn from another. The influential tripartite vision of women's history encompasses a wide range of evidence. The claim that bodies, gender and sexuality were redefined because of debates in political theory subsumes a wide range of genres under only

[21] Londa Schiebinger, *Nature's Body: Gender in the Making of Modern Science* (Boston: Beacon Press, 1993), p. 143. See also Londa Schiebinger, *The Mind Has No Sex? Women in the Origins of Modern Science* (Cambridge, Mass.: Harvard University Press, 1989), p. 216.
[22] Burke, 'Overture', p. 4.
[23] Patrick H. Hutton, 'The History of Mentalities: The New Map of Cultural History', *History and Theory* 20 (1981), p. 258.
[24] For example, see Darnton, *Forbidden Best-Sellers*, passim; Nigel Smith, *Literature and Revolution in England, 1640–1660* (New Haven: Yale University Press, 1994).

one. It implies that novels, sermons and other didactic material, plays, legal records, philosophy, scientific tracts and medical books were all simultaneously saturated with the motivations of political writers. This implies an understanding of culture as undifferentiated, a second limitation of much work on women and gender. The idea that change in one genre led to simultaneous and comparable changes in others relies on a model of culture as monolithic; it obscures the ways in which different types of material might have drawn on a range of resources and performed different functions. In this analysis of erotica, I discuss the cultural resources that erotic culture drew on, and consider both the similarities and differences between erotic and non-erotic sources. As eighteenth-century culture was not a monolith, so discreet genres – or even single texts – were rarely one-dimensional. For example, erotica presented male and female bodies as having many different qualities. Male bodies were violent and powerful, but also soft and vulnerable; female bodies were both passive and devouring. The multi-vocal nature of texts shifts our understanding of change and transformation: a plurality of female bodies complicates the argument that one type of early-modern female body was replaced by one type of modern female body at some point during the eighteenth century.

A third limitation of much work on women arises from the use of evidence, and in particular from the approach to the relationship between representation and experience. Often based on texts regarded as 'fictional' or 'prescriptive', much of this work assumes that this evidence enjoyed predictable contemporary responses, and that there is a knowable and predictable relationship between representation and practice. Precisely how this material affected individuals remains murky, but we assume the connections are straightforward enough for historians to use representation as an index to people's experience of the past. In examining representations of gender roles, authors claim, 'we find the greater repression of women'.[25] The problems with this approach become particularly acute when dealing with the history of the body. Despite pleas for physical bodies to be brought into our accounts of the past, the object of research for historians of the body remains emphatically 'discursively constituted' – created through and located in image and text.[26] This work has been profoundly

---

[25] Hitchcock, 'Redefining Sex', pp. 77, 78.
[26] Quote from Laqueur, *Making Sex*, p. 15. See Lyndal Roper, *Oedipus and the Devil: Witchcraft, Sexuality and Religion in Early Modern Europe* (London: Routledge, 1994), pp. 21, 17, for discussion of the physical body. In contrast to historians, cultural anthropologists make attempts to grapple with the physicality of bodies. See, for example, Thomas Buckley and Alma Gottlieb (eds.), *Blood Magic: The Anthropology of Menstruation* (Berkeley: University of California Press, 1988), especially p. 47; Bruce M. Knauft, 'Bodily Images in Melanesia: Cultural Sub-stances and Natural Metaphors', in M. Feher (ed.), *Fragments for a History of the Human Body: Part Three* (New York: Zone, 1989), p. 201; Françoise Héritier-Augé, 'Semen and Blood: Some Ancient Theories Concerning their Genesis and Relationship', in Feher (ed.), *Fragments for a History of the Human Body*, p. 160.

influenced by Michel Foucault's prioritization of discursive over non-discursive practices and his claim that sexuality was 'the correlative' of the 'discursive practice' of sexual science.[27] In Foucault's *The History of Sexuality* (1976), 'the body' emerged as a screen onto which non-discursive power projected effects.[28] A related view has been given by Judith Butler, who regards gender as 'the discursive/cultural means by which "sexed nature" or "a natural sex" is produced and established as "pre-discursive", prior to culture'.[29] Historians of the body generally argue that bodies are discursive products of political forces; however, historians of women and gender have embedded understandings about bodies in their accounts of women's and men's lives.[30]

We need to be cautious about over-simplifying the relationship between texts and their readers; texts were never mere tools of influence that produced predictable behaviour.[31] Representations need to be understood as effects with complicated relationships to both the groups which produced them and those who consumed them. For example, erotic tales sometimes depicted men as sexually violent towards women, and incipient violence was expressed in gendered patterns of movement – women were stationary and men were mobile. While there is evidence that some actual readers of erotica adopted these patterns of movement in practice, erotica is not evidence of men's behaviour towards women. Erotic material is not an index of past experience, of being a body (embodiment) or of sexual activity in the eighteenth century; erotic culture celebrated the autonomy of the reader and this suggests that readers of

---

[27] Michel Foucault, *The History of Sexuality. Volume I: An Introduction* (1976; London: Allen Lane, 1979), pp. 68, 127. On Foucault's prioritization of non-discursive practices, see Andrew Thacker, 'Foucault and the Writing of History', in Moya Lloyd and Andrew Thacker (eds.), *The Impact of Michel Foucault on the Social Sciences and the Humanities* (Basingstoke: Macmillan, 1997), p. 43; Lois McNay, *Foucault and Feminism: Power, Gender and the Self* (London: Polity Press, 1992), p. 27.

[28] On Foucault's general approach to the body, see McNay, *Foucault and Feminism*, pp. 28, 38–40.

[29] Judith Butler, *Gender Trouble: Feminism and the Subversion of Identity* (New York: Routledge, 1990), p. 7. In *Bodies That Matter: On the Discursive Limits of Sex* (New York: Routledge, 1993), Butler failed to offer even a speculative model of the role of this matter in the production of identities and categories. 'Matter' was a process through which the '"materiality" of sex . . . is formed and sustained through and as a materialization of regulatory norms that are in part those of heterosexual hegemony' (p. 15).

[30] Even Laqueur, who rarely comments on practice, remarks 'my sense is that doctors, lay writers, and men and women in their beds shared a broad view on how the body worked in matters of reproduction'. *Making Sex*, p. 68.

[31] One particularly influential approach is Michel de Certeau's view of readers as poachers and active consumers. See his *The Practice of Everyday Life*, trans. Steven Randall (1984; Berkeley: University of California Press, 1988). A helpful case study is Anna Clark's consideration of Anne Lister, which presents a picture of an active and selective reader. See Anna Clark, 'Anne Lister's Construction of Lesbian Identity', *Journal of the History of Sexuality* 7 (1996), pp. 23–50. Clark regards cultural representations as just one of three resources available on which past individuals might draw in constructing their sexual identity. The other two are 'their own temperaments and drives', and 'their material circumstances' (ibid., p. 27). See chapter one for a discussion of active readers.

eighteenth-century erotica neither copied erotic depictions of sex nor inter-nalized statements about bodies. Instead, representations of bodies should be seen as both products of cultural, social and political debate and screens onto which cultural, social and political concerns were projected. Erotica was fan-tasy. And, as such, it is saturated with beliefs, desires and fears about sex and gender. Emphatically, this does not mean that such representations have no rel-evance for an understanding of social relations. Chapter six reveals the striking similarities between erotic representations of rape and reports of such assaults in court: the languages we find in erotica were part of a wider discourse which shaped individuals' understanding – and therefore experience – of such critical events.

If erotica can be related to the practice of any group in the eighteenth cen-tury, then it relates to groups of men. This book trains the light not solely on female bodies, but also on male bodies, and places all these in the con-text of masculinity. Work on masculinity is much less developed than work on women. Rather than engaging with change over the long term, most research tends to take place within limited periods. However, some sense of change over time is emerging. When aligned, published work suggests a move from a distinctively seventeenth-century honourable manhood resting on control over women's sexuality, through a polite and civil eighteenth-century masculinity, to a later-eighteenth-century and early-nineteenth-century man of distinctively English plain and often unpolished taciturnity.[32] The move from the rough and ready man, who will defend his honour and patriarchal authority through violence, to the polite gentleman engaging in sociable conversation is built in part on claims about changes in bodies. The shift from a one-sex to a two-sex model of sexual difference, and the redefinition of women as 'domesticated' and 'sexually passive', has been used to explain the reorientation of manhood away from honour grounded in the control of wives' sexuality, and towards an emphasis on restraint in social settings. Desexualized women in the home were no threat to men; instead sexual dangers lay outside marriage and outside the home, in '[m]asturbation, pornography, sex with prostitutes, and sex with other men'.[33] Indeed, the history of changing masculine sexualities tells a story of an

---

[32] Compare Elizabeth Foyster, *Manhood in Early Modern England: Honour, Sex and Marriage* (Harlow: Longman, 1999); Philip Carter, *Men and the Emergence of Polite Society: Britain 1660–1800* (Harlow: Longman, 2001); and Michèle Cohen, 'Manliness, Effeminacy and the French', in Tim Hitchcock and Michèle Cohen (eds.), *English Masculinities, 1660–1800* (Harlow: Longman, 1999), pp. 44–61.

[33] Foyster, *Manhood in Early Modern England*, pp. 212, 213–14. A similar case has been made by Randolph Trumbach. See his 'Sex, Gender, and Sexual Identity in Modern Culture: Male Sodomy and Female Prostitution in Enlightenment London', *Journal of the History of Sexuality* 2 (1991), pp. 186–203; and 'The Birth of the Queen: Sodomy and the Emergence of Gender Equality in Modern Culture, 1660–1750', in M. B. Duberman, M. Vicinus and G. Chauncey (eds.), *Hidden from History: Reclaiming the Gay and Lesbian Past* (Harmondsworth: Penguin, 1989).

increasingly rigorous and narrow conception of masculinity which is entirely compatible with the dominant narrative of women's history outlined above.[34]

The historiographical shift from seventeenth-century to eighteenth-century masculinity can be challenged in a number of ways. First, the men in these two contrasting images often belong to different social groups. The range of men who appear in Foyster's consistory court defamation cases are not of the same rank as the legal student or an Anglican clergyman considered by Carter.[35] Moreover, the witnesses, defendants and plaintiffs of the consistory court are situated in the home, whereas the eighteenth-century polite man is in the coffee house, so accounts move from a focus on men's domestic and sexual lives to a focus on their social lives.[36] Indeed, the work on eighteenth-century men's sexuality tends to remain distinct from work on men's social roles. Philip Carter has intimated the usefulness of this bifurcation, claiming that discussions about masculinity spun on social rather than sexual issues.[37] Carter rightly cautions that historians of masculinity run the risk of over-emphasizing sexuality, particularly sexual deviancy. Yet the sexual should not be cleaved from the social. By 'sexuality', I refer to the nature of sexual desire, the object of sexual desire, and the emotional and physical aspects of sexual desire. Sexuality was one area in which some of the basic tensions in eighteenth-century masculinity, and in eighteenth-century society more generally, were played out, and this was done in social contexts. The men who participated in erotic culture were of the kind for whom politeness would have been central. Yet they do not conform to the model of eighteenth-century polite masculinity, and many of their exploits were distinctly impolite. By situating erotic representations in such social and

---

[34] Hitchcock, 'Redefining Sex'; Tim Hitchcock, *English Sexualities, 1700–1800* (Basingstoke: Macmillan, 1997); Laurence Senelick, 'Mollies or Men of Mode? Sodomy and the Eighteenth-Century London Stage', *Journal of the History of Sexuality* 1 (1990), pp. 33–67; Trumbach, 'Sex, Gender, and Sexual Identity'; Trumbach, 'Birth of the Queen'. This change has been charted in other areas of North Europe. See Jonas Liliequist, 'Peasants against Nature: Crossing the Boundaries between Man and Animal in Seventeenth- and Eighteenth-Century Sweden', *Journal of the History of Sexuality* 3 (1991), pp. 393–423.

[35] Foyster's *Manhood in Early Modern England* is based largely on court depositions. Sometimes she mentions status and occupation, but usually not. She discusses this on pp. 10–15. Carter uses a range of sources, but his discussions of Dudley Rider and John Penrose are based on their diary and letters respectively. See *Men and the Emergence of Polite Society*, pp. 164–83.

[36] On men in eighteenth-century society, see Donna Andrew, 'The Code of Honour and its Critics: The Opposition to Duelling in England, 1700–1850', *Social History* 5 (1980), pp. 409–34; Philip Carter, 'Men about Town: Representations of Foppery and Masculinity in Early Eighteenth-Century Urban Society', in Barker and Chalus (eds.), *Gender in Eighteenth-Century England*, pp. 31–57; Carter, *Men and the Emergence of Polite Society*; Michèle Cohen, *Fashioning Masculinity: National Identity and Language in the Eighteenth Century* (Routledge: London, 1996); Lawrence Klein, 'The Third Earl of Shaftesbury and the Progress of Politeness', *Eighteenth-Century Studies* 18 (1984–5), pp. 186–214; Susan Staves, 'The *Man of Mode* and the Secrets of Genteel Identity', *Studies in Eighteenth-Century Culture* 19 (1989), pp. 117–28.

[37] Carter, 'Men about Town', p. 34.

cultural contexts, I will respond to work on men and masculinity as well as to the dominant narrative of women's history.

Eighteenth-century erotica

Erotic culture centred on the many hundred eclectic erotic books which included satirical prose essays, novellas, short poems and songs, and extended metaphorical poems. While there were important differences between these books, the many links between them forged a discrete and coherent genre. Style and theme linked a number of erotic sub-genres and numerous poems were reproduced in more than one of these texts.[38] This book is not intended to be a history of the erotic genre, though, nor have I attempted to include every item published during the eighteenth century that might be considered 'erotic'. On the other hand, this is not a micro-study of a handful of texts, and I hope that the scale of the book enables me to say something meaningful about erotic culture, gender and the eighteenth century. A language of 'representativeness' (with its intimations of statistically verifiable typicality) is inappropriate for a study of meaning, but there are a number of themes that recur often enough in this sample of over one hundred erotic texts for us to consider them relevant to our broader understanding of gender in this period.

Until relatively recently, fictional material concerned with sexual activity was regarded as the 'black sheep' amongst the family of evidence on sexuality.[39] Prior to the mid-1980s, historical investigations were generally of a bibliographical nature or were concerned with publishing history.[40] Peter Wagner's

[38] For example, 'The Female Contest' appeared in *Kick Him Jenny; A Tale. To which is added The Female Contest, A Merry Tale*, 11th edn. (For W. France near Leicest Fields, 1737), 22–4, and in *The Bacchanalian Magazine and Cyprian Enchantress. Composed Principally of New and Convivial and Amorous Songs* (For H. Lemoine, Bishopsgate Church-Yard, 1793), pp. 36–7. 'Addressed to Lady' appeared in *The Festival of Love; Or, a Collection of Cytherean Poems*, 6th edn. (For M. Smith, and by the editors permission, sold by the booksellers in Fleet-Street, Piccadilly, and Paternoster Row, [c. 1770]), pp. 1417, and in Charles Morris, *The Festival of Ancareon: Being a Collection of Songs*, 9th edn. (London: Printed for James Ridgway, opposite Sackville-Street, Piccadilly. Dublin: Reprinted for C. Jackson, [c. 1788]), pp. 22–5. [John Armstrong's] *The Oeconomy of Love: A Poetical Essay* (For T. Cooper, at the Globe in Pater-Noster-Row, 1736) appeared in *The Pleasures that Please on Reflection. Selected from the Album of Venus* (For W. Holland, Garrick's Richard, No. 50, Oxford-Street, 1789), pp. 5–34, and was mentioned in *The Fruit-Shop. A Tale* (For C. Moran, in Covent-Garden, 1765), pp. 161–2, and in [Thomas Stretser's] *Merryland Displayed: Or, Plagiarism, Ignorance, and Impudence Detected. Being Observations upon a Pamphlet Intituled A New Description of Merryland* (Bath: Printed for the Author and sold by J. Leake; and the booksellers of London and Westminster, 1741), p. 12.

[39] G. S. Rousseau in *Eighteenth-Century Fiction* 4 (1991–2), reviewing Peter Wagner (ed.), *Erotica and the Enlightenment* (Frankfurt: Peter Lang, 1991).

[40] David Foxon, *Libertine Literature in England, 1600–1745* (London: Shenval Press, 1964); P. J. Kearney, *A History of Erotic Literature* (London: Macmillan, 1982); David Loth, *The Erotic in Literature: A Historical Survey of Pornography as Delightful as it is Indiscreet* (New York: Julian

Eros Revived: Erotica of the Enlightenment in England and France (1988) marked a significant departure from this approach, although the breadth of focus meant that he was unable to explore the material in any depth.[41] Some work engages with the content of this writing, though there remains a dearth of detailed analyses of the content of this material. Moreover, most works are concerned specifically with pornography, just one category of this broader family of material.[42]

Erotic material has been subject to less detailed analysis. One reason for this is the difficulty in defining the genre. Eighteenth-century erotic culture was certainly porous and drew on many different literary and visual styles. The difficulties in placing and fixing this material can be illustrated by discussing just one element of erotic books – the images. Some of these images were designed specifically for these erotic texts, and refer to an incident described in the accompanying text. (Illustrations 15, 21 and 26, for example.) Such images can be regarded as 'actualizations' of a book.[43] However, many of the engravings bound with erotic books were not originally designed for this purpose. (Illustrations 3, 16 and 17, for example.) Several depict much less explicit scenes than the texts they accompany, and they often originate from thoroughly non-erotic sources. Illustration 1, for instance, was exposed as an example of 'Curlism', because the publisher Edmund Curll had used it for a number of other books of varying content before using it as a frontispiece to an erotic work.[44] Similarly, most of the engravings from the edition of *A Voyage to Lethe* (1741) used in this book date from well after its publication in 1741; they were inserted by a later bookseller or reader late in the century.[45] Illustration 2 was originally

[handwritten marginal note: Use of images problematic]

Messner, 1961); Roger Thompson, *Unfit for Modest Ears: A Study of Pornographic, Obscene and Bawdy Works Written or Published in England in the Second Half of the Seventeenth Century* (London: Macmillan, 1979).

[41] Peter Wagner, *Eros Revived: Erotica of the Enlightenment in England and France* (London: Secker and Warburg, 1988).

[42] The essays in Lynn Hunt (ed.), *The Invention of Pornography: Obscenity and the Origins of Modernity, 1500–1800* (New York: Zone Books, 1993), contextualize close readings with attention to wider social, political and cultural developments, though these essays are primarily concerned with European books. Iain McCalman, *Radical Underworld: Prophets, Revolutionaries and Pornographers in London, 1795–1840* (Cambridge: Cambridge University Press, 1988) omits a detailed analysis of the material in favour of a careful reconstruction of radical groups. Julie Peakman's *Mighty Lewd Books: The Development of Pornography in Eighteenth-Century England* (Basingstoke: Palgrave, 2003) looks to erotic literature for the roots of pornography (see p. 11).

[43] Philip Stewart, *Engraven Desire: Eros, Image and Text in the French Eighteenth Century* (Durham: Duke University Press, 1992), p. 2.

[44] See *Merryland Displayed*, p. 16.

[45] Captain Samuel Cock [pseud.] *A Voyage to Lethe; By Capt. Samuel Cock; Sometime Commander of the Good Ship the Charming Sally. Dedicated to the Right Worshipful Adam Cock, Esq; of Black-Mary's-Hole, Coney-Skin Merchant* (For J. Conybeare in Smock-Alley near Petticoat-Lane in Spittle Fields, 1741), British Library: Cup.1001.c.4.

PANDORA, *lovely Fair*, QUEEN - *Regent reign'd;*
And, with her Casket-dire, the Land inflam'd.

Illustration 1:   Pandora's Box. Frontispiece to *A New Description of Merryland*, 7th edn. (1741).

Illustration 2:   *The Dog* (1784). Inserted in *A Voyage to Lethe* (1741) BL:
Cup.1001.c.4.

published in *The Wit's Magazine* of 1784. The date of Illustration 24 has visibly
been changed to 1741 and it is a later engraving.[46]

There are other prints that were added to *A Voyage to Lethe* whose origins
and dates are unknown. This demonstrates that these books had a life extending
many decades after publication, It suggests that a book of 1741 may well be as
relevant to claims about the 1780s as to those about the 1740s. But the images
whose origins are unknown can be confidently dated to the eighteenth century.
They bear a close resemblance to images in related books of the same period
and several visual clues reinforce this.[47] We should not be surprised to find

[46] Illustration 24 appeared in *The Wit's Magazine*, November 1784 (Harrison and Co., no. 18,
Paternoster-Row, 1784). The engraving accompanied a suggestive poem by W. Whitehead,
'The Dog', in which the woman is encouraged to mount the dog while her husband is away. See
pp. 431–3. Similarly, the image of a man taking his bath, now in *A Voyage to Lethe*, originally
appeared in Voltaire's *Histoire de Jenni* in his *Romans et contes*, 3 vols. (Bouillon: Société
typographique, 1778), vol. III, p. 7.

[47] For images similar to those in erotica see the engravings published with *The Cuckold's Chronicle;
Being Select Trials for Adultery, Incest, Imbecility, Ravishment, &c.*, 2 vols. (For H. Lemoine,
Bishopsgate Church-Yard, 1793). The clues to dates in the erotic images added to *A Voyage
to Lethe* include the barrenness of the interiors. On such sparseness, see Charles Saumerez
Smith, *Eighteenth-Century Decoration: Design and the Domestic Interior in England* (London:
Weidenfeld and Nicolson, 1993), pp. 57, 109, 268. The plain-styled and typically six-panelled

them inserted in books. It was not unusual for engravings, which were printed on machines different to those which produced text, to be inserted in a book when bound. Moreover, it was quite typical for purchasers of books to choose the plate they wanted to have bound with a book.[48] The various origins of erotic illustrations point to a range of different possible relationships between text and image. This is explored at various points throughout this book. As some of the discussions below – particularly chapter five – illustrate, many of the techniques adopted in erotic writing had their visual companion, if not direct equivalent. In contrast – as chapter two points out – interrogating the irreconcilable differences between written and visual representations can reveal significant features about understandings of bodies and gender.

The different origins of these images raise questions about defining the genre. Those prints which came from quite different genres may have given erotica a feel of respectability, taking the edge off more explicit textual descriptions. Other such images, however, were quite graphic. Consider, for example, Illustration 3, in which the act of masturbation is openly depicted. Further devices pulled erotica towards pornography or bawdy humour. By referring to material conventionally regarded as explicit, erotic authors deepened the suggestiveness of their own material. For example, the author of *A Chinese Tale* (c. 1740) listed Ovid's 'Art of Loving', 'One *Rochester*, and two *Aristotle's*' as key examples of sexual explicitness from which he distances his own text, though at the same time associating it with them.[49] While known to discuss sex at length, these books did not necessarily deal in the degree of sexual explicitness suggested by this erotic author. A seventeenth-century translation of Ovid's *Art of Love* may have warned 'modest maids' away, but the fulfilment of the seduction instructions were not discussed, and the muse was left standing at the bed-chamber door.[50] The case of Rochester is more complicated. Two

doors suggest that these images date from after c. 1760. See Dan Cruickshank and Peter Wyld, *Georgian Town Houses and Their Details* (1975; London: Butterworth Architecture, 1990), p. 82; and Geoffrey Beard, *The National Trust Book of the English House Interior* (1990; Harmondsworth: Penguin, 1991), pp. 175, 177, 222. The floor coverings in the images provide other clues. Carpet floor coverings were an exclusive preserve of the extremely wealthy until the very late part of the century; wall-to-wall carpets were a very late-eighteenth-century style, and most carpeted floors would have had a border before this time. See Peter Thornton, *Authentic Decor: The Domestic Interior, 1620–1920* (London: Weidenfeld and Nicolson, 1984), pp. 59–60, 101–2, 155. Most of the interiors inserted in *Voyage to Lethe* have carpet, generally with a border of uncovered floor (Illustrations 14, 16, 18, 19, 20, 25). This is a good indication that they were executed after the book's publication in 1741, but prior to the end of the century.

[48] Edward Hodnett, *Image and Text: Studies in the Illustration of English Literature* (London: Scolar Press, 1982), p. 24; Stewart, *Engraven Desire*, pp. 11, 317.
[49] [William Hatchett], *A Chinese Tale. Written Originally by that Prior of China the Facetious Sou ma Quang, A Celebrated Mandarine of Letters; Under the Title of Chamyam Tcho Chang, or Chamyam with her Leg upon a Table . . . Inscribed to Thomas Dawson Esq; Cornet in Lieutenant-General Honeywood's Dragoons* (For J. Cooper in Fleet-Street; and sold by all the Pamphlet-sellers of London and Westminster, [c. 1740]), pp. 15–16.
[50] *Publii Ovidoo Nasonis de Arte Amandi or, The Art of Love* (no publication details, [trans. Thomas Heywood, c. 1600]), pp. 2, 61.

Illustration 3: Masturbation in the kitchen. Inserted in *A Voyage to Lethe* (1741) BL: Cup.1001.c.4.

traditions of Rochester developed in the eighteenth century: 'a "polite", classicizing one', and 'a semi-pornographic one'.[51] While there was certainly a 'vividness' to descriptions of bodies in the seventeenth-century poetry of John

---

[51] Harold Love, 'Refining Rochester: Private Texts and Public Readers', *Harvard Library Bulletin* 7 (1996), p. 47. I am grateful to Justin Champion for guiding me to Love's work.

Wilmot, Earl of Rochester (as will be noted below), some of his poems used the innuendo of metaphor so central to erotic material.[52] Finally, descriptions of bodies and sex in some versions of the popular medical book *Aristotle's Compleat Master-Piece* may have been largely devoid of innuendo and suggestion, but the edition of 1725 interspersed the anatomical depictions with poetry not dissimilar from that of erotic collections. The author even recommended such 'amorous Rapture' to heighten the sexual pleasure of the bridegroom on his wedding night.[53] Nevertheless, in naming Ovid, Rochester and Aristotle in his own work, this erotic author was trading on myths of explicitness in order to lend his own work greater frisson. A related way in which erotica drew meaning as a genre was through its immediate textual contexts. A poem which would have been fairly innocuous in some books became heavy with sexual implication when placed alongside more explicit works. As Harold Love has put it, 'a Pindaric ode on the bible means one thing read as part of a collection of godly verse and quite another wedged between two segments of "Seigneur Dildoe": equally clearly it would not be within all communities of readers that such a juxtaposition would have been possible'.[54] In this sense, the social contexts of erotica – how and where it was read – would have transformed the meaning of some works.

The consumption of erotica in gatherings where pornography was also read would have similarly transformed the meaning of texts; it also points up the difficulties in establishing definitions.[55] Some of the most engaging work on pornography, erotica and other genres concerned with sex explores the blurred boundaries of literary genres. Philip Stewart's consideration of French erotica couches the problems in terms of 'decency' and 'indecency', and claims that the task is to explore why such uncertainty has persisted.[56] Similarly, Bradford

---

[52] Quote from Rachel Weil, 'Sometimes a Sceptre is Only a Sceptre: Pornography and Politics in Restoration England', in Hunt (ed.) *Invention of Pornography*, p. 131. For the poetry, see John Wilmot, *The Works of the Right Honourable and the Late Earls of Rochester and Roscommon*, 2nd edn. (For Edmund Curll, at the Peacock with-out Temple-Bar, 1707), for example, pp. 15–17, 66–70.

[53] *Aristotle's Compleat Master-Piece. In three parts. Displaying the Secrets of Nature in The Generation of Man . . . To which is added, A Treasure of Health; Or, the Family Physician: Being Choice and Approved Remedies for all the Several Distempers incident to Humane Bodies*, 11th edn. (Printed and sold by the Booksellers, [1725]), pp. 9, 14, 32–3. There were several versions of this book. See Roy Porter, ' "The Secrets of Generation Display'd": Aristotle's *Master-piece* in Eighteenth-Century England', in Robert Purks Maccubbin (ed.), *'Tis Nature's Fault: Unauthorized Sexuality during the Enlightenment* (Cambridge: Cambridge University Press, 1987), pp. 1–21.

[54] Harold Love, *Scribal Publication in Seventeeth-Century England* (Oxford: Clarendon, 1993), p. 230.

[55] See chapter one for the reading contexts of erotica. Thanks to Arthur Burns for alerting me to this point.

[56] Stewart, *Engraven Desire*, p. 371. For other examples of the fruits of this approach, see Paul-Gabriel Boucé, 'The Secret Nexus: Sex and Literature in Eighteenth-Century Britain', in Alan

Mudge has tried to reproduce the 'Curllian chaos' of the eighteenth-century literary marketplace, a world in which works by Mary Delarivier Manley, Daniel Defoe, Samuel Richardson and John Cleland jostled without the constraints of strict generic boundaries. By the early nineteenth century, Mudge argues, pornography and literature were distinguished, though they grew from common roots.[57] Nevertheless, though there were blurred boundaries and substantial areas of overlap, some distinctions were drawn in the eighteenth century between the different kinds of material which discussed sex. This is demonstrated by the prosecution of some texts and not others. Moreover, it is my contention that in eighteenth-century England it meant one thing to read an erotic poem with some claims to refinement, and quite another to read a pornographic novel in which people fucked.

In defining fictional material pertaining to sex, scholars have been most exercised by pornography. Indeed, some writers have categorized erotic works negatively as 'not pornography', rather than as texts bearing distinctive qualities and having their own history.[58] Though not discussing the material considered in this book, these attempts to define pornography can help us think about how we might define a literary genre. A classic definition of pornography focuses on the intention of the author, defining pornography as material intended to sexually arouse.[59] Other approaches try to combine intent with content. This is the approach taken in Peter Wagner's important *Eros Revived*. The book begins by defining the four components of a broad category of 'erotica': bawdy is 'the humorous treatment of sex', obscene is 'a description whose effect is shocking or disgusting', and erotic is 'the writing of sex within the context of love and affection'. Each category is defined on slightly different grounds: style, audience response and subject respectively. While these three are dispensed with in a phrase, much more space is devoted to defining the fourth component of 'erotica' – pornography. After acknowledging the problems in identifying what an author intended their work to mean, and how audiences interpreted the work, Wagner's final definition of pornography is given as 'the written or visual presentation in a realistic form of any genital or sexual behaviour with a deliberate violation of existing and widely accepted moral and social taboos'.[60] This succinct definition combines style, subject and authorial intention. Similarly, though Lynn Hunt concedes that pornography was not 'a wholly separate and distinct category of written or visual representation before the early nineteenth

Bold (ed.), *The Sexual Dimension in Literature* (London: Vision, 1982), pp. 70–89; and David O. Frantz, *Festum Voluptatis: A Study of Renaissance Erotica* (Columbus: Ohio State University Press, 1989), esp. pp. 186–207, 208–52.

[57] Bradford K. Mudge, *The Whore's Story: Women, Pornography, and the British Novel, 1684–1830* (Oxford: Oxford University Press, 2000), p. 200 and passim, particularly pp. 121–222.

[58] Wagner, *Eros Revived*, p. 192; Margaret C. Jacob, 'The Materialist World of Pornography', in Hunt (ed.), *Invention of Pornography*, p. 198.

[59] Frantz, *Festum Voluptatis*, p. 4.   [60] Wagner, *Eros Revived*, pp. 5–7.

century', her definition combines content and authorial intention: pornography is 'the explicit depiction of sexual organs and sexual practices with the aim of arousing sexual feelings'.[61]

In including reception or authorial intent in their definitions, these approaches involve a degree of guesswork and speculation about what an author meant and how a work was received. Ultimately, though, these assumptions derive from the historian's interpretation of the content of the material, and it is upon this that most definitions rest. It is therefore unfortunate that analyses of the content of pornography are generally brief. In Wagner's definition, for example, there is no discussion of the term 'realistic'; in Hunt's definition, there is no explanation of the term 'explicit'. By contrast, in elaborating my own definition of erotica, I want to spend some time focusing on content and techniques of representation.[62] Working within the context of a genre already loosely shaped by historians and bibliographers, the term 'erotica' is used in this book to describe *material about sexual pleasure which depicted sex, bodies and desire through illusions of concealment and distance: bodies were represented through metaphor and suggestion, and depictions of sexual activity were characterized by deferral and silence.*[63]

Erotica versus pornography

My use of the term 'erotica' in this book is significantly different from other common usages. Erotica in this book does not mean 'an overarching description for all books on sex'; nor is it used to refer to an antecedent of pornography: clusters of material we can refer to as 'erotica' and 'pornography' are different genres of material which have coexisted and which have their own histories.[64] Crucially, I do not use erotica to refer to a non-offensive counterpart to pornography. Defining erotica and pornography can become 'the problem of sorting out the good sex from the bad, the non-violent from the violent', with pornography being defined as 'bad/too-explicit/violent/too-fast and too-rough/loveless

---

[61] Lynn Hunt, 'Introduction', in Hunt (ed.), *Invention of Pornography*, p. 10.

[62] This is reminiscent of a strand of feminist thought which sees the pornographic as a form of representation informing various media and distinguished by particular techniques. See Carol Smart, *Feminism and the Power of the Law* (London: Routledge, 1989), pp. 124–8. An example of this approach is Susan Griffin, *Pornography and Silence: Culture's Revenge against Nature* (London: Women's Press, 1982).

[63] This sample of erotic books was selected largely from a corpus of literature loosely defined as erotic. Erotica is also the term used most widely in bibliographies and catalogues to refer to material depicting sex. The most important bibliography is P. J. Kearney's *The Private Case: An Annotated Bibliography of the Private Case Erotica Collection in the British (Museum) Library* (London: Jay Landesman, 1981). *A Directory of Rare Book and Special Collections in the United Kingdom and Republic of Ireland* (London: Library Association, 1985) also refers to 'erotica' rather than 'pornography'.

[64] Peakman, *Mighty Lewd Books*, p. 7.

sex'.[65] This approach is reflected in historical work, as in the case of Alan Bold's distinction between 'good erotica' and 'carnography' (the latter meaning 'nastily impure work' written by 'male chauvinists' and imbued with 'the sense of a desire to masticate flesh'), or Colin Wilson's statement that 'pornography is a more civilised version of rape'.[66] Such comments are understandable responses to depictions of sexual violence, but not only do they allow us to exclude material regarded as unpalatable from analysis, they also risk conflating explicitness with power differentials and suggestiveness with equality. In using the term erotica, I emphatically do not mean a more pleasant version of pornography. Eighteenth-century erotica was saturated with masculinist themes, privileging male pleasure and power and suggesting insidious violence towards women, but this is not integral to my definition, nor is it how the material was selected.

In order to flesh out my definition of erotica, I propose to show how it differs from other closely related types of material. First, let me explain how erotica differed from pornography. In the definitions of pornography considered above, Hunt's prioritizing of 'explicit' echoes Wagner's stress on the 'realistic' nature of pornographic depictions. Similarly, Joan DeJean sees classic French pornography as existing 'at the intersection of sexual explicitness or obscenity and political dissidence', while Lucienne Frappier-Mazur describes the 'description of the sexual action' as 'the central, indispensable unit of pornography'.[67] There are two key elements of early-modern pornography here: the *explicit* depiction of sexual *action*. The material examined in my book differs from pornography both in terms of the nature of the description, and in terms of the object or narrative of the description. Historians have claimed that the explicitness or realism of pornography was produced by language which negated metaphor and abandoned the figurative in order to achieve a closer mimetic relation to real bodies. Findlen claims that sixteenth-century pornographers 'loudly proclaimed that their work laid bare the truth, stripped of all the metaphorical witticisms and allegories that characterised the contemporary culture of learning'.[68] Similarly, according to Frappier-Mazur, eighteenth-century French pornography contributed to the impression of greater verisimilitude through use of the obscene word. Such language 'calls up corporeal representations, which it endows with a hallucinatory quality', thus unmasking the body.[69] This theme

---

[65] Susanne Kappeler, *The Pornography of Representation* (Cambridge: Polity Press, 1986), pp. 39, 47.

[66] Alan Bold, 'Introduction', in Bold (ed.), *Sexual Dimension in Literature*, p. 11; Colin Wilson, 'Literature and Pornography', in Bold (ed.), *Sexual Dimension in Literature*, p. 212.

[67] Joan DeJean, 'The Politics of Pornography: *L'Ecole des Filles*', in Hunt (ed.), *Invention of Pornography*, p. 121; Lucienne Frappier-Mazur, 'Truth and the Obscene Word in Eighteenth-Century French Pornography', in Hunt (ed.), *Invention of Pornography*, p. 207.

[68] Paula Findlen, 'Humanism, Politics and Pornography in Renaissance Italy', in Hunt (ed.), *Invention of Pornography*, p. 77.

[69] Frappier-Mazur, 'Truth and the Obscene Word', p. 212.

of greater proximity to the body, together with the stripping away of illusion to reveal the truth, is found in many historical analyses of pornography.

If pornography portrayed sexual activity as realistic or explicit, then erotica was characterized by metaphor or suggestion, deferring or avoiding the sexual denouement. Pornography claimed to abandon the figurative for the literal, while erotica was determined to retain this metaphorical technique of expression. This was most evident in those erotic texts which employed an extended metaphor, apparently a peculiarly English phenomenon.[70] The first erotic text to use an extended metaphor of land for the female genitalia was *Erotopolis. The Present State of Bettyland* (1684).[71] Thomas Stretser's *A New Description of Merryland* (1741) was in the same tradition. At pains to distance his work from those 'uncertain Guesses and fabulous Relations' of false travel books, Stretser disingenuously claims to recount only 'Truth and Nature'.[72] Other authors employed botanical metaphors, thereby drawing on the work of botanists amongst whom the sex life of plants was being discussed, reflected in the work of Phillip Miller (who published his *Catalogus Plantarum* in 1730) and Carl Linnaeus (1707–78). Later in the century, experiments in electricity received satirical attention. The erotic *Teague-Root Display'd* (1746), for example, is dedicated to William Watson, Fellow of the Royal Society, who published *Experiments and Observations tending to Illustrate the Nature and Properties of Electricity* in 1745. Watson had reported that he had succeeded in creating an electric current by rubbing a glass tube to create 'electrical Fire' or an electrical 'stroke'. In response, the author of *Teague-Root Display'd* jokes that when the male teague-root came into contact with its female equivalent, they engaged in 'just such a Motion as you make when you are making your Glass Tube to be Electrical, by Means of Friction'.[73]

The metaphorical aspects of erotica – generally understood as satirical – are what seem to be at the root of denouncements of this material as 'naive',

---

[70] Kearney, *History of Erotic Literature*, pp. 53–7.

[71] [Charles Cotton], Ερωτσπολιζ or *Erotopolis. The Present State of Bettyland* (For Tho. Foy, at the White-Hart, over and against St Dunstan's Church in Fleet-Street, and at the Angel in Westminster-Hall, 1684).

[72] Roger Pheuquewell [pseud., alias Thomas Stretser], *A New Description of Merryland. Containing a Topographical, Geographical, and Natural History of that Country*, 7th edn. (Bath: Printed and sold by J. Leake there; and by E. Curll, at Pope's Head in Rose-Street, Covent-Garden, 1741), p. x. This was a very popular book, going through ten editions between 1740 and 1742. See Kearney, *History of Erotic Literature*, pp. 56–7. On false travel books, see Percy G. Adams, *Travelers and Travel Liars, 1660–1800* (1962; New York: Dover, 1980).

[73] William Watson, *Experiments and Observations tending to Illustrate the Nature and Properties of Electricity* (By Jacob Ilive, for the author, London, 1745), pp. 6, 11; Paddy Strong-Cock [pseud.], *Teague-Root Display'd: Being Some Useful and Important Discoveries tending to Illustrate the Doctrine of Electricity, in a letter from Paddy Strong-Cock, Fellow of Drury Lane, and Professor of Natural Philosophy in M. King's College, Covent-Garden, to W M W N, F. R. S. Author of a late Pamphlet on the Subject* (For W. Webb, near St. Paul's, 1746), p. 17.

'primitive', 'mundane', and 'childish'.[74] It has also been suggested that metaphor was employed in order to evade legal penalties or avoid breaking taboos.[75] But metaphor was not employed simply (if at all) because it avoided prosecution, or because the author lacked an imagination. Rather, metaphors were selected because they were thought appropriate to the topic, and they can thus reveal important and otherwise unspoken understandings about bodies and gender. This kind of depiction also forged a distinctive genre. Indeed, just as pornography made claims to explicitness, erotic authors announced themselves masters of metaphor. In contrast to popular medical guides such as *Aristotle's Master-Piece* – intent on 'displaying the secrets of nature' – erotic authors presented their work as discreet and decent. The author of the preface to *A Chinese Tale*, who was ostensibly the translator of the original Chinese text, notes the way in which the 'dark' and 'perplex'd' Chinese style has been cleared up and wrapped in 'an *English* dress'.[76] *Consummation* (1741) similarly begins by contrasting its own style of 'Softer Music' with 'keen Satire' and 'rough Verse'.[77] In a similar comparison in *Seventeen Hundred and Seventy-Seven* (1777), the veiled language of the poem is favourably placed against 'satyr impudence, expos'd and bare'.[78] When their works are compared to John Wilkes' notorious *An Essay on Woman* (1763), these claims of erotic authors appear convincing. Descriptions of sexual intercourse as 'a few good Fucks' and of 'Prick, Cunt and Bollocks in Convulsions hurl'd' were anathema to erotica.[79] Despite the impression of veiling, though, metaphor could convey a great deal. For example, an eighteenth-century botanical writer explained that, though 'Nature' had 'hid from us the manner of Working in the Generation of *Animals*', she was 'more enclin'd to open that Mystery to us in the *Vegetable* Kingdom'.[80] Erotic authors repeatedly invoked botany in part because these metaphors could transmit copious detail.

---

74 Kearney, *History of Erotic Literature*, p. 57; Thompson, *Unfit for Modest Ears*, p. 191; Wagner, *Eros Revived*, p. 192.

75 Kearney, *History of Erotic Literature*, p. 57; Thompson, *Unfit for Modest Ears*, p. 190; Wagner, *Eros Revived*, p. 191; Peter Wagner, 'The Discourse on Sex – or Sex as Discourse: Eighteenth-Century Medical and Paramedical Erotica', in G. S. Rousseau and Roy Porter (eds), *Sexual Underworlds of the Enlightenment* (Manchester: Manchester University Press, 1987), p. 46; Peakman's *Mighty Lewd Books*, p. 187.

76 *Chinese Tale*, p. 5.

77 *Consummation: or, the Rape of Adonis* (For E. Curll, at Pope's Head, in Rose Street, Covent-Garden, 1741), p. 1.

78 *Seventeen Hundred and Seventy-Seven; Or, a Picture of the Manners and Character of the Age* (For T. Evans, near York-Buildings, in the Strand, 1777), p. 8.

79 [Pego Borewell; pseud., John Wilkes], *An Essay on Woman* (1763), reproduced in Adrian Hamilton, *The Infamous Essay on Woman: Or, John Wilkes Seated between Vice and Virtue* (London: André Deutsch, 1972), pp. 213, 229.

80 Richard Bradley, *A Philosophical Account of the Works of Nature* (For W. Mears, at the Lamb, without Temple-Bar, 1721), p. 29.

These points can be illustrated by comparing two descriptions of sex, one pornographic, one erotic. The first appeared in John Cleland's pornographic *Memoirs of a Woman of Pleasure* (1748–9), commonly known as *Fanny Hill*, and it uses metaphor only intermittently:

Her petticoats, thrown up with her shift, discovered to the company the finest turned legs and thighs that could be imagined, and in a broad display that gave us a full view of that delicious cleft of flesh into which the pleasingly hair-grown mount over it parted and presented a most inviting entrance, between two close ledges, delicately soft and pouting. Her gallant was now ready, having disencumbered himself from his clothes . . . But giving us no time to consider dimensions, and proving the stiffness of his weapon by his impatience of delay, he threw himself instantly over his charming antagonist, who received him without flinching, . . . we could observe the pleasure lighten in her eyes as he introduced his plenipotentiary instrument into her, till at length, having indulged her its utmost reach, its irritations grew so violent, and gave her the spurs so furiously that, collected within herself, and lost to everything but the enjoyment of her favourite feelings, she retorted his thrusts with a just concert of springy heaves.[81]

The second extract, taken from the erotic book *A Voyage to Lethe*, not once abandons one of a range of extended metaphors:

The Main-Mast being a Long-side, we strove to heave it in, but found much Difficulty; indeed I thought once I should never have got it righted in her, being somewhat of the largest; but by the greasing and working it to and fro, the third Day it went tolerably plumb into the Socket. I work'd Night and day upon the rest of her Rigging – we took in her cargo, Stores and Ammunition, and were to deliver in the Gulph of *Venus* – provided myself next with a very able Pilot, whose name was *Philip Handcock*, . . . and now being thoroughly equipp'd and mann'd, after examining her Bottom, which was as white as Hound's Tooth, I order'd her Foresail to be unbent, as a Signal for sailing.[82]

It should be clear that both extracts describe sex. An unwillingness to abandon metaphor in *A Voyage to Lethe*, in other words, did not preclude a detailed description of this encounter. Indeed, the perceived 'realistic' and 'explicit' qualities of early-modern pornography were an illusion, just as erotica manufactured the illusion that sexual activity was not being described and that bodies were hidden. Indeed, a key element of the pleasure offered by erotic texts was achieved by seeing through the illusion.

Not all erotic texts employed extended metaphors, though. Many erotic books instead used suggestion and allusion to insinuate sexually charged activity, avoiding descriptions of the body or sexual action. To illustrate this feature of erotica I want to again juxtapose extracts from an erotic and a pornographic text,

[81] John Cleland, *Fanny Hill: Or, Memoirs of a Woman of Pleasure* (1748–9; Harmondsworth: Penguin, 1985), p. 151.
[82] *Voyage to Lethe*, p. 13.

this time published in the same year. Though Robert Darnton has questioned whether the book *Thérèse philosophe* (c. 1748) can be described as pornography, he does recognize it as 'the supreme work . . . that took sex far beyond the boundaries of decency that had been generally recognized under the Old Regime'. It was one of the top three clandestine bestsellers in France, and was lauded by the notorious pornographer the Marquis de Sade (1740–1814) as the publication which embodied 'the idea of an immoral book'.[83] Consider this extract:

I distinctly saw His Holiness's ruby red member take the canonical path, after he delicately opened its purple lips with the thumb and index finger of each hand. This work was begun with three forceful thrusts which caused half of it to enter . . . His head was bent and his glistening eyes were fixed on the work of his battering ram, whose thrusts he controlled in such a manner that, as it retracted, it did not leave its sheath completely and, as it shot forward, his stomach did not come into contact with the thighs of his charge . . . I saw also that with each backward movement of the father's rump, as the cord withdrew, and its head appeared, the lips of Eradice spread open, revealing a crimson hue wondrous to behold.[84]

Wagner has pointed out that eighteenth-century readers did not make a clear distinction between French and English literature, and *Thérèse philosophe* was translated and published in English just a year after it appeared in France.[85] Yet this French pornographic fiction is far removed from English erotica. As the phrase 'battering ram' indicates, the author of *Thérèse philosophe* does not relinquish metaphor altogether. But in the context of a passage which generally eschewed figurative speech, such phrases are rendered only more pronounced and the body part they denoted made more palpable. Moreover, words such as 'member', 'lips', 'thrusts' and 'thighs' may not be regarded as obscene, but they certainly reveal an avoidance of allusion.

The descriptions of sex in the erotic *A Spy on Mother Midnight* (1748) are very different to those in *Thérèse philosophe*. The former concludes with the sexual consummation of the relationship between the male narrator and Maria. Believing her companion was a woman, Maria has welcomed him into her room and accepted his offer to masturbate her with a dildo. He soon dispenses with the dildo and penetrates her:

I put out the Candle and soon follow'd, clasp'd her fast in my Arms, and scarce permitted her to draw Breath, before she might know the Difference between Mr. *F* and a poor

---

83 Darnton, *Forbidden Best-Sellers*, p. 89.
84 [Jean-Baptiste de Boyer], *Thérèse philosophe, ou mémoires pour servir à l'histoire du P. Dirrag et de Mlle Eradice* (*Thérèse philosophe, Or, Memoirs about the Affair between Father Dirrag and Mademoiselle Eradice*) (c. 1748), translated by and quoted in Darnton, *Forbidden Best-Sellers*, pp. 260–1.
85 Wagner, *Eros Revived*, pp. 231–2, 375.

insensible Implement. 'Bless me!' says she, 'What!' She had not Power to ask the Question, but was immediately convinc'd what Sort of a Bedfellow she had got. Great was her Confusion, but not so great as to spoil our Sport; she had gone too far to recede. However we soon found Leisure to come to an Explanation of the Mystery.[86]

A reader might easily miss the sexual action, indicated most clearly by Maria's exclamation 'What!'. These two extracts depict penetrative sex, but in very different ways. In particular, the allusiveness of the erotic passage hides the sexual activity, while the absence of bodily detail removes the action from the reader. The sexual practice was the same, but the erotic and pornographic treatments of this were different.

These two categories can also be distinguished by the action they described and particularly by the narrative they employed. While erotica often avoided describing bodies engaged in sexual activity, pornography is defined by modern authors as repeatedly depicting the sex act. Goulemot identifies eighteenth-century French pornography by the 'moments of pleasure repeated and narrated through the course of episodes which are always different and yet basically the same'.[87] The proliferation and repetition of bodies engaged in sex is also central to Stewart's definition of 'indecent' material, which is contrasted with 'decent' material set only before or after (never during) sex.[88] Cleland's *Fanny Hill* has been identified as pornography, in part because it sacrifices 'linear development to the monotonous rhythm of desire . . . [an] endless cycle of arousal, satisfaction, and the reawakening of desire'.[89] In only the first quarter of the book, Fanny watches a couple have penetrative sex twice while being masturbated, before spending nearly two weeks in a room in a Chelsea tavern, during which episode there are three lengthy and detailed descriptions of penetrative sex.[90]

Often paraded as '*the* original work of pornography'[91], and sold in England throughout the eighteenth century, *L'Ecole des Filles* (1655) contains descriptions of male and female genitalia which resemble those found in eighteenth-century erotica. Susanne's descriptions of 'this device with which boys pass water . . . known as the *yard*', together with 'two globes which hang in a pouch and are called his *stones*', and a woman's '*sheath* or the *thingummy*, the *little hole*, the *mossy hole*', for example, were not that dissimilar from some of the

---

[86] *A Spy on Mother Midnight: Or, The Templar Metamorphos'd. Being a Lying-in Conversation. With a Curious Adventure. In a Letter from a Young Gentleman in the Country, to his Friend in the Town* (For E. Penn, near St Paul's, 1748), pp. 33–4.

[87] Jean-Marie Goulemot, *Forbidden Texts: Erotic Literature and its Readers in Eighteenth-Century France*, trans. James Simpson (1991; Cambridge: Polity Press, 1994), p. 61.

[88] Stewart, *Engraven Desire*, p. 272.

[89] Ruth Bernard Yeazell, *Fictions of Modesty: Women and Courtship in the English Novel* (Chicago: University of Chicago Press, 1991), p. 103.

[90] Cleland, *Fanny Hill*, pp. 65–71, 76–84.   [91] DeJean, 'Politics of Pornography', p. 110.

depictions in erotica.[92] However, the descriptions in *L'Ecole des Filles* were transformed because these organs are repeatedly portrayed engaged in sexual activity.[93] Following the description of the penis, a boy is envisaged inserting 'his long instrument into the hole she pees through', while immediately after the description of the vulva, he 'lodged it in the girl's opening, [and] pushes forward with his rump'.[94] Similarly, though some of the earlier poetry of Rochester – recently reclaimed as a pornographic writer – could resemble erotica in language, the relentless repetition of sexual activity he portrayed in some works prefigured later French pornography.[95]

Such repeated episodes are missing from erotica, in which sex was often put off and unattained. In many ways, the erotic book *A Description of the Temple of Venus* (1726) is a lengthy meditation on this mode of discussing sex. The narrator was born at Cybaris where rewards were given to those who were 'fruitful at inventing new Scenes of Voluptuousness'. There was no deferral of the gratification of sexual desire at this place, and little value was placed on the preambles to sexual liaisons, praised by the narrator as 'those inestimable Nothings; . . . every Thing that is a Kind of Prelude to the happy Minute; . . . so many enjoyments before the last'.[96] Cybaris celebrated not the erotic joy of preliminaries but the myopia of pornography. In contrast, the narrator of *A Description of the Temple of Venus* refuses to give 'the particulars' of a story 'entirely made up of the most passionate sentiments'. Rather, 'he just gives us a *Hint* of it . . . but goes no farther, to prevent his falling into a vicious Uniformity'.[97] This is clear when the narrator joyfully describes the sexual act:

I'll go to the Mead, and gather Flowers, which I will stick in her Bosom. I may, perhaps, have an Opportunity of leading her to the Grove, and when we have wandered to the most lonely Part of it, I'll give her a balmy Kiss, and this Kiss will embolden me to – but Love that inspires my Breast, forbids me to reveal his Mysteries.[98]

Little more is revealed at the close of the book when, after a long search and chase through the forest, the narrator is finally reunited with his lover. Despite his forceful attempts to persuade her to have sex with him, he fails to do so.[99] In *A Chinese Tale* there is a similar climb towards a deferred denouement. A man follows Cham-Yam through her palace and into her cabinet to watch her undress and masturbate. Now stashed away in a large jar adjacent to her sofa, the effect on him is considerable:

[92] [Michel Millot and Jean L'Ange], *The School of Venus* (1655; trans. Donald Thomas; London: Panther, 1972), pp. 83, 85. Compare to the erotic descriptions discussed in chapter two.
[93] *School of Venus*, pp. 87, 89–90, 98, 99, 101–4.   [94] Ibid., pp. 84, 85.
[95] Weil, 'Sometimes a Sceptre', passim; Wilmot, *Works of Rochester*, pp. 63–71.
[96] *A Description of the Temple of Venus, at Cnidus* (Printed and sold by Tho. Edlin, 1726), pp. 29, 31.
[97] Ibid., pp. viii, ix.   [98] Ibid., p. 16.   [99] Ibid., p. 62.

He burst His prison and the Floor
Resounded with tremendous Roar:

. . . .
He bore to th' adjacent Bed,
And what was done need not be said.[100]

The sexual act is indicated by the man's bursting from the jar, and by the refusal
to describe what occurred upon the bed, but not by a description of the act itself.

This lack of description could be made convincing in a number of ways. *The
Genuine Memoirs of the Celebrated Miss Maria Brown* (1766) is a very different
type of text from the ones just considered. An example of what Wagner has
referred to as the 'whore biography', it is a first-person account of one woman's
life.[101] The first-person narration posed problems for the author seeking to limit
what was described, but Maria's role as narrator is repeatedly debilitated and
the amount of detail conveyed curtailed. This is clear during her first sexual
experience when, after having been plied with alcohol and drugs, Maria is
raped by her fiancé Mr Fitzherbert. His actions rouse her from sleep, but by
this time 'the deed was done'. On the next occasion Maria and her fiancé have
sex, she describes how he followed her into her bed-chamber, 'caught me in
his arms, and, almost drowning me with kisses, threw me upon the bed, whilst,
in a kind of trance, I granted all he could desire'.[102] Unlike the prostitute-
narrator in *Fanny Hill*, who might faint away after sex had taken place, Maria
is repeatedly thrown into a mental state which prevents her from conveying any
details of the incident.[103] Placing sexual action off the page flew in the face of
the pornographic mode, in which the description of the sexual act was placed
at the centre of the narrative. In contrast, techniques that created an illusion of
distance between the reader and the bodies engaged in sexual action were key
to erotica. As we will see in chapter one, they were also highly significant for
the readers of erotica.

Erotica versus romantic and amatory fiction

If erotica made a virtue of concealing sex and the body from the reader, then how
can we separate it from the fiction of the eighteenth century which deals with
desire, love and romance and which was also non-explicit? It was Richardson's
Pamela (1740) that inaugurated 'the moral romance novel'.[104] In some ways,
this novel follows the contours of an erotic narrative, teasing the reader with
a series of attempts at seduction which are repeatedly thwarted. After a series

---

[100] *Chinese Tale*, pp. 19–20, 24–5.   [101] Wagner, *Eros Revived*, pp. 216–20.
[102] *The Genuine Memoirs of the Celebrated Miss Maria Brown. Exhibiting the Life of a Courtezan in the Most Fashionable Scenes of Dissipation*, 2 vols. (For I. Allcock, near St Paul's, 1766), vol. I, pp. 111, 117.
[103] Cleland, *Fanny Hill*, p. 78.   [104] Mudge, *Whore's Story*, p. 187.

of anti-climaxes, a climax is reached, and this is the marriage between Mr B and Pamela. Needless to say, this resolution is hardly an erotic one. Indeed, in *Pamela*, 'femininity is transformed into the renunciation of desire', and 'the popular romance novel is translated into an edifying literary scripture whose pleasures remain from beginning to end beyond reproach'.[105] But Richardson's novels have been credited with inventing 'the terms of Moral Femininity in the English novel'.[106] He grounded his stories in the here and now of the 1740s, the social issues of the mid eighteenth century.[107] The moral seriousness and the rootedness of Richardson's novels render them not pleasurable discussions of desire and sex, but ruminations on the relationship between the private world and the social world. The morality of the moral romance novel distinguished it from erotic fiction, switching the focus away from sexual pleasure.

Less easily distinguished from erotic fiction is the genre of amatory fiction. Amatory fiction comprises the works of three women: Aphra Behn (1640–98), Mary Delarivier Manley (1672?–1724) and Eliza Haywood (1693?–1756). Ros Ballaster describes it as 'a particular body of narrative fiction by women which was explicitly erotic in its concentration on the representation of sentimental love'.[108] For Ballaster, amatory fiction is distinct from 'male pornography': 'The primarily anatomical, procreative and instructional emphasis of this literature bears little relationship to the erotic-pathetic drive of the seduction and betrayal narratives of Behn, Manley and Haywood.'[109] On the other hand, amatory fiction, 'with its voyeuristic attention to the combined pleasures and ravages of seduction', is also distinct from 'female-authored pious and didactic love fiction, stressing the virtues of chastity and sentimental love'.[110] Laid out in this way, amatory fiction sounds very much like female-authored erotica; indeed, Ballaster regards it as a kind of 'pornography for women'.[111] Yet many of the distinctive features of amatory fiction set it apart from erotica, drawing amatory fiction closer to more conventional love fiction.

Amatory fiction places events firmly in the context of sentimental love. Current scholarship is divided over whether female authorship produced fresh ways of representing sexual activity and gender relations,[112] or simply replicated

[105] Ibid., p. 191.
[106] Susan Ostrov Weisser, A 'Craving Vacancy': Women and Sexual Love in the British Novel, 1740–1880 (New York: New York University Press, 1997), p. 52.
[107] Ibid., pp. 38–40, 51.
[108] Ros Ballaster, Seductive Forms: Women's Amatory Fiction from 1684 to 1740 (Oxford: Clarendon Press, 1992), p. 31.
[109] Ibid., p. 32.   [110] Ibid., pp. 32, 33.   [111] Ibid., p. 35.
[112] Ros Ballaster, 'Seizing the Means of Seduction: Fiction and Feminine Identity in Aphra Behn and Delarivier Manley', in Isobel Grundy and Susan Wiseman (eds.), Women, Writing, History (London: Batsford, 1992), pp. 93–108; Alison Conway, 'The Protestant Cause and a Protestant Whore: Aphra Behn's Love-Letters', Eighteenth-Century Life 25 (2001), pp. 1–19; Paula McDowell, The Women of Grub Street: Press, Politics, and Gender in the London Literary Marketplace, 1678–1730 (Oxford: Clarendon Press, 1998), pp. 262–3.

patriarchal visions.[113] But amatory fictions certainly encased sexual events in a moral story. For example, the build-up to a rape scene in Mary Delarivier Manley's *The New Atalantis* (1709) reads very much like an erotic tale. The young woman Charlot is an orphan left in the Duke's care. Having earlier eschewed the romances, novels and poetry that might soil a girl's innocence, the Duke encourages her to read 'Books dangerous to the Community of mankind; abominable for Virgins, and destructive to Youth; such as explain the Mysteries of Nature, the congregated Pleasures of *Venus*, the full Delights of mutual Lovers, and which rather ought to pass the Fire than the Press'.[114] Having been prepared in this way, the gullible and adoring Charlot is raped:

> *Charlot* no sooner arriv'd, but the Weather being very hot, she order'd a Bath to be prepar'd for her. Soon as she was refresh'd with that, she threw her self down upon a Bed, with only one thin Petticoat and a loose Nightgown, the Bosom of her Gown and Shift open; her Night-cloths tied carefully together with a Cherry-colour'd Ribon [sic], which answer'd well to the yellow and silver Stuff of her Gown. She lay uncover'd, in a melancholy careless Posture, . . . when raising herself a little, at a gentle noise she heard from the opening of a Door that answer'd to the Bed-side, she was quite astonished to see enter the amorous Duke. Her first emotions were all Joy, but in a minute she recollected herself, thinking he was not come there for nothing: She was going to rise, but he prevented her, by flying to her Arms, where, as we may call it, he nail'd her down to the Bed with Kisses; his love and resolution gave him a double vigour, he wou'd not stay a moment to capitulate with her, whilst yet her surprise made her doubtful of his designs, he took advantage of her confusion to accomplish 'em; neither her prayers, tears, nor struglings [sic], cou'd prevent him, but in her Arms he made himself a full amends for all those pains he had suffered for her.[115]

The profuse apology of the Duke, rapid forgiveness of Charlot, and happiness of the couple that immediately follows this event could all sit quite happily in an erotic book. What distinguishes this from erotica, though, is the framing of the sex in a wider story that is not simply or even primarily about sexual pleasure. This encounter is preceded by a romantic love affair: a young woman growing aware of her sexual desire, and an older man realizing his feelings for her are more than simply paternal.[116] By the same token, the rape has far-reaching consequences: ultimately, the story transforms into Charlot's descent into 'one continu'd Scene of Horror, Sorrow, and Repentance: She dy'd a true Landmark: to warn all believing Virgins from the shipwracking their Honour upon (that

---

[113] Toni O'Shaughnessy Bowers, 'Sex, Lies and Invisibility: Amatory Fiction from the Restoration to Mid-Century', in John Richetti (ed.), *The Columbia History of the British Novel* (New York: Columbia University Press, 1994), p. 59.

[114] Mary Delarivier Manley, *Secret Memoirs and Manners of Several Persons of Quality, of Both Sexes. From the New Atalantis, an Island in the Mediteranean*, in Patricia Koster (ed.), *The Novels of Mary Delariviere Manley* (1709; Gainesville, Fla.: Scholars', Facsimiles, 1971), vol. I, pp. 339–40.

[115] Ibid., pp. 343–4.   [116] Ibid., pp. 322–38.

dangerous Coast of Rocks) the Vows and pretended Passion of Mankind'.[117]
One of Manley's tragic heroines, Charlot dies 'loath'd, and unlamented'.[118]

The work of Eliza Haywood frames sex in similar ways. Though Haywood
wrote domestic fiction from the 1740s, and produced *The Female Spectator*
(1744–6), her early amatory novels were notorious. Indeed, she famously styled
herself the 'Great Arbitress of Passion'.[119] In her short novel *The Mercenary
Lover: or, the Unfortunate Heiress* (1726), a rape takes place. In the build-up to
this, the focus is primarily on the vice-ridden and 'industriously mischievous
Clitander'.[120] Through a number of sinister and underhand methods, including
priming her with books of Ovid and Rochester, he encourages his sister-in-law
Althea to return his affections. Left alone in his house, he rapes her:

Action was now his Business, and in this Hurry of her Spirits, all unprepar'd, incapable
of Defence, half yielding, half reluctant, and scarce sensible of what she suffer'd, he bore
her trembling to the Bed, and perpetuated the cruel Purpose he had long since contriv'd.

The Scene of Ruin over, the barbarous Author of it, now began to exert his utmost
Wit and Eloquence to dry her Tears, and hush the Remonstrances of violated Virtue . . .
[but] tho' he stirr'd not from her the whole Day, he found all his Efforts to compose her
ineffectual.[121]

The focus on the flaws of Clitander means that the progression towards the
rape is not a simple source of anticipatory pleasure – the narrator is judging
the man's every move. And after the attack, it is not the frisson of the sex that
lingers, but the devastating impact it has on Althea and her sister Miranda: six
months pregnant, Althea dies from poisoning, while her sister Miranda remains
estranged from Clitander, who himself is now destined to suffer 'Bitterness of
Soul' in Eternity.[122] The terrible consequences of the rape are long-lasting. The
sexual encounters in amatory fiction are an opportunity to relish erotic pleasure;
but this is not their primary purpose, it seems to me. Rather, the sexual incidents are exemplary of serious moral arguments regarding men's and women's
interactions. This moral framing of sex significantly alters the presentation of
sexual activity, rendering it different in kind from the descriptions of sex found
in erotica.

The fictional short stories in women's magazines might be considered a
slightly less explicit form of amatory fiction – they were women-centred tales
in which sex was discussed, but was wrapped up in moral tones. As *The Lady's
Magazine* informed its readers in 1784, the authors were 'moral Writers' whose
intention was to provide a forum for women's voices, but also to arm women

---

[117] Ibid., p. 355.   [118] Ibid., p. 356.   [119] Quoted in Ballaster, *Seductive Forms*, p. 158.
[120] Eliza Haywood, *The Mercenary Lover: or, the Unfortunate Heiress* (1726), in *Selected Fiction
and Drama of Eliza Haywood*, ed. Paula R. Backscheider (New York: Oxford University Press,
1999), p. 129.
[121] Haywood, *Mercenary Lover*, p. 135.   [122] Ibid., p. 162.

against the perils of seduction.[123] In part, the placing of these stories in magazines which also featured many 'anti-erotic' pieces on the perils of seduction and the virtues of female chastity gave clear signals that these stories were not about erotic pleasure. This was made absolutely plain in the stories themselves. In 'Celadon and Florella; or, The Perils of a Tête-à-Tête', which appeared in 1774, Florella is a beautiful and charming woman who regards men as 'play-things', and who becomes intimate with them in order to add them to her list of conquests. Celadon, an attractive young man who women adore, sets out 'to get the better of her *virtue*'. Left alone with Florella at her toilette, Celadon 'urged her to infringe the inviolable laws of female honour', but he is thwarted by the rekindling of Florella's early religious education, and she banishes him from her house: 'Florella exulted in the consciousness of approved virtue, and was cautious for the future of granting any indulgences that might expose her to the attacks of vice, or subject her to the censures of malevolence'.[124] This story does indulge erotic pleasure, but the conclusion provides a moral-religious climax, not a sexual one. Sex does not take place even after the narrative ends.

It was characteristic of stories in women's magazines to avoid explicit discussion of sex and end with an anti-erotic climax. In 'The Unwary Sleeper', also from *The Lady's Magazine*, Dulcetta is the reluctant friend of the more frivolous Amelia. As the latter strikes up an intimacy with the more worldly-wise Mr D, Dulcetta retreats from the friendship, but warns Amelia of the danger Mr D poses. Dulcetta then hears that her friend has eloped with Mr D, who is now suspected of being married with children. One month later, Dulcetta travels with her parents to an estate of her father's, where she wanders through the woods alone:

One day, which was excessively sultry, I found myself very much fatigued, and laid myself down under a large tree, with my elbow reclined on the turf, that grew upon a kind of a bank underneath it. Sleep insensibly closed my eyes, and I was immediately transported into the land of dreams. I thought I was in a solitary place, and that a person was attempting to be rude with me. I shrieked – the shriek waked me – and who should stand before me but the treacherous Mr D, who seemed to have no good design.

A servant comes to her rescue, and Mr D flees, ensuring that Dulcetta escapes ruin. This story mirrors erotic narratives until the final denouement, at which point there is no sexual finale or even the suggestion of one, but instead a pronouncement on the necessity of women's constant vigilance against sexual encounters.[125] These magazine stories left no hint of sex or desire, but

---

[123] *The Lady's Magazine; or Entertaining Companion, for the Fair Sex, Appropriated solely to their Use and Amusement* (Printed for G. Robinson, 25, Paternoster-Row), January 1784, p. iv.
[124] 'Celadon and Florella; or, The Perils of a Tête-à-Tête', *Lady's Magazine*, February 1774, pp. 65–6.
[125] 'The Unwary Sleeper', *Lady's Magazine*, May 1774, pp. 233–4.

rather the aftertaste of women's moral superiority and a sense of their narrow escape. Furthermore, both amatory fiction and the stories in women's magazines differed from erotica in tone. Amatory fiction sometimes hinted at obscenity in the references to risqué reading matter, but generally none of this writing implied that there are things done but left unspoken, that there is something going on between the lines or behind the page. Puns, allusions and knowingness were central to erotica; the tone of amatory fiction is, in contrast, earnestness.

Erotica depicted sex, bodies and desire through illusions of concealment and distance: bodies were represented through metaphor and suggestion, and depictions of sexual activity were characterized by deferral and silence. Despite these illusions, sexual pleasure and the sexual act were primary. Sex might be deferred until after the narrative closed, or it might be hidden by metaphor, but the reader was in little doubt that something took place or was going to take place. These texts were not meditations on men's and women's behaviour. This is indicated by the lack of seriousness in erotica and the willingness to joke about almost anything, including sexual violence. This lack of seriousness, combined with the primacy of sexual pleasure (however disguised), lent erotica a considerable capacity for sexual innuendo. In this regard, erotica was distinct from both pornography and amatory fiction.

Erotica shared with pornography an interest in sex, and shared with amatory fiction a desire to hide it from the reader. This combination situated the genre on the cusp between refined restraint and liberated libido. Erotica is a useful source for thinking about the collision between these apparently competing facets of eighteenth-century culture. It is also a genre that, despite techniques of concealment and distance, contained rich depictions of bodies, sex and gender. This book undertakes a close reading of erotica against the backdrop of the narrative of the emergence of a new discursive woman, changes in understandings of sexual desire, and the invention of modern, opposite sexes. In bringing the relatively under-studied material of erotica into the historical repertoire, I do not want to reduce erotica to this narrative but to reflect on arguments for a momentous transformation in understandings of the body. In chapters two and three I reassess the claim that a model of sexual difference replaced one of sexual sameness, and propose alternative ways of analysing representations of bodies and of reading change in such evidence. The book also seeks to revise the view that understandings of female bodies, gender and desire can be united in one general narrative. It teases apart these three elements and considers the themes of bodily difference (chapter two), active/passive gender roles (chapter three) and sexual passion (chapter seven) separately. Dominant narratives may tell a story of a sexual, active, independent woman being superseded by a desexualized, passive, domestic woman, but (as discussed in chapter five) being deeply associated with sex did not equate with sexual autonomy. Moreover, the later chapters seek to broaden the history of the body by considering bodies not simply in terms of anatomical and physiological difference and sexuality, but also in terms of space (chapter five), movement (chapter six) and the senses (chapter seven). This close reading of erotica is framed by an exploration of its social and cultural contexts. In chapter one, the reconstruction of a model of readership for eighteenth-century erotica, together with the ritual contexts of this readership, reveal that erotic cultures were male gatherings characterized by civility, sociability, learning and wit. The content of erotic culture was also indubitably masculinist: understandings of bodies, sex and gender celebrated male force and pleasure (as chapters four and six argue). Meanings are created, received and transmitted at specific times and places, and eighteenth-century ideas about bodies and gender were shaped by and interacted with these material contexts. The erotic culture of eighteenth-century England can only be fully understood by exploring both the discursive and the material aspects – the content and the contexts – of this culture.

1   Contexts

Jean-Jacques Rousseau was referring to pornography when he described 'those dangerous books' which 'can only be read with one hand.'[1] Historians have concurred with this sentiment, adding that this sexually explicit writing had other powerful effects, and writing pornography into the history of the French Revolution.[2] At the level of both the body and the polity, then, pornography has been endowed with a potent capacity for incitement, and we have a number of contexts within which we can read the evidence of pornography. The less explicit material of erotica was no less embedded in eighteenth-century society and culture; in order that we might interpret its significance, this chapter yokes the content of erotic writing to a context of reading and ritual. The history of reading is plagued by a dearth of examples of actual readers. Even personal testimony is unreliable, subject to the disparity between deed and word: one eighteenth-century preacher exhorted his congregation against the evils of romances, but confessed to his diary that he was reading *Memoirs of the Fortunate (Country) Maid, a Romance*.[3] Faced with such problems of evidence, we need to take a multi-faceted approach. This chapter therefore interrogates the full range of evidence we have for the contexts of eighteenth-century erotica: the books as objects, the producers, the texts and their cultural milieu, and external evidence of the groups who read erotica and where they did so. Different kinds of readers then emerge: the 'likely readers' suggested by clues within and around the books, 'implied' readers deducible from the structure of the texts themselves, the 'imagined' readers portrayed in representations contained within the material, the 'stated readers' noted by the authors and the 'actual readers' indicated by external evidence.

[1] Quoted in Goulemot, *Forbidden Texts*, p. 36.
[2] See, for example, Roger Chartier, 'Book Markets and Reading in France at the End of the Old Regime', in Carol Armbruster (ed.), *Publishing and Readership in Revolutionary France and America* (Westport, Conn.: Greenwood Press, 1993), pp. 117–36; Robert Darnton, *The Corpus of Clandestine Literature in France, 1769–1789* (New York: Norton, 1995) and his *Forbidden Best-Sellers*; Hunt (ed.), *Invention of Pornography*. For pornography and political radicalism in England, see McCalman, *Radical Underworld*.
[3] Richard Beale Davis, *A Colonial Southern Bookshelf: Reading in the Eighteenth Century* (Athens: University of Georgia Press, 1979), p. 122.

Given that it is a non-canonical genre, it would be very difficult to answer the question 'who read erotica?' with any certainty. Nor would this be the most valuable question to ask if our aim is to understand the content of the material; it will be more revealing, I suggest, to know who was thought to read it, who was supposed to read it and who said they read it. These are the questions which will help us understand erotica and its place in eighteenth-century society. We must also ask not simply who, but *how*, paying attention to what James Raven has called 'different performative modes' of reading.[4] By combining different kinds of readers we produce a socio-cultural model of reading for erotica, one which was socially, culturally and gender specific. Erotic culture was one aspect of a particular kind of homosociability united around a number of activities – such as drinking, singing, viewing naked women and prostitution – through which communities of manly good fellowship were forged. And yet for these readers sexual pleasure was potentially troublesome, because pleasure – and men's possible surrender to it – threatened the loss of manly self-control. Stylistically a less explicit genre than pornography, erotica promised sexual pleasure of a kind which kindled fewer difficulties for dominant modes of masculinity based on restraint. Moreover, as this chapter argues, erotica was situated in contexts with pretensions to refinement. The socio-cultural model of reading produced by male authors and readers stressed civility not boorishness, merriment not masturbation, and placed erotica in sociable environments. In this way the reading of sexually suggestive material became both a pleasurable and a permissible encounter.

The books

Books are not simply repositories of textual meaning: they are material objects whose physical characteristics are central to an understanding of their place in the past. To build a profile of likely readers of erotica, we have to consider the books themselves: access to them, their material nature, their cost, distribution and retail. Access to erotic books was dictated partly by legal constraints. But though erotic authors may have ridiculed those who called for tighter censorship, presenting them as hypocrites with a secret penchant for flagellation, the distribution of their work was unlikely to have been considerably curtailed by censorship.[5] Donald Thomas' account of English literary censorship in *A Long Time Burning* (1969) suggested a rather haphazard approach to the prevention and punishment of publications considered immoral, profane or obscene. The Licensing Act of 1662 required that all books had to be licensed and then entered

[4] James Raven, 'New Reading Histories, Print Culture and the Identification of Change: The Case of Eighteenth-Century England', *Social History* 23 (1998), p. 270.

[5] *Did You Ever See Such Damned Stuff? Or, So-Much-the-Better. A Story without Head or Tail, Wit or Humor* (For C. G. Seyffert, in Pall-Mall, 1760), pp. 153–6.

in the Registers of the London Stationers' Company, and published only in London, Cambridge, Oxford and York. The lapsing of this Act in 1695 not only removed the need for pre-publication licensing, but also lifted the numerical and geographical limitations on printing houses.[6] Thereafter, pre-publication censorship was replaced by post-publication prosecution. Prior to 1725, publishers or authors of blasphemous or defamatory material could be punished for the offence of obscene libel under common law if it could be proved that specific persons had been libelled. The publishers of *The Fifteen Plagues of a Maiden-Head* (1707) were brought to Queen's Bench, for example, but punishment was not enforced because the court found that no named individuals had been libelled.[7] Only after the prosecution of Edmund Curll at King's Bench in 1725 for publishing two pornographic books was obscene libel redefined as a book which threatened morality or the peace, rather than defamation of a person or group.[8]

However, the material prosecuted as obscene libel at Queen's and King's Bench was considerably more explicit than erotica.[9] The blatant descriptions of sex in *Venus in the Cloister* (1725), for example, and for which Curll was prosecuted, are quite unlike those which appeared in erotica.[10] Other examples of prosecution help sketch out eighteenth-century distinctions between the explicit and the suggestive. Warrants were issued for the arrest of the author, publisher and printer of *A Compleat Sett of Charts of the Coasts of Merryland* in 1745, a book which probably cashed in on the success of the erotic text *A New Description of Merryland* (1741). It appears that the former (of which no copies are extant) included graphic images of female bodies, making the book deserving of legal action.[11] Similarly, *Harris's List of Covent Garden Ladies*, published in the 1780s and 1790s, in which the descriptions of women's bodies resemble some of those found in erotica, claims to list actual women working as prostitutes, thereby exploding any illusions of metaphor. This is likely to explain the prosecution of James Roach in 1794 for selling

---

[6] See Michael Treadwell, '"1695–1995": Some Tercentenary Thoughts on the Freedoms of the Press', *Harvard Library Bulletin* 7 (1996), pp. 3–19.

[7] Donald Thomas, *A Long Time Burning: The History of Literary Censorship in England* (London: Routledge, 1969), pp. 77–8; Foxon, *Libertine Literature*, pp. 12–13. The report of this trial differs in Loth, *Erotic in Literature*, pp. 104–5. See also W. Thompson and J. Annetts, *Soft-Core: A Content Analysis of Legally Available Pornography in Great Britian 1968–90 and the Implications of Aggression Research* (London: W. Thompson, 1990), pp. 1–9, for a review of censorship in this period.

[8] Thomas, *Long Time Burning*, pp. 79–83.

[9] For a discussion of definitions of erotica and related genres, see Introduction.

[10] Consider two of the passages for which Curll was prosecuted, in *Venus in the Cloister: Or, The Nun in her Smock* ([Edmund Curll], 1725), pp. 122–3, 137. This was a French pornographic book written in 1683 and first translated into English in 1692. For a lengthier comparison of erotica and pornography, see chapter one.

[11] Foxon, *Libertine Literature*, pp. 15–16.

the book.[12] In any case, by 1787 'there had not been a prosecution involving a newly-written piece of pornography since 1750'.[13] Attempts to prosecute intensified after the establishment of William Wilberforce's (1759–1833) Proclamation Society in 1787, but the eighteenth-century English book trade faced few constraints.[14] Erotica circulated relatively unfettered.

The size, paper and price of books, combined with information regarding distribution and availability, are avenues which might lead to a 'sociology of texts' and ultimately to a sociology of likely readers.[15] For example, Roger Chartier has argued that a transformation in the physical nature of books contributed to a change in reading practices during the eighteenth century. Less durable books might have been read in a different way: paper binding of the seventeenth century indicated a book designed for one or two readings.[16] Similarly bound books in the eighteenth century may only have been sufficient to stand a few readings before the book would have to be discarded or rebound, though books were still most commonly advertised sewn in paper or boards at the end of the century.[17] The books considered here varied from thin publications with flimsy pages bound with string[18] to more substantial leather-bound books of higher-quality paper.[19] The vast majority were medium octavo size, usually reserved for popular books with 'a certain distinction'.[20] Far fewer were small duodecimo or the larger-sized quartos or folios. In other words, these erotic books were not lavish items to be treasured by successive generations, though they appear to have been too substantial to be discarded after just one reading.

---

[12] Thomas, *Long Time Burning*, p. 120. See, for example, *Harris's List of Covent Garden Ladies: or Man of Pleasure's Kalendar, for the Year 1788* (For H. Ranger, at No. 9, Little Bridges-Street, near Drury-Lane Play-House, 1788).

[13] Thomas, *Long Time Burning*, p. 117. I have interpreted Thomas' 'pornography' to include what I have defined as 'erotica', based on his elision of the differences between books such as Madam B—l [pseud.], *The Fifteen Plagues of a Maiden-head* (By F. P. near Fleet-Street, 1707) and *Venus in the Cloister*.

[14] John Feather, *A History of British Publishing* (London: Croom Helm, 1988), p. 90.

[15] Quote from William Sherman, *John Dee: The Politics of Reading and Writing in the English Renaissance* (Amherst: University of Massachusetts Press, 1995), p. 56. See also Daniel Roche, 'Printing, Books and Revolution', in Armbruster (ed.), *Publishing and Readership*, pp. 6–7.

[16] Chartier, 'Book Markets', p. 132; Margaret Spufford, *Small Books and Pleasant Histories: Popular Fiction and its Readership in Seventeenth-Century England* (Cambridge: Cambridge University Press, 1981), pp. 48–9.

[17] Terry Belanger, 'Publishers and Writers in Eighteenth-Century England', in Isabel Rivers (ed.), *Books and Their Readers in Eighteenth-Century England* (Leicester: Leicester University Press, 1982), pp. 8, 19; James Raven, 'The Book Trades', in Isabel Rivers (ed.), *Books and Their Readers in Eighteenth-Century England: New Essays* (London: Leicester University Press, 2001), p. 24.

[18] *The Natural History of the Frutex Vulvaria* (For E. Hill, in White-Fryers, Fleet-Street, 1741); *The Secret History of Pandora's Box* (For T. Cooper in Pater-Noster-Row, 1742).

[19] *The Electrical Eel: Or, Gymnotus Electricus. Inscribed to the Honourable Members of the R***l S*****y* (No publication details, [c. 1770]); *The Old Serpent's Reply to the Electrical Eel* (For M. Smith, and sold by the Booksellers near Temple-Bar, and in Pater-Noster Row, 1777).

[20] Raven, 'Book Trades', p. 24.

Finding the reader

In trying to locate the social status of readers, we need to be cautious; the content of erotic material complicates any association between erotica and a specific social group. Significantly, many of the books referred to in erotic texts cost substantially more than the erotic books themselves. This might suggest that erotic books were the cheap and dispensable items in the otherwise highly priced collections of wealthy readers, or it could suggest an appeal to a broad range of readers. Erotic books were certainly reproduced in a range of formats, so that the more expensive items would have been familiar to those who read or listened to cheaper items. *Arbor Vitae; Or, The Natural History of the Tree of Life*, for example, was produced in a variety of formats, many of which are still extant. In 1732 both a poem and a prose version were available in a 32-page collection priced at 6d, a prose version was available in a book of 1741 priced 1s 6d, while paraphrased poetic versions were found in collections at 4s 6d in 1770 and at 2s 1d in 1788.[21] Other items which appeared singly in a cheap format found their way into the more expensive items. For example, *The Riddle* (c. 1725) was a six-page folio poem sold at 6d. This closely resembled the poem 'A Riddle', which appeared in *The Festival of Love* (1770): a several-hundred-page collection which, selling for 4s 6d, was the second most expensive item considered in this book.[22] A shared erotic culture which straddled demarcations of social status and purchasing power clearly existed in eighteenth-century England.

Our knowledge about those who could read certainly suggests that these books could have been read by most people. Though James Raven has argued that it was not until the early nineteenth century that literacy rates shot up, 60 per cent of men and 40 per cent of women could sign their names in 1753. This, claims Jonathan Barry, underestimates people's ability to read, because writing was only taught after reading.[23] Nevertheless, information on the price of books suggests that the likely readers of erotica were drawn from a more exclusive social group. The most expensive book was half a guinea and most were much cheaper, but these were still relatively costly objects. Of the thirty-seven items priced on the title page, twenty-eight sold for between 1s 6d and 6d (ten at 6d, seven at 1s and eleven at 1s 6d). A further five can be

21 'The Arbor Vitae; Or, Tree of Life. A Poem' and 'The Natural History of the Arbor Vitae; Or, the Tree of Life, in Prose', both in *The Ladies Delight* (For W. James in the Strand, 1732), pp. 5–12, 13–20; 'Arbor Vitae: or, the Natural History of the Tree of Life', in *New Description of Merryland*; *Arbor Vitae: Or, the Natural History of the Tree of Life* (For E. Hill, in White-Fryers, Fleet-Street, London, 1741); 'The Tree of Life. By Captain M[orri]s', in *Festival of Love*, pp. 305–7; Morris, *Festival of Ancareon*, pp. 26–7.
22 *A Riddle: Of a Paradoxical Character of an Hairy Monster, Often found under Holland*, 2nd edn. (Printed for A. Moore, near St Paul's; and sold at most of the Pamphlet-Shops in London and Westminster, [c. 1725]); *Festival of Love*, pp. 149–50.
23 Raven, 'Book Trades', pp. 26–7; Jonathan Barry, 'Literacy and Literature in Popular Culture', in Tim Harris (ed.), *Popular Culture in England, c. 1500–1850* (Basingstoke: Macmillan, 1995), p. 76.

priced at 6d, two at 1s and two at 1s 6d.[24] These were not very expensive books, but they were in a different price band than the popular chapbooks and ballads which sold for 2–3d in the 1680s.[25] Contextualizing these prices is difficult. Bought new, the cheapest erotic book of 6d would have cost a well-paid servant receiving 40s a year in 1743 the equivalent of 60 per cent of a week's pay.[26] At the same time, this book would have cost an averagely paid agricultural labourer half a day's pay, a building labourer around a third of a day's pay and a building craftsman one quarter of a day's pay.[27] The vast differences between the pay of a servant (who was provided with bed and board) and that of a farm labourer (who may have had additional payments in kind but whose work was less secure) expose some of the problems of using this evidence in contextualizing the price of books. At best such figures are suggestive, because retail price is not equivalent to perceived value. It is therefore instructive to compare the prices of other forms of entertainment: the cheapest erotic book at 6d cost half as much as a ticket to a pleasure garden or a cheap seat at the theatre, though most erotic books cost about the same or more. John Brewer has claimed that these public entertainments were available to an artisan earning between £40 and £60 a year.[28] Erotic books were available to a similar, though broader, group. Despite claims that this material was read by lower ranks, it seems unlikely that even the cheapest erotic books were bought by servants and labourers on a regular basis, if at all.[29] The cheaper books were within reach of craftsmen and similarly paid workers receiving £20–30 a year, and the more expensive items (of which there were many) could have been afforded only by people enjoying large incomes. A reasonable speculation is that erotic books were bought by the 'middle sort' and above.[30]

---

[24] The pricing of these additional nine items is based on the title-page price of similar editions of the same texts.
[25] Spufford, *Small Books*, p. 48.
[26] T. H. Baker (ed.), *Records of the Seasons, Prices of Agricultural Produce, and Phenomena Observed in the British Isles* (London: Simpkin, Marshall and Co., [c. 1888]), p. 191.
[27] Peter Bowden, 'Statistics', in Appendix III of Joan Thirsk (ed.), *The Agrarian History of England and Wales* (Cambridge: Cambridge University Press, 1985), vol. V, section 2: 1640–1750, pp. 877, 878.
[28] John Brewer, *The Pleasures of the Imagination: English Culture in the Eighteenth Century* (London: HarperCollins, 1997), pp. 92–3. Many thanks to Mike Braddick for discussing this point with me.
[29] Julie Peakman, 'Medicine, the Body and the Botanical Metaphor in Erotica', in Kurt Bayertz and Roy Porter (eds.), *From Physico-Theology to Bio-Technology: Essays in the Social and Cultural History of Biosciences* (Amsterdam: Clio Medica, 1998), p. 199. Peakman renews this claim in her *Mighty Lewd Books*, pp. 33–4.
[30] Commentators began to refer to a middle group in society during the civil war, and the language of 'sorts' became increasingly common in descriptions of social structure. See Keith Wrightson, 'Estates, Degrees and Sorts: Changing Perceptions of Society in Tudor and Stuart England', in Penelope Corfield (ed.), *Language, History and Class* (Oxford: Basil Blackwell, 1991), pp. 49–52. By 'middle sort' I refer to those whom contemporaries identified as the top 40–50

geography

The extent to which this shared erotic culture was spread geographically is hard to ascertain. Invariably erotic books were printed and sold in London. Some participating printers, publishers and booksellers were based in Fleet Street and the Strand, and in Covent Garden, Piccadilly and Pall Mall to the West, but most were concentrated around St Paul's Church-Yard and Paternoster Row. This distribution is interesting, given that '[t]he Row was not Grub Street – it manufactured a certain stateliness and gentility'.[31] It suggests that an erotic book was not an entirely disreputable kind of publication. The distribution of these books outside London is difficult to chart, though. Unlike the situation in France, where strict censorship encouraged pedlars to carry those books which could not be sold openly in booksellers, the relatively lax censorship laws in England allowed erotic material to be produced and sold more freely. Pedlars were therefore likely to have carried only the cheapest erotic books.[32] For their erotic reading matter, therefore, provincial readers probably relied on visits to the metropolis, contacts with booksellers in London, provincial dealers who had London connections, or subscription.[33] It seems likely that the market for erotic books was predominantly urban, if not solely metropolitan. Moreover,

per cent of the population. According to the work of Gregory King (1688), Joseph Massie (1759) and Patrick Colquhoun (1801–3), this group *excluded* individuals such as labourers, common soldiers, cottagers, miners and seamen. For these estimates, see Douglas Hay and Nicholas Rogers, *Eighteenth Century English Society* (Oxford: Oxford University Press, 1997), pp. 19–21. This is a generous definition which probably encompasses groups who could not afford erotic books. Note that this discussion of price is based on first-hand prices; it is likely that a second-hand market in erotic books existed and allowed greater access.

[31] James Raven, 'Memorializing a London Bookscape: The Mapping and Reading of Paternoster Row and St Paul's Churchyard, 1695–1814', in R. C. Alston (ed.), *Order and Connexion. Studies in Bibliography and Book History: Selected papers from the Munby Seminar, Cambridge, July 1994* (Cambridge: Brewer, 1997), p. 196. Many of these businesses were listed in contemporary trade directories. See Ian Maxted, *The London Book Trades, 1775–1800: A Preliminary Checklist of Members* (Folkestone: Dawson, 1977); Ian Maxted, *The London Book Trades, 1735–1775: A Checklist of Members in Trade Directories and in Musgrave's 'Obituary'* (Exeter: Exeter Working Papers in British Book Trade History, University of Exeter, 1983); Henry R. Plomer, *A Dictionary of the Printers and Booksellers . . . in England, Scotland and Ireland from 1668 to 1725* (Oxford: Oxford University Press, 1922); Henry R. Plomer, G. H. Bushell and E. R. McC. Dix, *A Dictionary of the Printers and Booksellers . . . in England, Scotland and Ireland from 1726 to 1775* (Oxford: Oxford University Press, 1932). Alternative sources of information on those in the book trades are maps and land tax assessments. For details see the website of the University of Oxford project started by James Raven at http://members.tripod.co.uk/bookhistory. Another rich resource is the British Book Trade Index at the University of Birmingham, which uses a vast range of published material and archival research to provide bibliographic material on those in the trades. See www.bbti.bham.ac.uk.

[32] Darnton, *Corpus of Clandestine Literature*, pp. 225–6; Spufford, *Small Books*, pp. 111–28.

[33] Terry Belanger, 'Publishers and Writers in Eighteenth-Century England', in Rivers (ed.), *Books and Their Readers*, pp. 11–13; Raven, 'Book Trades', pp. 12–13. Eighteenth-century Northern gentry relied on friends' trips south or on relations residing in London for a range of goods. See Amanda Vickery, 'Women and the World of Goods: A Lancashire Consumer and Her Possessions', in John Brewer and Roy Porter (eds.), *Consumption and the World of Goods* (London: Routledge, 1993), pp. 280–1; Amanda Vickery, *The Gentleman's Daughter: Women's Lives in Georgian England* (New Haven: Yale University Press, 1998), p. 183.

while there is evidence of a shared erotic culture spanning a range of social status groups, we can place this material most securely in a context comprised of the middling sort and above.

Producers

Access to erotic books was shaped by legal constraints, rank and geography, and information on the size, quality and price gives more clues to the likely readership. Yet purchasing power plus access does not necessarily equal acquisition: other factors also affect the decision to buy or borrow a book. With this in mind, historians have looked to the production of books in order to help them locate a likely readership, arguing that there are links between the producers, writers and readers of eighteenth-century print.[34] Here the issue of gender comes to the fore. Women were clearly active in the eighteenth-century printing trades. Paula McDowell goes so far as to argue that the book trade after 1680 constituted 'a new mode of association for women', though they were increasingly excluded from the trade after 1730.[35] Throughout the century women performed a diverse range of roles in print, including the publication of controversial or illicit material and the street selling of ephemeral material as hawkers or mercuries. Margaret Hunt concludes that women's publications demonstrated 'a well-developed libertine aspect'.[36]

One of the items of erotica considered in this book was published by a woman. Mary Cooper (d. 1761) dealt in a considerable range of items.[37] Like many women who worked in the book trade, Cooper had worked with her husband Thomas from 1732 to 1743, and they were prolific printers who advertised under both their names. The erotic *A Secret History of Pandora's Box* (1742), published a year before Thomas' death, however, was printed with just his name on the title page. When Thomas died in 1743, Mary continued to publish

---

[34] Rivers, 'Introduction', in Rivers (ed.), *Books and Their Readers*, p. 2. See also Paula McDowell, 'Women and the Business of Print', in Vivien Jones (ed.), *Women and Literature in Britain, 1700–1800* (Cambridge: Cambridge University Press, 2000), p. 136.

[35] McDowell, *Women of Grub Street*, p. 17.

[36] Margaret Hunt, 'Hawkers, Bawlers, and Mercuries: Women in the London Press in the Early Enlightenment', in Margaret Hunt, Margaret Jacob, Phyllis Mack and Ruth Perry (eds.), *Women and the Enlightenment* (New York: Haworth Press, 1984), pp. 41–68 (quote at p. 46); Hannah Barker, 'Women, Work and the Industrial Revolution: Female Involvement in the English Printing Trades, c. 1700–1840', in Hannah Barker and Elaine Chalus (eds.), *Gender in Eighteenth-Century England: Roles, Representations and Responsibilities* (London: Longman, 1997), pp. 90, 93; McDowell, *Women of Grub Street*, p. 85.

[37] Beverly Schneller, 'Using Newspapers Advertisements to Study the Book Trade: A Year in the Life of Mary Cooper', in O. M. Brack (ed.), *Writers, Books, and Trade: An Eighteenth-Century English Miscellany for William B. Todd* (New York: AMS Press, 1994), pp. 123–43. The British Book Trade Index at the University of Birmingham puts Mary Cooper's trading dates as 1736–61, and describes her as a bookseller, publisher and printer of a newspaper. See www.bbti.bham.ac.uk.

alone, apparently producing *The Man-Plant* (1752) amongst her list.[38] Yet it is misleading to claim that the activities of businesswomen like Mary Cooper demonstrates that women were both 'sellers *and* buyers of erotica'.[39] Cooper's business does not show that a widespread female readership existed or was condoned, and it assuredly does not indicate that women purchased the material as independent consumers. Mary Cooper was unusual in several ways. First, she was a trade publisher, of whom there were no more than five in London before 1750. As such, Cooper occupied a place in the trade more lowly than that of the bookseller; she and her husband would have published for those who held the copyright, partly to conceal the latter's involvement.[40] Second, Cooper was highly unusual because she was a woman. Indeed, McDowell offers Cooper not as one of the economically independent, politically expressive women involved in early-eighteenth-century print, but as an exception at a time when women were being pushed out of the trade.[41] Cooper's activities in the erotic trade were a continuation of her husband's work rather than her own autonomous business, and she was far outnumbered by male publishers.

Unfortunately, many of those involved in the production and sale of erotic books are now invisible to us, and this includes the authors. The vast majority of the items used here were published anonymously or pseudonymously. The only author acknowledged on the title page was Charles Morris (1745–1838), author of *The Festival of Ancareon* (1788) and *A Complete Collection of Songs* (1788). However, Peter Wagner provides much detail about other likely authors. Thomas Stretser was the author of *A New Description of Merryland*, *Merryland Displayed* (1741), *Arbor Vitae: Or, the Natural History of the Tree of Life* (1732; 1741) and, I would argue, *The Natural History of the Frutex Vulvaria* (1737; 1741), though no information on his life is extant.[42] Charles Cotton (1630–87) wrote *Erotopolis* and also published a satirical work mocking Virgil's *Aeneid* and a gardening book called *The Planter's Manual* (1675).[43] Likewise Edward Ward (1667–1731) produced a considerable range of books including the monthly *London Spy* (1698–1700) and *History of the London Clubs*

---

[38] Vincent Miller (pseud.), *The Man-Plant: Or, a Scheme for Increasing and Improving the British Breed* (For M. Cooper, at the Globe in Pater-Noster-Row, 1752). On the Coopers' careers, see Plomer et al., *A Dictionary of the Printers and Booksellers . . . 1726 to 1775*. Mary Cooper's career resembles that of some French widows who published political pornography in France, and whose primary concern was to produce a bestseller. See Darnton, *Forbidden Best-Sellers*, pp. 36–7.

[39] Peakman, 'Medicine, the Body', p. 199 (emphasis added). Peakman's claim that 'it is evident that women read and enjoyed obscene literature' is based on just one actual example, a female reader of Enlightenment works on sex. See *Mighty Lewd Books*, p. 37.

[40] Michael Treadwell, 'London Trade Publishers 1675–1750', *The Library* 5 (1982), 6th series, pp. 102, 106–7, 118, 120–1.

[41] McDowell, *Women of Grub Street*, pp. 114–15.

[42] Wagner, *Eros Revived*, pp. 193, 195.   [43] Ibid., p. 165.

(1709–11).[44] *The Oeconomy of Love*, first published in 1736 and then repeatedly throughout the century, was written by John Armstrong, a doctor who also wrote popular health books.[45] James Perry (1756–1821), the son of a builder who made money writing poetry and essays before becoming a newspaper proprietor, is thought to have been the author of *The Electrical Eel* (1774) and *Mimosa; or, the Sensitive Plant* (1779).[46] For many authors, writing erotica was part of a varied literary career.

Of those authors named in erotic books, only two are women. The title page of the collection *The Festival of Love* lists twenty-four unnamed male authors (including five Dukes, four Lords, three Doctors, and two Knights), but 2 of the 150 poems in this collection are ascribed to 'Mrs R' and 'Mrs S', names that are significantly noted with the poem rather than on the title page.[47] We have to be extremely cautious of ascribing female authorship to erotic books when this cannot be verified with other sources, as we know that publishers marketed many novels as being female-authored when they were not, because they sold more.[48] So Mrs R and Mrs S could be men. They might also be only the visible tip of a much larger body of unnamed female authors. Although in the case of novels the balance between male and female authors shifted in women's favour only after 1779, publications by women did rise over this period.[49] While women capitalized on their femaleness in their presentation of themselves as authors, however, there remained real restrictions on women's ability to enter print.[50] It is possible that some of the pseudonymous or anonymous authors of erotica were women, but Mrs R and Mrs S remain the only named (possible) female authors of erotica, overshadowed by a larger body of named male authors about whom we are sure. Women's role in the production of erotic print culture appears highly circumscribed.

The texts

Moving away from the book as a material object and product, we need to consider the content of erotic texts as a source of information on reading.

---

[44] Ibid., pp. 36, 249, 453; Leslie Stephen (ed.), *Dictionary of National Biography* (London: Smith, 1885–1903).

[45] Wagner, *Eros Revived*, p. 14.   [46] Ibid., pp. 196, 194; *DNB*.

[47] 'Song', pp. 8–9, 'On Lady T r C l's Ring', p. 165, both in *Festival of Love*.

[48] See James Raven, 'Historical Introduction: The Novel Comes of Age', in James Raven and Antonia Forster with the assistance of Stephen Bending (eds.), *The English Novel 1770–1829: A Bibliographical Survey of Prose Fiction Published in the British Isles. Volume I: 1770–1799*, general eds. Peter Garside, James Raven and Rainer Schöwerling (Oxford: Oxford University Press, 2000), pp. 42–3.

[49] Cheryl Turner, *Living by the Pen: Women Writers in the Eighteenth Century* (London: Routledge, 1992), pp. 152–216. See also Raven, 'Historical Introduction', pp. 45–9, which shows that, for novels where authorship can be identified, in the 1790s women accounted for 37 per cent of titles, compared to men's 31 per cent.

[50] Catherine Gallagher, *Nobody's Story: The Vanishing Acts of Women Writers in the Marketplace, 1670–1820* (Oxford: Clarendon Press, 1994).

Sexually explicit and implicit material has been placed at the heart of accounts
of new types of reading practice in the late-seventeenth and eighteenth centuries.
New forms of writing, particularly the novel, were designed for private, solitary *where*
and domestic reading, and pornography was the epitome of this new privatized
literature.[51] Reading practices themselves became eroticized in the eighteenth
century, Butler has argued, as the relationship between the text and lone reader
was amplified.[52] The notorious marker of this privatized, eroticized form of
reading was the encounter between Samuel Pepys (1633–1703) and a French
pornographic novel, recorded partly in code in his diary.[53] Pepys had considered
buying the book for his wife on 13 January 1668, but decided it was too 'bawdy,
lewd'. He returned to the booksellers on the Strand on 8 February to purchase
'that idle, roguish book' but resolved to burn it as soon as he had read it. After
drinking with friends, he retired to his chamber to read 'for information sake',
masturbated and, true to his word, reported 'after I had done it, I burned it'.[54]
This lone masturbating figure with his pornographic book stalks the history of
early-modern reading practices.

   This figure is supported by theories of the implied reader. According to
Wolfgang Iser, a reader 'actualizes' the 'prestructured' meaning of a text, and
thus experiences the literary effects embedded in the writing; 'response-inviting
structures' of a text, in other words, dictate reader response.[55] For these reasons,
an implied reader can be reconstructed from the text. It is this approach which
Jean-Marie Goulemot adopts in *Forbidden Texts* (1991), the only thoroughgoing
published account of reading sexually explicit or suggestive material in the

---

[51] Peter Brooks, *Body Work: Objects of Desire in Modern Narrative* (Cambridge, Mass.: Harvard
   University Press, 1993), p. 32. Also see Ruth Perry, *Women, Letters and the Novel* (New York:
   AMS Press, 1980), p. xii.
[52] Gerald Butler, *Love and Reading: An Essay in Applied Psychoanalysis* (New York: Peter Lang,
   1989), p. 29.
[53] Francis Barker, *The Tremulous Private Body: Essays on Subjection* (1984; Ann Arbor: University
   of Michigan Press, 1995), pp. 1–7. Though Ian Frederick Moulton regards Pepys as atypical of
   the seventeenth century, he also claims that Pepys was suggestive of a post-Enlightenment form
   of reading. See his 'Before Pornography: Explicitly Erotic Writing in Early Modern England',
   unpublished PhD thesis, Columbia University (1995), pp. 262–4. The argument for a move from
   communal to private reading between the sixteenth and eighteenth centuries is also noted in his
   book, though not developed. Ian Frederick Moulton, *Before Pornography: Erotic Writing in
   Early Modern England* (Oxford: Oxford University Press, 2000), p. 37.
[54] Robert Latham and William Matthews (eds.), *The Diary of Samuel Pepys* (London: Bell, 1976),
   vol. IX, 13 January and 8 February 1668, pp. 21–2, 57, 59.
[55] Wolfgang Iser, *The Implied Reader: Patterns of Communication in Prose Fiction from Bunyan to
   Beckett* (Baltimore: Johns Hopkins University Press, 1974), p. xii; Wolfgang Iser, *Prospecting:
   From Reader Response to Literary Anthropology* (Baltimore: Johns Hopkins University Press,
   1993), p. vii. For introductions to German reception theory and Anglo-American reader-response
   theory, see Robert Holub's *Reception Theory: A Critical Introduction* (London: Methuen, 1984);
   Elizabeth Freund, *The Return of the Reader: Reader Response Criticism* (London: Methuen,
   1987). This approach has been much used by medievalists. See, for example, David F. Hult,
   Self-Fulfilling Prophecies: Readership and Authority in the First Roman de la Rose (Cambridge:
   Cambridge University Press, 1986); Robert Sturges, *Medieval Interpretation: Models of Reading
   in Literary Narrative, 1100–1500* (Cardondale: Southern Illinois University Press, 1991).

eighteenth century. Goulemot sets out to extrapolate reader response from the strategies employed by the author. He claims that an eighteenth-century erotic novel produced 'the desire for physical pleasure in the reader, [placing] him or her in a position of tension and lack, the only escape from which can be provided by a recourse to the extra-literary'.[56] These books, in other words, led inexorably to a search for a sexual partner or to masturbation.

This approach, which deduces the reading context and response from the texts, provides only a partial account of readership and context. Indeed, other research has demonstrated that claims for the private, eroticized relationship between novel and reader have underestimated the extent of other forms of reading in this period. Middling-sort families enjoyed the latest novels while gathered around a male reader who edited and commented on the text as he read, and wives read aloud to their husbands.[57] In addition, to equate the structure of the text with a single possible reading experience leaves – in Goulemot's own words – 'absolutely no freedom of choice' for the reader.[58] Yet texts were open to a range of readings. Vivien Jones argues that even eighteenth-century conduct literature allowed space for women to read these books resistantly, rather than submissively.[59] Moreover, a variety of materials might have produced the exact response Goulemot identifies with erotic narrative structure. John Cannon (b. 1684), for example, was caught masturbating in possession of a midwifery text, soon confiscated by his mother.[60] Theories that proclaim that discrete genres are linked to distinct reader responses can be easily dislodged with micro studies, because textual structure was just one factor which manufactured reader's responses.

Yet eighteenth-century writers were certainly concerned that particular texts compelled particular responses. Worries about men and women retiring alone to their closet with immoral novel in hand were certainly rife, and much writing catalogued the physical perils awaiting those who read regardless of warnings.[61] The reading of suggestive material was considered a serious threat for women in particular. In 1695, the feminist Mary Astell cautioned that 'Plays and Romances' encouraged fellow womenfolk 'in the practice of the greatest

[56] Goulemot, *Forbidden Texts*, p. 115.
[57] Patricia Howell Michaelson, 'Women in the Reading Circle', *Eighteenth-Century Life* 13 (1990), pp. 59–69; Naomi Tadmor, ' "In the Even my Wife Read to Me": Women, Reading and Household Life in the Eighteenth Century', in James Raven, Helen Small and Naomi Tadmor (eds.), *The Practice and Representation of Reading in England* (Cambridge: Cambridge University Press, 1996), pp. 162–74.
[58] Goulemot, *Forbidden Texts*, p. 117. See also pp. 58–60.
[59] Vivien Jones, 'The Seductions of Conduct: Pleasure and Conduct Literature', in Roy Porter and Marie Mulvey Roberts (eds.), *Pleasure in the Eighteenth Century* (Basingstoke: Macmillan, 1996), p. 112.
[60] Hitchcock, *English Sexualities*, p. 14.
[61] Roy Porter, 'Reading is Bad for your Health', *History Today* 48 (1998), pp. 11–16; Adrian Johns, 'The Physiology of Reading in Restoration England', in Raven et al. (eds.), *Practice and Representation of Reading*, pp. 138–61.

Follies'.[62] Throughout this period, women were warned off '[t]hose despicable romances, which inflame the passions, or deprave the taste of the reader', or might even have 'fatal effects'.[63] The dangers were acute, because women were thought to have 'a *decided taste*' for romances.[64] Female writers of fiction themselves portrayed reading as a standard tool of seduction and cause of women's downfall.[65] Some men also harboured a belief in women's special vulnerability to the seductions of print. In his defence during his trial for adultery in 1793, Captain Hook responded to allegations that he had attempted to seduce his married niece with 'obscene prints' bought by his valet by trying to render the allegations improbable:

[S]upposing that I had the design of inflaming the passions, and seducing the virtue of this young woman, by exhibitions of obscenity; is it probable that I should have desired a common servant to have been the purchaser of such a thing? Even if I had been abandoned enough to have meant them for the private gratification of my own profligacy, it is a kind of secret I should have kept to myself, and therefore would have been myself the purchaser; and I should have been still more anxious to have concealed such a purchase, had I meant them for the secret purpose of corrupting an other.[66]

Though denying the allegation, Hook was especially concerned to point out that it was the publicity of the purchase – not the idea of seducing a vulnerable woman with the aid of print – that made the claim unconvincing.

These ideas about women's responses to erotic material were reflected in the imagined readers depicted within erotic texts. Some books envisage the reading of erotica as a socially and sexually democratic experience, being read disguised as 'Marriage Ceremony with Notes' by 'prudes, or women who would wish to be considered so', as 'An Essay on increasing the Poll-Tax' by statesmen, or as 'The pleasant Art of becoming a Bankrupt with Expedition and female Pity' by tradesmen, for example.[67] Equally playful are depictions of poor countrymen reading Ovid in translation or tracts examining 'the inconveniences of chastity'.[68] More typically, however, it is women who are depicted reading erotic material. Women's reading – which included French pornography – was a symptom of their supineness: 'having nothing else to do as they sit upon the Plains, they are always reading *Cassandra, Cleopatra, Grand-Cyrus, Amadis*

[62] [Mary Astell], *A Serious Proposal to the Ladies, for the Advancement of their True and Greatest Interest. By a Lover of that Sex*, 2nd edn. (Printed for R. Wilkin, at the King's-Head in St Paul's Church-Yard, 1695), p. 67.
[63] 'On Pleasures', *Lady's Magazine*, September 1774, p. 522; 'On Reading', *Lady's Magazine*, March 1775, p. 143.
[64] Ibid., p. 142.
[65] Mary Delarivier Manley, *Secret Memoirs and Manners of Several Persons of Quality, of Both Sexes. From the New Atalantis, an Island in the Mediterranean*, ed. Ros Ballaster (1709; London: Pickering and Chatto, 1991), pp. 30, 35–7.
[66] *Cuckold's Chronicle*, vol. 1, pp. 177, 189, 254. I am grateful to Seth Denbo for bringing this case to my attention.
[67] *Festival of Love*, p. iv.
[68] *Kick Him Jenny*, p. 8; *Did You Ever See Such Damned Stuff?*, p. 61.

de Gaul, Hero and Leander, the School of Venus, and the rest of the Female-Classics'.[69] The woman who masturbates in *A Chinese Tale* possesses a library bursting with suggestive material, while the modest Princess in *Did You Ever See Such Damned Stuff?* (1760) is discovered reading 'a new romance', rendering her subsequent sexual responsiveness more convincing.[70] The idea of female vulnerability frequently appeared in depictions of the use of suggestive material as a tool in female seduction. In *The Genuine Memoirs of the Celebrated Miss Maria Brown* (1766), a bawd scoffs at conventional moral hierarchies of literature, naming Richardson's *Pamela* (1740–1) as an example of 'bad books' which 'turned' her girls' brains. Instead, she provided 'Memoirs of a Woman of Pleasure [*Fanny Hill*] with cuts; or such lascivious prints for those who cannot read, as may tend to inflame their passions'.[71] Such was the power of books on women's brains, that one author begs for 'pages fraught with am'rous lore' to waft into the night-time bedchambers of young virgins.[72] Women are also envisaged reading those texts which depict the exploration of the female body as land. In his mock criticism of his own book, the author of *Merryland Displayed* complains that women as well as men are reading *A New Description of Merryland*. They were discussing it at the tea-table, he reports, pretending 'there is not a baudy Word in it' while relishing the 'smutty Allusion' gracing every page.[73] The references to tea and women were intimately connected, as tea-drinking was regarded as an activity associated with female laziness, gossip and frivolous expense.[74] The image is saturated with fears about female reading. But these imagined readers are not evidence of the nature of the reading experience.[75] A corollary of this interpretation would be that the relative lack of images of men reading erotica demonstrates that men did not read this material, an assertion which is unsustainable in the light of evidence for actual readers considered later in this chapter.

---

[69] [Charles Cotton], 'Erotopolis; Or, of the Situation of Bettyland', in [Philo-Brittanniae, pseud.], *The Potent Ally: Or, Succours from Merryland. With Three Essays in Praise of the Cloathing of that Country; and the Story of Pandora's Box. To which is added . . . The Present State of Bettyland*, 2nd edn. (Printed by direction of the author, and sold by the booksellers of London and Westminster, 'Paris', 1741), pp. 30–1.

[70] *Chinese Tale*, pp. 15–16; *Did You Ever See Such Damned Stuff?*, p. 20.

[71] *Genuine Memoirs of . . . Miss Maria Brown*, vol. I, pp. 156, 157.

[72] *Seventeen Hundred and Seventy-Seven*, p. 4.

[73] *Merryland Displayed*, pp. 5–6. Tea-drinking was culturally associated with the wealthy, but equipment for hot drinks was more commonly found amongst the possessions of manufacturing or commercial trades, rather than rich farmers or even the gentry. Lorna Weatherill, *Consumer Behaviour and Material Culture in Britain, 1660–1760* (London: Routledge, 1988), pp. 157–9, 166–89, esp. Table 8.4 on p. 188.

[74] See, for example, *The Good and Bad Effects of Tea Consider'd* (For John Wilkie, behind the Chapter-House, St Paul's Church-Yard, 1758), pp. 41–6. For an alternative reading of this erotic text, see Hitchcock, *English Sexualities*, p. 13.

[75] Though this is how they are sometimes used. See Goulemot, *Forbidden Texts*, pp. 30–50; Darnton, *Forbidden Best-Sellers*, pp. 222, 229–31.

Take, for example, the theme of women's vulnerability to print in depictions of imagined readers. Assumptions of female passivity have underpinned claims that the new female gender roles of the eighteenth century were created through new forms of print culture.[76] But not all women necessarily conformed to the image of the passive absorber of literary prescription. Warnings of women's vulnerability and the risks posed to them were grounded partly on exaggerated reports of women's corruption. The author of *The Unsex'd Females* (1798), for example, laments the saturation of women's art and writing with licentiousness, but one of the engravings used as evidence of this decline, designed by Emma Crewe, is much more demure and restrained than the images by Henry Fuseli in the same volume.[77] Margaret Spufford has used the depictions of women in seventeenth-century chapbooks to speculate about female readership, suggesting that because women were present as characters in the texts they may also have been present as readers of them.[78] In using evidence which apparently proclaimed women's consumption of sexual writing, however, we must ask what role these depictions perform in the context of the text. The claim that actual women wanted to read books in which women were portrayed as sexually active, for example, belies the assumption that such images were regarded as somehow 'positive'. Yet images of women being sexually active may have worked to undermine female reputations built on chastity.[79] Even the association between women and novels – commonplace in the eighteenth century – can be questioned. As Jan Fergus has suggested, moralists' claims of female addiction to novel reading reflect not women's activity, but 'fear of female fantasy or sexual stimulation'.[80]

Rather than see these imagined readers depicted within erotic texts as evidence of actual readers, we must ask how these images of women reading in erotica worked in the context of eighteenth-century culture. In eighteenth-century manuals on how to read, women were the focus for widespread fears about the dangers of private and intimate reading. They served as exemplars of the dramatic physical and psychological effects that books could have on

[76] Armstrong, *Desire and Domestic Fiction*; Kathryn Shevelow, *Women and Print Culture: The Construction of Femininity in the Early Periodical* (London: Routledge, 1989).
[77] *The Unsex'd Females: A Poem, Addressed to the Author of the Pursuits of Literature* (For Cadell and Davies, 1798), pp. 20–1. The engraving criticized was *Flora at Play with Cupid*, and appeared in Erasmus Darwin, *The Botanic Garden; A Poem, in Two Parts. Part 1 containing The Economy of Vegetation. Part 2. The Loves of the Plants*, 2 vols. (For J. Johnson, St Paul's Church-Yard, 1791), frontispiece, vol. II.
[78] Spufford, *Small Books*, pp. 63–4. Significantly, she cites no examples of actual women readers in support of this claim; the only examples produced are of men. See pp. 74–5.
[79] On the significance of chastity to the reputations of women, men and households, see Laura Gowing, *Domestic Dangers: Women, Words, and Sex in Early Modern London* (1996; Oxford: Clarendon Press, 1998). See, for example, pp. 85–6, 94.
[80] Jan Fergus, 'Women Readers: A Case Study', in Jones (ed.), *Women and Literature in Britain*, pp. 155–76. Quote from p. 173.

impressionable readers.[81] In addition, though material by and for women covered a range of topics, their reading was thought to comprise mainly imaginative genres while men's reading provided intellectual development.[82] The figure of the woman reader therefore emphasized the sensual effects of reading. In situating the reading of erotica in female-only environments, and in employing the exemplar of the female reader, erotic authors reinforced notions of women's laziness, their perpetual availability for sex and their uncontrollable sexual desires when exposed to an effective stimulus. They also seemed to insist that it was women, rather than men, that were susceptible to erotic literature and the perils of solitary reading.[83]

Similar caution is needed when dealing with other evidence from erotic texts, particularly forms of address and dedication. In comments on intended readership, there was often inconsistency. Texts are dedicated 'To our Fair Readers', or authors might direct their declarations to 'You heedless Maids', but men and women are often addressed together.[84] *The Fifteen Comforts of Matrimony* (1706), for example, is dedicated to those without lovers: 'Batchelors, Maids & Widowers'; while the readers that the author professes to be 'most desirous of pleasing' in *The Fruit-Shop* (1765) are 'L A D I E S and Gentlemen'.[85] Common was the stated male reader. '[T]he Reader' of *A New Description of Merryland* is indubitably a 'he' according to the author,[86] and, bearing many similarities to this spoof travel book, *A Voyage to Lethe* (1741) is targeted at 'that learned Body of Men, which composes the Royal Society'.[87] The epistolary *A Spy on Mother Midnight* (1748) is addressed to the male narrator's friend 'Jack', and, not surprisingly, the account of 'our Wives' good Nature to others' in the

---

[81] Peter de Bolla, *The Discourse of the Sublime* (Oxford: Basil Blackwell, 1989), pp. 249, 250 and passim; Jacqueline Pearson, *Women's Reading in Britain, 1750–1835: A Dangerous Recreation* (Cambridge: Cambridge University Press, 1999), p. 219.

[82] Pearson, *Women's Reading*, p. 19. For advice on what women should read, see 'A Compendious Abstract of Ancient History', *Lady's Magazine*, January 1773, pp. 25–7; 'A Chronological Account of the most Remarkable Discoveries in the Arts and Science', *Lady's Magazine*, December 1773, pp. 639–40. Dr Gregory advised women to read history, art and science. See *Lady's Magazine*, November 1783, p. 588.

[83] The depictions of readers as women also facilitated the representation of a range of male bodies. See chapter five.

[84] *The Surprize: Or, the Gentleman Turn'd Apothecary. A Tale written originally in French Prose; afterwards Translated into Latin; and from thence now Versified in Hudibrastics* (Printed and sold by the Booksellers of London and Westminster, 1739); *Fifteen Plagues of a Maiden-Head*, p. 6. Indeed, authors were sometimes inconsistent regarding the gender of the reader they addressed within a single text. See, for example, *Genuine Memoirs of . . . Miss Maria Brown*, vol. II p. 165, where the readership is first noted as male, and subsequently as encompassing men and women.

[85] *The Fifteen Comforts of Matrimony: Or, A Looking-Glass for All those who have Enter'd in that Holy and Comfortable State* (no publication details, 1706); *Fruit-Shop* (1765), vol. I, p. xviii.

[86] *New Description of Merryland*, pp. xiv, viii.

[87] *A Voyage to Lethe* (For Mrs Laycock, at Mr Clevercock's [pseud.], in Smock-Alley, Glasgow, 1756), p. 9.

preface of *The Fifteen Comforts of Cuckoldom* (1706) figures the readers as male.[88]

Such comments have been used as a guide to likely readers of the material.[89] Yet to take the claims of erotic authors on trust ignores the panoply of tricks of the erotic book trade. These books were not simply printed anonymously and without publication details, but were also furnished with blatantly pseudonymous authors and places of publication. Invariably, these were exploited as opportunities for punning. *A New Description of Merryland* is supposedly written by 'Roger Pheuquewell', whose family are 'remarkable for their being Red-Headed, of great Note, and of *long standing* in that Country'.[90] Other authors, such as 'Lucretia Lovejoy', Philogynes Clitorides ('*Botanist, and one of the Missionaries of the Society of* Jesuits *for* propagating KNOWLEDGE in foreign Parts'), and Captain Sam Cock, descendent of the Cock family of '*Coney-Hatch*' and the Laycock family of '*Cunnington* in *Huntingdonshire*', are similarly and obviously fictional.[91] Such references were not innocent jibes, however, but functioned as useful signals to prospective buyers, indicating the type of publication on offer.[92]

Moreover, there was sometimes a disparity between the gender of the stated reader and the gender of the reader who emerges from closer textual analysis. For example, in the riddle *Little Merlin's Cave* (1737) the object is the female genitalia, and just as the riddle is recited to a woman by the male gardener, so the explicitly stated reader is female.[93] The main text of the poem, however, imagines the reader as male. Initially, men are simply described enjoying the 'cave' in heterosexual encounters, but in verse 14 the use of the word 'us' serves to unify the male narrator with the readers.[94] Subsequently, the author repeatedly

[88] *Spy on Mother Midnight*, p. 1; *The Fifteen Comforts of Cuckoldom. Written by a Noted Cuckold in the New-Exchange in the Strand* (no publication details, 1706), p. 2.
[89] Penelope Wilson, 'Classical Poetry and the Eighteenth-Century Reader', in Rivers (ed.), *Books and their Readers*.
[90] *New Description of Merryland*, pp. i–ii.
[91] Lucretia Lovejoy, sister to Mr Adam Strong, author of the Electrical Eel [pseud.], *An Elegy on the Lamented Death of the Electrical Eel, or Gymnotus Electricus. With the Lapidary Inscription, as Placed on a Superb Erection, at the Expence of the Countess of H—, and Chevalier-Madame D'Eon de Beaumont* (For Fielding and Walker, No. 20 Pater-Noster-0, 1777); Philogynes Clitorides [pseud.], *The Natural History of the Frutex Vulvaria, or Flowering Shrub: As it is Collected from the Best Botanists both Ancient and Modern* (Publication details and date torn off, [c. 1737]); and *Voyage to Lethe* (1756), p. 4. The author of *The Fruit-Shop* explained that the word 'Philogynists' was a compound of the Greek words for 'lover' and 'women': i.e. lover of women. See vol. II, p. 113. 'Coney' appears to be a reference to female genitalia or pubic hair. See 'The Coney-Skin Merchant', *Bacchanalian Magazine*, pp. 118–19.
[92] The same techniques were used in France. See Goulemot, *Forbidden Texts*, pp. 79–105.
[93] [Edward Ward], *Little Merlin's Cave. As it was Latel'y Discover'd by a Gentleman's Gardener, in Maidenhead-Thicket to which is added, A Riddle: Or a Paradoxical Character of an Hairy Monster, often found under Holland*, 4th edn. (For T. Read, in Dogwell-Court, White Fryers, 1737), p. 1.
[94] *A Riddle: Of a Paradoxical Character*, p. 5. This poem is identical to *Little Merlin's Cave* apart from the two-verse introduction in the latter.

aligns himself with a male audience, making comments which situate this 'us'
against the object of the riddle.[95] These comments suggest the author's intended
readership, but these intentions were not necessarily satisfied by actual readers.
Indeed, when discussing the response they expected to produce in a reader,
these authors expected readers to actively engage with their writings. These
statements are suggestive, if not about likely readers, then certainly about the
likely ways of reading. Aiming at 'Pleasure and Satisfaction', the author of *A
New Description of Merryland* recognizes that reception might vary, and hopes
that 'If it affords him no *Improvement*, I may venture to promise it will at least
give him some *Entertainment*'.[96] Most authors recognized that the autonomy
of readers produced a lack of uniformity of response. The author of *A Voyage to
Lethe* explains that he would be disappointed if the reader was not 'delighted'
with the book, but acknowledges that 'it will be in the Power of every Reader,
Beau or Belle, from his or her Experience to give me the Lye.'[97]

Significantly, erotic authors did not proclaim their work as aids to masturbation, but suggested they wanted to make people laugh. The story recounted
in *The Surprize* (1739), for example, has apparently 'excited many a Joke'.[98]
Published in 1765, *The Fruit-Shop* assures its readers that they have 'hit upon
facetious company', rather than 'fallen into a gloomy club', though the author
recognizes that 'no author or authors, can be so vain as to expect, or even to
think that they shall please all readers'.[99] Later in the century, as Illustration 4
suggests, *The Bacchanalian Magazine* (1793) was placed in the context of Bacchus and Venus (the gods of wine and love), and the collection *Hilaria* (1798)
was similarly situated in the context of 'the delights of love and the joys of wine,
happily blended'.[100] But it is not expected that all readers of *Hilaria* will react
alike to the poems. '[T]he cynic, the sanctified hypocrite, and the misanthrope,
will eagerly condemn many of them,' for example, 'but the man of the world,
who thinks liberally, and acts up to his feelings, the *bon vivant*, the friend of
the fair sex, the bottle and song, will, it is hoped and presumed, place them
under their private care and protection'.[101] Some historians have suggested that
likely responses to material can be deduced from the responses expected by
authors, but English erotic authors denied the possibility of predictable reader
response.[102]

[95] *A Riddle: Of a Paradoxical Character*, see for example, p. 6 (verse 23) 'It tempts us',
(verse 27) 'To pay us back', p. 7 (verse 28) 'it lets us taste', (verse 29) 'in we pop', (verse
32) 'stops our ruin', p. 8 (verse 36) 'it draws us in'.
[96] *New Description of Merryland*, p. xiv.   [97] *Voyage to Lethe* (1756), p. 3.
[98] *Surprize*, p. 137.   [99] *Fruit-Shop*, vol. I, pp. 20, 79.
[100] [William Hewardine or Hewerdine?], *Hilaria. The Festive Board* (Printed for the Author, 1798),
p. i.
[101] Ibid., p. vii.
[102] James Raven has also noted an eighteenth-century 'sense of contingency' with regard to reception. See 'New Reading Histories', p. 283. For some instances where authorial comment has

Illustration 4: *Entwine. The Myrtle of Venus with Bacchus's Vine.* Frontispiece to *The Bacchanalian Magazine* (1793).

A model of critical reading was reinforced by the liberal plagiarism of non-erotic texts by erotic authors. The debt of erotic authors to other fiction and non-fiction books was wonderfully illustrated in *Merryland Displayed*, in which Thomas Stretser exposed the degree to which he had plagiarized in his previous book, *A New Description of Merryland*. Not only did he produce a list of thirty-five books he had used or claimed to have used, he also revealed precisely which lines of *A New Description of Merryland* were lifted from which non-erotic texts.[103] Dissecting his earlier text phrase by phrase, Stretser's *Merryland Displayed* is testimony to a faith in the ability of readers to have critical responses to a text.[104] Readers were thus plunged into an ethos of critical reading. Erotic books satirized botany, science, travel literature and much more,

plagury

---

been used as guidance for readership, see Chartier, 'Book Markets', pp. 123–4; Darnton, *Forbidden Best-Sellers*, pp. 223, 226. See also Robert L. Montgomery, *Terms of Response: Language and Audience in Seventeenth- and Eighteenth-Century Theory* (Philadelphia, Pa.: Pennsylvania State University Press, 1992).

[103] Wagner, *Eros Revived*, pp. 303–9; Paul-Gabriel Boucé, 'The Secret Nexus: Sex and Literature in Eighteenth-Century Britain', in Alan Bold (ed.), *The Sexual Dimension in Literature* (London: Vision, 1982), pp. 70–89; *Merryland Displayed*, pp. 54–6.

[104] There are several examples of borrowing in erotica. Lawrence Sterne was praised in *The Rake of Taste, Or the Elegant Debauchee: A True Story* (For P. Wicks, in Pater-Noster-Row, 1760), p. 9, and criticized in [Helenus Scott], *The Adventures of a Rupee* (Dublin: Printed by W.

but they also satirized a one-dimensional way of reading in which claims to verisimilitude were unquestioningly accepted by the reader. The evidence for readers within erotic texts is slippery, but while it offers little concrete information about actual readers, it does show how authors styled the consumption of their material. Erotica was portrayed as having a powerful and sensual effect on its imagined female readers; in contrast, authors presented the consumers of erotica as autonomous, free-thinking and united in merriment.

Cultural milieu

The very playfulness of erotic texts allows us to situate this material culturally, and there are other kinds of evidence that can help locate erotica in a cultural milieu. Adverts are suggestive of the literary setting of erotic writing. Few erotic books carried adverts, but those that did promoted a range of reading. *The Festival of Love* (1770), for example, carried advertisements for the romance *Santmaria: Or, the Mysterious Pregnancy. A Novel* and the suggestive *Emily de Varmont: Or, Divorce Dictated by Necessity*.[105] Yet this erotic collection also recommended *The Festival of Wit* – supposedly selected by King George III, described as 'not a delicate *Moreceau* for the polite Circles only', but as a book which 'must suit the taste of every Man who loves cheerful conversation and Attic Wit' – and *Advice to the Officers of the British Army*.[106] An earlier edition of the latter book was advertised in the erotic *The Prostitutes of Quality* (1757). The author of *Advice to the Officers of the British Army* (1783) was quite clear that erotic and pornographic material was staple reading matter for young officers passing the 'tedious hours in camp or garrison'. Cleland's

Spotewood, for Messrs Price, Whitestone, Walker, White, Beatty, Burton, E. Cross and Bryne, 1782), pp. viii–ix. The series of volumes which contained John Hawkesworth's edited versions of James Cook's and Joseph Banks' journals of their voyages of 1768–71, first published in 1773, were mentioned by the author of *Seventeen Hundred and Seventy-Seven*, p. 20. One man tried to seduce a woman 'in the Style of the *Whole Duty of Man*', one of the most popular devotionals by Richard Allestree. See *Spy on Mother Midnight*, p. 6.

    On critical dialogues between erotic texts see, for example, *Natural History of the Frutex Vulvaria* ([c. 1737]), p. 19, and *Arbor Vitae* (1741); Adam Strong [pseud., James Perry?], *Electrical Eel*; *Elegy on the Lamented Death of the Electrical Eel*, and *Old Serpent's Reply to the Electrical Eel*; *The Torpedo, A Poem to the Electrical Eel. Addressed to Mr John Hunter, Surgeon: and Dedicated to The Right Honourable Lord Cholmondeley* (Printed and sold by all the Booksellers in London and Westminster, 1777); *A Riddle: Of a Paradoxical Character* and *A Riddle. In Answer to the Hairy Monster, by a Young Lady* (No publication details, [Dublin?, 1725?]).

[105] The editions consulted here were *Emily De Varmont; Or Divorce Dictated by Necessity; to which are added the Amours of Father Sévin*, 3 vols. (For G. Kearsley, no. 46, Fleet-Street, 1798) and *Santa-Maria; Or, The Mysterious Pregnancy. A Romance* (For G. Kearsley, no. 46, Fleet-Street, 1797).

[106] *Festival of Love*, p. xii; see the collection of reviews reproduced in *Advice to the Officers of the British Army*, 6th edn. (By W. Richardson, for G. Kearsley, in Fleet-Street, 1783), pp. 1–4.

'*The Woman of Pleasure*' and Rochester's poems, for example, promise to 'warm the imagination and inspire to military achievements'; while '*Trials for Adultery*', packed with sexual scandal and intrigue, will lend 'a fund of historical and legal information'.[107] Readers of *The Prostitutes of Quality* were also directed towards *The Letter-Writer's New and Complete Instructor* and *The Youth's Pocket-Companion*. The latter was marketed as a book 'for every young Man',[108] and the book itself apparently contained 'what is absolutely necessary for every young Man to know and practice'.[109] Advertisements in and for erotic books suggest that erotica was one component of a spectrum of material, much of it explicitly aimed at men.

A great deal of information about the cultural setting of erotica can be gleaned from the texts. This is because the kind of knowledge required for the comprehension of a book can help in identifying 'not only the class of reader the author is addressing (for example the reader's age, sex, social status or level of education, information about which can often be learnt simply from the title page or preface), but, more importantly, the moral, intellectual, or social assumptions that he shares with his reader.'[110] In taking this route we come close to the approach of Stanley Fish, and begin to reconstruct an 'interpretive community' of eighteenth-century erotica, a setting in which the interpretation and meaning of texts were shared.[111] In order to comprehend all the jokes and innuendoes in erotica, a reader required access to varied cultural resources. These included novels and poetry, classical mythology, biblical tales, theology, ancient and modern world history, European conflicts, ancient medicine, recent science and contemporary quackery, botany, natural history, reports of voyages and expeditions, the love-lives of the rich and famous, and the popular haunts of prostitutes, to name but a few. Certainly, erotica was comprehensible to those who did not possess substantial libraries. The richness and density of this material stemmed partly from the way it performed on different levels. Complex

---

107 Ibid., p. 79.
108 *The Prostitutes of Quality; or, Adultery a-la-mode. Being Authentic and Genuine Memoirs of Several Persons of the Highest Quality* (For J. Cooke & J. Coote, opposite Devereux-Court, in the Strand, 1757), pp. 223–4.
109 George Wilson, *The Youth's Pocket-Companion: Or, Universal Preceptor*, 2nd edn. (For J. Coote, at the King's Arms, Pater-noster-row, 1749), title page. I have not been able to locate a book of the exact title *The Letter-Writer's New and Complete Instructor*. However, J. Cooke (one of the publishers of *The Prostitutes of Quality*) did publish James Wallace's *Every Man his own Letter-Writer: Or, The New and Complete Art of Letter-Writing* (For J. Cooke, no. 17, Pater-noster Row, 1780), directed at the 'man of quality, the gentleman, the tradesman, the mechanic, the servant' (p. xi). The copy at the British Library, pressmark 10923.a.29, is inscribed 'Tho[mas]. Benson's Book 1785, Newcastle July 17.'
110 Rivers, 'Introduction', in Rivers (ed.), *Books and their Readers*, p. 1.
111 Stanley Fish, *Is there a Text in this Class? The Authority of Interpretive Communities* (Cambridge, Mass.: Harvard University Press, 1980). Kevin Sharpe points out that this approach has been neglected by historians. See Kevin Sharpe, *Reading Revolutions: The Politics of Reading in Early Modern England* (New Haven: Yale University Press, 2000), p. 60.

puns stood alongside bawdy innuendo, and so the varieties of humour ensured appeal to an audience of some breadth. However, the historical, scientific and classical allusions in erotica allow us to position this material more firmly in terms of rank and gender. As already discussed, erotica resists simple categorization in terms of labouring/non-labouring, popular/elite, but the types of knowledge alluded to in erotica suggest that the material should be situated in a masculine context in which elite learning was familiar.

The use of Latin and classical history and mythology in erotic material is a useful example with which to illustrate some key points. Familiarity with the Classics certainly aided the reader of erotica in the comprehension of style, plot and characterization, and a knowledge of Latin was indispensable for understanding parts of some texts.[112] Poems such as 'Loaves and Fishes' in *The Bacchanalian Magazine* used Latin extensively, and would barely have been understood without some grasp of the language.[113] Eighteenth-century women writers certainly read Latin, though even a poet of the 'Augustan Age' such as Mary Leapor (1722–46) would have possessed a patchy knowledge at best.[114] Lady Mary Wortley Montagu (1689–1762) used Latin extensively in her letters, while Anne Lister (d. 1840) learned Latin and Greek in order to seek out references to love and sex between women.[115] At the same time, however, Montagu's letters suggest an awareness that her knowledge of Latin was unusual or unsuitable for a woman, while Lister publicly denounced classical learning as improper for women.[116] The thirst for classical obscenity displayed by the extraordinary Lister seems poor evidence for numbers of eighteenth-century women secretly learning Latin in search of the sections censored by contemporary translators. But the duplicity practised by Montagu and Lister may have been widespread. Moreover, women did read English books detailing ancient history, myth and literature, while others read the Classics in translation, devoid

---

[112] There is a use of the Classics in *Natural History of the Frutex Vulvaria* ([c. 1737]), pp. 2, 3; *The Whim! Or, the Maid-Stone Bath. A Kentish Poetic* (For J. Williams, in Paternoster-Row, 1782), p. 7; *Description of the Temple of Venus*, pp. 6–10; and *Man-Plant*, pp. 10–11.

[113] 'Loaves and Fishes', in *Bacchanalian Magazine*, p. 36.

[114] Martha Rainbolt, 'Their Ancient Claim: Sappho and Seventeenth- and Eighteenth-Century British Women's Poetry', *The Seventeenth Century* 12 (1997), pp. 112–4; Richard Greene, *Mary Leapor: A Study in Eighteenth-Century Women's Poetry* (Oxford: Clarendon Press, 1993), pp. 167–70.

[115] Joseph W. Lew, 'Lady Mary's Portable Seraglio', *Eighteenth-Century Studies* 24 (1991), p. 435; Anna Clark, 'Anne Lister's Construction of Lesbian Identity', *Journal of the History of Sexuality* 7 (1996), pp. 31–5.

[116] At the age of 20, Montagu's comments on her self-taught knowledge of the classical languages suggest a degree of hesitancy and self-deprecation in keeping with an endeavour not widely condoned. In her mid-sixties, she was bold enough to suggest that her eldest granddaughter be educated in 'the Languages', but counselled that it was 'absolutely necessary' that the girl conceal all such learning. See Mary Wortley Montagu, *Selected Letters*, ed. Isobel Grundy (London: Penguin, 1997), pp. 5–6, 9, 378–82. On Lister, see Clark, 'Anne Lister's Construction of Lesbian Identity', p. 32.

of the more explicitly sexual content.[117] Thus, some women were equipped to understand the many classical references which peppered erotica. Indeed, some women rivalled men with the knowledge necessary to understand most erotic allusions. The substantial reading list of Anna Larpent (b. 1758), wife of a successful civil servant, for example, was dominated by English and French works of fiction, but also included books on travel, botany and history.[118] Larpent was well-placed to understand many of the satirical intricacies of eighteenth-century erotica, though it seems unlikely that the devout Larpent would have coveted or countenanced erotica.

And here lies the rub: an individual's reading of erotica was not wholly determined by his or her library. Readers did not actually require any foreign languages or classical knowledge in order to read most erotic writing. Indeed, erotic books were educative on all these issues: the accounts of the lives of the gods were partial, admittedly, but provide more detail than most modern dictionaries of classical mythology. Even the author of *A New Description of Merryland*, who quoted from Latin and Arabic texts, confessed he was unable to read these languages and had relied heavily on English translations.[119] To be sure, it was typically female ignorance of classical languages which authors commented on. One fictional female author of erotica supposedly translates a Latin inscription while apologizing that it was 'far beyond the flight of a feminine pen', and the author of *The Fruit-Shop* explains that the Latin citations have been translated 'for the sake of the ladies'.[120] Yet such translations would have proved helpful to those men whose competency in Latin was limited. In any case, both with and without translations, substantial parts of the texts remained absolutely comprehensible.

Regardless of a person's library, then, understanding of much of these texts was perfectly possible. Reading was not only governed by social, economic and educational factors, however, but also by cultural factors which condoned or delimited certain forms of reading for certain individuals. In a number of areas, historians have begun to grapple with the gendering – the association primarily with either men or women, or with masculine or feminine traits – of written and spoken words in both representation and practice. It is clear, for example, that languages were gendered in the eighteenth century. Though in the late seventeenth century Latin was thought by some to render men's conversation awkward, by the late eighteenth century Latin was characterized

---

[117] Vickery, *Gentleman's Daughter*, pp. 258–9, 343; John Brewer, 'Reconstructing the Reader: Prescriptions, Texts and Strategies in Anna Larpent's Reading', in Raven et al. (eds.), *Practice and Representation of Reading*, p. 229.

[118] Brewer, 'Reconstructing the Reader', p. 229.

[119] *Merryland Displayed*, pp. 55–6. Here, the author of *A New Description of Merryland* reveals how he had written the earlier book.

[120] *Elegy on the Lamented Death of the Electrical Eel*, p. 29; *Fruit-Shop*, vol. I, p. xx.

as a masculine subject, disciplining the mind and accentuating appropriate gender differences. French, in contrast, was increasingly regarded as a feminine language.[121] Accordingly, one characteristic of medical books directed at an elite, male audience between 1500 and 1750 was the use of Latin.[122] A classical education was central to elite male culture; it became the 'most popular way of instilling manliness'.[123] Indeed, Samuel Johnson described his programme of classical reading as 'all literature, Sir, all ancient writers, all manly'.[124]

Gendered differentiation took place in other eighteenth-century publications. Although the polite world of early-eighteenth-century periodicals such as the *Tatler* (1709–11) and the *Spectator* (1711–13) tried to forge a community inclusive of men and women, the tone of the writings changed dramatically according to the assumed audience.[125] Books on various subjects were geared in different ways towards women: a female reader commented approvingly that a book was 'written in a light and easy style, to make it palatable to a lady's taste'.[126] Women writers also produced very different material for male and female readers. The topics, tone and language of Lady Mary Wortley Montagu's letters, for example, were based partly on whether the recipient was male or female. Men were given accounts of the distant past, religion and poetry, often using lengthy Latin quotations, while women were sent tales about contemporary women in English.[127] Of course, the fact that a woman was so flexible in her writing demonstrates how norms of gendered forms of writing could be exploded. Ultimately, however, Montagu's letters reveal the extent to which strong-willed women condoned notions of gendered speech and writing.

With regards to literature on sex, subtle gradations differentiated those materials deemed suitable for men or women. Women were surely as eager to learn about sex as men: mixed audiences apparently attended the frank lectures on sex and reproduction given by the notorious quack Dr James Graham in the late eighteenth century, for example.[128] Nevertheless, material explicitly designed for women was written and packaged in distinctive ways. Early-eighteenth-century

---

[121] Cohen, *Fashioning Masculinity*, pp. 26–7, 82–8.

[122] Patricia Crawford, 'Sexual Knowledge in England, 1500–1750', in Roy Porter and Mikuláš Teich (eds.), *Sexual Knowledge, Sexual Science: The History of Attitudes to Sexuality* (Cambridge: Cambridge University Press, 1994), p. 94.

[123] Pearson, *Women's Reading*, pp. 69–71. Quote from Carolyn D. Williams, *Pope, Homer and Manliness: Some Aspects of Eighteenth-Century Classical Learning* (London: Routledge, 1993), p. 38.

[124] Johnson quoted in Williams, *Pope, Homer and Manliness*, p. 39.

[125] Stephen Copley, 'Commerce, Conversation and Politeness in the Early Eighteenth-Century Periodical', *British Journal for Eighteenth-Century Studies* 18 (1995), p. 68. See also Pearson, *Women's Reading*, p. 19, for details of the gendering of literary genres.

[126] This comment was made in 1813 by the governess Ellen Weeton about R. Morgan's *Letters on Mythology addressed to a Lady*. See Ellen Weeton, *Miss Weeton's Journal of a Governess*, ed. Edward Hall (1939; Newton Abbot: David and Charles, 1969), vol. II, p. 77.

[127] Lew, 'Lady Mary's Portable Seraglio', p. 435.

[128] Eric Jameson, *The Natural History of Quackery* (London: Michael Joseph, 1961), p. 125.

women writers of amatory fiction may have produced work which was 'explicitly erotic in its concentration on the representation of sentimental love', but the writing was still affected by 'a publishing industry that differentiate[d] between the desires of male and female readers'.[129] In addition, while erotica was male-centred, amatory fiction was female-centred, not only expressing female sexuality without fear of condemnation, but communicating women's power and agency.[130] Desirous to attract female readers and protect female modesty, authors of other books on sex chose sober styles and titles for their books.[131] The author of a natural history book of 1802 assured female readers that 'every indelicate subject is scrupulously excluded'.[132] No doubt some women openly or covertly eschewed such delicacies. Unhindered by notions of feminine delicacy, female writers invented gruesome tales of childbirth and infanticide.[133] Similarly, a few women penned frank midwifery texts, though they claimed this safeguarded the modesty of all other women.[134] Women also censored their own publications. An English female translator of a travel book on Africa 'softened' the parts concerning the 'Hottentot Venus' – African women thought to have unusual genitalia – citing both 'the temper and genius of English readers' and 'the delicacy of a female translator' as justification.[135] Women were not necessarily the passive imbibers of moral warnings, but it is clear that some chose to bow to the force of expectation or felt that these gendered distinctions should be maintained.

Women were also warned against 'low puns, and obscene innuendoes'.[136] But while much erotica undoubtedly fell into this category, the humour was often couched in quite different terms. Readers were expected to recognize puns based on their elite knowledge, and this is suggestive not only of the rank and gender of readers, but perhaps also of the style of reading. Goulemot argues that eighteenth-century pornographic novels excluded jokes because humour created a distance between reader and text which disrupted the masturbatory effect of pornography.[137] In contrast, a liberal use of humour in erotica gave the impression that erotic material catered for other pleasures besides the sexual and the physical. Erotic authors were here negotiating a taxonomy of pleasures developed by moralists, in which emphasis was placed on the satisfaction of natural but controlled impulses: 'the meer necessities of Nature' rather than

---

[129] Ballaster, *Seductive Forms*, pp. 31, 35.   [130] Ibid., pp. 34–5.

[131] Crawford, 'Sexual Knowledge', pp. 93, 94.

[132] William Bingley, *Animal Biography; or, Authentic Anecdotes of the Lives, Manners and Economy of the Animal Creation*, 3 vols. (1802; For Richard Phillips, No. 6, Bridge-Street, 1805), vol. I, p. vi. I am grateful to Nick Webb for this reference.

[133] See, for instance, Manley, *New Atalantis*, pp. 83–4.

[134] Crawford, 'Sexual Knowledge', p. 95.

[135] François Le Vaillant, *Travels from the Cape of Good-Hope into the Interior Parts of Africa*, trans. Elizabeth Helme (For William Lane, Leadenhall-Street, 1790), vol. I, p. x.

[136] 'On Pleasures', *Lady's Magazine*, September 1773, p. 523.

[137] Goulemot, *Forbidden Texts*, p. 91.

'the desires of voluptuousness and idleness'.[138] This distinction between 'the *Cravings of Nature*' and 'the *Wantonness of Appetite*' was discussed in the context of luxury.[139] Luxury threatened moral corruption, bodily degeneration, the dilution of English culture and the compromising of national security. It also threatened to 'deface Manhood' with effeminacy.[140] One of the key themes in this discourse on luxury was pleasure. Pleasure could be 'a real good', but only when enjoyed in moderation.[141] The point of crisis came when the senses became 'wild Masters' of the 'Reasonable Creature'.[142] There was, Thomas Cole explained, 'a wide difference between voluptuousness, and insensibility; between renouncing one's animal nature entirely, and being a perfect slave to it'.[143] In order to resist 'unmanly Gratifications', men had to be equipped with autonomy and self-control.[144]

As a genre which discussed feelings of sexual passion and pleasure, erotic material appeared to threaten readers' self-governance. But the nature of erotic humour, and the knowledge from which much of it was drawn, transformed the genre into an appropriate diversion in which specialized and elite knowledge was confirmed. Contrary to the sensual reading symbolized by the imagined female readers, much of the content of erotica suggested quite a different mode of reading. Not simply (if at all) about physical gratification, erotica seemed to yield pleasure of a largely intellectual nature. Authors situated their writings within a wide range of reading, and they emphasized the autonomy of individual readers, readers whom they distanced from the workings of the passions with which erotic writings were concerned.

External evidence

How do these likely, implied, imagined and stated readers compare to the actual readers of eighteenth-century erotica? In ascertaining the actual readers of

---

[138] Anthony Horneck, *Delight and Judgment: Or, a prospect of the Great Day of Judgment, And its Power to damp, and imbitter Sensual Delights, Sports, and Recreations* (H. Hills Jun. for Mark Pardoe at the Sign of the Black Raven, over against Bedford House in the Strand, London, 1684), p. 139.

[139] *Of Luxury, More Particularly with respect to Apparel* (For T. Green, over-against Falstaff's-Heed, near Charing-Cross, London, 1736), p. 34.

[140] George MacKenzie, *The Moral History of Frugality. With its Opposite Vices, Covetousness, Niggardliness, Prodigality and Luxury* (Edinburgh, 1691), p. 11. See also *Faustina: or the Roman Songstress, A Satyr, on the Luxury and Effeminacy of the Age* (For J. Roberts, at the Oxford Arms, in Warwick Lane, London, [1726?]), pp. 4, 5.

[141] *Luxury no Political Evil, but demonstratively Proved to be Necessary to the Preservation and Prosperity of States* (Sold by R. Baldwin, Paternoster-Row, London [1780]), p. 23.

[142] *Luxury no Political Evil*, p. 33. Quote from MacKenzie, *Moral History*, p. 33.

[143] Thomas Cole, *Discourses on Luxury, Infidelity, and Enthusiasm* (For R. and J. Dodsley, in Pall-Mall, London, 1761), pp. 4–5.

[144] *The Tryal of the Lady Allurea Luxury* (For F. Noble, at his Circulating-Library in King-Street, Covent-Garden and J. Noble, at his Circulating-Library, in St Martin's Court, near Leicester-Square, London, 1757), p. 88.

erotica, the most illuminating evidence must be references of reading external to the books. Such references are rare, and the bleakness of the English field
is highlighted when compared with Robert Darnton's work on France which,
though based on sources far superior to evidence available for England, is itself
built on 'scraps of evidence'.[145] For England, Lawrence Stone's analysis of a
Norwich group of men and women stands alone and the integration of pornography into the affair, Stone conceded, was based on pure conjecture.[146] Yet
other evidence does exist, and this confirms the model of the male homosocial
reader.[147] Few extant copies of erotic books are inscribed: the erotic books *A
Voyage to Lethe* and *Adventures of a Rupee* were signed 'James Comerford' and
'John Warnford Armstrong' respectively.[148] More fulsome evidence exists for
the social contexts of reading, and this situates erotica in exclusive, sociable,
all-male environments. While there were surely other forms of erotic reading
which went unrecorded, these examples facilitate an exploration of 'the *event
of reading*'.[149] The final section of this chapter explores not simply who read
erotica, therefore, but how the material was consumed and (crucially) what this
consumption meant in an eighteenth-century English context.

Erotica circulated in the homosocial environment of clubs and coffee houses,
which served as libraries and venues for book sales. One edition of *The Secret
History of Pandora's Box* (1742), a spoof essay typical of many erotic texts, is
inscribed 'N2 Tom's Coffee House Sep 29 17—', for example.[150] Moreover,
for decades coffee houses had featured a particular kind of reading: one of reading aloud, perhaps with the audience interjecting, or of reading as a prelude to
conversation.[151] Coffee houses were thus exemplary of an increased possibility
for 'shared and formalized reading', arising from the greater number of smaller
book formats available.[152] And erotica was part of this oral culture. The Beef-
Steak Society, an all-male club which met in London coffee houses from 1709,

---

[145] Darnton, *Forbidden Best-Sellers*, p. 219.
[146] Lawrence Stone, 'Libertine Sexuality in Post-Restoration England: Group Sex and Flagellation
among the Middling Sort in Norwich in 1706–07', *Journal of the History of Sexuality* 2 (1992),
pp. 521–5.
[147] Goulemot's examples of erotic reading in France also pertain to men. See *Forbidden Texts*,
pp. 13–29.
[148] *A Voyage to Lethe*, BL: Cup.1001.c.4; *Adventures of a Rupee* (1782), BL: 1607/1648.
[149] Janice Radway, *Reading the Romance: Women, Patriarchy, and Popular Literature* (1984;
London: Verso, 1987), p. 7.
[150] *Secret History of Pandora's Box*, BL: RB.23.a.14343. There were at least six Tom's Coffee
Houses in London at that time. See Bryant Lillywhite, *London Coffee Houses: A Reference
Book of Coffee Houses of the Seventeenth, Eighteenth and Nineteenth Centuries* (London:
Allen and Unwin, 1963), pp. 580–96. Sexually explicit material was also sold at the select
Tom's Coffee House in Oxford in 1774. See Norma Aubertin-Porter and Alyx Bennett, *Oxford
Coffee Houses, 1651–1800* (Oxford: Hampden, 1987), p. 21. On the link between coffee houses
and libraries see ibid., p. 15, and John C. Day, *Coffee Houses and Book Clubs in Eighteenth-
and Nineteenth-Century Northumberland* (Newcastle upon Tyne: John Day and Society of
Antiquaries, 1995), pp. 3–6.
[151] Love, *Scribal Publication*, pp. 206–7.   [152] Raven, 'New Reading Histories', p. 281.

crowned the erotic writer Charles Morris as its bard and caroused to the singing of his songs and poems.[153] Poems in *The Festival of Love* (1770) were allegedly sung at 'the Anacreontic Society', which may have met at the Anacreon Coffee House in Covent Garden.[154] Bonnel Thornton (1724–68), the author of a contribution to a similar collection – *The Pleasures that Please on Reflection* (1789) – regularly visited coffee houses,[155] while 'pornographic verses' were read at the famous Kit-Kat Club in earlier decades.[156] Appropriately, perhaps, Cesar de Saussure, a traveller to England, referred to coffee houses as 'temples of Venus'.[157]

Coffee-house culture was no monolith. Though coffee houses have been closely associated with politeness, and identified as 'a key site of masculine social discipline', many displayed 'a carnivalized sociability, more popular than polite', constructed partly around the female proprietors and their unruly, transgressive sexuality.[158] Helen Berry has argued that some coffee houses could be assuredly impolite, providing a space in which refined behaviour could be 'suspended'.[159] Indeed, recent work demonstrates that not all coffee houses of the late seventeenth century were exclusive in terms of social status or gender.[160]

[153] John Timbs, *Club Life of London, with Anecdotes of the Clubs, Coffee-Houses and Taverns of the Metropolis during the 17th, 18th, and 19th Centuries* (London: Richard Bentley, 1866), vol. I, pp. 123–57; Louis C. Jones, *The Clubs of the Georgian Rakes* (New York: Columbia University Press, 1942), pp. 149–52. On the lack of women at the club, see Timbs, *Club Life*, pp. 147–8. Timbs does not mention where the Society met, but Lillywhite reproduces a reference to John Wilkes dining with the 'Beef-Stake Club' at the Piazza Coffee House, Covent Garden in June 1773. See Lillywhite, *London Coffee Houses*, p. 448.

[154] 'The Marriage Morn', pp. 89–90, 'Song', pp. 288–9, both in *Festival of Love*. Both poems were also in *Bacchanalian Magazine*, pp. 114, 14–15; and 'The Marriage Morn' was in *Hilaria*, pp. 8–9. This coffee house was located on Great Russell Street, Covent Garden, and was used for masonic meetings from 1787 to 1794. Anacreon was a Greek poet, and 'anacreontic' signalled a particular metre, but also a convivial or erotic style. Lillywhite speculates that the name might have suggested the character of the coffee house. See *London Coffee Houses*, pp. 670–1.

[155] 'The Birth of the Rose', in *Pleasures that Please on Reflection*, pp. 39–40; Lillywhite, *London Coffee Houses*, p. 692.

[156] John Brewer, *The Pleasures of the Imagination: English Culture in the Eighteenth Century* (London: HarperCollins, 1997), pp. 40, 41.

[157] Quoted in Markham Ellis, 'Coffee-Women, 'The Spectator' and the Public Sphere in the Early Eighteenth Century', in Elizabeth Eger, Charlotte Grant, Cliona o Gallchoir and Penny Warburton (eds.), *Women, Writing and the Public Sphere, 1700–1830* (Cambridge: Cambridge University Press, 2001), p. 32.

[158] Brian Cowan, 'What was Masculine about the Public Sphere? Gender and the Coffeehouse Milieu in Post-Restoration England', *History Workshop Journal* 51 (2001), p. 142; Ellis, 'Coffee-Women, 'The Spectator' and the Public Sphere', pp. 37, 39 (quote at p. 57).

[159] Helen Berry, 'Rethinking Politeness in Eighteenth-Century England: Moll King's Coffee House and the Significance of Flash Talk', *Transactions of the Royal Historical Society* 6th series, 11 (2001), p. 74.

[160] Steve Pincus, ' "Coffee Politicians Does Create": Coffeehouses and Restoration Political Culture', *Journal of Modern History* 67 (1995), esp. pp. 815–16; Helen Berry, ' "Nice and Curious Questions": Coffee Houses and the Representation of Women in John Dunton's *Athenian Mercury*', *The Seventeenth Century* 12 (1997), pp. 257–76.

Unlike the imagined community of erotica, the virtual reading community of the late-seventeenth-century coffee-house periodical the *Athenian Mercury* did include women.[161] However, it does appear that the women who attended in the late seventeenth and early eighteenth centuries were either workers (servants, keepers or owners) or members of the nobility and upper gentry attending select and exclusive establishments.[162] This was in stark contrast to the habitual use by men of various ranks. According to one French visitor to London, coffee-house clubs were one of 'the two resorts in which Englishmen pass the greater part of their lives' (the second being taverns).[163] Moreover, by the later eighteenth century it seems that coffee houses were increasingly associated with men. By the beginning of the nineteenth century coffee houses were regarded as meeting places for 'the gentry, merchants and principal inhabitants', 'military gentlemen and strangers', and particularly 'mercantile men'.[164] The paucity of comment on women's attendance in the eighteenth century cannot be equated with their absence, but the evidence of men reading and listening to erotic material in such environments is not matched by examples of women doing the same.

Erotica was also consumed in the more libertine environment of the Beggar's Benison. The 'Beggar's Benison and Merryland' of Anstruther, Scotland, was a notorious group which ran from 1732 well into the nineteenth century. It is likely that there were groups throughout the union, as an advert from a Manchester newspaper of 1773 suggests:

By Order of the SOVEREIGN.
A CHAPTER of the most Antient and Honorable Order of the BEGGARS BENNISON, is to be held at the *Old* Coffee House, in *Manchester*, on *Wednesday* the 6th of *October*

---

[161] Helen Berry has reiterated this point in her *Gender, Society and Print Culture in Late-Stuart England: The Cultural World of the Athenian Mercury* (Aldershot: Ashgate, 2003).
[162] Pincus, 'Coffee Politicians', p. 816, Berry, 'Nice and Curious', pp. 261–2.
[163] Rochefoucauld, François de la, *A Frenchman in England: Being the* Mélange sur l'Angleterre *of François de la Rochefoucauld*, ed. Jean Marchand, trans. S. C. Roberts (1784; Cambridge: Cambridge University Press, 1933), p. 20.
[164] These are descriptions of the clientele of the Coffee Room, Briggate, Leeds. See *The Leeds Directory for 1809, Containing an Alphabetical List of the Merchants, Traders and Inhabitants in General* (Leeds: Printed for the compiler, and for M. Robinson & Co. Booksellers, Commercial-Street, 1809), p. 13; *Directory, General and Commercial, of the Town & Borough of Leeds, for 1817* (Leeds: Printed by Edward Baines, at the Mercury-Office, 1817), p. 11. This particular coffee room adjoined the Commercial News-Room. This was frequented by 'tradesmen and other respectable inhabitants', 'gentlemen', and was 'peculiarly convenient and agreeable to Men of Business'. See *Leeds Directory for 1809*, p. 14; *The Leeds Mercury* (Edward Baines, Briggate, Leeds), 23 December 1809. Similarly, The White Bear Inn in Basinghall Street, London, had a coffee room, and also boasted 'suites of apartments for gentlemen' and 'every convenience for conducting business with facility'. See the advert for sale in the *Manchester Mercury; and Harrop's General Advertizer* (Manchester: Printed at the printing-press, opposite the Exchange), 4 November, 1817. Dunn's coffee house in Doncaster appealed to 'gentlemen' for business. See advert in *Sheffield Mercury* (W. M. Todd, head of the Market Place, Sheffield), 20 September 1817.

Instant, on special Affairs; when it is hoped the K N I G H T S C O M P A N I O N S in the Town and Neighbourhood will attend.

D I N N E R on the Table at Three o'Clock.

R.A. S.L.[165]

As supported by this request for the attendance of 'Knights', the notorious Scottish group was male, apart from female prostitutes paid to attend. Members included merchants, writers, a naval officer, a lawyer, a parish minister, a bishop, a clerk of customs and a chief magistrate.[166] Erotic material formed an important component of this group's meetings. Knights were required to read 'amorous' passages aloud during the initiation ceremony, and later in the meetings the men sang songs, recited toasts and bons mots, read classic erotic texts, '[a]natomy and anatomical Bible texts', and 'enriched the Society with lecherous Articles of Vertu'.[167] There was also much erotic language shared between the Knights of the society and eighteenth-century erotic books. Members were devotees of 'our Celebrated Territories of M E R R Y L A N D', committed to 'the encouraging of Trade, Manufacture, and Agriculture in that delightful Colony'.[168] Echoes of the book *A New Description of Merryland* (1741), in which the female body (Merryland) was described as a continent, and treated as a place with its own 'commodities', 'language' and 'customs', are clear.[169] Indeed, the inhabitants of Merryland in this erotic book were thought to engage in similar activities at 'Merry-makings', beginning 'over a Bottle . . . with drinking a Health to M E R R Y L A N D'.[170] The rituals described in erotica and those conducted at the Beggars' meetings mirror one another. The numerous toasts reported to have been made at the Beggar's Benison were much like those which peppered *The Bacchanalian Magazine*,[171] while the

[165] *The Manchester Mercury*, 5 October 1773. This advert resembles those placed in Scottish papers for the Benison. See David Stevenson, *The Beggar's Benison: Sex Clubs of Enlightenment Scotland and their Rituals* (East Linton: Tuckwell Press, 2001), pp. 175–6.

[166] Ibid., pp. 151–2, 170–1. See also *Records of the Most Ancient and Puissant Order of the Beggar's Benison and Merryland, Anstruther* (Anstruther: for private distribution, 1892), pp. 5–6, 21–6. Information on the Beggar's Benison derives largely from the nineteenth-century publications purporting to be the records of the society. The status of these records is questionable, but thoroughgoing research by David Stevenson shows that much of the content is authentic. Stevenson, *Beggar's Benison*, pp. 23–43. We are right to be cautious about these materials, though as an attempt to characterize erotic culture they are invaluable.

[167] *Records of the Most Ancient and Puissant Order*, p. 10. The extracts from the Bible reported as having been read out at the meeting refer to childbirth and/or sex. The 'Song of Songs' is also listed; this discusses sex in richly metaphorical language.

[168] Ibid., pp. 6–7.

[169] See *New Description of Merryland*, passim. For the Beggar's Benison and the term 'Merryland', see Stevenson, *Beggar's Benison*, pp. 18–19.

[170] *New Description of Merryland*, p. 21.

[171] For the toasts, see *Supplement to the Historical Portion of the* Records of the Most Ancient and Puissant Order of the Beggar's Benison and Merryland, Anstruther, *Being an Account of the Proceedings at the Meetings of the Society* (Anstruther: for private distribution, 1892),

'Sea-Captains from Holland and Denmark' were probably sexually experienced men whose euphemistic titles relied on the references to female genitalia as Holland in erotic material.[172] Much of the material supposedly read at the Beggar's Benison was stylistically and thematically compatible with the corpus of eighteenth-century erotica,[173] and at least one of the poems reproduced in the records of the group appeared in a contemporary erotic collection.[174]

This group demonstrates the extent to which reading erotica was part of a culture of texts and practices, because for members of the Beggar's Benison reading aloud was one ritual among many. The initiation ceremony involved rubbing erect penises together, while late in the century men masturbated into the ceremonial dish engraved with the words, 'THE WAY OF A MAN WITH A WOMAN. TEST PLATTER'.[175] In the same way, inhabitants of the continent of Merryland were determined to '*spend all they can*, and glory in who *spends most*'.[176] This notable phallicism, which has been likened to pagan fertility rituals, echoed an interest in male bodies reflected in much erotica.[177] But while the meetings of the Beggar's Benison may have involved a degree of homoeroticism, these gatherings also focused on women's bodies. For example, men inspected the bodies of women paid to display themselves. The records of the society report that 'One Feminine Gender, 17, was hired for One Sovereign, fat and well-developed. She stripped in the Closet, nude; and was allowed to come in with face half-covered. None was permitted to speak or touch her. She spread wide upon a seat, first before and then behind.'[178]

Physical activity was central to the Beggar's Benison, whether onanistic, phallic or heterosexual. Yet these physical encounters were not reckless or abandoned. The description of the observation of the seventeen-year-old woman at the Beggar's Benison – in which 'every Knight passed in turn and surveyed the Secrets of Nature' – is suggestive of attempts to intellectualize this

---

pp. 17–32; *Bacchanalian Magazine*, pp. 50, 74, 98, 120. For example, the former included 'The Radical Moisture from the Female Cave; the open space for Cupid's Rudder; the fine Sheath for the bold Dagger' (p. 21), while the latter included 'Old Wine and Y O U N G Wenches' (p. 54), 'Maiden hair, or the F U R that suits all weather' (p. 74) and 'May the tide of Fortune float us in the Harbour of Content' (p. 120).

[172] *Records of the most Ancient and Puissant Order*, p. 10; *A Riddle: of a Paradoxical Character . . . Often found under Holland.*

[173] The poem 'A Pastoral', which appeared in *Supplement to the Historical Portion*, p. 56, illustrates many of the points made in chapters six and seven of this book.

[174] The poem 'Botany Bay', which appeared in the *Supplement to the Historical Portion*, pp. 71–3, was printed in *Hilaria*, pp. 16–20.

[175] *Records of the Most Ancient and Puissant Order*, pp. 6–10.

[176] *New Description of Merryland*, p. 19.

[177] Jones, *Clubs of the Georgian Rakes*, p. 177. See chapter five of this book for relevant representations of male bodies in erotica.

[178] *Supplement to the Historical Portion*, p. 13. This is the element of the records that Stevenson is most cautious about, although he thinks it is entirely possible that such activities took place, as they did in other venues during this period. See Stevenson, *Beggar's Benison*, pp. 37–9.

voyeuristic and supposedly deeply physical enjoyment.[179] Similarly, members of the Beggar's Benison were required to read erotic texts aloud but interject 'with comments', just as erotic texts depicted readers as autonomous and free-thinking.[180] There were other aspects of these meetings which seemed to mitigate the potentially disorderly elements of the group. Tim Hitchcock has claimed that the 'pseudo-Masonic' rituals of the Beggar's Benison reflect the extent to which eighteenth-century sociability was shaped by clubs and voluntary societies.[181] The tone of the society's meetings can certainly be aligned with the irreligion and the emphasis on good fellowship of the early radical Whig strand of Freemasonry.[182] But there are also links between the Beggar's Benison and traditional, official Masonry. Comprising part of the philosophical underpinnings of Masonry was pantheistic materialism, interpreted by some contemporaries as legitimizing sexual freedom.[183] This alone might explain why the Beggar's Benison considered Masonic rituals to be a suitable model for their own activities. But in addition, the tenor of Masonry offered much to eighteenth-century men keen to indulge in erotic pleasures but desirous to avoid a descent into a disorderly sensual revelry. Apart from religious devotion, much of the 'mentality of official Masonry – its taste for science, its craving for order and stability, its worldly mysticism, as expressed in fanciful rituals, passwords and mythology, its love of secrecy' was echoed in the meetings of the Beggar's Benison.[184] In mimicking Masonic rituals, the tone of the meetings as described in the formal records of the society – and to some extent the records themselves – presented a controlled and restrained gathering of intellectual gentlemen.

The Beggar's Benison can be aligned with other groups whose activities combined reading sexually explicit or suggestive material with physical, sexual activity. The infamous 'Hell-Fire Club' was convened by Sir Francis Dashwood (1708–81) at West Wycombe. As in the case of the Beggar's Benison, most of the women known to have been present were prostitutes.[185] The importance of

---

[179] *Supplement to the Historical Portion*, p. 13. See chapters four and seven of this book for relevant images of female bodies.

[180] *Records of the Most Ancient and Puissant Order*, p. 10.

[181] Hitchcock, *English Sexualities*, pp. 22, 23.

[182] See Margaret C. Jacob, *The Radical Enlightenment: Pantheists, Freemasons and Republicans* (London: Allen and Unwin, 1981), pp. 116–19, 267–9, 275.

[183] Ibid., pp. 229–30.   [184] Ibid., p. 133. See also pp. 282–3 on restraint in Masonic lodges.

[185] Jones, *Clubs of the Georgian Rakes*, pp. 128–9, 141. Though one author has considered the possibility of twelve women attending Hell-Fire meetings, this does not compare with the thirty-seven men certainly or probably present at the club. Donald McCormick, *The Hell-Fire Club: The Story of the Amorous Knights of Wycombe* (London: Jarrolds, 1958), pp. 148–63, 195–8. Of the twelve possible 'Nuns' of the 'Order' considered by McCormick, the attendance of seven was probably based on their relationship with one of the male Knights, while the presence of another two was highly unlikely. The presence of the remaining three has been founded on little more than rumour. This is in contrast to the list of twenty-six certain male

Scribal ?

reading to Dashwood's Hell-Fire Club, or Medmenham Monks as they were also known, is demonstrated in the manuscript 'The Medmenham Garland', inscribed 1755.[186] The Garland – a kind of erotic commonplace book – begins with an invitation for the current reader to pass it on to another when he has finished with it, suggesting a community of private readers, perhaps. But as the author recalls with characteristic drollery, the poems had been part of a sociable encounter:

Well do I recollect all (or nearly all) of the Verses here transcrib'd & the Occasions upon which they were deliver'd to our holy Fraternity . . .
   The sole Object of our little Society of Franciscans was but to escape from Dullness; & our Proceedings were by no means so licentious as Rumour hath since charitably alleg'd. True, we improvis'd a few hundred bawdy Songs; but we also strung together some very respectable Verses, as several herein do testify.[187]

Harold Love has argued that in seventeenth-century England scribal publications suggested a private rather than a public audience, and thus a 'more intimate community of readers'.[188] Certainly, like earlier manuscript texts which 'bond[ed] groups of like-minded individuals into a community', the Garland bound together the fraternity of the Hell-Fire Monks.[189] Yet the relationship between a private audience, an intimate community of readers and manuscript was perhaps not as strong by the eighteenth century. At least in the case of the Hell-Fire Club, both manuscript and printed material – of both a sexually implicit and explicit nature – was read, reminding us that clear distinctions between erotica and pornography are not easily drawn.[190]
   As with the Beggar's Benison, the irreligious nature of the meetings is clear. Indeed, the third page dedicates the manuscript 'To That Multitude of Clerical Jack = asses / whose / Remarks & "*candid* Criticisms" will be plung'd in the Abyss of Oblivion'.[191] This was to be expected from a group whose famous clientele included John Wilkes, renowned for his combination of 'religious libertinism' and 'sexual libertinism'.[192] As with the Beggar's Benison,

---

members, eleven probable male members, and seventeen possible and doubtful male members 4 people produced by McCormick.
[186] 'Eros in Monachium or the Medmenham Garland Cull'd from the Franciscan Originals' Erotic (c. 1760). Clark Library: MSS. E71M1 ca. 1760 Bound. This document was apparently written Common between 1753 and 1759 by the Medmenham monks. place
[187] Ibid., f. 1. book
[188] Love, *Scribal Publication*, p. 148. See Harold Love, 'Refining Rochester: Private Texts and Public Readers', *Harvard Library Bulletin* 7 (1996), pp. 40–9, where Love argues that the shift from manuscript to print changes 'the whole set of reading practices' (p. 49). On manuscript erotica of the late sixteenth and early seventeenth centuries, see Moulton, *Before Pornography*.
[189] Love, *Scribal Publication*, p. 177.
[190] See Introduction for a discussion of definitions of erotica and pornography.
[191] 'Eros in Monachium', f. 3.
[192] John Sainsbury, 'Wilkes and Libertinism', *Studies in Eighteenth-Century Culture* 26 (1998), p. 158.

the irreligion took on a practical form and also expressed the extent to which participants of the group were to be active readers. Many of the poems in this manuscript deal in biblical stories, but the author has resisted 'the mystic or allegoric Sense' adopted by those 'theoretic Theologists, & itinerant Enthusiasts, who have the Art and Mystery of finding out Meanings in an Author, which he never meant . . . in Order to serve a Purpose, or promote a Tenet, however illegal or heterodox'.[193] Such men, the author claimed, 'render what is really sacred & serious, prophane & ridiculous; or plain & obvious, abstruse and unintelligible by their endless Illustrations, Expositions, Animadversions & Annotations'.[194] This writer, however, has 'render'd them in their most literal & general Acceptation'.[195]

At both the Beggar's Benison and the Hell-Fire Club, reading and sociable sexual activity were integrated. Erotica was not a substitute for an engagement with actual bodies, therefore. And yet these men were engaged in active and intellectual pursuits. This was epitomized by practices of reading which served as a marker of both the serious and the satirical nature of their gatherings. In the eighteenth century, while certain books threatened ruin to certain readers, other books could guard against excess. Books, one author counselled, were prophylactics against drunken tavern revels, reeling forgetfulness and the twin foes of Bacchus and Venus.[196] Reading, another author wrote, furnished the true happiness of 'mental gratification', rather than the transitory joy of 'corporeal pleasures'. Indeed reading, particularly of the Classics, was celebrated as 'the universal remedy or grand panacea'.[197] The distinctions of moralist writers on luxury between different kinds of pleasure were thus mapped onto practices of reading. The mode of reading practised by male consumers of erotica alleviated accusations of excess, while providing ample opportunity for a satirical swipe at the notion of books as guardians of morals.

A continuum of good fellowship

How should we contextualize the diverse groups in whose midst we can locate erotic books? The Hell-Fire Club can be contextualized through connoisseurship. Sir Francis Dashwood was one of the founder members of the Society of Dilettanti, a society of connoisseurs formed in 1732 which soon wielded considerable influence in Britain's artistic world. The links between the society and libertinism were numerous. Horace Walpole denounced the Society, claiming that 'the nominal qualification for membership is having been in Italy, and the real one, being drunk'.[198] In addition, phallicism was a part of elite male

---

[193] 'Eros in Monachium', f. 3.   [194] Ibid.   [195] Ibid.
[196] 'On the Refined Pleasures of Reading', *Town and Country Magazine* (1769), p. 544.
[197] 'Essay on Reading', *Town and Country Magazine* (1769), pp. 544, 545.
[198] Brewer, *Pleasures of the Imagination*, p. 257.

Illustration 5:   Richard Cosway, *Group of Connoisseurs* (1771–5).

sociability, and the activities of groups such as the Beggar's Benison appear
less eccentric when placed in this context. The Society of Dilettanti used a wax
penis as the table centre-piece at their meetings, for example. William Hamilton
and Richard Payne Knight were other members of the Society who had a particular interest not simply in collecting antiquities, but in the history of sexuality,
Payne Knight printing a report of Hamilton's account of phallus worship.[199]

There were close links between these men which took the form of sexual,
artistic and classical appreciation. In Richard Cosway's *A Group of Connoisseurs* (1771–5), commissioned by Charles Towneley, another member of the
Society, we see the pleasure to be gleaned. The men in this painting are capti-
vated by the figures. (Illustration 5.) The seated man is certainly transfixed, but
sight is not the only sense to be enlivened: the right hand may hold the glass, but
the left is thrust firmly into the breeches. This is not one of the many satires or
criticisms aimed at the Society of Dilettanti and connoisseurs. It affectionately
displays men of quality, whose opinions were widely respected, gleaning an

[199] G. S. Rousseau, 'The Sorrows of Priapus', in his *Perilous Enlightenment: Pre- and Post-Modern
Discourses. Sexual, Historical* (Manchester: Manchester University Press, 1991), p. 85.

Illustration 6: William Hogarth, *A Midnight Modern Conversation* (c. 1732).

erotic pleasure from their collections. As Anne Bermingham and John Barrell have argued in relation to accomplishments and garden sculpture respectively, connoisseurship – particularly of a visual nature – was regarded as a masculine endeavour.[200] This painting is a witty depiction of what Brewer calls 'the connoisseur's prurient and lascivious gaze' upon the female object.[201] But as well as asking how this image portrays men's relationship to women, we might also ask what it says about men's relationships with each other. This image projected and fashioned a world populated by elite men engaged in artistic appreciation and conversation, united around the objects of classical culture and gleaning an erotic frisson from these objects.

This world can be juxtaposed with another often depicted in eighteenth-century visual culture, that of groups of men in merry union. This was a long visual tradition, drawing on seventeenth-century Dutch images, and beginning in England with portraits of the Kit-Cat club.[202] Typified by William Hogarth's *A Midnight Modern Conversation* (c. 1732), such images depict male groups in varying states of inebriation. (Illustration 6.) The ubiquitous toppled chair and innumerable discarded carafes suggest disorder and excess. Conversation was central to polite masculine status.[203] Hogarth's title – *A Midnight Modern Conversation* – is ironic: no one here is capable of conversation. And yet this is an affectionate portrayal of a group of professional men – Hogarth's friends, in fact – in St John's Coffee House. James Worsdale's painting *The Limerick Hell-Fire Club* (c. 1736) is of a different order. (Illustration 7.) We know little about the Irish Hell-Fire Clubs. The Limerick and Dublin clubs appeared later than those in England, but at the same time as the Beggar's Benison, in the early to mid-1730s. David Solkin places this painting in the context of an already outmoded country resistance to politeness, expressed through the 'merry company portrait'.[204] Juxtaposed against the earlier polite and commercial portraits of the Whig clubs, this portrait might be aligned more closely with what Solkin refers to as the 'impolite conviviality' of *A Midnight Modern*

---

[200] John Barrell, 'The Dangerous Goddess: Masculinity, Prestige and the Aesthetic in Early Eighteenth-Century Britain', in his *The Birth of Pandora and the Division of Knowledge* (Basingstoke: Macmillan, 1992), pp. 63–87; Ann Bermingham, 'The Aesthetics of Ignorance: The Accomplished Woman in the Culture of Connoisseurship', *Oxford Art Journal* 16 (1993), pp. 3–20.

[201] Brewer, *Pleasures of the Imagination*, p. 279.

[202] See Sheila O'Connell, *The Popular Print in England* (London: British Museum Press, 1999), pp. 120–2, and David H. Solkin, *Painting for Money: The Visual Arts and the Public Sphere in Eighteenth-Century England* (New Haven: Yale University Press, 1992), pp. 32–42.

[203] Cohen, *Fashioning Masculinity*; Lawrence Klein, 'Gender, Conversation and the Public Sphere in Early Eighteenth-Century England', in Judith Still and Michael Worton (eds.), *Textuality and Sexuality: Reading Theories and Practices* (Manchester: Manchester University Press, 1993), pp. 100–15.

[204] Solkin, *Painting for Money*, pp. 100–2, quote at p. 100. Also see Geoffrey Ashe, *The Hell-Fire Clubs: A History of Anti-Morality* (1974; Stroud: Sutton, 2000), pp. 60–61.

Illustration 7:   James Worsdale, *The Limerick Hell-Fire Club* (c. 1736).

Illustration 8: *The Jolly Bacchanals*. In *The Bacchanalian Magazine* (1793).

Conversation.[205] Certainly, the composition of this painting is similar to Hogarth's coffee-house painting; but Worsdale's image is not wholly rejecting polite pictorial conventions: all chairs are standing and all wigs are intact. This group is aping the refinement of the Society of Dilettanti rather than the excesses of Hogarth's conversation.

Nevertheless, there are connections between all three works. These three visual works locate erotic texts in a continuum of male homosociality and good fellowship. Erotic culture celebrated manly good fellowship. The image of 'The Jolly Bacchanals' depicted in one erotic collection glorified this form of boisterous sociability, and it was perhaps this glorification which explained why *The Potent Ally* (1741) was dedicated to Humphrey Parsons (c. 1676–1741), a Lord Mayor of London renowned for his love of beer.[206] (Illustration 8.) Recent work has highlighted the degree to which homosociality was key to the attainment of

---

[205] See Solkin, *Painting for Money*, pp. 27–47 on the club portraits, and pp. 79–81 on Hogarth's *A Midnight Modern Conversation*. Quote at p. 79.

[206] *Potent Ally*, 2nd edn., p. 1. Humphrey Parsons, a wealthy brewer and Tory MP from 1722 to 1741, was elected Lord Mayor of the City of London in 1730 and 1740. His popularity was demonstrated by the fact that, unusually, he was elected twice. His death in 1741 explains the dedication in this publication of the same year. See Valerie Hope, *My Lord Mayor: Eight Hundred Years of London's Mayoralty* (London: Weidenfeld and Nicolson, 1989), pp. 106, 108, 112–13; Romney Sedgwick, *The History of Parliament. The House of Commons, 1715–1754* (London: History of Parliament Trust, 1970), vol. II, pp. 326–7.

What about Politeness?

appropriate masculinity.[207] Yet the particular style of homosociality discussed in this chapter might seem anathema to the central theme in the historiography of eighteenth-century masculinity, and indeed the eighteenth century in general: politeness. Politeness was an ethos and a mode of behaviour which centred on refinement.[208] Philip Carter has explained how individual men – notably James Boswell – wrestled with the tensions between polite ideals and practice. One set of tensions related to sexuality and bad behaviour. Boswell inhabited a world in which 'manly behaviour was defined less by sexual prowess than such qualities as self-command, independence, dignity and politeness', and his sexual personae sat uncomfortably with his attempts to achieve appropriate manly behaviour.[209] Thus, Carter regards blackguards and other styles of bad behaviour as a 'counter-culture of anti-civility'.[210] A different but related approach is adopted by Anthony Fletcher, who argues that the sexual freedoms granted to men in the eighteenth century, and the resultant emphasis on virility, lurked '[b]eneath the veneer of civility and politeness'. Promiscuity and pornography were consolation for and relief from the demanding strictures of masculinity.[211] Both these approaches place sexuality outside or beneath polite masculinity.

Such models make it difficult to think about the ways in which the sexual and the social aspects of masculinity were formed within the same cultural conditions. The context of erotica discussed in this chapter demonstrates the extent to which the social and the sexual were entwined; in reading erotica, men strived to be refined while enjoying sexual pleasure. The tradition of good fellowship in which we can situate erotica had many strands, from elite connoisseurship to drunken cavorting, and the modes of erotic consumption displayed by the Knights of the Beggar's Benison and by the Medmenham Monks seem to straddle both forms of male sociability. In part, this is evidence for the longevity of traditional manly qualities. Erotic gatherings bore more than a passing similarity to the masculine sociability of the clubs which 'served as bastions of traditional male perceptions of sociable behaviour, against new, more refined notions of manners favoured by women and increasingly coloured by the culture of sensibility'.[212] The persistence of this traditional masculinity suggests that the rise of politeness after the late seventeenth century and the subsequent shift to

---

[207] Carter, *Men and the Emergence of Polite Society*, pp. 9–10; Cohen, 'Manliness, Effeminacy and the French', p. 60; Tim Hitchcock, 'Sociability and Misogyny in the Life of John Cannon', in Tim Hitchcock and Michèle Cohen (eds.), *English Masculinities, 1660–1800* (Harlow: Longman, 1999), p. 47.

[208] Carter, *Men and the Emergence of Polite Society*, p. 19.

[209] Carter, 'Men about Town', p. 129.

[210] Carter, *Men and the Emergence of Polite Society*, p. 135.

[211] Fletcher, *Gender, Sex and Subordination*, pp. 340–5. Quote at p. 343.

[212] Peter Clark, *British Clubs and Societies, 1500–1800: The Origins of an Associational World* (Oxford: Clarendon Press, 2000), p. 203.

sensibility in the final quarter of the eighteenth century tells only one part of the
story. There were occasions when eighteenth-century men revelled in a lack of
propriety, even a boorish excess, and there was plenty of space for men to enjoy
joviality and companionship with wine but without women.[213] Michèle Cohen
has explored the waning of politeness from the 1760s, as a growing emphasis
on domesticity led to an imperative to prove masculinity through homosocial
encounters.[214] Women writers were also ambivalent about masculine politeness, questioning the extent to which there had been a shift from 'sanctioned
violence to refinement'.[215] Certainly later writers freely admitted the extent
to which 'the true harmony' of social gatherings was actually the effect of 'a
pretty quick circulation of the bottle, which composes animosity and drowns
discordance'. Sociability was precarious and quarrels only just contained.[216] It
appears that the dominance of politeness was relatively short-lived, sandwiched
between mid-seventeenth-century and late-eighteenth-century ideals of manliness which had much in common. Helen Berry has alerted us to how the rules
of politeness could generate the impolite.[217] From at least the 1730s erotic culture engaged with and questioned politeness. Its smooth polish, together with
the bonding of manners and morals, sat somewhat uncomfortably with erotic
culture.[218] But erotic culture was not an alternative to politeness. The keywords
associated with politeness – 'form, sociability, improvement, worldiness, and
gentility' – were also central to erotic culture.[219] Politeness was not hegemonic,
but it was a key referent. Erotic culture did not constitute an 'impolite' world;
rather, it had politeness at its heart, both as something to mock and as something to aspire to. Erotic encounters thus combined the rough homosociality
increasingly regarded as central to English masculinity and the restraint placed

[213] Vickery, *Gentleman's Daughter*, pp. 195–284; Anne Taylor, *Bacchus in Romantic England: Writers and Drink, 1780–1830* (Basingstoke: Macmillan, 1999). The key difference between erotic gatherings and these literary ones is that the latter eschewed Venus as incompatible with Bacchus. In erotica, these two forces – sex and drink – are twinned.
[214] Cohen, 'Manliness, Effeminacy and the French', passim.
[215] Laura L. Runge, 'Beauty and Gallantry: A Model of Polite Conversation Revisited', *Eighteenth-Century Life* 25 (2001), p. 44 and passim.
[216] 'Descriptions of a Club', *Lady's Magazine*, November 1783, pp. 583–5.
[217] Berry, 'Rethinking Politeness', p. 68.
[218] On manners and morals, see Philip Carter, 'Polite Persons: Character, Biography and the Gentleman', *Transactions of the Royal Historical Society* 12 (2002), pp. 333–54. David M. Turner has also commented on the relationship between politeness and sexuality, demonstrating that adultery was seen less in terms of sin and was increasingly described through the 'soft words of civility'. See his *Fashioning Adultery: Gender, Sex and Civility in England, 1660–1740* (Cambridge: Cambridge University Press, 2002), quote at p. 195.
[219] Lawrence E. Klein, 'Politeness and the Interpretation of the British Eighteenth Century', *The Historical Journal* 45 (2002), p. 877. For a more detailed discussion of politeness and mas-culinity, see Karen Harvey, 'The History of Masculinity, c. 1650–1800', in *The History of Masculinity, c. 1500 to the Present*, a special issue of *The Journal of British Studies* (forthcom-ing), ed. Karen Harvey and Alexandra Shepard.

at the heart of politeness, and the result was a refined and learned bawdiness that catered to both politeness and prurience, refinement and ribaldry.

The model of reading that emerges from external evidence is quite distinct from Pepys' coded report of his solitary encounter with *L'Ecole des Filles*. More typical of erotic reading was the case of Thomas Thistlewood, the English owner of a plantation in Jamaica. On 24 May 1759, aged 28, Thomas Thistlewood recorded in his diary, 'Lent Mr Parkinson the Oeconomy of Love'.[220] *The Oeconomy of Love* was a popular erotic poem published repeatedly throughout the century. Regardless of the detail with which Thistlewood reported his numerous liaisons with women, he did not record a heterosocial perusal of this or other works. Moreover, Thistlewood's diary entry was neither in code nor did it have the tone of a guilty confession. On the contrary, he failed to differentiate between the ways he read erotic and other types of material. He circulated this erotic poem amongst a network of male friends, in the same way that he and his friends swapped and discussed political treatises, botanical dictionaries, natural histories, scientific and medical books, and popular fiction. The encounter between Thistlewood, his friend Parkinson and the erotic poem remains obscure. Yet the case is suggestive of a number of important characteristics featured in the model of reading reconstructed here. Firstly, this was situated in male environments. Men and women did not enjoy a 'shared appreciation' of erotica.[221] It is more accurate to argue that erotica was a 'male-centred genre' read by 'some women'.[222] In the publishing trade, one widow continued her late husband's business and published erotic material. At the Beggar's Benison, women were present as prostitutes. And at coffee houses, women served and managed. But in such circumstances, if women read erotic material at all they were paid workers governed by business acumen, not pleasure-seeking consumers guided by desire. Eighteenth-century women were not more passionless, ignorant of sex, or naïve than eighteenth-century men. They had access to material which discussed sex and sexual pleasure, particularly through an oral culture.[223] Yet though some women may have read it, erotica was not a corpus of material which catered to women's sexual curiosity, desire or pleasure.

Secondly, this was a civil and sociable model of reading which allayed fears associated with solitary, sensual reading. When combined, the different approaches to readership reveal that the archetypal implied readers of textual analysis are not matched by external evidence of actual readers. Moreover, there

[220] Thomas Thistlewood, *In Miserable Slavery: Thomas Thistlewood in Jamaica*, 1750–86, ed. Douglas Hall (London: Macmillan, 1989), p. 87. I am grateful to A. D. Harvey for bringing this diary to my attention.
[221] Peakman, 'Medicine, the Body', p. 199.
[222] Emma Donoghue, *Passions Between Women: British Lesbian Culture, 1668–1801* (New York: HarperCollins, 1993), pp. 14–15.
[223] Though even here, restrictions on women's talk were likely to have moulded female discussion of sexual matters differently from men's. See Crawford, 'Sexual Knowledge', pp. 94–5.

is a clear disparity between the imagined female readers in erotica texts and the actual male readers of external evidence. The latter leads us to regard the former not as proof of female readership, but as one of a range of techniques which characterized women (and men) in a particular way. As their reading practices demonstrated, women possessed latent, uncontrollable sexual desires waiting to be aroused. Images of women as enthusiastic and receptive readers of erotica were not a source of pleasure for women, but a source of sustenance for erotica's male readers. Erotic narratives depicted female readers having sex while reading erotica. In contrast, men's reading of erotica was not sex: it was wit, sociability, enquiry and improvement and it embodied some of the classic civic virtues of Georgian England. Erotica was consumed and positioned alongside a wide range of elite texts, it was as much a social as a solitary experience, and the reading of erotica was one facet of homosocial occasions attended by men from a range of middling, gentry and aristocratic groups. The evidence of the content of erotic texts, the production and distribution of the books, the visible authors, and the evidence of actual readers external to the texts – this all suggests that erotica was designed for and by men. In other words, erotica was a masculinist genre where certain masculine values and pleasures were valorized and validated. Such knowledge about the material contexts of erotica must shape our understanding of its content.

2   Sexual difference

The nature of the relationship between male and female bodies has dominated the history of the body, and underpinned many claims about gender in the eighteenth century. Thomas Laqueur, whose important work is central to historians' understandings of sex differences, proposes that the relationship between male and female underwent a major transformation during the eighteenth century. In the early-modern world, a 'one-sex model' was dominant. This model was based on the humoral system, which portrayed the body as comprising four humours of different qualities – cold, hot, moist and dry – and according to which individuals were believed to vary in humoral composition. Though women were always dominated by cold and moist humours, and men by hot and dry humours, differences of sex were differences of degree. The way in which this became clearest was in the apparent parity of male and female genitals: 'The penis becomes the cervix and vagina, the prepuce becomes the female pudenda.'[1] During the eighteenth century, this way of understanding was replaced by a 'two-sex model' in which women and men were now anatomical opposites.

This argument for the growing hegemony of models of difference in discussions of gender mirrors work on race and nationality. The eighteenth century saw the rise of 'racial science', according to Nicholas Hudson, which replaced the notion of 'nation' as a way of describing political and social differences between groups with the notion of 'races' that displayed 'common traits of body and mind'.[2] Londa Schiebinger has gone so far as to name the eighteenth century as 'the great age of classification', in which 'age, sex, and nation . . . emerged as the central categories of analysis'.[3] Physical differences were stressed in new languages and new ways of thinking, and changing visions of male and female bodies were therefore part of a more general rise of new forms of classification, a united process of 'the *ontologising via embodiment* of sex and

[1] Laqueur, *Making Sex*, p. 26. See pp. 23–35 for a detailed account of this parity.
[2] Nicholas Hudson, 'From "Nation" to "Race": The Origin of Racial Classification in Eighteenth-Century Thought', *Eighteenth-Century Studies* 29 (1996), p. 248.
[3] Londa Schiebinger, *Nature's Body: Gender and the Making of Modern Science* (Boston: Beacon Press, 1993), pp. 117–18.

racial difference'.[4] In theorizing on both sex and race, difference was based on the physical rather than the cultural. While in the one-sex world physical differences were the product of a cultural 'gender', for example, during the eighteenth century these physical 'sex' differences were redefined as foundational to gender.[5]

New ideas about bodies were not the result of empirical findings about the human body, though, and Laqueur is adamant that changes in understandings of bodies derived not from medical discoveries but from wider political transformation. Nevertheless, the account of the emergence of incommensurable sex differences during the eighteenth century is common to most histories of the body and gender, and it is generally upon the highly distinct and specialized discourses of science and medicine that these claims about bodies are based. For many historians, the two hundred years after 1650 witnessed a bifurcation in men's and women's social roles and in ideas about gender. The chronology of these accounts matches closely that of Laqueur; indeed the shift from a one-sex to a two-sex model of sexual difference often underpins the larger claims. For Anthony Fletcher, changing understandings of bodies which increasingly stressed opposites rather than hierarchy were central to the 'new framework of gender relations' after the seventeenth century.[6] Robert B. Shoemaker identified 'the development of the two-sexed body' as part of the 'increasing value placed on the distinct sexual roles of men and women'.[7] Randolph Trumbach outlines a sexual revolution which produced a third gender – the 'new effeminate adult sodomites' – and which was constituted by both a splitting of men's sexual desire (into exclusively heterosexual or homosexual) and the emergence of sexed bodies.[8] Finally, Tim Hitchcock incorporated the move from a one-sex to a two-sex vision of the human body into a more general sexual revolution, linking this to the rise of separate spheres ideology.[9]

This widespread integration of Laqueur's thesis has not taken place without qualification. Fletcher adjusts Laqueur's timing, characterizing sixteenth- and seventeenth-century England as 'a curious transitional world of neither one sex nor two'; similarly, Mary Fissell describes how vernacular medical books question the hegemony of the one-sex model in the second half of the seventeenth century.[10] Recent work, then, implies that the stress on bodily difference existed much earlier than Laqueur allows. Shoemaker has cautioned that continuities

[4] Nancy Leys Stephan, 'Race, Gender, Science and Citizenship', *Gender and History* 10 (1998), p. 29.
[5] Laqueur, *Making Sex*, pp. 8, 149–54.
[6] Fletcher, *Gender, Sex and Subordination*, quote at p. 407. On bodies, see pp. xvii–xvii, 291, 402.
[7] Shoemaker, *Gender in English Society*, p. 85. See also pp. 31–5, 313–14.
[8] Trumbach, *Sex and the Gender Revolution*, pp. 1–11. Quote from p. 9.
[9] Hitchcock, 'Redefining Sex', pp. 72–90; Hitchcock, *English Sexualities*, esp. p. 49.
[10] Fletcher, *Gender, Sex and Subordination*, p. 41; Mary Fissell, 'Gender and Generation: Representing Reproduction in Early Modern England', *Gender and History* 7 (1995), pp. 433–56.

are as significant a feature as change in the history of the body and sexuality, in common with many historians of women and gender who increasingly stress persistence as much as transformation.[11] Hitchcock and others have questioned the relevance of elite published works to popular understandings and the experiences of men and women, and Laura Gowing argues that ordinary men and women between c. 1560 and 1640 stressed sexual difference rather than similarity.[12] Aspects of the one-sex model can be found in popular culture, then, but people did not subscribe to the entire vision.

Criticisms of Laqueur have therefore focused on timing, the over-emphasis on change, the representativeness of evidence and the collapse of a number of elements into singular models. I want to build on some of these criticisms by considering how erotic discussions of bodies compare to those which have been found in elite medical and scientific works. Producers of erotica were fascinated by bodies, by how they worked and by the relationships between them. Later chapters explore how bodies were conceived in terms of space, movement and the senses, but in this chapter I want to focus on those issues which dominated scientific and medical writing and were also discussed in erotica: conception, the genitals, other bodily markers of sexual difference, and sexual desire. The erotic treatment of these topics was shaped by the deeply satirical nature of erotic writing, part of which was the depiction of bodies in a myriad of guises. Many erotic texts drew on new botanical classifications, for example. Indeed, erotic texts which satirized contemporary scientific material were published so frequently that erotica would seem a likely candidate for the take-up of the new forms of medical and scientific thinking about bodies. Despite this, the one-sex and two-sex models of medical and scientific writing were not present in erotica. In fact, representations of bodies in eighteenth-century erotica fail to display the solidity and inflexibility that the language of models implies. In this chapter, therefore, I will consider two different themes (rather than models) which featured in discussions of the relationship between male and female bodies – sameness and difference – and chart how and when these themes were used.

Though Laqueur aligns the themes of sameness and difference with the one-sex and two-sex models respectively, these themes were not discrete or mutually

---

[11] Shoemaker, *Gender in English Society*, p. 61. Also pp. 20–1, 86. See also Sara Mendelson and Patricia Crawford, *Women in Early Modern England, 1550–1720* (Oxford: Clarendon Press, 1998), pp. 18–30; and Laura Gowing, *Common Bodies: Women, Touch and Power in Seventeenth-Century England* (New Haven: Yale University Press, 2003), for example p. 205. On continuity more generally, see John Tosh, 'The Old Adam and the New Man: Emerging Themes in the History of English Masculinities', in Hitchcock and Cohen (eds.), *English Masculinities*, p. 238; Gowing, *Domestic Dangers*, pp. 28–9.

[12] Hitchcock, *English Sexualities*, p. 49; Shoemaker, *Gender in English Society*, p. 60; Tosh, 'Old Adam and the New Man', p. 227; Gowing, *Domestic Dangers*, p. 7.

exclusive.[13] Dichotomy in language and thought has been powerful in the past, but dichotomies are not unchanging: each term carries a number of meanings which can disrupt apparently stable oppositions.[14] Indeed, distinctions are not always binary in nature and apparently dichotomous terms are not exhaustively defined by each other. For example, man can be opposed to woman, but also to beast and child. In erotica white man was opposed to black man, English man to Irish man, and fertile man to infertile man. By the same token, male and female bodies were not fixed and immutable and always defined in the context of dichotomy; rather they were dense and malleable. As Barbara Duden has written of eighteenth-century Germany, the 'analogous, dissymetrical complementarity of the sexes, in which the difference was established through complex relationships among similar things, arose from a culture in which gender was constructed only through diverse relationships to each other and to the environment.'[15] In eighteenth-century erotica male and female bodies were imagined as distinctive and commensurable, as both different and the same. There were patterns in when and how male and female bodies were discussed, though these patterns were not chronological but were determined by the current topic and the general context of a genre which valorized heterosexual desire and procreative sex. Moreover, there was a striking degree of persistence in the ways in which sexual difference was imagined.

Conception

Laqueur identifies changing understandings of conception as 'the initial necessary step' in the move from a one-sex to a two-sex model in the eighteenth century.[16] In a traditional Aristotelian one-seed theory of conception, the male *sperma* was the active substance which worked on the passive female *catamenia*, contained in her menstrual blood. As women did not produce seed, female ejaculation was unnecessary; female orgasm was therefore not required for conception.[17] This was later challenged by Hippocratic and Galenic two-seed theories. In the Hippocratic vision, the ejaculate of the man and woman were deemed to be of the same quality, while in the Galenic vision a woman's seed was regarded as having less powerful a role. In both, however, two seeds were

---

[13] Laqueur, *Making Sex*, p. 10.
[14] Lawrence E. Klein, 'Gender and the Public/Private Distinction in the Eighteenth Century: Some Questions about Evidence and Analytical Procedure', *Eighteenth-Century Studies* 29 (1995), pp. 98–100.
[15] Barbara Duden, *The Woman Beneath the Skin: A Doctor's Patients in Eighteenth-Century Germany* (Cambridge, Mass.: Harvard University Press, 1991), p. 119.
[16] Laqueur, *Making Sex*, p. 8.
[17] McLaren, 'Pleasures of Procreation', p. 326; Vern L. Bullough, 'Medieval Medical and Scientific Views of Women', *Viator* 4 (1973).

required to work on the matter provided by the female.[18] In Laqueur's one-sex model, two-seed theories dominated: 'both sexes experienced a violent pleasure during intercourse that was intimately connected with successful generation; both generally emitted something.'[19] During the eighteenth century, however, two-seed theories were undermined. Ultimately women's sexual pleasure – symbolized by female orgasm – was seen as dispensable to conception and women were reimagined as desexual and maternal.

In this account, female physical pleasure and sexuality are reduced to 'orgasm', and views of sex differences crystallize in discussions of conception. Two omissions from this chapter are immediately suggestive of the deviations of erotica from some other evidence. First, though the question of female pleasure was intimately linked to conception in erotica and will be discussed briefly here in that context, representations of female sexuality and desire were complex and not limited to female emission or orgasm. Second, it is significant that not all discussions of conception in erotica took place within the context of male and female similarity or difference; some focused on men or women alone. I will return to these issues in the following two chapters.

For the moment, I shall focus on those instances where conception is discussed explicitly in the context of the relationship between male and female bodies. Such discussions of conception were common in those erotic texts which used botanical and topographical metaphors. For a modern reader, these texts appear quintessentially eighteenth-century, influenced by recent developments in botany and exploration. If 'modern' sex differences can be found in any eighteenth-century erotic books, surely it is in these? Certainly these writers were fully aware of scientific and medical theories. For example, the author of *The Natural History of the Frutex Vulvaria* (1737), one of several texts which relied on an extended botanical metaphor to discuss female bodies, begins by recounting the theories of Hippocrates and Galen. These theories 'very obstinately' contended that the female plant 'had a balmy *Succus*, or *viscous Juice*, . . . of the same Nature with that discharg'd at the *Pistillum* of the *Arbor Vitae*, which was absolutely necessary in order to its bearing.' Specifics are withheld, but some qualitative equivalence of male and female seed is implied. Others, he writes, including 'the celebrated *Harvey*', denied this and affirmed that the female 'is impregnated solely by the *Succus* of the *Arbor Vitae*, without contributing any Juice there-to itself, insomuch that this Opinion [Hippocratic/Galenic] is now entirely exploded.'[20] This short piece

[18] Thus, it was sometimes claimed that women could fertilize themselves without male assistance. See Crawford, 'Sexual Knowledge', p. 90.
[19] Laqueur, *Making Sex*, p. 46.
[20] Philogynes Clitorides [pseud., alias Thomas Stretser?], *The Natural History of the Frutex Vulvaria, or Flowering Shrub: As it is Collected from the Best Botanists both Ancient and Modern* (Publication details and date torn off, [c. 1737]), pp. 7, 8.

highlights the mutability of apparently discrete theories of conception. William Harvey, who carried out groundbreaking work on the female egg published in 1651, is celebrated along with a vital male contribution reminiscent of older Aristotelian theories. New information about female eggs – not necessarily interpreted as a passive element in conception – melded with ancient theories.

It thus appeared that the idea of female seed had been jettisoned in favour of an older Aristotelian view which saw men's seed as the active agent. Yet this same author later reaffirmed female involvement in conception. The author is writing in response to a story which implied that women took little role in conception, recounted in the companion text on male bodies, *Arbor Vitae; or, The Natural History of the Tree of Life* (1732; 1741).[21] To this the author of *The Natural History of the Frutex Vulvaria* retorts, 'this could not have been done without the Assistance of our *Shrub*, which, *at least*, *went halves* in the *Operation*.'[22] This author upholds a vital role played by women in conception, against claims of men's 'sole' contribution. Popular medical books aired the gamut of conception theories, and the complex discussion of conception in these two erotic books seems to have been lifted from Mauriceau's late-seventeenth-century midwifery book *The Diseases of Women with Child*.[23] Erotic authors did not simply rehearse medical opinion, however, but moulded discussions in the light of their own motivations. Overall, they displayed an ambivalence towards the mechanics of conception, seeking to assure the reader that women played a crucial role in conception, but simultaneously wishing to stress the qualitatively superior contribution of the male. In wanting to emphasize both, this erotic author struggled to find a vision of conception that performed the necessary work. Discrete theories merged as the author forged a combination that conveyed the desired meaning.

Similar complexities can be found in *The Man-Plant* (1752). This book charts the progress of a fictional experiment which sought to increase the country's population by reducing the period of gestation and thereby increasing the number of babies a woman could conceive in her lifetime. A young woman, who had reached 'that critical Season, when the Integrity of a Girl hangs upon a single Hair' was chosen, and the success of the conception depended on 'her True Love's laying the foundation of a future *Foetus*'. The author therefore ensured she had sex with a similarly potent young man, displaying the 'flush of Health and Vigour'.[24] The embryo was extracted from the woman after thirty-nine days, placed in a bladder full of liquid, and 'planted' in a wicker basket of soil. Not only was the male contribution to conception apparently the crucial one – it

---

[21] *Arbor Vitae* (1741), p. 8.   [22] *Natual History of the Frutex Vulvaria* ([c. 1737]), p. 19.

[23] Francis Mauriceau, *The Diseases of Women with Child: As also the Best Means of Helping them in Natural and Unnatural Labours*, 7th edn., trans. Hugh Chamberlain (London: T. Cox and J. Clarke, 1736), pp. 10–11.

[24] *Man-Plant*, pp. 25, 27, 26.

laid the foundations of the foetus – but the entire book relies on an association between the womb and a fertile container of soil. In adopting such images, the author of this erotic book betrayed a debt to ancient understandings of conception, and one which was wielded in medical works. As Mauriceau baldly states, 'We may, with good reason, compare the Womb to a fruitful Field'.[25] Indeed, those 'Aristotelian images of the womb as field' to which Laqueur refers abound in eighteenth-century erotica.[26]

However, the woman's contribution to conception in *The Man-Plant* cannot be reduced to an Aristotelian vision. Firstly, a remarkable extended Latin description of the female body in this book, aping Offray de La Mettrie's *L'homme plante* (1748), grants women active seed as in Hippocratic or Galenic theory:

PERICARPIUM {seminis involucrum}. Capsula ovalis unilocularis.
SEMEN. Unicum, saepe duplex, raro triplex.[27]

The wrapper of the seed, or *pericarpium*, encases small capsules which, presumably, contain the single, double or triple seed. Yet this glimpse of the comparability of the male and female role in procreation is eclipsed by a third view of conception which appears in *The Man-Plant*, one which incorporates the late-seventeenth-century discoveries regarding human female ovaries:

[L]ike the Females of other Animals, she is furnished for Fecundation with an Ovary, and Eggs, a Discovery made by modern Naturalists, and which constitutes the Basis of my Improvements. These Eggs are well known to be no other than the Conceptacles, or temporary Capsules of the male-seed, which is itself the Integument, or Wrapper of a Spark or Particle of Fire, essentially quickened with the vivifying electric Touch produced by the Friction of the generative Process, and radiated up the Womb, where that individual Animacule fostered by a Heat congenial to its igneous Essence, grows and develops into the human Form.[28]

Not until the nineteenth century were the precise activities of sperm and eggs observed, and therefore in the eighteenth century new knowledge regarding female eggs and male sperm could be interpreted in different ways. In preformationist theories, the egg contained the new life which the sperm simply initiated; alternatively, the sperm contained the new life for which the egg was

---

[25] Mauriceau, *Diseases of Women with Child*, p. xxv.

[26] Laqueur, *Making Sex*, p. 272, note 83. See chapter three on these land metaphors.

[27] *Man-Plant*, p. 11. The relevant extract of La Mettrie's book is almost identical:

PERICARPIUM. Capsula ovalis unilocularis.
SEMEN. Unicum, saepe duplex, raro triplex &c.

See Julien Offray de La Mettrie, *L'Homme-plante* (Potsdam: Chretien Frederic Voss, 1748), p. 29.

[28] *Man-Plant*, pp. 16–17.

Erotica — ~~a~~ conception taking some of old theory; some of new theory.

the sustenance.[29] The author of *The Man-Plant* was most definitely of the latter, animalculist, opinion. Once again, the idea that male sperm contained the crucial ingredient for new life was easily accommodated within the Aristotelian vision suggested by the image of woman as fertile earth.

Such moves might be evidence of the persistence of the one-sex model and the resulting interpretation of new knowledge – potentially suggestive of a two-sex model – according to one-sex priorities. But it is not so clear cut. First, the dominant view of the woman's contribution is Aristotelian: her womb was merely a passive and fertile location in which the active male sperm would gestate. This meant that no female ejaculation was required, though in the one-sex model this aspect was crucial. Second, this erotic text contains a lengthy description of the female anatomy explicitly in the classification style introduced by Linnaeus. For Laqueur, such a style and language was emphatically a two-sex feature.[30] *The Man-Plant* thus eludes placement in a one-sex to two-sex story because, as with the botanical satires, the discussion of conception in this text combines elements of both the one-sex and two-sex models.[31]

While some writers reduced women's contribution to conception to the state of a fertile receptacle, others fiercely defended the equal participation of men and women in the process. Consider the satirical book *The Fruit-Shop* (1765). This uses biblical stories to mock contemporary medical debates, ridiculing the idea that women could conceive without men's contribution in a description of the Immaculate Conception. The votaries of 'a new religion', the author explains, asserted that their founder 'had come into the world in a very extraordinary manner; the organic faculties of the female form, being only employed, to the absolute exclusion of those that characterize the superiority of males'. This story, the author scoffs, is 'the very triumph of absurdity'.[32] Insisting that men and women play comparable roles in conception, this author also appears to reject the theory of male sperm and female egg. Though these had been discovered over a hundred years earlier, another century would elapse before the process of fertilization was observed. This view of conception is consequently inadequate for the author of *The Fruit-Shop*, who questions how conception could take place if male and female contributions were different:

equal effort req.

---

[29] Laqueur, *Making Sex*, p. 173. Debates about these different theories took place from the later seventeenth century, but the major clash occurred during the years 1758–68. See Shirley A. Roe, *Matter, Life, and Generation: Eighteenth-Century Embryology and the Haller-Wolff Debate* (Cambridge: Cambridge University Press, 1981).

[30] Laqueur, *Making Sex*, pp. 172–3.

[31] *The Man-Plant* also resists McLaren's schema of 'high' and 'low' culture medical texts which bifurcated in the eighteenth century. The former were allegedly concerned with the organization and development of the embryo, while the latter were increasingly interested in older questions of conception and gestation. See McLaren, 'Pleasures of Procreation', p. 329.

[32] *Fruit-Shop*, vol. II, pp. 78–9, 87.

[E]xtraordinary emanations were to proceed from the circumference of each; and, like the primogenial ramified particles of certain philosophers, were to struggle towards a mutual adhesion at first: and then, by degrees, blend and associate into an animated consistence. Thus the form in whose composition the particles exhaled from the male should prevail (they wearing, as a characteristic token, an appendaged prominence) was to be declared of the masculine gender. But that form, in whose composition the particles emitted from the female should be prevalent, accompanied with the characterising mark of a vermillion-edged involution of substance elegantly fringed around, should be declared of the feminine gender . . . Three blue beans in a blue bladder! – Here is a fine chimerical jargon truly![33]

In a later discussion of '*corporeal*' and '*spiritual*' conception, the same opinionated author expressly rejects the classic Aristotelian theory of conception in which the man contributed 'spiritus' and the woman 'animus': '*Corporeal conception*, . . . hath been assigned over to females by the all-wise disposer of things; the *spiritual* was arrogated by man . . . How would they purposely set about, good Heaven knows, what *odd conceptions*!' One criticism of the idea of male and female particles – that these particles were themselves gendered – resurfaces: female corporeal conception and male spiritual conception are deemed unworkable because such differences prevented an effective encounter. Instead, this author favours the side of the 'materialists', claiming that conception occurred through 'the mutual efforts, and kindling collision, of animated substance, till they lie all dissolving in a state of beatific intoxication'.[34] What this idea admitted, but the two previously eschewed views did not, was some degree of equivalence in male and female contributions to conception which made 'mutual efforts' in conception. The author of *The Fruit-Shop* denounced biblical, new scientific and Aristotelian views of conception, ultimately celebrating a vision akin to the one-sex, two-seed model.

The texts discussed so far in this chapter, spanning the middle decades of the eighteenth century, offer a complex set of understandings regarding conception and resist a chronological pattern. The most unequivocal statement of the process of conception occurs in *The Fruit-Shop*, where the author is adamant that male and female sameness, in terms of potent emission, facilitates human procreation. In contrast, the views of conception offered in *Arbor Vitae* and *The Natural History of the Frutex Vulvaria* encompass classical myths of solitary male procreation, Aristotelian visions of active male seed working on passive female substance, Hippocratic notions of equal male and female ejaculate, and a Galenic theory of two seeds in which the male contribution was nonetheless qualitatively superior. Similarly, the author of *The Man-Plant* manages to include a range of supposedly one-sex visions, incorporating female eggs only to reduce them to a much older Aristotelian vision.

[33] Ibid., vol. I, pp. 131–2.   [34] Ibid., vol. II, p. 85 [emphasis in original]; vol. I, p. 132.

To some extent, this complexity reflects the nature of the erotic genre. While a scientific or medical text had to conform to expectations of reasonable and demonstrable claims, authors of erotica were free from such constraints. For them the purpose was not to convey information regarding conception, but partly to satirize contemporary medical and scientific concerns. This was clearest in a distinctive cluster of texts published in the 1770s which mocked recent experiments with electricity, particularly the work of the Royal Society Fellow John Hunter on the ray fish or 'torpedo'.[35] Hunter's essay to the Royal Society in 1774 presents work on the ray fish, and commemorates those scientists 'who have originally surmised a similitude between the properties of the torpedo and those of the electrical eel, and between the properties of both and those of the Leyden phial'.[36] This scientific concern with analogy was a rich seam for erotic satirists. The erotic poem *The Torpedo* (1777), for example, describes male and female bodies as the eel and the torpedo respectively, and compares them in terms of desire, potency and fertility using the metaphor of electricity. Sexual equivalency is noted, but the female torpedo emerges as a much more powerful force with 'sparkling fires' and 'stronger flames'. Indeed, not only is the electricity of the torpedo more powerful than that of the eel, but the eel's electricity 'From the TORPEDO came'.[37] As with the botanical texts, the playful element in these electrical satires is pronounced; they mimic and poke fun at attempts to decipher similarities and differences between conduits of electricity, staging a playful comparison of male and female. In so doing they characterized the relationship between male and female as an irresolvable conundrum, and reflected the extent to which questions about sexual difference were still being asked in the final decades of the eighteenth century.

Despite playfulness, though, there were consistencies in how theories of conception were selected and modified. Though a Hippocratic/Galenic approach did find some support amongst erotic books of the eighteenth century, this was a much-tempered support because female orgasm was not causally connected to conception. Certainly, as will be discussed at greater length in the following chapter, erotic literature showed women experiencing heady and climactic pleasure during sex, which at times produced an emission: 'When tickl'd most',

---

[35] *Torpedo* (Printed and sold by all the Booksellers in London and Westminster, 1777); *Electrical Eel* (No publication details, [c. 1770]); *Elegy on the Lamented Death of the Electrical Eel; Old Serpent's Reply to the Electrical Eel*.

[36] Sir John Pringle, *A Discourse on the Torpedo, Delivered at the Aniversary Meeting of the Royal Society, November 30, 1774* (London: The Royal Society, 1775), p. 22. The Leyden phial was a machine designed to conduct electricity, delivering a shock to a willing participant. This cluster of erotic texts also responded to the satirical work of John Hill, which rejected the theory that women could conceive without men. See Giancarlo Carabelli, *In the Image of Priapus* (London: Duckworth, 1996), pp. 22–3.

[37] *Torpedo* (Printed and sold by all the Booksellers in London and Westminster, 1777), pp. 10, 9.

for example, *Little Merlin's Cave* (1737) 'will weep'.[38] Frequent references to the flames, heat and electricity of desire may also have been intended to imply orgasm.[39] Moreover, an image of female climactic pleasure itself was perhaps intended as a metaphor for ejaculation. However, in view of the emphasis placed upon reproductive sex in the erotic genre, female orgasm would surely not have been represented so discreetly if it was thought indispensable to conception. Yet female orgasm was omitted from erotic discussions of conception, and the male contribution to conception was championed. This aspect of difference smacked of hierarchies of potency and pleasure, and in both male bodies enjoyed the privileged position.

And yet, while resisting the theory of potent female seed, erotic authors sought to reinforce sexual equivalence in conception because sameness made the workings of that process comprehensible. The stress on male and female equivalency, for example, was particularly noticeable when authors wanted to show that men and women could procreate. The male plant in *Wisdom Reveal'd* (c. 1732), for example, is able to breathe its '*succus Genitalis*' (its sperm) onto the female plant precisely because 'this the Female, that the Male is'.[40] Sexual equivalence facilitated impregnation, and thus clear statements of sameness were introduced when reproduction was being extolled. Reversing the argument employed in *Wisdom Reveal'd*, the author of *The Natural History of the Frutex Vulvaria* uses the possibility of human reproduction to support an unequivocal statement of similarity: 'To shew that the Frutex Vulvaria is absolutely of the same Genus, one need only to observe, that upon the Inoculation of the *Arbor Vitae* thereupon, it will bear both an *Arbor Vitae*, and a *Vulvaria*'.[41] In this case, human reproduction was evidence of similarity.

Two-seed theories were thus attractive to erotic authors because of the equivalence they implied, yet both these two-seed theories and the modern egg and sperm theories were coloured with an Aristotelian brush. Other medical texts engineered the same manoeuvre.[42] Rather than representing the 'before' to a modern 'after', any pre-eminence of the two-seed Galenic theory seems to have been a relatively short-lived blip sandwiched between enduring support for Aristotelian-derived theories of conception, both of which downplayed women's active participation. This is not a linear narrative, then, but a circular one. Furthermore, in erotic discussions of conception neither sameness nor difference adequately captured the sum of relationships envisaged between male and female. Erotic culture drew on a range of competing theories of conception

---

[38] *Little Merlin's Cave*, p. 4.   [39] Laqueur, *Making Sex*, pp. 99–103.

[40] *Wisdom Reveal'd: Or, the Tree of Life Discover'd and Describ'd* (W. Shaw, [c. 1732]), p. 11.

[41] *Natural History of the Frutex Vulvaria* ([c. 1737]), pp. 8–9.

[42] *Aristotle's Compleat Master-piece. In three parts. Displaying the Secrets of Nature in the Generation of Man*, 11th edn. (Printed and sold by the Booksellers, [1725]), p. 17; McLaren, 'Pleasures of Procreation', p. 336; Merchant, *Death of Nature*, p. 162; Laqueur, *Making Sex*, pp. 143–4.

for particular ends and modified them according to the multiple purposes of erotic texts. Each theory performed different work for the author and was used strategically at specific stages in a text. In particular, these authors seem driven by a concern to stress a degree of male and female sameness or equivalence for the purposes of conception, while at the same time professing male superiority and thereby relieving female orgasm of a causal role in the process.

Genital structure

The sameness or equivalence of male and female bodies was indicated through other topics, particularly that of genital structure. Like the two-seed view, the homology between male and female genitals was a crucial aspect of Laqueur's one-sex model. Anatomically, structurally and functionally the same, men's genitals differed from women's only because they were outside the body. One of the most striking examples of this was the likeness between depictions of male and female genitalia in medical illustrations.[43] Robert Martensen has reassessed the iconic images of human genitalia in Vesalius' medical text and concluded that men and women could be conceived 'as both similar and different, as both one-sex and two-sex'.[44] Indeed, while the illustrations of the cervix and penis were similar, there were also undeniable likenesses between the illustration of the rectum and those of both the penis and cervix. Illustrations of internal human parts often looked remarkably similar.[45] Similarly, erotic discussions of genital structure described both the likeness and difference of men and women. Genital homology was invoked particularly when vaginal penetration was depicted, where it served to legitimize penetrative vaginal sex. When attempting to justify heterosexual intercourse, for example, the narrator of *Wisdom Reveal'd* explains that 'Gard'ners' used only specific (female) 'cases' for their plants because '[t]heir entrances exactly fit'.[46] This use of male and female structural equivalence was clearest in the poems *Arbor Vitae*, which describes the male tree, and *The Natural History of the Frutex Vulvaria*, which describes the female shrub. As already seen in their treatment of conception, this duo of texts establishes a complicated relationship between male and female bodies. The opening of *Arbor Vitae* employs a rich botanical metaphor:

[43] See illustrations in Laqueur, *Making Sex*, pp. 82–4.
[44] Robert Martensen, 'The Transformation of Eve: Women's Bodies, Medicine and Culture in Early Modern England', in Roy Porter and Mikulás Teich (eds.), *Sexual Knowledge, Sexual Science: The History of Attitudes to Sexuality* (Cambridge: Cambridge University Press, 1994), p. 113. The text considered is *De humani corporis fabrica* (1543).
[45] See Andreae Vesalius, *De humani corporis fabrica Libri septum* (Basle: Ioannem Oporinum, 1555), pp. 392, 396, 584, 586. Also see the illustrations of male and female genitals and torsos in William Cowper, *The Anatomy of Humane Bodies* (Oxford: Printed at the Theatre, for Sam. Smith and Benj. Walford, Printers to the Royal Society, at the Princes Arms in St Paul's Church Yard, London, 1698).
[46] *Wisdom Reveal'd*, p. 15.

The *Tree of Life* is a *succulent Plant*, consisting of one only straight Stem, on the Top of which is a *Pistillum*, or *Apex* . . . Its Fruits, contrary to most others, grow near the Root; they are usually no more than two in Number, their Bigness somewhat exceeding that of an ordinary *Nutmeg* . . . the whole Root of the plant, is commonly thick set with numerous *Fibrillae*, or *Capillary Tendrils*. The Tree is of slow Growth, and requires time to bring it to Perfection, rarely feeding to any Purpose before the Fifteenth year.[47]

The female plant is described in much the same way in the opening section of *The Natural History of the Frutex Vulvaria*:

The *Frutex Vulvaria* is a low flat shrub, which always grows in a moist warm Valley, at the Foot of a little Hill, which is constantly water'd by a Spring, whose Water is impregnated with very saline Particles, which nevertheless agree wonderfully well with this *Shrub*; it is guarded round with *Fibrillae*, or *Capillary Tendrills*, of the same Nature, and Use, with those at the Root of the *Arbor Vitae*. It is of slow Growth, like the *Arbor Vitae*, especially in those *Northern* Countries, where it seldom comes to Perfection before the fifteenth or sixteenth Year.

The language is strikingly similar. Moreover, these extracts display the same concerns for structure, appearance and development. Indeed, direct parallels are drawn between the appearance and growth of these two plants in the description of the female, regarding pubic hair and the onset of puberty. A further similarity is again referred to in *The Natural History of the Frutex Vulvaria*, in which the author explained that the *frutex vulvaria* possessed 'a natural *Fissura* or *Chink* in the Middle, much like the *Eye* which we shall see in some Trees'.[48]

Significantly, these similarities were offered as justification for particular types of sexual liaison. As the author writes of the *arbor vitae*, 'natural Soil is certainly best for their Propagation, and that is in hollow Places, that are warm and near salt Water, best known by their producing the same Sort of *Tendrils* as are observ'd about the Roots of the *Arbor* itself'. Pubic hair was a sign of similarity, as well as of sexual maturity. Indeed, employing the increasingly popular language of classification, this author confuses bodily similarity with sexual practice, claiming that there is 'the greatest Sympathy between this tree and the Shrub, *They are . . . of the same Genus, and do best in the same Bed; the* Vulvaria *itself being no other than a Female* Arbor Vitae'.[49] This is strong evidence for the adherence of these authors to a strictly one-sex model of sexual difference. It is a striking rendition of the Galenic view of male and female genital homology, of male and female differences of degree plotted on a vertical axis, of the female as 'no other' than a version of the male.

If such statements are to be interpreted as claims for male and female sameness, then this vision held sway throughout the century. In a much later poem

[47] *Arbor Vitae*, pp. 1–2.
[48] *Natural History of the Frutex Vulvaria* ([c. 1737]), pp. 6, 8.   [49] *Arbor Vitae*, pp. 5, 2–3.

lock + key
exact fit [handwritten annotation]

of 1793, the botanical metaphor has been dropped, only to be replaced by the metaphor of the lock and key, another carrier of the notion of male and female genital structural parity. This poem also confirms the work that the image of parity performed for these authors. The advice to the man to 'whip your key in Beauty's Lock' was legitimate precisely because these bodies are moulded for each other – the lock and key fit together perfectly.[50] The equivalence of male and female anatomy emphasized the kinds of activity in which they should engage. This late-eighteenth-century image rings of the structural parity of male and female genitals in the one-sex model, a parity that has generally been associated with an earlier period. In fact, in erotic writing throughout the century, genital structural homology was presented as a prerequisite to sex, and it also functioned to explain and legitimize heterosexual vaginal penetration. *as opposed to anal* [handwritten annotation]

However, as the discussion of conception suggested, different visions of relationships between bodies could coexist. The tree-shrub analogy of the 1730s and 1740s did not offer simply a vision of male-female genital homology. This can be illustrated by examining the two engravings that accompanied editions of the poems *Little Merlin's Cave* and *Arbor Vitae*. *which looked alike* [handwritten annotation] The first of these accompanies a written description of the female body, and depicts a moist and darkened recess with lush foliage. (Illustration 9.) It deviates little from the description of the female in *A Natural History of the Frutex Vulvaria* discussed above, apart from employing the metaphor of a cave rather than that of a shrub. The second engraving initially looks like a reproduction of the first, but a closer examination reveals that the engraving now possesses a title, 'Merryland'. (Illustration 10.) This refers to the popular book *A New Description of Merryland* (1741), which describes the female genitals at some length.[51] The copper plate used to make the engraving has also been altered and an addendum added to the lower left of the image. While the cave once stood alone, 'she' is now joined by an unequivocally male presence: at the foot of the waterfall and directed straight at the entrance to the cave, there is now a penis and testicles thinly disguised as a tree. The direction of the slanting tree suggests vaginal penetration and this is mirrored in the entwined trees reflected in the water. There is little doubt about the heterosexual nature of this particular encounter. Appearing alongside a poem which spoke so obviously of male and female structural parity, the second engraving could easily be interpreted as a visual translation of this element of commensurability. Yet this is not quite the case. While the accompanying text describes the plants the *arbor vitae* and the *frutex vulvaria*, this image depicts a tree and cave. This difference occurred for a number of reasons. First, the English book-buying public does not seem to have been prepared to pay

---

[50] 'Beauty's Lock', in *Bacchanalian Magazine*, p. 67.
[51] Not only were both texts available in the same collection, but they share a densely metaphorical style. It is highly likely they were penned by the same author.

Illustration 9:   A female body as grotto. Frontispiece to *Little Merlin's Cave* (1737).

Illustration 10:   Female genitals as grotto and the male genitals as tree. *Arbor Vitae: Or, the Natural History of the Tree of Life* (For E. Hill, 1741).

substantial prices for this type of literature, in apparent contrast to their French counterparts.[52] The publisher would have saved design and production costs by reusing an engraving.[53] Second, the analogy of a shrub and a tree might convey penetration when delivered in a written format, but it is more difficult to translate into a visual image.

[52] Illustrations to French erotic books were more common and more lavish than these English texts. See the illustrations in Stewart, *Engraven Desire.*
[53] Reusing plates happened elsewhere. The author of *Merryland Displayed* criticizes the publisher of *A New Description of Merryland* for using a frontispiece that had already been produced in his earlier publications. See *Merryland Displayed*, p. 16.

The difficulties in demonstrating visually a tree and shrub engaging in penetrative sex highlights the limits of the tree-shrub analogy for heterosexual sex. Revisiting the written material with doubt cast on the efficacy of the structural parity of tree and shrub, it appears that these limitations are admitted in the text. Indeed, though comparable in terms of pubic hair and development, the *arbor vitae* and *frutex vulvaria* are explicitly differentiated in three ways: genital moisture, genital size and genital structure. While the *arbor vitae* produces a 'Juice of balmy *Succus*' which is 'from Time to Time discharg'd at the *Pistillum*,'[54] the *frutex vulvaria* is 'constantly water'd by a Spring'. Male moisture was intermittent, female moisture was constant. The second difference is size. Considering the sizes generally deemed most favourable for men and women, the author states, 'Contrary to the *Arbor Vitae*, which is valued the more, the larger it is in Size, the *Vulvaria* that is least is most esteem'd'.[55] To some degree, these different requirements were also revealed in the third distinction between male and female. This crucial difference was one of structure. In *Wisdom Reveal'd* (c. 1732) the tree-shrub motif does allow the author to make a statement of sexual commensurability: 'this the Female, that the Male is'. But difference is also articulated precisely through this distinction: '[c]onscious his Tree was like a Shrub', the male narrator begins to speak of the length of his penis in order to distinguish it from the female body.[56] The parity between male and female conveyed in the distinction between tree and shrub did not preclude difference. The analogy was elastic, facilitating a depiction of both sameness and difference.

This elasticity was present in the source of the analogy. The authors of *Arbor Vitae* and *Wisdom Reveal'd* lifted the distinction of tree and shrub from the work of the eighteenth-century botanist Richard Bradley.[57] Bradley saw a degree of 'sympathy' between the tree and shrub: '[a] *Shrub*', he writes, 'is that Genus of *Plant*, which in every Circumstance, but in its Bigness and Duration, imitates a *Tree*'. Yet they are also distinct: '[a] *Tree*', he explains, 'is that sort of *Plant*, which of all the others is the most lofty in its Growth, and has its Parts more robust, firm and lasting than any kind of *Plant* yet mention'd; and to these its Perfections we may add, that it enjoys a longer Share of Life than any other *Vegetable*'.[58] Indeed, Bradley writes that the term 'frutex' denotes 'such Plants as are the next below the Dignity of Trees . . . The Shrubs have no Stem or Body

---

[54] *Arbor Vitae*, p. 2.   [55] *Natural History of the Frutex Vulvaria* ([c. 1737]), pp. 6, 7.
[56] *Wisdom Reveal'd*, pp. 11, 9.
[57] *Arbor Vitae*, p. 2; *Wisdom Reveal'd*, p. 7. There are many similarities between *Arbor Vitae* and *Wisdom Reveal'd*, and the author of the latter clearly read the former and referred to it in his preface as 'a late ingenious Essay' (p. i). In one erotic book, both the male and female genitalia are described as shrubs. See *Voyage to Lethe*, p. 65.
[58] Bradley, *Philosophical Account*, pp. 35, 37.

like a Tree, but grow like Brushes from the Root'.[59] The original comparison of shrub and tree not only indicated a degree of comparability, but simultaneously implied differences both of degree and of kind, differences which contained notions of hierarchy and superiority. Indeed, in claiming that the tree and shrub were 'of the same genus', rather than species, the author of *The Natural History of the Frutex Vulvaria* and *Arbor Vitae* indicated how male and female were considered part of a large group which included a range of assorted types.[60] The erotic depiction of genitals illustrated the commensurability necessary for penetrative sex, therefore, but the metaphors that represented these parts were flexible and could convey important differences.

Other bodily markers of difference

Images of genitals were key to discussions of sexual difference, but they could also disrupt those distinctions. One of the most significant markers of difference was the penis.[61] In the poem 'The Toy', published in *Hilaria* (1798), an accusation is hurled at two men – a captain and his ensign – alleging they had engaged in sex, and a crowd assemble in order to determine the truth of the matter. The captian defends himself by revealing that the ensign is actually a woman and, to satisfy the incredulous crowd, he opens her waistcoat to reveal 'a pair of bubbies'. The disbelieving cook rejects this as insufficient evidence:

> You *Sodomiters*, people say,
> Have breasts as dumplings big, sir.

Searching for genuine proof, she thrusts her hand into the ensign's breeches:

> She'd laid her hand upon the place,
> That spreads the ensigns p—s, sir,
> Then looking humbly in his face,
> Said, 'beg your pardon MISS – SIR'.[62]

The penis was here the key to establishing sex, as it could be in seventeenth-century Anglo-America.[63] In this erotic poem, individuals who disrupted bodily differences were those who engaged in reprehensible sexual practices: bodily differences and heterosexuality were constructed simultaneously. However, in

---

[59] Richard Bradley, *Dictionarium Botanicum: Or, a Botanical Dictionary for the Use of the Curi-ous in Husbandry and Gardening*, 2 vols. (For T. Woodward at the Half-Moon over-against St Dunstan's Church in Fleet-Street, and J. Peele at Locke's Head in Pater-Noster-Row, 1728), vol. I, unpaginated.

[60] *Natural History of the Frutex Vulvaria* ([c. 1737]), p. 9; *Arbor Vitae*, p. 5. 'Genus' meant 'a class of being, comprehending under it many species'. See Samuel Johnson, *A Dictionary of the English Language*, 2nd edn., 2 vols. (London: By W. Strahan, 1755), vol. I.

[61] See, for example, *Voyage to Lethe*, p. 10.   [62] 'The Toy', in *Hilaria*, pp. 96–7.

[63] See Brown, "Changed . . . into the Fashion of Man", for a case of undecided sex tested by an individual's possession or not of a working penis.

floating the idea that 'sodomiters' possessed breasts, the author allowed for the disruption of these associations. There were bodily possibilities, fastened to reprehensible sexual activities, which undermined strict sexual distinctions.

Though breasts were generally used as crucial determinants of a female body, as the last example indicated they could not always be relied upon to indicate unequivocal differences. In the tale of puberty told in *The Fruit-Shop*, breasts are portrayed as the fulfilment of a female sex already established, but a fulfilment which does not always occur:

The first budding orbs on the breasts of young girls, and the first downy appearance on the chins of young lads, the prologue of a beard, are nature's criteria, indicating to each sex to think betimes of the principle end they were sent for into this world.

In accoutring each she is at a different expense of plastic power . . . Hence it obviously appears, that the particular expending of nature in one sex, is an equivalent to that in the other; and that she cannot afford a double gift of the requisites in both to either.

Now, in order to illustrate this doctrine, be it remembered, that most of those errors of nature, those manlike females, odiously remarkable for beards or great-whiskers, are scraggy-breasted.[64]

This extract offers a complex vision of sex differences. On the one hand, only absolute differences between men (those with beards) and women (those with breasts) appear possible. Sex differences were not differences of degree, and were mutually exclusive: 'Nature' could not serve the 'double gift' of both a beard *and* breasts to one body. On the other hand, the author concedes that some 'manlike females' display facial hair and scraggy breasts, thus posing two problems for what had appeared to be a two-sex vision. First, though retaining the logic of the mutually exclusive and opposite differences of sex (there could be no 'double gift'), these women threatened to assume the status of a median category because they were 'females' with beards and breasts. Sex distinctions were not absolute. Second, despite developing a male characteristic during puberty, these women remained female, suggesting that their sex preceded puberty and the bodily changes that took place at this stage. Beards and breasts might be important consequences of a person's sex, but they were not the defining aspects of it. *The Fruit-Shop* thus envisaged absolute difference, the transgression of that difference, and differences of degree.

Breasts could signal both the construction and the disruption of sex differences, and beards had the same potential. Beards were deemed markers of bodily distinction in this period which 'not only drew a sharp line between men and women, [but] also served to differentiate the varieties of men'.[65] Consequently, for some natural historians and scientists, the beard was the marker of

---

[64] *Fruit-Shop*, vol. I, pp. 149–50.   [65] Schiebinger, *Nature's Body*, p. 120.

a more civilized and noble class of human beings from which women and non-European men were excluded. For one young woman in *The Genuine Memoirs of the Celebrated Miss Maria Brown* (1766), the beard was the vital clue to sexual difference:

I had observed his beard, which he constantly shaved every day, and was from thence led to conjecture, that there must be some difference between men and women, besides their dress; and my curiosity was never completely satisfied upon this score, till such time as he manifestly convinced me of the distinction.[66]

The man's beard aroused suspicions of sex difference, but these were satisfied only when he revealed his genitals. In common with the author of *The Fruit-Shop*, this writer regarded men's facial hair as a secondary characteristic which simply confirmed the status established by the genitals. Like breasts, beards were secondary sexual characteristics of opposite sexes defined by genitals. They could be ascribed incorrectly, but heterosexual women and men who behaved in an appropriately gendered manner possessed the correct accoutrements.

As a distinguishing marker of the male sex, however, the beard did not go unchallenged. In their classification of human beings, men of science focused on facial hair to the exclusion of other types of body hair, of the armpit or groin, for example.[67] Women were classified not only according to their lack of facial hair specifically, but also through recourse to their general hairlessness. In view of this, the fascination that erotic writers of this period had with female pubic hair is significant.[68] One poem of the late eighteenth century charts a contest between four women vying for the parts that were 'best supply'd / With that which *pleases* man.' As each woman lifts her dress to reveal her genitals, the narrator describes only their pubic hair: black, brown, blonde or non-existent. Though the narrator's adoration is reserved for the young pre-pubescent girl, this poem does not disparage female body hair. The black pubic hair is 'all-alluring', the golden hair is 'noble' and the 'nut brown' hair is deemed deserving of special comment. The narrator is impressed by the 'sumptuous arch' of brown hair which grows high up to the woman's stomach and across each thigh, while the brown-haired woman acknowledges the mighty effect her pubic hair could

---

[66] *Genuine Memoirs of... Miss Maria Brown*, vol. II, pp. 178–9.

[67] Schiebinger, *Nature's Body*, p. 125.

[68] See also an alleged letter to *The Covent-Garden Magazine; Or, Amorous Repository: Calculated Solely for the Entertainment of the Polite World, and the Finishing of a Young Man's Education* (London: G. Allen, 1773), vol. II, p. 60, in which a woman adorns her own dark pubic hair with hair obtained from a white rabbit. This interest in female pubic hair was reflected in the histories of the Beggar's Benison and the Wig Club, which used a head-wig supposedly made from the pubic hair of Charles II's mistresses, after which the Wig Club was named. See Jones, *Clubs of the Georgian Rakes*, pp. 192–3.

have on men, declaring, 'Tis *this* can make the hero droop / And tame the stoutest fellow'.[69] The greatest expanse of female pubic hair, therefore, astonished the male narrator and indicated this woman's capacity to control men. In view of eighteenth-century scientific claims regarding the significance of the beard to white European men, it is easy to see how hair could be associated with power.

Pubic hair was invariably an integral feature of descriptions of women's genitals. The vulva is described favourably as 'a ring set round with hair', 'a thing so hairy' and 'by moss circled round'.[70] It has an inside which is hot but an outside which is 'furr'd',[71] or features a 'blazing hairy appendage'.[72] And though this hair was often imbued with the power to instil trepidation in men, the word 'beard' was used in positive descriptions of female pubic hair: the female genitals were 'set off by a *beard*',[73] while 'the beard of *Venus*' was a repeated phrase.[74] If hair, particularly a beard, was a marker of the superiority of white European men, then the focus on women's pubic hair – and especially the language of the beard to describe it – might have constituted some disruption of this system of sexual difference. But women's pubic hair was important in erotica. First, it was regarded as one of the most noticeable aspects of female genitalia and the only female genital protuberance, thereby indicating the sex of women's bodies. Second, in 'hiding' female genitals to some extent, pubic hair may have been hailed as a kind of anatomical guard of modesty. Certainly, *Aristotle's Compleat Master-Piece* (1725) suggests that women's labia were designed as a veil, and this was how some ethnographers regarded the elongated labia of the infamous 'Hottentot Venus'.[75] Third, pubic hair was a crucial sign of sexual maturity in a genre deeply concerned with reproduction. An acknowledgement of female hair might be potentially disruptive of sex distinctions, but the concerns of the erotic genre served to bolster its status as a sign of sexual maturity and fertility. What in science and medicine indicated sexual difference took on quite a different meaning in erotica.

[69] 'The Warm Dispute', in *Bacchanalian Magazine*, pp. 36–7.
[70] 'On Lady T r C l's Ring', p. 165; 'The Squire', p. 198; and 'Song', p. 288, all in *Festival of Love*.
[71] 'Old Reeky', in *Forty Select Poems, on Several Occasions, by the Right Honourable The Earl of M* – (No publication details, [c. 1753]), p. 182.
[72] *Fruit-Shop*, vol. I, p. 66.
[73] 'The Fashionable That!', in *Bacchanalian Magazine*, p. 41.
[74] For example see *Rake of Taste*, p. 39; and *Did You Ever See Such Damned Stuff?*, p. 63.
[75] *Aristotle's Compleat Master-Piece*, p. 15. On the 'Hottentot Venus', or Sara Baartman, see Stephen Jay Gould, *The Flamingo's Smile: Reflections in Natural History* (New York: Norton, 1985), pp. 291–305; Sander L. Gilman, *Difference and Pathology: Stereotypes of Sexuality, Race, and Madness* (Ithaca, N.Y.: Cornell University Press, 1985), pp. 76–108; Schiebinger, *Nature's Body*, p. 165.

Historicizations of sex differences

The relationship between male and female in erotica was complex. Features which denoted difference might simultaneously signal sameness, but sameness was particularly employed during discussions of the mechanics of conception or vaginal penetration. When trying to relate heterosexual desire, though, authors made clear statements of stark sexual differences. In this final section, I want to consider erotic stories of the emergence of bodily sex differences. These historicizations of sex differences are intriguing in the context of the claim that cultural 'gender' was increasingly losing out to physical 'sex' as the foundation of difference. Erotic accounts of the birth of sex differences suggest a very different view. These accounts of the emergence of sex differences often focused on a cultural gender (encompassing behaviour, pose, activity), and though this was intimately connected to (and sometimes indistinguishable from) bodily sex and the genitals, sex was not layered over by gender. Indeed, quite the opposite story could be told. In 'The Spectacles', a short poem published in 1770, 'Dame Nature' equips men and women with laces to sew their bodies, and the different stitching produces male and female genitals.[76] Genital differences were given a history, but these differences were a fulfilment of pre-existing male and female categories: gender predated sex.

Typically, sex, gender and heterosexual desire were constructed in the same process. In 1726, the author of *A Description of the Temple of Venus* described two places where distinctions between men and women had collapsed. At Cibaris, the men dressed and behaved like women, so that 'one wou'd be apt to conclude there was but one Sex in the whole City'. Women also behaved immodestly and therefore in an unfeminine way: 'The Women rather throw 'emselves into the Arms, than yield reluctantly to the Embraces of their Lovers'. At Lesbos there existed the same pattern of effeminate men and unfeminine women, women who had lost their 'becoming Blush, their Weakness of Body' and become '*Lesbian* Maids'.[77] At both Cibaris and Lesbos men and women had lost their distinguishing traits, forging 'one Sex' by exchanging behaviours and objects of desire. Gendered roles and heterosexual desire were inseparable aspects of difference.[78] The development of men's beards and women's breasts during puberty described in *The Fruit-Shop* certainly took place within the context of heterosexual sex. Crucially, those 'errors of nature' or 'manlike females' discussed earlier are disruptive not only because they transgressed bodily distinctions, but because they lacked the 'gently swelling snowy orbs' that served

---

[76] 'The Spectacles', in *Festival of Love*, pp. 394–5.
[77] *Description of the Temple of Venus*, pp. 30, 34–5.
[78] The system posited by Judith Butler, in which the exigencies of heterosexual desire produced binary categories of gender and sex, therefore finds some support in this material. See Butler, *Gender Trouble*; also see discussion in the introduction to this book.

to 'tempt a lover's hand'. They were dangerous because their bodies precluded heterosexual sex. Indeed, as the author states, 'it is not to be supposed that the two sexes were discriminated one from the other by distinguishing criteria; but in order that they should be put to the very use they have since been found capable of through such a long series of, repeated, agreeable, and most alluring experiments.'[79] Bodily distinctions were functional, and sexual difference inspired heterosexual desire.

Some disruption of this triad of sex, gender and desire was permitted. Cross-dressing, for example, was sanctioned, but only when the occasion was the heterosexual pursuit of a lover. The narrator of *A Spy on Mother Midnight* (1748) is able to disguise himself as a woman and infiltrate the female group of which his intended lover was a member, partly because he had 'very little Hair upon my Chin'. Yet he insisted upon his heterosexual desire, revealing that 'the very Idea of a Petticoat, especially the Inside of one, put that Companion of mine into a mighty Fume'.[80] In a much later poem of 1798, cross-dressing by a man is again used in order to encourage three women to reveal their bodies to him.[81] Cross-dressing for women was similarly legitimate when it was done to facilitate greater contact with men. The cross-dressing of the 'Chevalier-Madame d'Eon de Beaumont' is reduced in erotica to her desire to be close to the men she loved.[82] Correspondingly, cross-dressing was unacceptable when it was part of a more general transgression of boundaries that undermined heterosexuality. The male worshippers who 'disguise 'emselves in Women's Apparel' in *A Description of the Temple of Venus* serve to 'emasculate 'emselves'; women were 'the Sex they have quitted, and that which it will be impossible for 'em ever to have.'[83]

The simultaneous forging of difference and heterosexual desire was clearest in *The Why and the Wherefore* (1765). This curious book seeks to address two questions, the first being 'Why Men have not much to boast of their greatness, nor women of their beauty, in certain very interesting parts'. In answering this, the male narrator tells a story of the creation of sexed human bodies. Before they joined to assemble 'perfect males and females', distinct 'tribes' of body parts existed: '*Eyes, Legs, Arms, Thighs, Breasts*, and so forth; but those names are now all lost, except just these of the more interesting ones, the *Poles* [penises], the *Flats* [vaginas], and the *Twinballians* [testicles].' Ultimately most of these body parts came to exist in a body along with a twin, apart

[79] *Fruit-Shop*, vol. I, pp. 150, 132.
[80] *Spy on Mother Midnight*, pp. 8–9.   [81] 'The Blue Vein', in *Hilaria*, pp. 57–64.
[82] *Elegy on the Lamented Death of the Electrical Eel*, pp. 14–17. The author of this poem concurred with the view existing during 'her' lifetime, that d'Eon was a woman who had spent the first half of her life cross-dressed as a man; but her death in 1810 revealed that 'she' was actually a 'he' who had lived the second half of his life as a woman. See Gary Kates, 'The Transgendered World of the Chevalier/Chevalière d'Eon', *Journal of Modern History* 67 (1995), pp. 558–94.
[83] *Description of the Temple of Venus*, p. 11.

from the 'Poles' and 'Flats'. In his explanation of the resulting sexed bodies, this author argues that heterosexual desire caused sexual differences. Before forming distinct bodies, the different parts were animated by desire: 'The *Eyes* saw one another with pleasure and mutual complacency; the *Arms* embraced; the *Mouths* kissed one another. The *Poles* were a free sort of a people, but no freer than welcome, especially to the *Flats*'.[84] The logic of desire governing most body parts led them to desire their twin, but the genitals are driven by a desire for difference. The second question answered in *The Why and the Wherefore* is, 'Wherefore is it that both sexes are so eternally dear lovers of that same?' In the response, heterosexual desire was given a history in which female desire for men ultimately originated from women's excessive desire, and men's desire for women was an attempt to placate women.[85] If the first part of *The Why and the Wherefore* offered a fantastical history of sexed bodies shaped by heterosexual desire, then the second part furnished the sustaining tale of that desire. This was an erotic fantasy that demonstrated the enduring fascination with sexual difference, in which heterosexual desire was not only inseparable from sexual difference, but actually produced that difference.

When the author of *Teague-Root Display'd* (1746) claimed 'There are two Kinds of this Root, the Male and Female', he suggested an apparently straightforward model of sex differences: male and female were placed alongside one another and understood as of the same 'kind'.[86] Yet analogous did not mean identical; according to Samuel Johnson it meant to be 'Resemblance between things with regard to *some* circumstances or effects'. In the same way, to be 'commensurable' meant to be 'Reducible to *some* common measure'; 'same' meant 'being of the like kind, sort or degree'; 'sort' meant 'A kind; a species', while 'kind' was capable of indicating a broad collective within which there were many variations.[87] Analogy was a tool which conveyed the mechanics of vaginal penetration and conception, but did not preclude considerable difference. In fact, in erotic discussions of fertility and reproduction, male and female bodies were discussed in terms of both sameness and difference, and placed in a framework allowing both analogy and distinction. There was considerable flexibility in erotic representations of bodies, then, and metaphors used to illustrate the equivalence of female and male bodies were also used to show their thoroughly sexed nature. But there were also patterns in emphasis depending

---

[84] *The Why and the Wherefore: Or, the Lady's Two Questions Resolved. Question the First; Why Men have not much to Boast of their Greatness, nor Women of their Beauty, in certain very Interesting Parts'. Resolved in the History of the Political, Natural, and Moral, of a Primitive Commonwealth. Question the Second. Wherefore is it that both Sexes are so eternally Dear Lovers of that Same? Resolved in a Story intitled The Female Embassy* (For J. Lamb, in the Strand, 1765), pp. 27–30.

[85] Ibid., pp. 131–70.   [86] *Teague-Root Display'd*, p. 11.

[87] Johnson, *Dictionary* [emphasis added]. Johnson claimed that '*Kind* in Teutonic English answers to *genus*, and *sort* to *species*; though this distinction, in popular language, is not always observed'.

on whether the topic was the process of conception, the act of penetration or the state of desire. It is very difficult to map these patterns chronologically, and this suggests that erotic representations of sexual difference cannot be encapsulated in period-specific models. Indeed, the language of models seems better suited to an analysis of scientific and medical modes of thought than to an analysis of erotic writing. Understandings of bodies in erotica drew on but did not replicate discussions in science and medicine; knowledge about bodies was not created in the fields of science and medicine and then rearticulated in other domains. In other words, erotica did not occupy a position in a cultural landscape in which all genres told the same story. Culture operates not through synecdoche, but through metonymy.[88] A cultural state cannot be deduced from one set of evidence, because neither 'culture' nor any single genre was monolithic or uni-vocal. Attention to the multi-vocal nature of texts reveals not a cacophony of voices, but complex patterns of meaning.

Such a view modifies the dominant narrative of the history of the body. The vision of sexual difference in erotica also raises questions regarding the treat-ment of change, endurance and variety in the history of gender. There was a significant degree of persistence in representations of the relationship between male and female bodies.[89] But this is not the same as saying the picture remained static. Indeed, while displaying many enduring qualities, eighteenth-century erotica was a genre which changed rapidly in response to contemporary events. Throughout the eighteenth century, authors wanting to depict bodies could draw on a number of ways of representing male and female. In erotica, though, changes were short-term and insubstantial rather than long-term and transfor-mative. Widespread claims for linear transformation are undermined by this striking combination of short-term shifts in language combined with a range of persisting themes. Eighteenth-century erotica was characterized by an enduring synchronic diversity in representations of sexual difference. However, represen-tations of male and female bodies were subject to distinctive patterns of trans-formation. The next chapter explores change and persistence in representations of female bodies, analysing the interplay of (supposedly) ancient, early-modern and nineteenth-century understandings of bodies during the eighteenth century.

[88] Susan Hegeman, 'Imagining Totality: Rhetorics of and versus Culture', *Common Knowledge* 6 (1997), p. 55.
[89] Some nineteenth-century scientific theories, for example, placed men and women on a hierarchy comparable to Laqueur's one-sex, early-modern, hot/dry, cold/wet grid. See Laqueur, *Making Sex*, p. 208, note 36, and Elizabeth Fee, 'Science and the Woman Problem: Historical Perspec-tive', in M. S. Teitelbaum (ed.), *Sex Differences: Social and Biological Perspectives* (New York: Anchor Books, 1976), pp. 175–223.

3   Female bodies

Despite the focus on difference in the history of the body, it is the female body that lies at the heart of narratives of bodies and gender: changing understandings of sexual difference comprised changing understandings of female – rather than male – bodies. Existing work on female bodies tells the story of a shift from one female body to another, and central to this shift were changing understandings of female sexuality. In the move from one-sex to two-sex, women were reimagined as sexually passive, and the key marker of this was the 'demotion of the female orgasm' in the elite scientific and medical discourses of the late eighteenth century.[1] This vision echoes earlier claims that the eighteenth century saw a shift from depictions of female sexuality as legitimate, necessary and 'earthy' in medical literature of the sixteenth and seventeenth centuries to images of 'the passive Victorians lying back and thinking of the empire'.[2] Indeed, the passionlessness of Victorian women is a well-established theme in women's history.[3] And this passionless woman contrasts markedly with the libidinous woman of the one-sex world. In a history of women, this is significant because changes in understandings of female sexuality are believed to have produced a position for women which was qualitatively poorer than the one which preceded it, bringing to a close the 'fairly egalitarian' situation in which 'the bed was one place in which men and women were more or less equal', and ensuring that 'the rights of women to sexual pleasure were not enhanced, but eroded'.[4] Sexuality has become part of a much larger picture, though, and the modern sexually disenfranchised woman has merged with the domesticated woman of the middle class. For example, Carolyn Merchant tied changing scientific attitudes to 'Nature' to the reassertion of women's passive role in reproduction, the concomitant repression of 'sexual passion' and

[1] Thomas Laqueur, 'Orgasm, Generation, and the Politics of Reproductive Biology', *Representations* 14 (1986), p. 3.
[2] McLaren, 'Pleasures of Procreation', pp. 324, 330. Many more recent examples could be marshalled. See Accati, 'Spirit of Fornication'; Crouch, 'Public Life of Actresses'; Schiebinger, 'Skeletons in the Closet'; Schiebinger, 'Gender and Natural History', p. 163.
[3] See especially Nancy Cott, 'Passionlessness: An Interpretation of Victorian Sexual Ideology, 1790–1850', *Signs* 4 (1978), pp. 219–36.
[4] McLaren, 'Pleasures of Procreation', pp. 340, 341.

102

the increasingly powerful association of middle- and upper-class women with domesticity.[5] This narrative of women's containment and loss of power mirrors statements of women's narrowing work opportunities, in which the decline of the family economy allegedly eroded 'something approximating to a working partnership with their husbands'.[6] Female independence has thus been located in specific configurations of home, work and sexuality, and, for some historians, in terms of all three the eighteenth century witnessed a downturn for women.

Although still in its infancy, the history of erotica and pornography bears traces of the account of changes in female sexuality. Some notable exceptions stress the alternative visions offered by this material.[7] But historians have also begun to use erotica and pornography to confirm standard narratives, rather than to complicate or refute them.[8] An important statement in this regard is by Bridget Orr, particularly relevant here because it is concerned exclusively with erotica. Orr's account is based largely on a comparison of *Erotopolis. The Present State of Bettyland* (1684) and *A New Description of Merryland* (1741), which both employed a metaphor of land for the female body. Enlisting this material, Orr argues for a transformation in female gender roles during the first half of the eighteenth century, claiming that the transgressive, sexual, independent and threatening women in the earlier text compared favourably with the constrained, sexually passive and conquered female body observable in the later book. '[M]odes of feminine subjectivity, hardening around new, more domestic and maternal ideals in the mid-eighteenth century', she writes, 'were rather more fluid in the late Restoration.'[9] Merryland was less sexualized

---

[5] Merchant, *Death of Nature*, p. 148. A related argument is offered in Felicity Nussbaum's *Torrid Zones: Maternity, Sexuality, and Empire in Eighteenth-Century English Narratives* (Baltimore: Johns Hopkins University Press, 1995). Nussbaum argues that the stress on motherhood and domesticity for middle-class women was part of the same process that rendered women of the empire and prostitutes at home sexualized and 'other'. It is important to note, however, that Nussbaum also seeks to resist the emphasis on the formation of two opposite sexed bodies in the eighteenth century, and explores the complexities of sexuality as suggested by pornography. See especially pp. 95–113.

[6] Hill, *Women, Work and Sexual Politics*, p. 46. See also Keith Snell, 'Agricultural Seasonal Unemployment, the Standard of Living, and Women's Work in the South and East, 1690–1860', *Economic History Review* 2nd series, 34 (1981), pp. 407–37.

[7] See Kathryn Norberg, 'The Libertine Whore: Prostitution in French Pornography from Margot to Juliette', in Hunt (ed.), *Invention of Pornography*, pp. 225–52; Dorelies Kraakman, 'Reading Pornography Anew: A Critical History of Sexual Knowledge for Girls in French Erotic Fiction, 1750–1840', *Journal of the History of Sexuality* 4 (1994), p. 534.

[8] For example, see Randolph Trumbach, 'Modern Prostitution and Gender in *Fanny Hill*: Libertine and Domesticated Fantasy', in G. S. Rousseau and Roy Porter, *Sexual Underworlds of the Enlightenment* (Manchester: Manchester University Press, 1987), pp. 67–85; Hitchcock, *English Sexualities*, pp. 8–23; Shoemaker, *Gender in English Society*, pp. 65–7.

[9] Bridget Orr, 'Whore's Rhetoric and the Maps of Love: Constructing the Feminine in Restoration Erotica', in Clare Brant and Diane Purkiss (eds.), *Women, Texts and Histories, 1575–1760* (London: Routledge, 1992), p. 214. I am grateful to Helen Weinstein for directing me to this piece. Orr's narrative owes much to Carolyn Merchant's claim that the new science of the

and less threatening than Bettyland; the earthy early-modern woman faded, and the path was cleared for Victorian passionlessness.

As an example of a much broader historiography, this argument provides a useful entry point to several issues concerning representations of female bodies in erotic culture. Orr's account of change is based in part on the argument that, while the author of the 1684 text tried but failed to contain 'transgressive feminine sexuality', by 1741 this threat had been erased by 'the judiciary, the new sciences and the Society for the Reformation of Manners'.[10] The later censure of female sexuality was not evidence that writers were anxious about the existing sexuality of women; instead, Orr claims that the 'extra-discursive female persona' which disrupted Bettyland no longer existed to intrude into Merryland. In other words, the lives of actual, less sexualized women were imprinted on erotic texts. Another important aspect of Orr's argument is the half-century separating the publication of these books. It is important to note, however, that Bettyland remained intelligible for readers of the mid-eighteenth century: Erotopolis was in fact reprinted in a collection of 1741 alongside A New Description of Merryland.[11]

While the 1684 text of Erotopolis was not greatly altered for a 1741 audience, though, there is one key difference between Erotopolis. The Present State of Bettyland and A New Description of Merryland, and this is the absence from the latter of anything approximating the account in Erotopolis of the narrator's tour through London's brothels. The women encountered on this tour, Orr argues, forged their own disruptive and powerful, liberated femininity which resisted the male-centred view of the rest of the book.[12] Their absence from the later A New Description of Merryland, she asserts, was evidence of the silencing of women's voices and the removal of their agency from erotica. This claim can be challenged in a number of ways. First, 'independent' female prostitutes continued to act as narrators in numerous eighteenth-century books.[13] Second, and more importantly, it is problematic to equate dangerous and libidinous figures with an independent female identity. The women of Bettyland were certainly presented as fierce characters to be reckoned with, but they were notable for their grotesque features rather than for a proto-feminist independence. The first woman 'lookt as if she had been eaten and spew'd up again',

sixteenth and seventeenth centuries determined that 'Disorderly female nature would soon submit to the controls and the experimental method and technological advance'. See Merchant, Death of Nature, p. 149.
[10] Orr, 'Whore's Rhetoric', pp. 201, 202.
[11] 'Erotopolis; Or, Of the Situation of Bettyland', in Philo-Brittanniae [pseud.], The Potent Ally (1741). In this chapter, the quotes from Erotopolis will be taken from 'Erotopolis; Or, Of the Situation of Bettyland' in The Potent Ally, as this edition does not differ substantially from the earlier edition of 1684, Ερωτοπολιζ or Erotopolis. The Present State of Bettyland. When this earlier has been used it will be noted.
[12] Orr, 'Whore's Rhetoric', p. 214.   [13] Norberg, 'The Libertine Whore', passim.

while the second woman was a 'ruinous piece of Antiquity with a Voice as hoarse as if her throat had been lin'd with Seal Skins: she had as much flesh below her Chin, as would have serv'd to have made another Face: she was pufft up like a shoulder of Veal blown up with a Tobacco-Pipe.'[14] The interpretation of such images as 'positive' ignores their depiction of women as monstrous.

In this chapter I respond to this work in three ways. First, I insist on diversity in past ideas about bodies. If, as suggested in chapter two, the themes of difference and sameness were not mutually exclusive, then the exemplary female body of the past must be plural, not singular. In other words, representations of female bodies did not simply transform from one type to another. In addition to the trust placed in Hippocratic and Galenic models of conception and an unmistakable degree of analogy and similitude in imaginings of male and female bodies, representations of female bodies in erotica reveal an emphasis on women's sexual pleasure and a stress on flow and moisture. This suggests a lingering humoral system of sexual difference. Yet the presence of more 'modern' elements – such as a focus on women's distinctiveness and their role as mothers – demonstrate that the one-sex model did not hold universal sway. In fact, the early-modern sexually voracious woman and the desexualized, domesticated woman who supposedly took her place appeared alongside one another. Rather than singularity, then, what emerges is *diversity* in past representations of female bodies. Second, this chapter argues for *endurance*. The combination of diversity and endurance in depictions of women's bodies suggests not that constructions of the female body radically transformed, but that change operated at a number of different levels. There was variety (for example, female bodies were depicted as both irresistible and fear-inspiring), but there were also notable constants which shaped all representations (for example, the stress on the fertility of female bodies). Third, this chapter thinks about how we should assess representations of female bodies in eighteenth-century erotic culture. We cannot simply plunder erotic writing for positive images of female bodies, to be used as evidence for a golden age of sexuality for women. The assessment of representations as simply positive or negative must be forged in the masculinist context of erotic culture, not assumed contexts of women's actual sexual identities or lives.

Sexuality

Throughout this period, female bodies inspired both fear and desire. The menacing images of women in seventeenth-century writing were clearly visible in mid-eighteenth-century erotic texts. Indeed, despite the claim that the female body in

[14] *Erotopolis* (1684), pp. 72–3, 73–4.

eighteenth-century texts was 'measured, mapped and known', many metaphors adopted in the representation of female genitalia appear to be designed precisely to convey a sense of unknowability. The practice of representing women's bodies as maps confirmed this sense of these bodies as mysterious.[15] In a similar vein, voyage metaphors were commonly used to depict sexual activity, and in these female bodies were often envisaged as alien and obscure. The opening description of the location of Merryland explains that the latitude and longitude of the country has never been 'fixed to any certain degree'.[16] Similarly, the canal that runs through the middle of the land is of such depths that the author has never reached the end: 'perhaps', he ponders, 'had my Sounding-line been a *few Fathoms* longer, it might have reached the Bottom'.[17] The voyage metaphor could also give the sense of a foreign land which had to be negotiated with caution. At the close of the book a guide to vaginal intercourse is couched in terms of 'Directions for strangers steering safe into Merryland':

[M]ake first for that Part of the Continent called L P S, where they generally *bring to*, and salute the Fort; and sometimes it is required that they *pay the Customs* and *Duties* here, before they are allowed to proceed further; but this is not always demanded. Then if you find the Wind favourable, steer along Shore to the *Bby-Mountains*, where there is *good Riding*; and if you meet with no Storm, but find it calm and quiet, you may then safely venture to run on with the Tide, and push in Boldly for the Harbour: But if you find rough and tempestuous Weather, as sometimes happens at touching the *Bby*, and the Tide strong against you, it is best to *lie-by*, till the Storm is appeased, and a fairer Prospect offers a prosperous Voyage.[18]

The shipman would eventually enjoy a successful 'landing', but the process could be a hazardous one.

The poem *Little Merlin's Cave* (1737) provides a sustained account of the ominous obscurity of the female genitals, portraying the vagina as 'Extremely pleasant, but unsafe'.[19] Men who have tried to explore the cave had failed to find its 'utmost limits' and 'the Upper-end' of the place, leaving hidden and potentially threatening parts uncharted.[20] The theme of women's unknowability

[15] Quote from Orr, 'Whore's Rhetoric', p. 215. The representation of women's bodies as maps is discussed below in chapter six.

[16] *New Description of Merryland*, p. 3.   [17] Ibid., p. 11.

[18] Ibid., pp. 44–5. Vowels were removed from a number of nouns. The author provided '*An Explanation of the Technical Abbreviations made use of in the New Description of Merryland*'. 'B B Y' meant 'bubby' or breast. The author did not give an explanation for L P S in his glossary, but there are a number of possibilities. The Latin may have been dropped (as it was in the case of 'B B Y'), so that the author meant 'Lips'. An alternative might be the Latin 'Lupa' (meaning prostitute or vile woman). This would render the subsequent comments about paying duties understandable. See 'Arbor Vitae: or, the Natural History of the Tree of Life', in *New Description of Merryland*, p. 7 verso.

[19] *Little Merlin's Cave*, p. 4.   [20] Ibid., pp. 6, 7.

Strong (Adam) pseud.

THE
ELECTRICAL EEL;
O R,
GYMNOTUS ELECTRICUS:
A N D,
THE TORPEDO;
A POEM.

The Torpedo

I am not what I seem.

Shakespear.

Illustration 11: *The Torpedo or I am not what I seem.* Title page of *The Electrical Eel; or Gymnotus Electricus: and, The Torpedo* (c. 1774).

was central to many of the poems in the bawdy collection *Hilaria* (1798), demonstrating that it had currency in a range of sub-genres and throughout the century. In 'Botany Bay', for example, Adam has tried but failed to discover the extreme reaches of this bay:

> he try'd the B A Y 's bottom to sound,
> But his L I N E was too short by a Y A R D   F R O M   T H E   G R O U N D. [21]

Even romantic and idyllic portrayals of female genitalia described them as 'dangerous to tread'.[22] Despite the trepidation that women's genitalia inspired, however, this quality could be prized: one author argued that women's genitals should be worshipped precisely because of their 'mysterious and incomprehensible nature'.[23]

The mystery of women's genitals is often conveyed by a potentially life-threatening hole or a void. The female genitals are variously referred to as 'Venus's Sphere', 'a larger *sphere*' and 'hollow Places'.[24] And this void possesses autonomy. It can open and close spontaneously, and it can suck things in, having been known to 'swallow brave Estates'.[25] The empress of the 'flats' (vulvas) in *The Why and the Wherefore* (1765) is appropriately called 'Ingulpha', and when she appeared before a group of 'poles' (penises) she made 'a mouth as if she would speak', reducing the crowd to a trembling mass who feared 'she would swallow them all'.[26] Some of the visual images used to represent female genitalia in erotic books employed this motif of a void. Illustration 1 was the frontispiece to the seventh edition of *A New Description of Merryland*. In the heavens, Jupiter hands a box to Pandora, and the inscription provides the narrative gloss: 'Pandora, lovely Fair, Q U E E N -Regent reign'd / And, with her Casket-dire, the Land inflam'd'. The association between Pandora's Box and female genitals might be used to varying effect, but in this case the stress is on apprehension and impending disaster.[27] The image on the title page of *The Torpedo* (1777) is a more simple depiction of a void, perhaps all the more threatening because of its emptiness. (Illustration 11.) The darkness in the centre of the image, together with the inscription beneath – 'I am not what

---

[21] 'Botany Bay', in *Hilaria*, p. 19.

[22] 'Song', in *Festival of Love*, p. 288. For similar representations of female bodies as threatening, see 'The Squire', in *Festival of Love*, p. 198; 'The Plenipotentiary', in Morris, *Festival of Ancareon*, p. 32; 'Venus and Love', in *Bacchanalian Magazine*, p. 15.

[23] *Secret History of Pandora's Box*, p. 49.

[24] *Man-Plant*, p. 37; *Torpedo* (Printed and sold by all the Booksellers in London and Westminster, 1777), p. 10; *Arbor Vitae*, p. 4.

[25] *Little Merlin's Cave*, p. 6.   [26] *Why and the Wherefore*, p. 76.

[27] Similarly, in *Little Merlin's Cave*, for example, the cave contains 'the Risque of greater Plagues, / Than ever fill'd *Pandora's* Box' (p. 6). But in *Secret History of Pandora's Box*, the image of Pandora's cave was emptied of a wholly threatening content. See also 'The Story of Pandora', in *Potent Ally*, pp. 17–26, in which the theme of curiosity is to the fore.

I seem' – hint at a metamorphosis reminiscent of much earlier imaginings of female bodies.[28]

Disease

There was, then, a palpable fear of the vulva's independent ability to transform itself and to damage men. A concrete source of this fear was venereal disease, which was particularly associated with prostitutes. Numerous texts vividly describe how venereal disease devoured male bodies, ultimately causing death.[29] Women are subject to the same risks: 'As the *Tree* is liable to be poison'd by the Contact of a foul *Vulvaria*, the *Shrub* is liable to be infected by the Contact of an envenom'd *Tree*.'[30] Nevertheless, male bodies were the ones perpetually exposed to these hazards, and men are advised to guard against the risks. In Merryland protection takes the form of a condom tied with a scarlet ribbon 'for Ornament'.[31] Elsewhere, men are transformed into soldiers preparing for battle: a '*well cas'd Warriour*', 'in *Armour* clad', who 'with *C*[ondo]*m* arm'd . . . wages Am'rous fight'.[32] Such depictions emphasize the imperilled situation of male bodies rather than a flexible and liberating identity for women.

A great deal of unease surrounded female sexual desire, which in eighteenth-

Desire

century erotica could be powerful. The passion of the female shrub (the *frutex vulvaria*) is incessant – signalled by 'the continual Opening of the Fissura, or Chink' – and is therefore deemed a disorder.[33] This female body's yearning for sex is to be treated by 'the Distillation therein of the balmy Succus of the Arbor Vitae', or, if this does not suffice, by removing the shrub 'to a Hot-House, where there are several Trees provided, in order to compleat the Cure'.[34] The 'Hot-House' was a brothel, and excessive female desire was used to legitimize prostitution. Ostensibly written by the famous prostitute Betsy Wemyss, *Great News from Hell* (1760) similarly explains, 'what we *once* called *Pleasure*, is

---

[28] Page duBois speaks of 'openings' in female bodies being associated with liminal, dangerous rituals in the ancient world in *Sowing the Body: Psychoanalysis and Ancient Representations of Women* (1988; Chicago: University of Chicago Press, 1991), pp. 58–9. Vern L. Bullough considers medieval ideas of the womb as animal in 'Medieval Medical and Scientific Views of Women', *Viator* 4 (1973), p. 494. This image was reproduced in a similar form on the Test Platter used by the Beggar's Benison. See Stevenson, *Beggar's Benison*, chapter two and Figure 5.

[29] 'Erotopolis' (1741), pp. 2–3; *Little Merlin's Cave*, p. 8; *New Description of Merryland*, p. 8; *Arbor Vitae*, p. 6.

[30] *Natural History of the Frutex Vulvaria* ([c. 1737]), p. 10.

[31] *New Description of Merryland*, p. 9.

[32] 'ΚΓΝΔΓΜΟΓΕΝΙΑ. A Tale', p. 15; 'Horace's Integer Vitae', p. 27; 'Armour. An Imitation of the Splendid Shilling', p. 3. All in *The Potent Ally*.

[33] *Natural History of the Frutex Vulvaria* ([c. 1737]), p. 14.

[34] Ibid., p. 14. Sex as a cure for certain maladies and excessive sexual desire is a common theme in many medieval and early-modern writings on female bodies, usually in order to purge women of their excess humours. See, for example, H. R. Lemay, 'Anthonius Guinerius and Medieval Gynecology', in J. Kirshner and S. F. Wemple (eds.), *Women of the Medieval World* (Oxford: Basil Blackwell, 1985), p. 335.

the most intense *Pain*'.[35] Wemyss' work on earth was thus supposedly driven by her own desires. It is little surprise, therefore, that a book such as *The Prostitutes of Quality* (1757) should contain so many depictions of sexually desiring women.[36] Even when not associated with prostitutes, women's sexual desire could be depicted as considerable. *Erotopolis* refers to the 'fury' of female sexual desire, illustrated with a series of mythic women who satiate their desires through incest and bestiality.[37] It was precisely in their sexual appetites that the draining potential of women was located. The dangerous *Little Merlin's Cave* (1737) is 'never satisfy'd', while the inhabitants of the hazardous Merryland are 'greedy and insatiable', forcing men to work hard to satisfy their 'voracious Appetites'.[38] Nothing inspired such trepidation as the potentially excessive and destructive nature of female sexuality.

Yet alongside this presentation of female sexual desire as a threat to men stood the view that sexual desire in women was healthy. In *A New Description of Merryland* the clitoris is recognized as an important site of female sexual pleasure. This 'Metropolis' was a 'pleasant Place, much delighted in by the Queens of M E R R Y L A N D, and is their chief Palace, or rather *Pleasure Seat*'. This description of the clitoris is exceptional, but other erotic texts discussed female sexual pleasure in positive tones.[39] The author of *The Man-Plant* (1752) explains that 'Nature, in its Distribution of the Pleasurable Sensation to the two Sexes, has been far from illiberal to the Fair. It is even pretended that their Allotment is greater than ours.'[40] Much the same idea is floated in *The Secret History of Pandora's Box* (1742), the author claiming that, in terms of desire, '[t]hese parts enjoy many advantages, which our nature is deprived of'.[41] In Bettyland, women's desires are placed in the context of a healthy community in which 'the Flames of Desire, like a Candle, [discover] the secret Paths and

---

[35] Betsy Wemyss [pseud.], *Great News from Hell, or the Devil Foil'd by Bess Weatherby. In a Letter from the Celebrated Miss Betsy Wemyss, the Little Squinting Venus, to the no Less Celebrated Miss Lucy C—r* (For J. Williams, on Ludgate-hill; and sold by J. Dixwell, in St Martin's Lane, near Charing-Cross, 1760), p. 9.

[36] See, for example, *Prostitutes of Quality*, pp. 1–2, 6, 100.

[37] 'Erotopolis' (1741), pp. 24–5.

[38] *Little Merlin's Cave*, p. 6; *New Description of Merryland*, p. 33. This notion of women's sexual insatiability had saturated centuries of thought and literature. See, for example, Elizabeth Robertson, 'Medieval Medical Views of Women and Female Sexuality in the *Ancrene Wisse* and Julian of Norwich's *Showings*', in L. Lomperis and S. Stanbury (eds.), *Feminist Approaches to the Body in Medieval Literature* (Philadelphia: University of Pennsylvania Press, 1993), p. 147.

[39] *New Description of Merryland*, p. 15. C L T R S was Clitoris. For the glossary, see 'Arbor Vitae', in *New Description of Merryland*, p. 7 verso. Nussbaum writes that a number of eighteenth-century texts describe the clitoris, and that in these descriptions we see how the sex of the prostitute is not fixed in a binary. See *Torrid Zones*, pp. 100–3. I agree with the sentiment, but contend that most of the texts Nussbaum discusses actually depict female genitalia in general rather than the clitoris.

[40] *Man-Plant*, pp. 2–3. The author was here referring to the myth of Tiresias, recounted in Ovid.

[41] *Secret History of Pandora's Box*, p. 47.

Labyrinths which the *Shepherds* and *Shepherdesses* of all Sexes, Ages, Degrees, and Humours, chuse in pursuit of their Amorous Designs'.[42]

When satisfied inappropriately or when excessive, female sexual desire was portrayed negatively, but sexual appetite in women which was satisfied in appropriate ways was condoned. As noted in the previous chapter, female orgasm was not depicted very clearly in eighteenth-century erotic culture. Nevertheless, in later erotic material in particular, there was a strong emphasis upon the mutuality of sexual pleasure: men and women share in 'mutual transports', display 'inclinations equal' and enjoy equally the 'height of pleasure' while 'mutually melting' in the exchange of '*mutual love*'.[43] A language of mutuality did not mean that men's and women's sexual pleasure and behaviour was in any way symmetrical, but it demonstrates that representations of female bodies were not stripped of sexual desire in the eighteenth century.[44] Indeed, orgasm or ejaculation was not the only motif of sexuality, and the failure to discuss female orgasm in erotica did not deny women's passions.

Fertility

Another consistency in erotic depictions of female bodies is the concern for fertility, most evident in the language of land used to describe female bodies. These metaphors were of considerable vintage, but by the eighteenth century writers of erotica could also draw on a well-established discourse of agricultural improvement, emphasizing certain components of that discourse for their own ends. A context of social and economic uncertainty had led to intensified pressures for increased agricultural activity. It had also produced a discourse of agrarian improvement which utilized metaphors of marriage, sexual intercourse and female bodies as part of a discussion of productivity, depicting the land laid out for the diligent, hard-working farmer.[45] Many elements of the erotic texts echo this discourse, particularly the emphasis on beauty and productivity: the 'gardens of pleasure and fields of profit' in pre-Restoration pastoral were echoed in later erotic writings.[46] Erotic female landscapes offer visual gratification: Bettyland 'shews you a very fair Prospect, which is yet the more delightful, the more naked it lies'.[47] Yet these depictions also stress the productivity of the land. In *Erotopolis*, female genitals are 'Private Enclosures'

---

[42] 'Erotopolis' (1741), p. 25.

[43] 'The Joke: Or, Mutual Transports', p. 39; 'Saucy Jack; Or, the Bladish Adonis of Tottenham Court Road', p. 62; and 'The Electrifying Kiss', p. 13, all in *Bacchanalian Magazine*; 'Mutual Love', in *Festival of Love*, p. 5.

[44] For a more detailed discussion of 'mutuality', see below, chapter seven.

[45] Andrew McRae, *God Speed the Plough: The Representation of Agrarian England, 1500–1660* (Cambridge: Cambridge University Press, 1996), pp. 135–68, 200, 231–61, 243, 258–9. McRae does not explore the gendered aspect of the material.

[46] Ibid., p. 299.   [47] 'Erotopolis' (1741), p. 7.

to be ploughed, watered and sowed by a husbandman 'every Night'.[48] Accordingly, Jupiter is glorified because he was 'industrious and indefatigable' in husbandry: 'the very *Sea, Rivers* and *Lakes* were full of his *Husbandry*'.[49] The same impression of a female body to be acted upon is given in *A New Description of Merryland*. In this later book, the female body is described as a continent in which the female genitals are the most important part. Merryland is situated 'in a *low* Part of the Continent, bounded on the upper Side, or to the Northward, by the little Mountain called MNSVNRS, on the East and West by COXASIN and COXADENT, and on the South or lower Part it lies open to the TERRA-FIRMA'.[50] It is the vagina which is the focus of interest, to be explored by the 'instrument' of 'a *large Radius*, and in perfect order' which the narrator proudly introduces to the readers.[51] This incarnation of the penis is later transformed into a plough, with which a man 'falls to labouring the Soil with all his Might'.[52] Metaphors of farming are accompanied by descriptions of what this husbandry might yield: '[t]he Country is generally fertile enough, where duly manured; and some Parts are so exceedingly fruitful as to bear two or three Crops at a Time . . . Other Provinces are so utterly barren, that tho' a Man should leave no Stone unturn'd, but labour and toil for ever, no seed will take Root in them'.[53] Sex, it is implied, is superfluous when the possibility of conception is removed. The concern for fertility in this book is confirmed by the anatomy which the author describes. The labia majora, clitoris, nymphae and hymen are all explored and the vagina is a particular focus. But the author of *A New Description of Merryland* also wonders at 'the great Treasury or Storehouse called UTRS', which is 'so admirably well contrived, that its Dimensions are always adapted to its Contents'.[54] Merryland was a place of both pleasure and production.

Such descriptions were part of a well-defined sub-genre of erotica that employed extended landscape metaphors, but this depiction appeared in a range of erotic material. In *The Polite Road to an Estate* (1759), for example, sex is a form of commerce or exchange in which women became 'lands, tenements, &c.' to be bought and sold.[55] Several books described women as the fertile land which would nourish male plants. *The Natural History of the Frutex Vulvaria* (c. 1737) advises women on how to handle the *arbor vitae*:

---

[48] Ibid., pp. 11, 3.   [49] Ibid., p. 17.
[50] *New Description of Merryland*, p. 3. MNSVNRS was Mons Veneris (mount of Venus, of love), COXASIN was Coxa Sinistra (left hip), and COXADENT was Coxa Dextra (right hip). See 'Arbor Vitae', in *New Description of Merryland*, p. 7 verso. However, COXASIN and COXADENT in *A New Description of Merryland* are used to mean left and right thighs. See *Merryland Displayed*, p. 28.
[51] *New Description of Merryland*, p. 3.   [52] Ibid., p. 21.   [53] Ibid., p. 12.   [54] Ibid., p. 16.
[55] *The Polite Road to an Estate; Or, Fornication one Great Source of Wealth and Pleasure* (For J. Coote, at the King's-Arms in Pater-Noster-Row, 1759), p. 21.

Be sure you take your *Trees* when they are very *erect* and in full *Vigour*, in order which nothing is better than to *warm* their *Roots* with generous *Wines*, . . . which will invigorate their *Sap*, and make their *Juices* full of volatile Particles, and apt to impregnate: Then remove them for a while into a *Hot-Bed*, with a soft but artful Hand, and placing the *Vulvarias* under their *Shades* secundum Artem, *you need not fear but they will answer your Ends to the full, and crown your utmost Wishes.*[56]

The word 'impregnate' signals productive vaginal sex; foreplay is designed to increase a man's potency, and the sexual position is chosen to facilitate the fulfilment of this potential. The Mimosa was to be similarly planted in 'the true and native *soil* of England, [which] is exquisitely *prepared* for the *reception* of the *plant*; will *raise* it to a very *vigorous extent*; *feed* it with the most *vegetative juices*; and *promote* its *articulations*'.[57] At the close of the century female land and male plough were still engaged in productive sex: '[t]he *lands* seem to ask for their seed', and the 'farmer' is advised:

> Ne'er think, like an idler, to stop,
> You ne'er need to *fallow* the *ground*,
> You may every year have a *crop*,
> If your *seed* falls but clean in the *pound.*[58]

Erotic authors switched metaphors with rapidity, and woman-as-land quickly became woman-as-plant. While likening women to 'those fertile Fields that yield two or three Crops in a Season', *The Man-Plant* also envisages the female body 'as a Flower Plant, in the method of *Linaeus* [sic]'.[59] The interweaving of older metaphors of women's bodies as land with botanical metaphors drawn from the new taxonomy is an example of how these texts integrated different languages. Yet while the language might change, the meaning remained consistent; the concern for reproduction was paramount. The author of *The Man-Plant* drew on the Linnean system of botanical classification, but he selects only the fructification of the plant – the part 'appropriated to generation' – rather than the root or herb.[60] Using the highly specialized language of botanical Latin, the description of the woman begins with what appears to be women's clothing ('calix') and moves on to the breasts ('nectarium'), before detailing various parts of the female genitalia: the womb ('pistillus'), vagina ('style unicus'), cervix ('stygma oblongum'), ovaries ('pericarpium') and seed ('semen').[61] Determined to

---

[56] *Natural History of the Frutex Vulvaria*, ([c. 1737]), p. 4.
[57] [James Perry?], *Mimosa: Or, the Sensitive Plant. A Poem. Dedicated to Mr. Banks, and Addressed to Kitt Frederick, Dutchess of Queensbury Elect* (For W. Sandwich, near the Admiralty; and sold by all the booksellers within the Bills of Mortality, 1779), p. v.
[58] 'The Natural Plough', in *Bacchanalian Magazine*, pp. 24–5.   [59] *Man-Plant*, pp. 35, 9.
[60] R. Hall, *Elements of Botany; Or an Introduction to the Sexual System of Linnaeus. To Which is Added an English Botanical Dictionary* (By E. Hudson, Cross-Street, Hatton Garden; for Vernor and Hood in the Poultry; T. Hurst, Paternoster-Row, and R. Bent, Coventry-Street, Haymarket, 1802), p. 17.
[61] *Man-Plant*, pp. 10–11.

convey details of women's reproductive organs, and the role that each part plays in the process of procreation, the author seeks to situate the plant firmly in a heterosexual context: the class is 'dieciae', which indicates that the stamens and pistils were on separate flowers and on different plants; the two orders of this class are 'monandria' and 'monogynia', the first indicating that each plant had one stamen, the second that each plant had one pistil.[62]

Though this description was indebted to new classificatory language, the depiction of a female body as a fertile, fruit-bearing plant in the later book *The Fruit-Shop* (1765) is openly drawn from 'modern and ancient authors, to wit, *French, Italian, Latin,* and *Greek*'. For example, 'a woman's being brought to bed' in French was '[t]he state of a woman delivered of her fruit'.[63] Indeed, the female body has been worshipped by peoples around the world, the author explains, because '[t]o its fertility they are indebted for their inhabitants'.[64] The resonance of this theme of reproduction was so powerful in erotica that it appeared even in descriptions of prostitutes. The decision to furnish *Great News from Hell* (1760), supposedly written by the notorious prostitute Betsy Wemyss, with an image of plant reproduction is suggestive. (Illustration 12.) Though entirely in keeping with the botanical metaphors used liberally throughout erotica, the connotations of reproduction and fertility suggested by 'Propagation by the Bud, and by the Branch' seem incongruous in a discussion of sex with prostitutes. The presence of this image in this book reveals the extent to which sex and reproduction, pleasure and procreation, were inextricably tied.[65]

What does the use of botanical metaphors tell us about understandings of bodies? We could conclude that the erotic interest in the sexual nature of plants reflected a growing concern with sexual difference. Yet as discussed in the previous chapter, these metaphors allowed considerable emphasis upon sameness. Moreover, the language used to describe male and female plants was at times indistinguishable.[66] We could argue that the precise and specialized language in botanical metaphors confirmed 'a masculine position of mastery and possession', demonstrating how the female body was increasingly presented as 'known'.[67] Yet an impulse to know could derive precisely from a feeling of vulnerable ignorance; furthermore, the use of the same language to describe male genitalia would suggest possession and mastery of men. Certainly, there was a degree of passivity in depictions of female bodies. Authors of erotica drew on eighteenth-century gardening writing, for example, in which the 'God-like actor/creator' worked on 'the passive, volitionless matter' of the personified,

[62] Ibid., p. 10; Hall, *Elements of Botany*, pp. 29, 36, 32. The use of the order 'monandria' is significant, because it was the only one of Linneaus' classes of plants which was 'monogamous'. See Schiebinger, 'Gender and Natural History', p. 169.
[63] *Fruit-Shop*, vol. II, p. 146.   [64] Ibid., vol. II, p. 143.
[65] *Great News from Hell* also included the engraving 'Propagation by the Root'.
[66] See chapter four below.   [67] Orr, 'Whore's Rhetoric', p. 214.

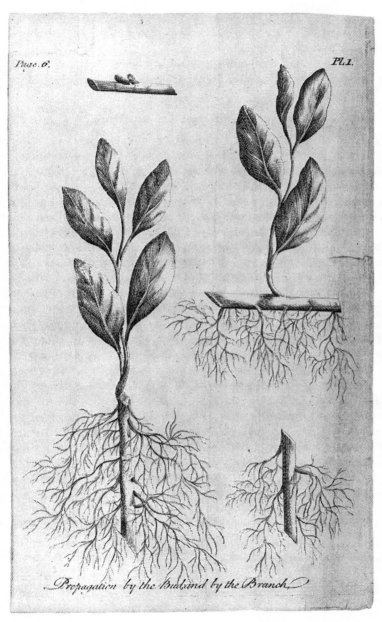

Illustration 12: *Propagation by the Bud; and by the Branch.*
Great News from Hell (1760).

feminized land.[68] But land is not necessarily passive. In erotica, women-as-land was as much about female bodies as active producers as it was about inert bodies. These descriptions could convey sameness or difference, passivity or activity. The constant, however, was the stress on women's fertility: whether treacherous places or pleasing vistas, female bodies as landscapes were always potentially productive.

Moisture

A concern for productivity meant that women's bodies needed to be suitably fertile and receptive. A crucial sign of female fertility was genital moistness. The poem 'The Crab-Tree; or, Sylvia Discover'd' (c. 1732) uses crab apples to pun with pubic lice; but whatever the joke, the story relies on an assumption that the female body is a fertile place that can bear fruit. A girl does a hand-stand for her sister, revealing her vulva; looking on, Jack plucks a fruit and throws it into her pudenda. This is a place where 'the Soil was fine' and 'the bubbling Fountain flows', and the tree puts down roots and thrives.[69] In another poem, published in 1770, a fountain is again one aspect of the 'little snug retreat' of a woman's body, in which '[s]eed flourish'd whensoever sown'.[70] And elsewhere in the same collection the female genitals are explicitly referred to as 'the fountain of Venus, the rivulet spring', whose 'nectar' was 'repaid with the choicest of fruit'.[71] Just as the male plant is the *arbor vitae* or 'tree of life', so the female plant is the 'fountain of life', 'a *Fons Vitae*, because it is the Fountain from whence all mankind first sprang'.[72] As we shall see in the following chapter, male bodies were also assessed according to their fertility in erotic material, and both male and female bodies displayed moisture. But female moisture differed from male moisture in at least two respects. First, women's moisture was regarded with some disdain as rather unpleasant. In *Little Merlin's Cave*, for example, 'the Sauce often proves sour'.[73] Similarly, the red (menstrual blood) and white (discharge) emissions of Merryland are 'not much to be commended'.[74] Second, the flow and moisture of female genitalia had to be continuous but controlled. The moistness of *Little Merlin's Cave* is a carefully monitored

---

[68] Carole Fabricant, 'Binding and Dressing Nature's Loose Tresses: The Ideology of Augustan Landscape Design', *Studies in Eighteenth-Century Culture* 8 (1979), p. 116. See also Fissell, 'Gender and Generation', pp. 440–1. For another use of the land metaphor for women, see [Astell], *Serious Proposal to the Ladies*, pp. 21–2, 26. Astell – often crowned the 'first English feminist' – depicted women as badly cultivated land in her passionate account of the obstacles to women's religious and intellectual fulfilment.

[69] 'The Crab-Tree; or, Sylvia Discover'd', in *Wisdom Reveal'd*, p. 27.

[70] 'A Riddle', in *Festival of Love*, p. 149.

[71] 'Song', in *Festival of Love*, pp. 288–9. This poem also appeared in *Bacchanalian Magazine*, as 'Venus and Love', pp. 14–15.

[72] *Natural History of the Frutex Vulvaria* ([c. 1737]), p. 17.   [73] *Little Merlin's Cave*, p. 6.

[74] *New Description of Merryland*, p. 26.

moistness '[t]hat never flows too little or too much'.[75] The author differentiates between the appropriate flow of a healthy woman and the dangerous excess flow which signalled chaos and disorder in the 'leaky' woman of early-modern humoral theory.[76] The extent to which flow was valorized in these female bodies suggests the continuing influence of a humoral understanding of the body, and this image of a flowing female body retained cultural purchase during the later part of the century.[77] This kind of moisture was distinctive to women's bodies.

Breasts

The issues of fluidity and difference resonate in representations of the breast. The breast has been regarded as the exemplar of the new female gender role of the later eighteenth century, seen as increasingly domesticated and 'colonized' over the period.[78] Erotic depictions of breasts could disrupt sexual differences, as discussed in the previous chapter, but they generally served as markers of women's distinctiveness. Moreover, several competing meanings were present in representations of the breast. After informing the reader of the occasional swelling of a particular mountain (the womb) at certain seasons, the author of *A New Description of Merryland* writes:

There are two other pleasant little Mountains called BBY, which 'tho at some Distance from MERRYLAND, have great Affinity with that Country, and are properly reckoned as an Appendage to it. These little Mountains are exactly alike, and not far from each other, having a pleasant Valley between them; on the Top of each is a fine *Fountain*, that yields a very wholesome Liquor much esteemed, especially by the younger sort of People. These Fountains often run quite dry; but it is observed, they seldom fail to run plentifully after the Swelling of the other Mountain aforementioned, and have in some Degree the same faculty of rising and falling; so that it is not without good Reason, Philosophers have imagined there is a secret Communication between these Places.[79]

[75] *Little Merlin's Cave*, p. 3.

[76] Gail Kern Paster, *The Body Embarrassed: Drama and the Disciplines of Shame in Early Modern England* (Ithaca, N.Y.: Cornell University Press, 1993), p. 92.

[77] See, for example, 'The Leaky Vessel', in *Festival of Love*, p. 336 (misnumbered in the original as p. 436). Helen Berry has stressed the persistence of 'ancient humoral ideas' about the body in the late-seventeenth-century periodical *The Athenian Mercury*. See *Gender, Society and Print Culture*, p. 153.

[78] Ruth Perry, 'Colonising the Breast: Sexuality and Maternity in Eighteenth-Century England', in John C. Fout (ed.), *Forbidden History: The State, Society, and the Regulation of Sexuality in Modern Europe* (Chicago: University of Chicago Press, 1992), pp. 107–37; Londa Schiebinger, 'Mammals, Primatology and Sexology', in Roy Porter and Mikulás Teich (eds.), *Sexual Knowledge, Sexual Science: The History of Attitudes to Sexuality* (Cambridge: Cambridge University Press, 1994), pp. 184–209.

[79] *New Description of Merryland*, pp. 28–9. BBY means Bubby (breast). For the glossary, see 'Arbor Vitae', in *A New Description of Merryland*, p. 7 verso.

The breast is placed in the context of the familiar association of moistness and fertility, though here the fountain does not emanate from the vagina but from the breast. Simon Richter has argued that eighteenth-century discussions of the breast were not indicative of a newly imagined system of sexual difference predicated on incommensurable biology. This was because the breast replaced the genitalia as the part of the female anatomy which was described analogously with the penis in an enduring system of comparisons. His work implies there were various enduring ways of thinking analogously about sexual difference.[80] In *A New Description of Merryland*, however, the clearest analogy is not between male and female, but between the breasts and the womb. Indeed, the inclusion of the breast denies the strict parity of male and female. Merryland was the female genitals, but the breasts were an appendage to these; female bodies were more than an inverted penis and scrotum.

The association of breasts with women's reproductive capacity was clear, but for eighteenth-century writers breasts were also irresistible objects of desire. One young bachelor confessed to a women's magazine his inability to control himself on seeing 'the finest bosoms nature ever formed', exhorting women to keep themselves covered for his sake.[81] While the fertility of the breast is stressed in *A New Description of Merryland*, the breasts in *The Man-Plant* are introduced as objects of aesthetic and sensual pleasure:

NECTARIUM {Mammae} duplex, rotunda-globosum, tenerum, niveum, Tacta suavissimum, aliquando Fuscum, nauseosum, mole, colore flacciditate horridum; cylindrulo papilliformi lacteo areola pulchre rubescente cincto, in medio sui gaudens, ad bafin utriusque, petali superioris positum.[82]

These breasts are round, tender, snow-white, very pleasant to touch, with a small nipple surrounded by a beautiful copper colour. Some indication of another purpose is given, though, by the inclusion of the word 'lacteo', or full of milk. It is to this function that the author later turns when he decries the practice of feeding children by wet-nurses. Women, he writes, 'renounce their Duty of nourishing the Fruit of their Womb; since, except a few, whom extream Indigence still obliges personally to discharge that homely and antiquated Function, they are all grown such very fine young Ladies, as to disdain the suckling of their Children'. The breasts of these women, he admits, are 'no longer to be of any use to them, but for Ornament, or Dalliance'.[83] This author admired the beauty of breasts, then, but this quality was not separate from their role in breastfeeding.

This depiction of breasts as objects of sexual desire and markers of women's sexuality but in the context of women's fertility and motherhood means that

[80] Simon Richter, 'Wet-Nursing, Onanism, and the Breast in Eighteenth-Century Germany', *Journal of the History of Sexuality* 7 (1996), pp. 1–22.
[81] 'Men-Seducers. An Adventure at Cox's Museum', *Lady's Magazine*, June 1775, p. 320.
[82] *Man-Plant*, p. 11.   [83] Ibid., p. 15.

erotic representations of breasts sit uncomfortably in those familiar narratives of the body and female gender roles which present women as increasingly desexualized over the eighteenth century. Breasts were not enlisted solely in a larger project of the maternalization of women to the corresponding exclusion of the sexual. In addition, though breasts might disrupt sex differences, they could not be accommodated in an analogous understanding of male and female bodies; rather they functioned as a sign for the ineluctable distinctiveness of female bodies.

Menstruation

A regular and predictable form of moisture associated with women was menstruation. Historians and anthropologists suggest that menstruation has been seen as a form of bleeding of which men had their equivalents.[84] However, the attitudes associated specifically with menstruation in erotica served to differentiate it as a unique female process. While the regularity of menstrual flow could allay some of the fears associated with the chaos of the flowing female body, some of the discussions of menstruation began very negatively. In *The Natural History of the Frutex Vulvaria*, menstruation is introduced in the section covering 'disorders', while men wishing to steer into Merryland are warned about 'the Time of *Spring-Tides*, which only flow for four or five Days, once a Month', when 'it best to *lie-by* till the Spring is over, tho' some People make no scruple of going in when the Spring-Tides are at the Height'.[85] Menstruation was not simply a hazard awaiting the traveller to Merryland, but was also a curse on women. In *The Why and the Wherefore* (1765), menstruation is a marker of female difference, unattractiveness and evil. During a battle between the '*Tall-Poles*' (large penises) and the '*Ugly-Flats*' (unattractive vulvas), the poles delivered vicious punishment on their rivals by 'making a great gash in the phyzz of them': 'the wound was so deep and venomous, that it bred a great deal of proud flesh, and could never be closed again; but from time to time breaks out a-bleeding afresh'.[86] A seventeenth-century view of menstruation as polluting persisted: menstruating women were portrayed as dangerous and powerful, and this unrivalled reaction to this form of bleeding gave menstruation a distinct status.[87]

Yet as with discussions of women's sexuality, genital moisture and the breast, discussions of menstruation featured both palpable fear and positive assessment.

---

[84] Barbara Duden, *The Woman beneath the Skin: A Doctor's Patients in Eighteenth-Century Germany* (Cambridge, Mass.: Harvard University Press, 1991), pp. 115–16; Knauft, 'Bodily Images in Melanesia', p. 207.

[85] *Frutex Vulvaria* ([c. 1737]), p. 13; *New Description of Merryland*, p. 46.

[86] *Why and the Wherefore*, pp. 91–2.

[87] Patricia Crawford, 'Attitudes to Menstruation in Seventeenth-Century England', *Past and Present* 91 (1981), pp. 57–65.

Menstruation may be classed as a disorder in *The Natural History of the Frutex Vulvaria*, but this not only 'very seldom proves of any ill Consequence', but it is precisely this disorder which provides 'Proof of the Shrub's being capable of bearing.'[88] Similarly, the author of *A New Description of Merryland* rejects the ancient view of the menses as threatening and writes: 'Some Naturalists have imagined these Flowers to be of a poisonous Quality; but that Notion is now sufficiently exploded, and it is observed, if they happen not to spring in their due Season, the Country generally proves unhealthy and barren.'[89] In other words, menstruation was a good because it was evidence of women's fertility.[90] It was in this context that female blood was invested with an almost magical potency, drops of which cause rose bushes to spring up from the ground.[91] Here we can see how the fear of menstruation could be a corollary of causally associating women's bleeding with their fertility and their reproductive power. The anthropologist Françoise Héritier-Augé has claimed that '*it is not sex but the capacity for fertility that makes up the real difference between male and female*'. It is menstruation, the process that represents women's fertility, that is 'the fundamental impetus for all the symbolic elaboration, at the outset, of the relations between the sexes'.[92] In eighteenth-century erotica, the connection between menstruation and fertility ensured that the former retained a unique status as a marker of women's distinctiveness. Moreover, as with other markers of female fertility, menstruation was treated with both fear and appreciation.

Pregnancy

In view of the complex ways in which female fertility was discussed in erotica, it should be no surprise that descriptions of pregnancy in eighteenth-century erotica were ambivalent. Pregnancy was often regarded with disgust and horror. Ostensibly this was partly due to the financial burden, but also because of the pain it caused women and the detrimental effect it could have on their subsequent

---

[88] *Natural History of the Frutex Vulvaria* ([c. 1737]), pp. 13–14.

[89] *New Description of Merryland*, p. 26.

[90] Anthropologists have also found that the centrality of menstruation to fertility has tempered negativity. See Thomas Buckley and Alma Gottlieb (eds.), *Blood Magic: The Anthropology of Menstruation* (Berkeley: University of California Press, 1988), p. 38.

[91] 'The Birth of the Rose', in *The Pleasures that Please on Reflection. Selected from the Album of Venus* (For W. Holland, Garrick's Richard, No. 50, Oxford-Street, 1789), p. 40.

[92] Françoise Héritier-Augé, 'Older Women, Stout-Hearted Women, Women of Substance', in M. Feher (ed.), *Fragments for a History of the Human Body: Part Three* (New York: Zone, 1989), pp. 295, 298. The nineteenth-century French historian Jules Michelet also placed much emphasis on the process of menstruation; it was the key to women's more 'natural' femininity, and therefore to a system of sex differences. See Ludmilla Jordanova, *Sexual Visions: Images of Gender in Science and Medicine between the Eighteenth and Nineteenth Centuries* (London: Harvester Wheatsheaf, 1989), p. 83.

experience of pleasure.[93] At times, however, this apparent sympathy for women
appeared to disguise a concern for the inconveniences that pregnancy, childbirth
and parenthood wrought to men's sexual enjoyment of women caused by the
'Over-dilatation [sic] of the Diameter of Venus's Sphere'.[94] In other texts,
the disparaging term 'tumour' is used for the foetus, though the process of
pregnancy is downplayed: the 'juice' of the *arbor vitae* often causes 'Tumours
in the Umbilical Region' of the *frutex vulvaria*, but these 'being of really no ill
Consequence, disperse of themselves in a few Months'.[95] The *Natural History of
the Frutex Vulvaria* similarly describes foetuses as 'Tumours', but sounds a more
cautionary note, explaining how they 'prove frequently destructive to both the
Shrub and the *Shoot*'. Nevertheless, the option of abortion, carried out by 'a Sort
of Female *Botanists* [sic]', is noted.[96] A positive view of pregnancy vied with
this disparagement, however. Contraception was rarely discussed: the spongy
plant found in Merryland and recommended 'not only as a *Cleaner*, but also
as an Antidote against the bad Effects of the Juice [semen]' was exceptional.[97]
Indeed, as will be more fully discussed in the next chapter, men's semen was
repeatedly judged for its reproductive potential; this was not a substance to be
wasted. While there were negative comments regarding pregnancy, then, they
were small in number and limited in impact compared to the representations of
women as the fertile receptacles of men's semen.

We have seen how erotica focused on female moistness as evidence of their
fertility and on menstruation as the essential key to women's reproductive power.
Such attitudes were appropriate to a genre that revered productive sex. In erotica, anal sex was unequivocally damned as preposterous and dangerous.[98] As
in manuals offering sexual advice, vaginal, penetrative, heterosexual and productive sex was esteemed.[99] A moist and fertile place, ready to receive potent
semen, was the place to which men must turn. At the same time, much of the fear
inspired by female bodies arose from their reproductive capacity. The power
with which women's fertility was endowed could be awesome, and this active,
fearsome capacity was considered an integral part of female sexuality. This is

[93] *New Description of Merryland*, pp. 6, 25, 28; *Little Merlin's Cave*, p. 8.
[94] *Man-Plant*, p. 37.   [95] *Arbor Vitae*, p. 9.
[96] *Natural History of the Frutex Vulvaria* ([c. 1737]), pp. 12–13. The word tumour is also used to
    describe a foetus in *A New Description of Merryland*, p. 25, and in the poem 'The Ink Bottle', in
    Forty Select Poems, p. 49, though in the latter it does not appear to have negative connotations.
    In Johnson's dictionary, the first meaning of 'tumour' is 'A morbid swelling', and the illustrative
    quotation from Wiseman describes it as 'a disease in which the parts recede from their natural
    state by an undue encrease of their bigness'. See Johnson, *Dictionary*.
[97] *New Description of Merryland*, p. 26. Though this mirrored the condemnation of such practices in
    sex manuals, it was in contrast to an apparently thriving trade in contraceptives and abortifacients.
    See Roy Porter, 'The Literature of Sexual Advice before 1800', in Porter and Teich (eds.), *Sexual
    Knowledge, Sexual Science*, p. 148; Crawford, 'Sexual Knowledge', p. 99.
[98] *New Description of Merryland*, p. 6; *Arbor Vitae*, p. 4.
[99] Porter, 'Sexual Advice before 1800', pp. 146–9.

significant because it urges us to view sexuality in the broadest terms. In many accounts of eighteenth-century women's sexuality, power, agency and orgasm have been pitted against maternity, passivity and desexualization. These oppositions are plotted over time to produce a tale of progressive worsening for women and, for example, they offer little room for passive sexuality or for maternal sexuality. In eighteenth-century erotica, maternity coexisted with female sexuality and could be associated with considerable power. Moreover, erotica also depicted a range of women's sexual desires, both gentle and fierce.[100]

In stressing women's fertility, presenting genital moisture and menstruation as signs of this fertility, and depicting pregnancy and breasts as distinctively female, eighteenth-century erotica revealed an understanding of female bodies as intrinsically and physically different from those of men. Sexual pleasure was not causally associated with conception, the nature of their genital moisture was distinctive to women, menstruation was a uniquely female process, and breasts were usually signs of women's anatomical distinction. In locating the distinctiveness of female bodies in their reproductive capacities, authors of eighteenth-century erotica rehearsed understandings which enjoyed considerable longevity. In medieval and early-modern cultures, a woman's health and bodily state were believed to be determined largely by the activities of her uterus. Similarly, some nineteenth-century scientific theories deemed women to be little more than 'an overgrown ovum', their entire physical and psychic existence determined by the functioning of the uterus and its attendant parts.[101] Persistence in erotica was accompanied by variety. Land was both inviting and ominous; menstruation was dangerous yet cherished. Female anatomical and physiological particularities – moisture, breasts, menstruation and pregnancy – were placed within a framework conditioned by responses of both fear and desire. There was not a diachronic shift between a threatening Bettyland and a pleasing Merryland, but a synchronic contrast. And this contrast derived not simply from the qualities of female bodies, but from the reactions those bodies inspired. Indeed, the form of female bodies actually remained remarkably similar; the texture of erotica derives more from the responses to those bodies incorporated into the representations: desire for the sensual pleasure and procreation that female bodies promised, apprehension of the loss of control and the destruction that female bodies threatened.

[100] See chapter seven for a discussion of passive sexuality.
[101] The quotation is Cynthia Russett's description of Patrick Geddes and J. Arthur Thomson's theory that sex differences arose from differences in the cell metabolism of male and female organisms. See Cynthia Russett, *Sexual Science: The Victorian Construction of Womanhood* (Cambridge, Mass.: Harvard University Press, 1989), p. 102. For the power of the reproductive organs over a woman, see Elizabeth Fee, 'Science and the Woman Problem: Historical Perspectives', in M. S. Teitelbaum (ed.), *Sex Differences: Social and Biological Perspectives* (New York: Anchor Books, 1976), pp. 196–7. For earlier understandings, see Bullough, 'Medieval Medical', p. 492.

Highly absorbent with regard to new trends in a range of genres, and accommodating of recent scientific and medical findings, there was much speedy change in erotic material. And yet this genre nonetheless displayed much of an enduring nature. In the context of representations of bodies, we can speculate that if material bodies are 'both objects and agents of practice',[102] then these agents were one of many factors which shaped the contours of somatic understanding. Enduring as other factors transformed, the substance of material bodies left a legacy of persistence in representations. Explaining longevity is difficult. However, many of the images of female bodies in these texts revealed male apprehension of those bodies. The images of women as passive recipients of male seed and as dangerous, libidinous and life-threatening beings were saturated with this apprehension. As Mark Breitenberg writes, 'the female body itself became a contested site of collective and individual masculine identities; anxieties about masculinity were projected onto female bodies and sexualities'.[103] Writers of eighteenth-century erotica were ostensibly more concerned with the female body than with the male, devoting much more literary space to descriptions of women. But the content of this material was tied to its context, and erotica was a masculinist genre. Not only were representations of female bodies as much about masculinity as they were about femininity, but male bodies as well as female bodies were at stake in eighteenth-century erotica; it is to examining these male bodies that we now turn.

[102] R. W. Connell, *Masculinities* (Cambridge: Polity Press, 1995), p. 61.
[103] Mark Breitenberg, *Anxious Masculinity in Early Modern England* (Cambridge: Cambridge University Press, 1996), p. 73. See also Linda Walsh, '"Arms to be Kissed a Thousand Times": Reservations about Lust in Diderot's Art Criticism', in Gill Perry and Michael Rossington (eds.), *Femininity and Masculinity in Eighteenth-Century Art and Culture* (Manchester: Manchester University Press, 1994).

4   Male bodies

Eighteenth-century erotic authors presented themselves as pioneers in the representation of male bodies. The author of *The Electrical Eel* (c. 1770), for example, claims he is retrieving the penis from the cloak of 'Fable, and metaphor'.[1] Rejecting figurative language, and asking that the reader 'Pardon the plainness of my diction', he stages a disingenuous act of revelation:

> Therefore the Serpent and the Tree,
> Divested of fring'd simile,
> Is a plain Eel of course.[2]

The author of *Wisdom Reveal'd* (1732) likewise claims that 'the *Arbor Vitae* has always been look'd upon as one of those *Arcana*, which are absolutely out of the Reach of human Wit'.[3] After stating that 'Quibbles' will be left to the writers of prose, the narrator promises that the action will be conveyed without 'jesting' or 'prating'.[4] Yet, whereas sober and matter-of-fact descriptions of male genitalia were the norm in pornography and popular medical works[5], figurative speech was never abandoned in erotica. Indeed, conversation ground to a halt at one point in *Wisdom Reveal'd*, as the male narrator struggled to find 'a *Simile*' for the Tree of Life. Male bodies, it seemed, were doomed to remain hidden, as the narrator admitted: 'our Tongue affords / Not Words sufficient'.[6] Regardless of the reliance on metaphor, male bodies were much discussed in erotic material, and authors were just as inventive in representing male bodies as they were in depicting female bodies. The author of *Merryland Displayed* (1741) chides himself for reinventing the penis on virtually every page of his earlier erotic book, *A New Description of Merryland* (1741): in describing 'the same thing turned into several Shapes, and differently described under different Names', he had 'outdone *Ovid* in Metamorphosing'.[7]

---

[1] *Electrical Eel* (No publication details, [c. 1770]), p. 9.   [2] Ibid., pp. 15, 10.
[3] *Wisdom Reveal'd*, pp. i–ii.   [4] Ibid., p. 2.
[5] See, for example, the popular medical text *Aristotle's Compleat Master-Piece*, pp. 3–7; and the pornographic book *School of Venus*, pp. 83–4.
[6] *Wisdom Reveal'd*, pp. 7, 11.   [7] *Merryland Displayed*, p. 43.

Until very recently male bodies were notably absent from explorations of both masculinity and bodies in the past. Indeed, in *Making Sex* (1990), Laqueur claimed that '[i]t is probably not possible to write a history of man's body and its pleasures because the historical record was created in a cultural tradition where no such history was necessary.'[8] Historians have explained this emphasis on women by claiming that sexual difference is not symmetrical; that the 'female' element has always been subject to greater variation and malleability, while male bodies have been the norm, the constant from which women have varied.[9] Male bodies were represented in erotica, though, and such representations demonstrate that male bodies were not imagined as monolithic and unchanging entities. Representations of male and female bodies were subject to different kinds of change, and depictions of male bodies display a sharper degree of historical specificity.

Much work on masculinity discusses a disparity between ideals of masculinity and male bodies on the one hand, and the actuality of experiences of men on the other. The disparity between the two injects anxiety into the heart of masculinity. In his exploration of early-modern masculinity, Mark Breitenberg argues that the 'necessary and inevitable condition' of 'anxious masculinity' was the result of a failure to paint over the internal contradictions of patriarchy.[10] Notions of masculinity at the level of rhetoric and representation, it is implied, translated into demanding and unattainable ideals at the level of practice. For many, this anxiety is often located in or on the male body. Thus the burden of much work on masculinity is to erode the myth of the 'monolithic, unchanging, unproblematic', 'unitary and transhistorical' male body.[11] As Lesley Hall ponders in her *Hidden Anxieties* (1991):

There are serious and searching questions to be asked about the frailty of sexual potency and its connection with the search for potency in other senses . . . The penis itself is a fragile, fleshy organ which, unlike the tools and weapons with which men equip themselves in pursuit of worldly domination, is very seldom completely under a man's conscious control.[12]

A variation of this approach can be found in some psychoanalytic accounts, in which male bodies and male authority are symbolically represented by the singular, majestic and imposing phallus and the actuality of male bodies as changeable, soft and various is overshadowed. For Susan Bordo this majestic phallus is challenged by male embodiment, and like Hall she wants to expose

---

[8] Laqueur, *Making Sex*, p. 22.
[9] Ibid., p. 270, note 58; Brown, "Changed . . . into the Fashion of Man", pp. 189–90.
[10] Breitenberg, *Anxious Masculinity*, p. 2.
[11] Joanna Bourke, *Dismembering the Male: Men's Bodies, Britain and the Great War* (London: Reaktion Books, 1996), pp. 15, 29, 251; Lesley A. Hall, *Hidden Anxieties: Male Sexuality, 1900–1950* (Cambridge: Polity Press, 1991), quote at p. 1.
[12] Ibid., p. 173.

the 'private and protected territory' of the male body, revealing the 'repressed', 'unarmoured, aroused penis'.[13] Whether writing from a psychoanalytical perspective or not, these authors tend to speak of anxiety and discord as fundamental to constructions of male bodies and masculinities. Revelations of the disparity between the ideals and practice of masculinity, particularly in relation to the male body, they argue, resulted in distress.

Erotic depictions of male bodies certainly reveal important concerns about masculinity. Male genitals stood for whole male bodies. These depictions were placed in the context of wider cultural, social, economic and political events, and concerns about these events emerged in discussions of the size, age, nationality and fertility of male bodies. Male bodies were compared along these axes, and this competitive aspect – particularly in a national and international context – was distinctive to depictions of men. Though ostensibly focusing on representations of bodies and genitals, then, this discussion is not simply about the sexual. These depictions exposed concerns about nationhood, military threats and the relative strength and potency of the male population, and demonstrate how male sexuality and male bodies were rooted in the social and political.

Erotic depictions of male bodies were predicated on male power: the responsibility for the state of the nation rested upon these bodies. In discussing male power, the concept of patriarchy has lost favour with many women's and gender historians of the eighteenth century. Lawrence Stone famously claimed that patriarchy abated in the eighteenth-century family, and only rarely is it employed in accounts of the eighteenth century to indicate a publicly sanctioned system with institutional support.[14] In contrast, patriarchy is still used by many historians of the sixteenth and seventeenth centuries to refer to a system of power, operating both formally and informally, which conferred authority on adult, house-holding men.[15] Yet patriarchy was not simply about women and men;

---

[13] Susan Bordo, 'Reading the Male Body', in Laurence Goldstein (ed.), The Male Body: Features, Destinies, Exposures (Ann Arbor: University of Michigan Press, 1994), pp. 267, 300. See also Kaja Silverman, Male Subjectivity at the Margins (New York: Routledge, 1992), pp. 1, 3.

[14] On the decline of the concept of patriarchy, see Judith Bennett, 'Feminism and History', Gender and History 1 (1989), pp. 251–72; Lawrence Stone, The Family, Sex and Marriage in England, 1500–1800 (1977; Harmondsworth: Penguin, 1979), passim. Anthony Fletcher argues that patriarchy found a new, firmer foundation in the eighteenth century, based not simply on household order but on stricter gender divisions and new ideas about the body. See Gender, Sex and Subordination, passim, esp. pp. 401–13. Susan Staves uses patriarchy to refer to the 'dominance and privilege of men' maintained by the legal system. See Susan Staves, Married Women's Separate Property in England, 1660–1833 (Cambridge, Mass.: Harvard University Press, 1990), p. 25.

[15] In Domestic Dangers, Laura Gowing uses patriarchy to mean 'the wide-ranging domination of women by men' (p. 5), and argues that 'at a personal and daily level men's power was consistently enforced at the expense of women's' (p. 273). Gowing's emphasis is on sexuality and the degree to which 'women's sexual culpability was not just greater than, but incomparable with, men's' (p. 4). Elizabeth Foyster has argued similarly in her Manhood in Early Modern England, in which she focuses on male sexual honour and the role women played in its loss and restoration. In contrast, David Turner has argued that men and women were judged by the

it was a broad system which incorporated hierarchies of age, rank and marital status.[16] Indeed, recent work shows that manhood was not made or lost through men's exercise of patriarchal authority over women: manhood was also forged through men's relationships with other men, and men as well as women 'undermined, resisted, or simply ignored patriarchal imperatives'. Manhood did not equate with patriarchy.[17] Although eighteenth-century erotica did not deliver all power to all men – women can inspire considerable fear, for example – this writing invested male bodies with considerable mastery, authority and command. The attainment of this mastery was achieved not simply by exercising power over women, but by men's control over themselves and the assertion of some men over others. Nor is the tone simply of men anxiously striving to fulfil patriarchal demands; instead the tenor of male power is easy and assured. These texts exhorted men to improve themselves and their nation through vigorous sexual activity, but they also operated as a space in which a range of male bodies were validated in a context of comfort and humour. While female bodies were often presented as unfamiliar and unknown, representations of male bodies are much more sympathetic to the limitations of those bodies. There were a multiplicity of states – of imposing erectness and soft vulnerability – in which male genitals were imagined and celebrated, and the chasm between the majestic phallus and the soft penis 'exposed' by some modern scholars was openly acknowledged by eighteenth-century writers of erotica.

Looking at male bodies

Looking at male bodies was problematic in the eighteenth century. In aesthetic theory, beauty was female, pleasing to look at, and it provided viewers with legitimate pleasure. In contrast, maleness was associated with the sublime, the powerful, the awe-inspiring, which resisted appropriation by viewers.[18] Depictions of male bodies straddled 'an erotic desirability conventionally most closely

same criteria. See David Turner, '"Nothing is so Secret but shall be Revealed": The Scandalous Life of Robert Foulkes', in Tim Hitchcock and Michèle Cohen (eds.), *English Masculinities, 1660–1800* (Harlow: Longman, 1999), pp. 169–92.

[16] See Michael J. Braddick, *State Formation in Early Modern England, c. 1550–1700* (Cambridge: Cambridge University Press, 2000), and Michael J. Braddick and John Walter, 'Grids of Power', in Michael J. Braddick and John Walter (eds.), *Negotiating Power in Early Modern Society: Order, Hierarchy, and Subordination in Britain and Ireland* (Cambridge: Cambridge University Press, 2001), pp. 1–42.

[17] Alexandra Shepard, 'Manhood, Credit and Patriarchy in Early Modern England', *Past and Present* 167 (2000), pp. 75–106; Alexandra Shepard, *Meanings of Manhood in Early Modern England* (Oxford: Oxford University Press, 2003), passim. Quote at p. 249.

[18] Anthony J. McGowan, 'The Sublime Machine: Conceptions of Masculine Beauty, 1750–1850', unpublished PhD thesis, Open University (1996), pp. 204–52; Alex Potts, *Flesh and the Ideal: Winckelmann and the Origins of Art History* (New Haven: Yale University Press, 1994), pp. 115, 114. Potts is providing a gloss on Edmund Burke's *A Philosophical Enquiry into the Origin of our Ideas of the Sublime and Beautiful* (1757).

associated with the female body, and suggestions of a powerful defeminized masculine presence'.[19] While an unequivocally sexual response to female bodies by men was often deemed reasonable, men voiced concerns over the freedom of women to gaze upon male bodies.[20] As John Moore commented in 1781, 'Ladies who have remained for some time at Rome and Florence . . . acquire an intrepidity and a cool minuteness, in examining and criticising naked figures, which is unknown to those who have never passed the Alps.'[21] Indeed, though there was 'something in the figure of the God of Gardens [Priapus], which is apt to alarm the modesty of a novice', this man had 'heard of female dilettantes who minded it no more than a straw'.[22] The 'prurient anecdotage' which built up around a naked statue of Achilles, commissioned by women in commemoration of Wellington in 1822, and the insistence of the male members of a committee that it be adorned with a strategically placed fig leaf demonstrates how this unease endured.[23]

As an artist, Angelica Kauffman (1741–1807) must have felt these limitations acutely. Her solution was to avoid the depiction of both male genitals and muscular nudes, sketching only the soft and beautiful male bodies that women were deemed able to view.[24] Kauffman was nonetheless chastised for producing a representation of 'her *Priapus*'.[25] But Kauffman's work indicates that women could legitimately look at certain kinds of male body, and indeed women were used strategically as imaginary viewers of some male bodies. Eighteenth-century male travel writers related the brawny male figures that they witnessed in Italy in their own words, but they used a female voice to admire the classical statues of softer male bodies.[26] The same device was employed in eighteenth-century poetry.[27] Such a framework was governed by 'a desire to acclaim the smooth-limbed male body as a source of pleasure, and the desire to keep imputations of effeminacy at bay'.[28] Muscular male bodies might be viewed by men, but softer male bodies had to be viewed by women.

By establishing women as the privileged viewers of male bodies in the form of imaginary authors and readers, erotica both played upon the possible titillation

[19] Potts, *Flesh and the Ideal*, p. 117.
[20] Walsh, 'Arms to be Kissed a Thousand Times,' esp. pp. 170, 165.
[21] John Moore, *A View of Society and Manners in Italy* (For W. Strahan; and T. Cadell, in the Strand, 1781), vol. II, pp. 424–5.
[22] Ibid., vol. II, p. 425.
[23] Linda Colley, *Britons: Forging the Nation, 1707–1838* (London: Pimlico, 1992), p. 258.
[24] Wendy Wassyng Roworth, 'Anatomy is Destiny: Regarding the Body in the Art of Angelica Kauffman', in Gill Perry and Michael Rossington (eds.), *Femininity and Masculinity in in Eighteenth-Century Art and Culture* (Manchester: Manchester University Press, 1994), pp. 44, 50.
[25] *Unsex'd Females*, p. 20.
[26] Chloe Chard, 'Effeminacy, Pleasure and the Classical Body', in Perry and Rossington (eds.), *Femininity and Masculinity*, p. 150.
[27] Potts, *Flesh and the Ideal*, p. 123.   [28] Chard, 'Effeminacy, Pleasure', p. 152.

of women observing men and excluded suggestions of male desire for the male body. The extended ode to the electrical eel, for example, is apparently written by Lucretia Lovejoy, while the statue of the eel which the ode advertises is to be financed by the 'Countess of H— ' and the 'Chevalier-Madame D'Eon de Beaumont'. Moreover, the first line of the poem – 'Ye lovely maids, ye amorous dames . . . Ye widows' – clearly figures the readership as female.[29] The reference to the opinions of women as 'your Ideas' in *Adam's Tail* (1774) also suggested that the readers were imagined to be female, a suggestion confirmed by the closing line: 'Thus, Ladies! I have told my Story.'[30] *Mimosa: Or, the Sensitive Plant* (1779) is addressed to a woman, and the text of the poem establishes her as the viewer and handler of the eponymous male plant, referring to 'thy eye', 'thy lovely *hand*', 'your face'.[31] Likewise, in *Wisdom Reveal'd*, Philander will only reveal the tree of life to Cloe. The heterosexual context is then reinforced as the author advises that any lady requiring further details concerning the plant 'may have the Experiment made familiar to her Senses, by applying to the Author, (who has never fail'd of giving satisfaction)'.[32] Female viewers disarmed the accusations of same-sex desire that depictions of male bodies might have provoked. Moreover, they exploited the sanctioning of women's looking at softer male bodies; female viewers allowed male bodies to be shown not only in states of grandeur and plenitude, but also as receptive and sensitive.

Beauty, size and vigour

The imaginary female viewers of male bodies were consistently characterized as insatiable in the face of male irresistibility. One of the most conspicuous scenarios where female insatiability and male irresistibility were married was in erotic renditions of the biblical story of the Fall. In *Arbor Vitae* (1741), the male tree is likened to that which grew in the middle of the garden of Eden 'whose Fruits were so alluring to our first Mother'.[33] In *Wisdom Reveal'd*, the conversation between Philander and Cloe begins when Cloe asks "Twas but an Apple ruin'd *Eve*?'[34] Following Philander's descriptions of the tree, culminating in a display of his own, Cloe's adoration leads her to exempt Eve from all responsibility in the Fall, suggesting it would be impossible for any woman to resist.[35] If the metaphor of the tree of life lent itself to a discussion of the Fall, so did the metaphors of the eel and the serpent. Here, emphasis was placed on the serpent (penis) whose attractiveness tempted Eve and aroused her desire. *The Electrical Eel* (c. 1770) is designed to prove that 'An Eel electrified

---

[29] *Elegy on the Lamented Death of the Electrical Eel* (No publication details, [c. 1770]), title page, p. 1.
[30] *Adam's Tail; Or, the First Metamorphosis*, 4th edn. (Printed for John Bell, near Exeter-Exchange, in the Strand, 1774), pp. 2, 27.
[31] *Mimosa*, title page and pp. 2, 3.   [32] *Wisdom Reveal'd*, p. i.
[33] *Arbor Vitae*, p. 8.   [34] *Wisdom Reveal'd*, p. 3.   [35] Ibid., p. 24.

dame Eve, / Nor Serpent – or a Devil.'[36] Not surprisingly, the author of *An Elegy on the Lamented Death of the Electrical Eel* (1777) commemorates this occasion: 'That Eel on earth, in Paradise the first', was the thing which led Eve to 'the tree accurst'.[37] Completing a trio of texts, *The Old Serpent's Reply to the Electrical Eel* (1777) takes issue with this state of affairs and asserts, 'I debauch'd fair Lady Eve.'[38] But it is for the eel that the adoration of women reaches its zenith:

> Women to thee shall dedicate their lives,
> And on their knees with gratitude revere,
> Thou wert the comfort of both maids and wives,
> And brush'd away the widow's ready tear.[39]

And on the 'superb erection' to be constructed in honour of the eel was to appear the inscription:

> HERE LIES
> THE ELECTRICAL EEL;
> ALAS! THE HOPE OF SHEPHERDESSES FLOCKS,
> LEFT, AND NEGLECTED
> ON
> THE NAKED STONES,
> WITHOUT
> THE HOPE
> OF THE RESURRECTION OF THE FLESH
> FINIS[40]

On occasion, women's desire for the penis reached comic proportions. The poem 'The Marriage Morn' (1798) recounts the attempts of a couple to consummate their marriage, and focuses particularly on the urgency of the new bride. Her lust would not be satiated until 'Manhood rose with furious gust'.[41] Generally, however, obvious hilarity was absent from these descriptions. In *Mimosa*, 'the plant, beloved' is held in 'the highest estimation', at least when these plants were 'grown up, vigorous and erect'.[42] The *arbor vitae* is similarly to be revered, not only having the capacity to solve domestic disputes, but also the ability to conclude the 'most destructive Wars' and produce 'the most friendly Treatises'.[43] Indeed, women are castigated should they not recognize the calibre of these penises:

> If your Ideas of them be
> Not full of Grace and Dignity;
> Attend, and it shall soon be shewn
> The Fault's not Nature's, but your own.[44]

---

[36] *Electrical Eel* (No publication details, [c. 1770]), p. 9.
[37] *Elegy on the Lamented Death of the Electrical Eel*, p. 1.
[38] *Old Serpent's Reply to the Electrical Eel*, p. 13.
[39] *Elegy on the Lamented Death of the Electrical Eel*, p. 5.   [40] Ibid., p. 29.
[41] 'The Marriage Morn', in *Hilaria*, p. 9.   [42] *Mimosa*, pp. 1, iii.
[43] *Arbor Vitae*, pp. 21, 10.   [44] *Adam's Tail*, p. 2.

As discussed in the previous chapter, though female bodies were often presented as irresistible, they also provoked fear. Male bodies were thus the unquestionable objects of adoration that female bodies never were. Often the charm of male bodies was believed to emanate from beauty. In *A Chinese Tale* (1740), a painting of a penis prompts the outburst:

> The World's great *Primum Mobile*;
> That Master-piece! that Source of Passion!
> That Thing that's never out of Fashion.[45]

A penis is 'That dear enchanting Rod', 'a Tree in all its Beauty', 'strong, lusty [and] beautiful'.[46] In the hierarchical relationship established between male and female bodies, this beauty was a trait that distinguished men. For example, *The Why and the Wherefore?* (1765) asks 'Why Men have not much to boast of their greatness, nor women of their beauty, in certain very interesting parts?'[47] When differentiating between male and female bodies, the author of *Teague-Root Display'd* (1746) claims that 'the Female is not so beautiful a Root' and has 'a very shocking Appearance'.[48] The 'chiefest Perfections of the Female-Sex', another author wrote, are incomparable to 'the Majesty of the Masculine-Form'.[49]

Male bodies were not only compared to female bodies, but to one another. One of the most important grounds on which comparisons were made was size. Such emphasis was not at all new in depictions of male genitalia, but had been central to depictions from at least a century before.[50] In the eighteenth century this endured: the priapic tradition depicted Priapus 'as a pigmy with a huge cock', and the penises which appear in John Cleland's pornographic *Fanny Hill* were notable for their size.[51] Similarly, erotic descriptions deemed penises most attractive when 'stiff, erect and high,' 'most streight of lovely Size' and 'Of such a size – of such a length'.[52] Cloe's curiosity regarding the tree of life in

---

[45] *Chinese Tale*, pp. 22–3.
[46] *Little Merlin's Cave*, p. 4; *Wisdom Reveal'd*, p. 24; *Teague-Root Display'd*, p. 14.
[47] *Why and the Wherefore: Or, the Lady's Two Questions Resolved. Question the First; Why Men have not much to Boast of their Greatness, nor Women of their Beauty, in certain very Interesting Parts?*.
[48] *Teague-Root Display'd*, pp. 14, 15.
[49] 'Erotopolis', pp. 28–9. The superiority of male bodies is further indicated by the use of Richard Bradley's distinction of tree and shrub to represent the male and female genitals respectively, in which the tree commanded greater perfections. See Bradley, *Philosophical Account*, pp. 35–7, and see chapter two.
[50] See Weil, 'Sometimes a Sceptre', pp. 125–53.
[51] G. S. Rousseau, 'The Sorrows of Priapus', in his *Perilous Enlightenment: Pre- and Post-Modern Discourses. Sexual, Historical* (Manchester: Manchester University Press, 1991), p. 93; Randolph Trumbach, 'Erotic Fantasy and Male Libertinism in Enlightenment England', in Hunt (ed.), *Invention of Pornography*, p. 266.
[52] *Mimosa*, pp. 2, 3; *Arbor Vitae*, p. 12; *Electrical Eel* ([c. 1770]), p. 25.

Wisdom Reveal'd is most urgent on the issue of size: 'But will you never tell the Size?', she excitedly interrupts the narrator.[53]

Size was certainly one criterion wielded in the mock vying between authors. While the *Elegy on the Lamented Death of the Electrical Eel* praises 'thy length', *The Old Serpent's Reply to the Electrical Eel* noted that the Eel was merely 'a Grig' or 'a small eel'.[54] Employing the popular metaphor of the tree for the penis, the author of *The Whim!* (1782) separates British men – except the Welsh – into their respective nations: 'The Irish *Shilaley*, the Scotch *Fir*, and the English *Oak*'.[55] Elsewhere, national or regional trees differed in size, with Kent and Ireland boasting the most impressive specimens. The tree of life in *Wisdom Reveal'd* is 'About two Hands of proper Length', but 'In *Kent* [it is] sometimes two Inches more', and 'in *Hibernia* Three or Four.'[56] The English tree in *Arbor Vitae* 'rarely passes nine, or even eleven Inches, and that chiefly in Kent; whereas in *Ireland*, it comes to far greater Dimensions'. Portraying women as land, Irish trees developed most fully because 'the *Irish* Soil is accounted the best'.[57] Similarly, in *Teague-Root Display'd* the author confides, 'I have seen it in most Countries of *Europe*; but I never met with any so good as in *Ireland*: There it arrives to the greatest *Perfection*'.[58] Party to this knowledge, 'a certain *Virtuosi*-lady' imported a 'cargoe of Male-Roots from *Ireland* to divert her'.[59] In 1798, Ireland was still believed to produce impressive specimens: ''Tis Ireland that boasts it, their sea-*rara avis* [rare bird].'[60] The legendary reputation of Irish penises must have informed 'Lucretia Lovejoy's' decision to deck the grave of the electrical eel with 'Some Irish Priapus'.[61]

Regional and national differences between female bodies were rarely noted, but numerous male bodily traits differed according to geography. A teague-root, for example, 'will grow in all Climates; but thrives best in our more Northern Countries. The warm Countries of *Spain* and *Italy* produce it in great Plenty; but it's too forward with them: it's suddenly ripe, and as soon rotten; and does not retain its Beauty, Vigour, nor Virtue, half as long as in Climates where the Heat is less intense'.[62] Vigour was particularly crucial in depictions of male bodies,

---

[53] *Wisdom Reveal'd*, p. 9.
[54] *Elegy on the Lamented Death of the Electrical Eel*, p. 7; *Old Serpent's Reply to the Electrical Eel*, p. 18.
[55] *Whim*, pp. ii–iii.   [56] *Wisdom Reveal'd*, p. 9.
[57] *Arbor Vitae*, p. 3. See chapter three on the metaphor of women as land.
[58] *Teague-Root Display'd*, pp. 13–14.   [59] Ibid., p. 18.
[60] 'An Extraordinary Fish', in *Hilaria*, p. 123.
[61] *Elegy on the Lamented Death of the Electrical Eel*, p. 7.
[62] *Teague-Root Display'd*, p. 13. For other references to the effects of weather and temperature on bodies, see *Natural History of the Frutex Vulvaria*, [c. 1737]), pp. 6–7; *Electrical Eel* ([c. 1770]), pp. 18, 27; *Arbor Vitae*, p. 4; *Teague-Root Display'd*, p. 15.

suggesting that strength, as well as size, mattered.[63] Adonis is a 'vig'rous Youth', a man mounts a bed 'in youth and vigour strong' and a 'vig'rous man' liaises with a 'rapturous fair'.[64] A toast in the *Bacchanalian Magazine* (1793) makes clear the sexual connotations of vigour: 'May the Cushion of Life be thumped by the Club of Vigour'.[65] Perhaps not surprisingly, vigour was implicated in acts of male sexual violence, as in a scene of rape in *The Prostitutes of Quality* (1757), in which one woman suffered 'all the Force of [the man's] vigorous Desire'.[66] And as vigour was a key attribute of the man who wished to have sex, so the absence of vigour prevented sex. Sam Cock in *A Voyage to Lethe* (1741) fails to have sex with one woman precisely because he and his crew do not have 'the Vigour or Courage we should have done'.[67]

Women were believed to find vigour very attractive in men, and strength and energy were distinctively male traits.[68] Discussing what women wanted in a man, the author of *The Fruit-Shop* (1765) explains that it was certainly not 'weakness in the Netherlands'.[69] Similarly, a woman in *The Why and the Wherefore* explains that 'the object of our desires should not only be the standard length and breadth on which we are agreed, but that its virtue, or power of action, should continue as long as the woman herself should wish it'.[70] Power and vigour here meant maintaining an erection. Indeed, the author notes earlier in the book that while the '*Small-Poles*' might have been more diminutive than other penises, 'in point of vigor and activity, some of them did not yield to the proudest of those huge, overgrown grandees'.[71] Vigour could be prized more highly than size.

Fertility, receptivity and age

Beauty, size and vigour were important qualities of admirable, attractive male bodies but, as in depictions of female bodies, the key characteristic of male genitalia was fertility. Like size, fertility depended on geographical difference. In *Mimosa*, botanists and women are agreed that the seed of the English mimosa is superior to that of the French:

---

[63] Samuel Johnson's dictionary definition gave 'vigour' three meanings: 'Force; strength'; 'Mental force; intellectual ability'; and 'Energy; efficacy'. The illustrative quotations spoke almost exclusively of men. Johnson, *Dictionary*.

[64] *Consummation*, p. 9; 'The Girdle of Venus Unlocked', in *Festival of Love*, p. 35; 'The Joke: or, Mutual Transports', in *Bacchanalian Magazine*, p. 39.

[65] *Bacchanalian Magazine*, p. 50.

[66] *Prostitutes of Quality*, p. 170. See chapter six on sexual violence in erotica.

[67] *Voyage to Lethe* (1741), p. 72.

[68] 'Ode to Lord Lincoln', in *Festival of Love*, p. 13.

[69] *Fruit-Shop* (1765), vol. II, p. 127.

[70] *Why and the Wherefore*, p. 146.

[71] Ibid., p. 56.

> The *motion* may not be so *strong*,
> The *pods* so full, the *stem* so long;
> So *succulent* the *root*.
> Yet Lady B—Y M O R E declares,
> Our *stamen* is as good as theirs;
> As exquisite the *fruit*.[72]

The importance of fertility is exemplified by the keen interest these authors expressed not only in the penis, but in the scrotum and testicles: those appendages which contribute 'very much to the Fruitfulness of the Soil' in Merryland.[73] The opening description of the *arbor vitae* includes a discussion of 'Its Fruits' which, 'contrary to most others, grow near the Root; they are usually no more than two in Number, their Bigness somewhat exceeding that of an ordinary *Nutmeg*, both contain'd in one strong *Siliqua*, or Purse'.[74] This echoes the description of the teague-root: 'At the Bottom of the Root issue two round Globes, that are pendulous in a Bag, where they seem to be loose, tho' bound to the Stem of the Root, by small yielding Fibres: The Outside of this Bag is wrinkly.'[75] Indeed, in *Wisdom Reveal'd*, the testes are one of the distinguishing markers of the male plant:

> Have you not seen some Plants that shoot,
> With all their Leaves about the Root?
> . . . .
> A Nutmeg's like, but often less than this –
> The common Crop is number two,
> Three are too many – one's too few.[76]

As discussed in chapter two, erotic discussions of conception were complex, but male contributions to conception were considered vital. Semen is 'The *Fruit of Life*', 'the vivid stream'.[77] The mimosa produces 'the most animating sap', and the tree of life in *Wisdom Reveal'd* administers a 'prolific Juice'.[78] Even the metaphor of the serpent allowed discussion of fertility, as the author of *The Old Serpent's Reply to the Electrical Eel* asserts the reproductive potency of the serpent *vis-à-vis* the eel.[79] In contrast, it is for his inability to imitate the productive fluid of semen that Seignior Dildo is railed against, appropriately by a midwife:

> *Monsieur*, by chance came in a Christening Room,
> Where he had like to have receiv'd his Doom:
> The Midwife bellowing, open mouth'd she cry'd,
> *If you're encourag'd, Villain, we're destroyed.*[80]

---

[72] *Mimosa*, p. 13.   [73] *New Description of Merryland*, p. 25.   [74] *Arbor Vitae*, pp. 1–2.
[75] *Teague-Root Display'd*, p. 14.   [76] *Wisdom Reveal'd*, p. 8.
[77] *Arbor Vitae*, p. 12; 'The Marriage Morn', in *Hilaria*, p. 9.
[78] *Mimosa*, p. vi; *Wisdom Reveal'd*, p. 11.   [79] *Old Serpent's Reply to the Electrical Eel*, p. 16.
[80] *Monsieur Thing's Origin: Or, Seignior D—o's Adventures in Britain* (For R. Tomson, near Cheapside, 1722), p. 19.

Illustration 13:   The great upright torch thistle on the left. Richard Bradley's *History of Succulent Plants* (1716).

Male bodies did not display the perpetual moistness and flow that was ascribed to female bodies, but semen was evidence of fertility, that most essential of male attributes.

A range of metaphors were employed to depict male bodies, but botanical metaphors were used most often. Such depictions used a highly specialized language, often focused on the reproductive capacity of plants. The author of *Mimosa*, for example, peppers his description of male bodies with an array of comments lifted from contemporary botanical writers:

'A funnel fashioned semi-quinquisid flower; its fruit is a long *pod*, containing a great many roundish *seeds*.' OWEN.

'The flower consists of one leaf, which is shaped like a FUNNEL, having many *stamina* in the *centre* – the flower is collected into a *round head*; – from the bottom rises the *pistillum*, which afterwards becomes an *oblong*, flat-joined *pod*, which opens both ways, and contains, in each partition, one roundish *seed*.' MILLER.[81]

Botanical metaphors were used repeatedly to convey the important male qualities of beauty, size and vigour. One author advises his readers to consider an illustration of the penis in a recent text by the botanist Richard Bradley. (Illustration 13.)[82] Of this plant, the torch thistle, Bradley wrote, 'It is wonderful to see this Plant rise out of the Earth in a Pillar-like Form, shooting directly upwards, . . . till it will attain to the height of about twenty Foot.'[83] The thistle has 'an extraordinary Face', and is praised for 'coming nearer the Perfection we look for' than other plants.[84] Other early-eighteenth-century discussions present the plant as grand enough to warrant comparisons with men: 'nothing is more frequent than for Plants and Trees, as well as Men, to carry a different Bulk and Heighth [sic], and yet to be in their full Perfection of Vigour and Strength; we often find, shorter Trees measure as much timber as taller, and shorter Men be as strong, as vigorous, as comely as taller'.[85] It was the upright nature of the torch thistle, combined with the beautiful, vigorous, dignified and superior nature of the plant, that made it an eminently suitable depiction of the male genitals.

Yet male plants were not always grand and imposing; they could be sensitive and receptive. For example, botanical penises often receded from the touch of women. 'If a Lady shou'd approach' them in *Wisdom Reveal'd*, 'beneath her Hand they shrink and crouch'.[86] The opening description of the mimosa similarly claims that it recedes from the touch, while a footnote expands: 'The *Sensitive Plant* is so denominated from its remarkable property of *receding* from the touch, and giving *signs* as it were of *animal life* and *sensation*.'[87] Of course, the penis does not simply recede from the touch of women, but ultimately rises to meet it:

> For, after we have touch'd the head,
> It does, as feelingly *recede*;
> And just as quickly *rise*.[88]

---

[81] *Mimosa*, p. 1.

[82] *Wisdom Reveal'd*, p. 7. The illustration referred to appears in Richard Bradley's *Philosophical Account*, and in a slightly altered form (used here) in his earlier *The History of Succulent Plants . . . Decade I* (For the Author, 1716).

[83] Bradley, *The History of Succulent Plants*, p. 1.   [84] Bradley, *Philosophical Account*, p. 23.

[85] *A True Account of the Aloe Americana or Africana . . . as also of Two other Exotick Plants, call'd, The Cereus, or Torch-Thistle* (For T. Warner, at the Black Boy in Pater-noster-Row, and sold by H. Whitridge in Castle-Alley at the Royal Exchange; and Mr Cowell at Hoxton, 1729), p. 42.

[86] *Wisdom Reveal'd*, p. 12.

[87] *Mimosa*, p. 1. John Cleland used the metaphor of 'the genuine sensitive plant, which, instead of shrinking from the touch, joys to meet it'. See Cleland, *Fanny Hill*, p. 198.

[88] *Mimosa*, p. 13.

In contrast to the movement of female genitals, which was invariably a source of fear, such descriptions seemed to praise the changeability and receptivity of the penis, showing it to be a tender thing of feeling.

Such receptivity to and dependence on the attentions of women allowed for a degree of vulnerability in the representations of male genitalia, themes which emerged most often in descriptions of the post-coital penis. Such images were not new to English literature. John Wilmot, Earl of Rochester, had described the 'imperfect enjoyment' of the premature ejaculation in the seventeenth century, lamenting the penis as '[s]hrunk up and sappless like a wither'd flower'. Here there is pathos and pity partly because the penis had failed to release the 'all dissolving Thunderbolt beloe', and had ejaculated into the woman's hand. But for Rochester the real tragedy was that while his penis would perform for whoring, it failed him when engaged in an act of love.[89] In erotica the interest was in reproduction not love. Sometimes, particularly in the more humorous texts, the limp post-coital penis is ridiculed. It was 'weary'd, worn out', 'lifeless, jaded and lame'; it entered the woman 'stoutly', but slipped out 'feebly'.[90] But generally, a post-coital penis had succeeded in performing its task, and was described without pity or humour. The mimosa, for example, 'sends the *tremor* to your heart, / And *shrinks* before your face'.[91] Other plants experienced the same metamorphosis. The teague-root 'shrinks into its original Limberless' after 'all the Electrical Fire is spent', and the tree of life in *Wisdom Reveal'd* discharges its 'vital *Succus*' and then 'faints, grows feeble, [and] hangs its Head'.[92] Even the fiery serpent 'lay awhile in sleep' after 'his wrath was spent'.[93] These spent and slumbering penises were not pathetic, because a flaccid penis after intercourse had done its job. Impotence, on the other hand, was treated more unkindly. Again, this had been dealt with before, for example in Aphra Behn's poem 'The Disappointment'. After a lengthy seduction, the 'too transported hapless Swain' finds himself 'slack'ned' at the crucial moment. The poem ends with the implication that his impotence is caused by Cloris' powers, as well as by his urgency.[94] In later erotica, images of men's impotence were often coupled with an appetitive, desiring woman. The wife in the poem 'Thomas and Joan' (1726) is 'most *impatient*, and *craving*', while her husband's

89 John Wilmot, Earl of Rochester, 'The Imperfect Enjoyment', in Harold Love (ed.), *The Works of John Wilmot, Earl of Rochester* (Oxford: Oxford University Press, 1999), p. 15, line 45 and p. 14, line 10.
90 'The High-Mettled P — o', p. 14; 'An Extraordinary Fish', p. 127, both in *Hilaria*.
91 *Mimosa*, p. 2.   92 *Teague-Root Display'd*, p. 16; *Wisdom Reveal'd*, p. 13.
93 *Old Serpent's Reply to the Electrical Eel*, p. 6.
94 Aphra Behn, 'The Disappointment', in Janet Todd (ed.), *The Works of Aphra Behn. Volume I: Poetry* (Columbus: Ohio State University Press, 1992), p. 67, lines 72, 84 and 78. I am grateful to Judith Hawley for this reference, and for the reference to Rochester, above.

penis is limp and unresponsive.[95] Too rapacious and overpowering a woman, it seems, prevented the transformation of a penis into a state of admirable erection.

The assumed impotence of older men was one reason why they received such short shrift in the material. As the author of *Arbor Vitae* explains, 'In the latter season they are subject to become weak and flaccid, and want support.'[96] Older men are therefore portrayed trying to increase their excitement 'by Cordials and Drugs', but also by other methods: 'sometimes to keep the Electrical Embers in some tolerable degree of Heat, they condescend to discover their Posteriors, and have them heartily flogg'd by their female Servants'.[97] Flagellation was the most common way in which elderly impotence was tackled. In *Arbor Vitae*, 'some Gardeners have thought of splintring them up with *Birchen Twigs*, which has seemed of some Service for the present, tho' the Plants have very soon come to the same, or a more drooping State than before'.[98] Many such efforts were doomed, however, because 'when Age brings on Decay' even the birch 'no more avail'd!'[99] The flaccidity of old age was treated more harshly than flaccidity immediately before or after sexual intercourse, because flaccidity in older men suggested a lack of size, vigour and fertility.

Eighteenth-century writers recoiled from the union of old men and younger women, and they were puzzled by how 'grey-bearded dotards, frozen with age' could possibly enjoy 'the amorous fire, and vivacity of ardent and passionate youth'.[100] This was reflected in erotica. Indeed, the premium placed on size, beauty, vigour and fertility and the ways in which these qualities were sometimes connected converged in these unfavourable depictions of old male bodies. The electrical desire which gave the teague-root its potency was weak in older men: 'Old Men are but slightly agitated by it; that is, the Effects of the Electrical Fire does not meet in their Bodies with a sufficient Quantity of *Pabulum* to make the Flame conspicuous to any but themselves.'[101] The effects that age might have on a man's body are vividly described. A man's 'querulous age' makes his limbs 'fail with unperceiv'd decay'.[102] Readers are thus counselled to court the affections of women while young, because when 'grown feeble with age,

---

[95] 'Thomas and Joan', published at the close of 'An Essay on Matrimony' in *The Sixpenny Miscellany. Or, a Dissertation upon Pissing* (Reprinted for A. Moore, near St Paul's, 1726), p. 28. For another example, see *The French King's Wedding: Or, the Royal Frolick. Being a Pleasant Account of the Amorous Intrigues, Comical Courtship, Caterwauling and Surprizing Marriage Ceremonies of Lewis the XIVth with Madam Maintenon* (By J. Smith, near Fleetstreet, 1708), p. 7.

[96] *Arbor Vitae*, p. 4.   [97] *Teague-Root Display'd*, p. 22.

[98] *Arbor Vitae*, p. 4.   [99] *Wisdom Reveal'd*, pp. 18–19.

[100] 'A Short Sermon on Matrimony', *Lady's Magazine*, October 1783, p. 520.

[101] *Teague-Root Display'd*, p. 21. See also *Arbor Vitae*, p. 4.

[102] 'The Bridal Night', in *Pleasures that Please on Reflection*, p. 50.

our feet will no longer carry us to their temples'.[103] Hence, one man hoped the Graces would come to him of their own accord because, he explained, 'I am sixty-three, / And that's too old to ravish'.[104] Sex involving old men was desperate. The unnamed 'distinguished personage' to whom the author of *The Fruit-Shop* dedicated his book is chided not for his excessive sexual behaviour, but because of his advanced age: 'and at such a time of life too! – Young fools may be excused, but old ones – O shocking turpitude.'[105] In particular, old age indicated an absence of vigour, constituting a 'horrid frost' which withdrew 'vigorous heat' from the body.[106] One young woman chooses a male lover because he possesses the vigour her old husband lacks, while another 'read want of vigour' in her old husband and sets out to have sex with a series of younger men.[107] Perhaps trying to avoid such a fate, another old man calls on Cupid to renew his 'dying embers' and 'give me back my vigour'.[108] These stories undermined old bodies and reinforced the majesty and reproductive capacity of younger men.

Race and nation

The combined emphasis on youth, vigour, fertility and national comparisons suggested an acute sense of Britain's place in the world and serious concerns over the nature of the population. It also revealed an ambivalence towards foreign men by erotic authors. These writers appear to have been worried about the ability of English or British men to satisfy their women, and they worried that foreigners would be more effective. This concern is displayed in *Seventeen Hundred and Seventy-Seven* (1777). The book is dedicated to 'Omiah, at Otaheite', the 'noble savage' brought from Tahiti to England after James Cook's second voyage in 1774, and the poem builds on the reputation of Otaheite as a place of wantonness, established by reports of voyages published throughout the 1770s. Echoing tales of British sailors valiently resisting the inviting allurements of the naked women of Otaheite, the author of *Seventeen Hundred and Seventy-Seven* asks how British men could remain 'cold' while sensual and beautiful women revealed themselves.[109] Wanting to revive heterosexual desire in men, the author hopes that the example of Omiah would

---

[103] *Secret History of Pandora's Box*, p. 55.
[104] 'Ode to Lord Lincoln', in *Festival of Love*, p. 14.   [105] *Fruit-Shop*, vol. I, p. iv.
[106] 'The Oeconomy of Love', in *Pleasures that Please on Reflection*, p. 30.
[107] 'The Ink Bottle', p. 47; 'The Squire', p. 146, both in *Festival of Love*.
[108] 'Horace, Lib. I. Ode XXX', in *Festival of Love*, p. 14.
[109] John Hawkesworth, *An Account of the Voyages . . . in the Southern Hemisphere . . . by Commodore Byron, Captain Wallis, Captain Carteret, and Captain Cook*, 3 vols. (For W. Strahan and T. Cadell in the Strand, 1773), vol. I, pp. 438–40, 481; *Seventeen Hundred and Seventy-Seven; Or, a Picture of the Manners and Character of the Age* (For T. Evans, near York-Buildings, in the Strand, 1777), p. 12.

> tempt the youths to rove,
> And bring their pleasures, and their arts of love!
> Let sooty throngs the cream-fac'd courtier shame,
> And southern lovers glad the curious dame.[110]

At the same time, though, southern men were anathema to British masculinity. At present, the erotic author writes, British men engage in sex without real pleasure; they were 'Debauched without desire' and a 'disgrace of manhood'.[111] The author aligns this with an effeminized, Italianate model of masculinity, exhorting his readers to 'Rise and be MEN, ye Macaroni train!'[112]

Foreign men could be more desiring, more vigorous; but they were often despicable. 'The Oeconomy of Love' portrays anal sex between men as foreign perversion, and vaginal intercourse and strict sexual differences as peculiarly British:

> For man with man,
> And man with woman (monstrous to relate!)
> Leaving the natural road, themselves debase
> With deeds unseemly, and dishonour foul.
> BRITONS, for shame! be male and female still.
> Banish this foreign vice.[113]

The same association is made when the narrator of *A Voyage to Lethe* (1741) is taken to a temple devoted to 'an Idol called PAEDERASTIA'. This temple is worshipped at by 'the *Sodomanians*, a very infamous People, of a mean sallow Complexion, and with an odious Squeak in their Voices', and though Britons are among their number the author is careful to point out that most worshippers are French or Italian.[114] In keeping with the ambivalent attitude of many eighteenth-century writers towards France, several authors were concerned about the effect French manners might have on the English. One of the male characters in *The Rake of Taste* (1760), for example, wonders why women are not taught 'good houswifery' rather than French, dancing and music.[115] A distaste for all things French permeates the *Genuine Memoirs of the Celebrated Miss Maria Brown* (1766), and is particularly clear in the description of Dorimont: 'that compendium of perfumery, who spoke only to hear his own sweet voice, smiled only to display his dimple, and laughed only to manifest the whiteness of his teeth; the unmeaning, insignificant, odoriferous Dorimont'.[116] French manners could engender sexual indiscretion. In *The Adventures of a Cork-Screw* (1775), for example, a young English man spends some time in France, only to return

[110] Ibid., p. 3.   [111] Ibid., p. 24.   [112] Ibid., p. 13.
[113] 'The Oeconomy of Love', in *Pleasures that Please on Reflection*, p. 33. See also Porter, 'Literature of Sexual Advice before 1800', p. 147.
[114] *Voyage to Lethe* (1741), p. 36.   [115] *Rake of Taste*, p. 30.
[116] *Genuine Memoirs of . . . Miss Maria Brown*, vol. I, p. 72.

and 'commit the grossest of crimes without a blush'.[117] Such exploits brought shame to England, and the perpetrators were criticized as being 'so unnatural, nay so undutiful to your mother country'.[118]

It was because of such behaviour that British trees were 'held in the utmost Contempt in all foreign Countries', reports the author of *The Natural History of the Frutex Vulvaria* (c. 1737).[119] This was one of a number of erotic texts, published in the late 1730s and early 1740s, which deployed botanical metaphors in a lament on the state of male bodies, and in particular the failure of men to reproduce. This cluster of texts certainly coincided with the burgeoning number of works which discussed the sex life of plants.[120] Yet this alone does not explain the frequency with which these erotic authors adopted these metaphors, because plant sex life had been discussed since the late seventeenth century.[121] Two other factors are key to understanding why these books were produced at this particular time. First, botanical texts facilitated a discussion of fertility, during a mortality peak across Europe in the early 1740s.[122] Emphases in botany worked well for the pro-natalist concerns of erotic authors: though most plants possess both male and female organs of reproduction, and are therefore technically hermaphrodites, eighteenth-century botanists discussed the sex life of plants in terms of heterosexuality.[123] Second, these writers made their complaints against the backdrop of what they saw as Britain's poor showing on the international stage. The poor fitness of British men's bodies meant that Britain was struggling to be a world power. As the 1737 edition of *The Natural History of the Frutex Vulvaria* declares, 'Since the *Peace of Utrecht* we have never done any *Great Feats*, but seem to be damnably *off our Mettle*. All these Misfortunes the *Naturalists* and *Botanists* ascribe (how truly I know not) to the Degeneracy

---

[117] *The Adventures of a Cork-Screw, in which under the Pleasing Method of a Romance, the Vices, Follies and Manners of the Present Age are Exhibited and Satirically Delineated* (Dublin: For W. Whitestone, 1775), p. 18.

[118] *Fruit-Shop*, vol. I, p. iii.   [119] *Natural History of the Frutex Vulvaria* ([c. 1737]), p. 3.

[120] See Wagner, *Eros Revived*, pp. 192–6; Paul-Gabriel Boucé, 'Chthonic and Pelagic Metaphorization in Eighteenth-Century English Erotica', in Robert Purks Maccubbin (ed.), *'Tis Nature's Fault: Unauthorized Sexuality during the Enlightenment* (Cambridge: Cambridge University Press, 1987), pp. 202–16.

[121] For example, Nehemiah Grew published *The Anatomy of Plants* in 1682, and this bore much resemblance to Linneaus' later work. See Schiebinger, 'Gender and Natural History', p. 165. Carl Linnaeus' (1707–78) most important book was *Philosophia botanica*, not published until 1751, though he had published *Systema naturae* in 1735. See Lisbet Koerner, 'Carl Linnaeus in his Place and Time', in Jardine, Secord and Spary (eds.), *Cultures of Natural History*, pp. 145–62. Indeed, the familiar botanical term 'vulvaria' used in eighteenth-century erotica to refer to the female genitalia was used in the seventeenth century. See *The Practical Part of Love. Extracted out of the Extravagant and Lascivious Life of a Fair but Subtle Female* (No publication details, [1660]), p. 51. I am grateful to Sarah Toulalan for this reference.

[122] See John D. Post, *Food Shortage, Climatic Variability, and Epidemic Disease in Preindustrial Europe: The Mortality Peak in the Early 1740s* (Ithaca, N.Y.: Cornell University Press, 1985), p. 17.

[123] Schiebinger, 'Gender and Natural History', pp. 166–7.

of our *Trees of Life*.[124] This author dates the decline from the Treaty of Utrecht, which had concluded the War of Spanish Succession (1702–13) and furnished overseas gains to Britain at the expense of France and Spain.[125] Britain did not suffer obvious military losses in the decades immediately following this success, however. As the author suggests, it was not military defeat that caused concern; rather it was the absence of obvious military success and the opportunity to prove Britain's mettle that this would provide. Nevertheless, by the time the 1741 edition of *The Natural History of the Frutex Vulvaria* appeared, the British had been defeated in their attempts to seize Spanish colonies in the Caribbean during the War of Jenkin's Ear (1739), and Britain's Caribbean army was all but destroyed by the spring of 1741. A new dedication for the 1741 edition of *The Natural History of the Frutex Vulvaria* now voiced concerns over the strength of British men and gave women some unequivocally pro-natal advice: 'you must not expect to gain your Ends so much from the Multiplicity of the Plants you raise, as from the Strength and Beauty of them'.[126] In the new international climate, quality not quantity of offspring was the key concern.

Nowhere was this apparent anxiety about British military strength clearer than in *The Man-Plant; or, a Scheme for Increasing and Improving the British Breed* (1752). Underpinning the experiment to discover a new way of gestating babies in this book lies a concern to improve the male population. Currently, the author explains, the population is 'like a Nursery of Plants when the Grub is got amongst them'.[127] His plan is to counter this by furnishing the country with healthy baby boys who will have

all that Strength of Sinew which strung the Arms of those Progenitors of ours, who antiently made such a Figure at the battles of *Crecy* and *Agincourt*, or of those who more lately drove whole Squadrons of their Enemies into the *Danube*, . . . Barbarous, rude, rough Work! and quite unfit for the dainty Hands of our present pretty Men; hands blanched with Almond-paste, brillianted with Diamonds, and be-delicated with *Dresden* Ruffles.[128]

The author unfavourably compares the fighting strength of Britain's present population with that of their ancestors who had defeated the French at Crecy (1346) and Agincourt (1415). Yet this author also mentions more recent successes, apparently referring to the Wars of Austrian Succession (1740–8), during which Britain had supported the ultimately successful Habsburgs against France and Spain.[129] Published in 1752, *The Man-Plant* appeared during a

---

[124] *Natural History of the Frutex Vulvaria* (c. 1737), p. 4.
[125] John Cannon (ed.), *The Oxford Companion to British History* (Oxford: Oxford University Press, 1997), pp. 880–1, 949.
[126] *Natural History of the Frutex Vulvaria* (1741), p. i.
[127] *Man-Plant*, p. 34.   [128] Ibid., pp. 38–9.
[129] Cannon (ed.), *Oxford Companion*, p. 69.

hiatus in Britain's involvement in conflict, though flanked by wars which proved successful: the Wars of Austrian Succession, and the Seven Years War (1756–63). Not until the American War of Independence (1775–83) did Britain suffer resounding defeat.[130] Once again, comments in erotic books concerning British military weakness coincided, not necessarily with vanquishment, but with the cessation of victorious combat. Sex, for the author of *The Man-Plant*, is 'practical Patriotism'.[131]

Like so much of the content of eighteenth-century erotica, these discussions of procreation constitute slippery evidence: they may have been a ruse designed to legitimize ever more sexual activity. Certainly, it is unlikely that this genre was designed primarily as pro-natal, nationalistic propaganda. But precisely because this was not the purpose of erotica, these frequent depictions of sex as a patriotic act do suggest deep-seated concerns. Sex was repeatedly seen as an activity which would restore the country's fearsome fighters, replacing the current insipid and ineffectual bodies. Despite periodic intensifications in this discourse, this concern remained prominent throughout the century. Like the male beasts in *The Why and the Wherefore*, men had sex not simply to satiate their desires, but to create 'a species so noble and so necessary to the laborers of the country, and to the decayed rakes of the town'.[132] In the same year, the author of *The Fruit-Shop* decried the intention of the Devil 'to stop the propagation of the human race, by leading the posterity of the first man into unnatural pursuits, and render them regardless of the *Fruit-shop*', praising a sect which advocated the 'begetting subjects to supply the place, / Of once an heav'nly, now an hellish race'.[133] As late as 1788, Charles Morris' *Complete Collection of Songs* contained the poem 'The Westminster Triumph', in which Britain is 'a falling Nation' whose 'drooping head / Can scarce withstand its foes'.[134] The national freedom secured by these men's forefathers was believed to be in jeopardy, no doubt thrown into relief by the loss of America. In all these examples, sexual decay is equated with national decay, and it is from men's sexual potency that Britain's national hope springs.

Sex was celebrated not simply as a source of simple pleasure, then, but as a way to repopulate the nation. According to the author, *Consummation: Or, the Rape of Adonis* (1741) is published at a time when 'War's rude Hand' has 'thinn'd the World'; it is thus intended that young men and women who read the book will 'Repair our Loss and fill our Isle again.'[135] Similarly, a large section

---

[130] Colley, *Britons*, pp. 52, 99 and passim.
[131] *Man-Plant*, p. 35.   [132] *Why and the Wherefore*, p. 135.
[133] *Fruit-Shop*, vol. II, pp. 81, 122.
[134] Charles Morris, *A Complete Collection of Songs*, 9th edn. (For James Ridgway, No. 1 York-Street, St James's Square, 1788), pp. 37, 36.
[135] *Consummation*, p. iv.

of the erotic-medical poem 'The Oeconomy of Love' is directed to those men for whom 'progeny thy views extend', and the advice given here gives some indication of the seriousness of the task:

> shun the soft embrace
> Emasculent, till twice ten years and more
> Have steel'd thy nerves, and let the holy rite
> License the bliss. Nor would I urge, precise,
> A total abstinence; this might unman
> The genial organs, unemployed for so long,
> And quite extinguish the prolific flame,
> Refrigerant. But riot oft unblam'd
> On kisses, sweet repast! ambrosial joy![136]

This author counsels men to balance their sexual pleasures, to walk a thin line between chastity and promiscuity. A degree of sexual play relieved men from abstinence before marriage and ensured their potency; it also meant their genitals would not be 'unmanned'. License was not to extend to 'Th' ungenerous, selfish, solitary joy' of masturbation, however, which would cause men to 'sow thy perish'd offspring in the winds'.[137] This concern for population seeped into even the most hedonistic and bacchanalian of erotic literature, in which men still sought to 'Have broods to succeed us a hundred years hence'.[138] It is evident that erotic writers were interested in the rejuvenation of the *male* population, in keeping with medical and religious discourses on sex.[139] The fictional experiment in *The Man-Plant* produces 'a fine full-formed Man-plant, a Male-infant, and vivacious'. Likewise, the birth at the centre of *A Spy on Mother Midnight* (1748) is of 'a lusty chopping Boy' to whom the women make the toast, 'thank the Lord, we may be merry when a Man-Child is born'.[140] Indeed, when Mrs. Spintext tries to convince one of the younger girls to court a particular man, she is careful to remark that he had 'twenty Boys in his Calves'.[141] In a poem of 1753, one woman's affair with a black man produces 'a tawny boy', while it is speculated in *The Fruit-Shop* that the Pope has fathered 'a chopping boy'.[142] Only in one poem of 1770 is the birth of a girl mentioned, and this was presented as the fulfilment of the woman's wish, but the failure of her male lover.[143] The

---

[136] 'The Oeconomy of Love', in *Pleasures that Please on Reflection*, p. 9.
[137] Ibid., pp. 10, 11.
[138] 'A Hundred Years Hence', in *Bacchanalian Magazine*, pp. 54, 55.
[139] Francis Mauriceau admired 'the great Passion many have, who complain of nothing with greater Regret than dying without Children, especially without Sons'. See Mauriceau, *Diseases of Women with Child*, p. 5. Also see Crawford, 'Sexual Knowledge', p. 91; Roy Porter, '"The Secrets of Generation Display'd": Aristotle's, *Master-Piece*', in Maccubin (ed.), *'Tis Nature's Fault*, p. 9.
[140] *Man-Plant*, p. 32; *Spy on Mother Midnight*, pp. 16, 24.   [141] Ibid., p. 20.
[142] 'The Ink Bottle', in *Forty Select Poems*, p. 49; *Fruit-Shop*, vol. II, p. 109.
[143] 'The Girdle of Venus Unbuckled', in *Festival of Love*, p. 36. In 'Epigram' in the same collection, another baby boy is born. See p. 6.

reproductive capacities of both men and women, it was hoped, would furnish Britain with a healthy and strong population of men.

In erotic texts, male bodies were craved for by women, revealed only to women, and responded only to women. But while the narratives of erotica established a heterosexual context, the techniques used to represent male bodies allowed men to look at those bodies in homosocial environments.[144] In many ways this confirms much of what we know about changing masculinities in this period. Expressions of desire between men were met with increasingly harsh reception in the seventeenth and eighteenth centuries.[145] An impulse to admire bodies of the same sex therefore needed to be framed in a heterosexual context in order to allay fears of same-sex desire. This material did not cater to 'homosexuality', then, but to homoeroticism, a source of pleasure for men well into the eighteenth century.[146] The delight of erotic texts did not lie simply in the pandering to readers' knowledge of the classics, botany or ethnography, or in the titillating stories of desire and sex. Depictions of male bodies in eighteenth-century erotica may have worked to police male bodies, spurning the old, the physically weak and the infertile; certainly, in the stress on fertility and the state of the population, concern and anxiety were present. Yet as much as they gave men something to live up to, erotic texts – and erotic culture more broadly – also provided a space where certain male bodies were celebrated. In guises of both hard, erect completeness and soft, sensitive receptivity, men were desired by insatiable and adoring women. These intimate depictions reveal something of the character of male power in the eighteenth century: it was flexible, and could appear quite precarious, but beneath it all was a profound and unshakeable belief that the future of the new nation lay in the male body. Only these bodies were capable of reproducing the children that Britain needed to be great. Fertility was critical to male and female, but depictions of male fertility were distinctive because they exposed specific concerns about the British population. Firmly rooted in an international and a military context, male fertility and sexuality were politicized and nationalized. Eighteenth-century erotica displayed considerable persistence in its discussions of female bodies; erotic representations of male bodies, in contrast, were more susceptible to the tides of contemporary developments.

[144] See chapter one for a discussion of contexts.
[145] Alan Bray, 'The Body of the Friend', in Hitchcock and Cohen (eds.), English Masculinities, pp. 65–84; Hitchcock, English Sexualities, pp. 58–75.
[146] G. S. Rousseau, 'The Pursuit of Homosexuality in the Eighteenth Century: "Utterly Confused Category" and/or Rich Repository', Eighteenth-Century Life 9 (1985), pp. 132–68.

5 Space

The modernity of eighteenth-century England has been located in the dramatic changes in both the urban landscape and the domestic interior. Eighteenth-century urbanization was remarkable in quantitative and qualitative terms. By the close of the century, around 30 per cent of the population lived in towns, which were larger and more evenly spread throughout the country than before.[1] Both the metropolis and provincial centres acquired new social spaces, in the form of broad walkways, ample squares and purpose-built venues of leisure in which social interaction was characterized by openness, politeness and the mixing of men and women. The street became a 'more obviously public space'.[2] Simultaneously, increasing subdivision and a stress on comfort within the house suggested a growing 'privatization and commercialization of the household'.[3] Such changes in the urban and domestic environment have been woven into a narrative of progress and the 'peculiar modernity of the Hanoverian age'.[4] This transformation of lived space was accompanied by changing understandings of human bodies, the birth of two modern opposite sexes concomitant with 'Enlightenment political theory [and] the development of new sorts of public spaces'.[5] Both the flesh and the city became modern.

Modern understandings of bodies and gender have been located in porno-graphic and erotic material, and this material has itself been regarded as part

---

[1] See Penelope J. Corfield, *The Impact of English Towns, 1700–1800* (Oxford: Oxford University Press, 1982). See also my introduction for a brief discussion of 'modernity'.

[2] Peter Borsay, 'Early Modern Urban Landscapes, 1540–1800', in Philip Waller (ed.), *The English Urban Landscape* (Oxford: Oxford University Press, 2000), p. 109. See also Peter Borsay, 'The English Urban Renaissance: The Development of Provincial Urban Culture, c.1680–1760', in his *The Eighteenth Century Town: A Reader in English Urban History, 1688–1820* (London: Longman, 1990), pp. 159–87; Peter Borsay, *The English Urban Renaissance: Culture and Society in the Provincial Town, 1660–1770* (Oxford: Oxford University Press, 1989), pp. 50–72; Ogborn, *Spaces of Modernity*, pp. 148–57. On the particularly 'feminine' nature of eighteenth-century polite interaction, see Klein, 'Gender, Conversation and the Public Sphere', pp. 100–15.

[3] Borsay, 'Early Modern Urban Landscapes', p. 102.

[4] Langford, *Polite and Commercial People*, p. 2. On urban improvement and domestic interiors, see pp. 70, 417–32.

[5] Laqueur, *Making Sex*, p. 11. On the Enlightenment, gender and bodies, see Merchant, *Death of Nature*.

of the Enlightenment.[6] In this chapter I want to reconsider the connections between erotica and modernity, whilst also suggesting a complication of narratives of gender and space. Historians of women have considered space in discussions of the public and private 'separate spheres', focusing particularly on where men and women carried out various activities.[7] Yet space is not simply physical; it is imaginary and mythic. My approach here is indebted more to the work of geographers who have combined the analytical categories of gender and space to demonstrate how specific spaces or places were gendered, and to show how gender may in part be created through the organization and representation of space.[8] Much of the burden of this work has been to subject the contemporary discipline of geography to a feminist analysis, revealing gendered approaches to space as historical products of the Scientific Revolution and the Enlightenment. Part of a general denigration of the feminine and a championing of masculine rationality and reason, these movements are supposed to reveal a desire to transcend, dominate, control, subordinate or regulate feminized space.[9] For example, eighteenth-century landscape design has been presented as the art of taming, controlling and possessing feminine nature.[10]

Configurations of gender and space in eighteenth-century erotica do not fit this model of the supposed redefinition of the feminine and concomitant ascendance of the masculine. Erotic authors were fascinated by bodies, and previous chapters have considered erotic discussions of subjects such as conception, genital structure and orgasm which were paramount in scientific and medical writing and are now central to existing historiography. Yet for erotic authors bodies bore qualities beyond the medically anatomical and physiological. I have argued in earlier chapters that understandings of sex differences were malleable, and that women were neither simply passive nor desexualized. I want

---

[6] For example, see Hitchcock, *English Sexualities*, pp. 8–23; Laqueur, *Making Sex*, 159–60; Orr, 'Whore's Rhetoric', pp. 195–216; Trumbach, 'Modern Prostitution and Gender in *Fanny Hill*', pp. 67–85. For accounts which place erotica in an enlightened context, see Hunt (ed.), *Invention of Pornography*; Wagner (ed.), *Erotica and the Enlightenment*; and Wagner, *Eros Revived*.

[7] For a review of this material, see Vickery, 'Golden Age to Separate Spheres?', pp. 383–414. For a recent restatement of the value of the public/private spatial dichotomy, see Hannah Barker and Elaine Chalus, 'Introduction', in Barker and Chalus (eds.), *Gender in Eighteenth-Century England*, pp. 17–24.

[8] See, for example, Doreen Massey, *Space, Place and Gender* (Cambridge: Polity Press, 1994); Alexander Ponte, 'Architecture and Phallocentrism in Richard Payne Knight's Theory', in Beatrix Colomina (ed.), *Sexuality and Space* (New York: Princeton Architectural Press, 1992), pp. 272–305; Gillian Rose, *Feminism and Geography: The Limits of Geographical Knowledge* (Cambridge: Polity Press, 1993).

[9] Genevieve Lloyd, *The Man of Reason: 'Male' and 'Female' in Western Philosophy* (London: Methuen, 1984), p. 2 and passim; Massey, *Space, Place*, pp. 7, 9–11; Rose, *Feminism and Geography*, pp. 6–7, 86–112; Mark Wigley, 'Untitled: The Housing of Gender', in Colomina (ed.), *Sexuality and Space*, pp. 353–7.

[10] Fabricant, 'Binding and Dressing Nature's Loose Tresses', p. 116; Simon Pugh, *Garden-Nature-Language* (Manchester: Manchester University Press, 1988), pp. 112–13.

to develop these points in this chapter, by considering how male and female sexuality were viewed spatially. Erotic writing was distinct from medical and scientific literature in being more clearly a site of fantasy and imagination: what eighteenth-century men and women termed 'fancy'.[11] Erotica was not documentary, therefore, and this also applies to sexualized locations, or the places where erotic encounters were imagined to occur. These locations appeared partly because they were particularly convenient for this activity, but the choice of locations in erotica was much narrower than convenience allowed, and this suggests that cultural factors – relating to the intellectual and emotional associations of a location – exerted considerable force. I hope to access some of the associations underpinning fancy by asking what it was about these locations that made them suitable for scenes of sex. What characteristics were considered essential attributes of sexualized locations in eighteenth-century erotica?

Generic conventions and cultural themes

The content of erotica was determined partly by the powerful generic conventions under which erotic authors laboured. For example, writing on sex had long been used as a tool of political and religious critique, often taken as an index of its Enlightened quality. French pornographic novels of the seventeenth and eighteenth centuries, available to the English market in translation soon after original publication, frequently placed sex within the context of Catholic worship,[12] while in Spain anti-clerical literature demonstrated vividly the risks posed to female penitents by confessors.[13] In England too, engravings revealed the pious to be forever preying on beautiful worshippers or engaging in sex with one another.[14] Many of the sexualized locations in erotica clearly reflected this established satiric role. Eager confessors were depicted probing young, innocent women for their sexual history, and seducing their vulnerable penitents within the secure confines of the closed confessional.[15] In placing sexual

---

[11] In Nathaniel Bailey, *A Universal Etymological English Dictionary* (London: E. Bell, 1721), the entry for 'Fantasy' begins 'Fancy, Imagination', and the entry for 'Fancy' reads simply 'Imagination'. Similarly, in Benjamin Martin, *Lingua Britannica Reformata: or, a New English Dictionary* (London: 1749), the entry for 'Fantasy' reads 'See *Fancy*'. This entry includes 'a faculty of the soul', 'notion, or conception' and 'foolish conceit, or illusion'. The second entry for 'To Fancy' reads 'to imagine, or conceive'. Johnson's *Dictionary* defines 'Fantasy' as 'Fancy; imagination; the power of imagining'.

[12] Darnton, *Corpus of Clandestine Literature*; Darnton, *Forbidden Best-Sellers*; Wagner, *Eros Revived*, pp. 45–86; Peter Wagner, 'Anticatholic Erotica in Eighteenth-Century England', in Wagner (ed.), *Erotica and the Enlightenment*, pp. 166–209.

[13] Stephen Haliczer, *Sexuality in the Confessional: A Sacrament Profaned* (Oxford: Oxford University Press, 1996).

[14] See, for example, the Bowles and Carver series of prints dating from c. 1760 in the British Museum, BM. Sat. 3775–7, 3780–1.

[15] 'Work for a Cooper', pp. 409–14, and 'The Mad Dog', pp. 439–40, both in *Festival of Love*; *Genuine Memoirs of . . . Miss Maria Brown*, vol. I, p. 43.

encounters in confessionals, monasteries and churches, erotic authors drew on a well-established tradition of associating the religious with the sexual.

Other common locations were shaped less by the specifics of erotic convention and Enlightened critique, and more by long-standing cultural tropes. A fine example of this is the pastoral. There was a vibrant pastoral tradition in the arts, exemplified by the penchant for the pastoral costume of shepherds and shepherdesses among eighteenth-century men and women of fashion.[16] Moreover, these places have an ancient association with erotic Elysium and sexual liberty: Venus and Priapus were garden deities and gods of fertility and love.[17] The impact of such classical precedents in eighteenth-century Augustan England was considerable. Lush, outdoor, rural settings and calm, tranquil spots were common locations in erotica. Lovers revelled on gentle rolling fields, village greens and grassy banks. The search for a lost Arcadia – which so many of the depictions of rural scenes seemed to represent – was a search for a place in which the inexorable passage of time was halted and the promise of perpetual youth fulfilled. The ravages of time on human bodies were vividly portrayed and frequently lamented. Life is a 'transient season' soon blighted by the 'frozen sway' of age, and the passage of time is a reason for both men and women to take many lovers while young.[18] Indeed, the sacred, unthreatening and idyllic rural locations in erotica produce a particular kind of fresh sexuality: a 'rural fair' and 'rosy nymphs'.[19] Women from 'the Country' are shameless but innocent: the narrator of *A Spy on Mother Midnight* (1748) is surprised to find a dildo in the luggage of one woman, because she is 'so young a Creature, so compleat a Prude, and a Country Girl too'.[20]

Such visions of country girls are found in eighteenth-century pastoral art and literature. Carson Bergstrom has argued that pastoral representations celebrate a polymorphous sexuality which downplays gender difference and gender hierarchy, depicting a range of sexual practices, de-emphasizing vaginal

---

[16] Anne Buck, *Dress in Eighteenth-Century England* (London: Batsford, 1979), pp. 39–40.

[17] Charles Barber, 'Reading the Garden in Byzantium: Nature and Sexuality', *Byzantine and Modern Greek Studies* 16 (1992), pp. 1–19; A. R. Littlewood, 'Romantic Paradises: The Role of the Garden in the Byzantine Romance', *Byzantine and Modern Greek Studies* 5 (1979), pp. 95–114; Michael Niedermeier, '"Strolling under Palm Trees": Gardens – Love – Sexuality', *Journal of Garden History* 17 (1997), pp. 186–207. On Priapus, see Eugene Michael O'Connor, *Symbolum Salacitatis: A Study of the God Priapus as a Literary Character* (Frankfurt: Peter Lang, 1989), pp. 16–25, and H. David Brumble, *Classical Myths and Legends in the Middle Ages and Renaissance: A Dictionary of Allegorical Meanings* (London: Fitzroy Dearborn, 1998), p. 278. On Venus, see Brumble, *Classical Myths*, pp. 337–42, and Pierre Grimal, *Dictionary of Classical Mythology*, trans. A. R. Maxwell-Hyslop (Oxford: Blackwell, 1986), p. 464–5.

[18] 'To Cynthia', in *Festival of Love*, p. 17; 'Miss and the Parson', in *Forty Select Poems*, p. 119; 'The Tooth-Drawer', in *Forty Select Poems*, p. 148.

[19] 'Strephon and Blowsalind. Or the Amorous Squire', p. 28; 'The Girdle of Venus Unbuckled', p. 30, both in *Festival of Love*.

[20] *Spy on Mother Midnight*, p. 32.

penetration and orgasm, and stressing the youth and childlikeness of characters.[21] The painted pastorals of the French artist Boucher (1703–70) depict a
gender ambiguity or androgyny that eroticizes the bodies of both sexes, while
English pastoral poetry is infused with an atmosphere of egalitarian liberty from
which violence is banished and in which sex becomes 'harmless pleasure'.[22] We
can over-emphasize this gender equality, however. According to Bergstrom, the
exemplary evocation of pastoral innocence and equality is Milton's *Paradise
Lost* (1667). Yet the happy innocence of Adam and Eve is fashioned through a
gendered relationship of submission and dominance: Adam's features 'declared
/ Absolute rule', Eve's implied 'Subjection', and the 'sweet reluctant amorous
delay' of the meeting is forged by her modest composure.[23] Implicit violence
is integral to Milton's vision, and any appearance of gender equality disguises
a stark gender hierarchy.

Yet for erotic writers the apparent innocence of the pastoral was important.
This is clearest in the satire *The Fruit-Shop* (1765). Milton's vision is used
to conjure a pastoral landscape by the erotic author, who then engages in a
careful process of selection. The premise of *The Fruit-Shop* is that the realm
of sexual intercourse and bodies is the garden of Eden, and the author lifts
several lines from Book IV of *Paradise Lost* to furnish his description. At two
points the author makes cuts, removing 'And of pure now purer air / Meets
his approach', and 'able to drive / All sadness but despair'.[24] These omissions
transform Paradise in important ways. It is not the reference to odour or to
favourable aspects of Eden in the first extract that the author of *The Fruit-
Shop* wants to excise; he does not omit later references to fine perfume or
attractive features. Rather, it is the reference to purity, suggesting spotless states
of sinlessness, that is inappropriate to the erotic garden. The second extract,
which refers to despair, inserts the only displeasing element into this part of
Milton's description; it suggests that pleasure has limits and that unpalatable
emotions can disrupt Eden. Erotic authors sought locations 'free from shame
and sense':[25] erasing these lines renders Eden a place solely of pleasure, though
not necessarily a morally pure pleasure.

The pastoral in erotica signified an imaginary flight from urban immoral-
ity. Early-modern anxieties about venality, lust and luxury in the city contrast

[21] Carson Bergstrom, 'Purney, Pastoral and the Polymorphous Perverse', *British Journal for Eighteenth-Century Studies* 17 (1994), pp. 149–63. Bergstrom's 'polymorphous sexuality' derives from Freud's 'polymorphous perverse', a term Freud used to refer to a period of child-hood in which sexuality is not organized around genitals or gender.
[22] Melissa Hyde, 'Confounding Conventions: Gender Ambiguity and François Boucher's Painted Pastorals', *Eighteenth-Century Studies* 30 (1996), pp. 41, 44; Bergstrom, 'Purney, Pastoral', p. 151.
[23] John Milton, *Paradise Lost*, Book IV, lines 300–1, 308, 311. In *Milton: Poetical Works*, ed. Douglas Bush (1966; Oxford: Oxford University Press, 1992), p. 282.
[24] Milton, *Paradise Lost*, in *Milton: Poetical Works*, p. 278, lines 153–4 and 155–6.
[25] *Seventeen Hundred and Seventy-Seven*, p. 13.

Rural-urban tension *(handwritten annotation)*

with the more favourable appreciation of cities that emerged during the mid-nineteenth century.[26] Writers in eighteenth-century England certainly felt that it was the Country which promised relief from 'the noxious Ills of Life'.[27] In French erotica, pastoral settings served as refuges from urban corruption. Amy Wyngaard has demonstrated that the work of Rétif de la Bretonne was a response to fears about corruption in burgeoning Paris, idealizing a rural world in which a lack of private space facilitated the community surveillance which prevented moral decline.[28] Against the anonymity of the metropolis, the rural was championed for its openness. However, as I will discuss below, the pastoral locations in English erotica displayed none of the openness observable in de la Bretonne. Indeed, the same developments could clearly produce very different responses. Orest Ranum has delineated the private spaces which in the early-modern period were cherished as 'refuges of intimacy' – often erotic intimacy – as part of a modernization process common to Western Europe.[29] The enclosed pastoral locations in English erotica bear much resemblance to those discussed by Ranum, as do many other English sexualized locations. Thus the appearance of the pastoral in the English material cannot be explained simply by the location (outdoors and non-urban). Indeed, the most common locations for sex in erotica are united not by their pastoral or religious features, but by a number of specific qualities which cut across urban/rural distinctions.

In examining the sexualized locations in erotica I will focus on spatial qualities, such as the nature of the light or texture of a place.[30] This approach makes it clear that gender was integral to the choices of location in erotica. Wyngaard and Ranum focus on specific places and the uses to which they are put, but do not attempt a gendered approach to those spaces. This is a striking omission: all the spaces in Ranum's discussion except the study (the walled garden, chamber, ruelle and alcove) are predominantly associated with women, whereas

---

[26] Stena Nenadic, 'English Towns in the Creative Imagination', in Waller (ed.), *English Urban Landscape*, pp. 316–41.

[27] *On Rural Felicity; in an Epistle to a Friend* (by J. Wilford, behind the Chapter-House, in St Paul's-church Yard, 1733), p. 6. The frontispiece to this poem is itself mildly risqué: it shows a man reclining while holding a musical instrument, with a woman seated between his knees exposing much of her breasts. On the rural as escape, see also Terry Castle, *Masquerade and Civilization: The Carnivalesque in Eighteenth-Century English Culture and Fiction* (London: Methuen, 1986), p. 18.

[28] Amy Wyngaard, 'Libertine Spaces: Anonymous Crowds, Secret Chambers, and Urban Corruption in Rétif de la Bretonne', *Eighteenth-Century Life* 22 (1998), pp. 104–22. On the pastoral and French erotica more generally, see Stewart, *Engraven Desire*, p. 237.

[29] Orest Ranum, 'The Refuges of Intimacy', in Roger Chartier (ed.), *A History of Private Life. Vol. III: Passions of the Renaissance*, trans. Arthur Goldhammer (Cambridge, Mass.: The Belknap Press of Harvard University Press, 1989), pp. 207–31.

[30] My approach in this quest is indebted to Henri Lefebvre's concept of spatial codes: the elements which determined the construction of a space, rather than the way it was interpreted. See Henri Lefebvre, *The Production of Space*, trans. Donald Nicholson-Smith (1974; Oxford: Blackwell, 1991), pp. 7, 17.

Wyngaard explores 'libertine spaces', a phrase suggestive of particularly masculine sexual exploits.[31] My argument is, by contrast, that understandings of
gender and the act of sex are key to the choice of sexualized locations in erotica
and to how such spaces were presented. The established social functions of
erotica and powerful cultural themes helped to shape the locations in which sex
was imagined to have occurred. Only by using gender as an analytical category
can we understand these locations and what they said about sex, bodies and
sexuality.

Shady enclosure

In the 'racy and titillating' work of the Frenchman Rétif de la Bretonne,
pastoral locations and village communities were set against the enclosed,
secluded spaces of Paris, where seduction, licentiousness and corruption
could thrive.[32] In English erotica, interiors display similar shady enclosure.
The newly-wed husband in one poem calls on 'Time' to 'haste the coming
night', and begins the sexual encounter only as 'the GOD of NIGHT draws
near'.[33] Indeed, while erotica performed an important role as religious satire,
shadiness was one of the enduring characteristics of these religious locations.
The congregation in *The Fruit-Shop* (1765) convene in an underground
chapel and embark on sex when the candles are extinguished, and the group
'disengage from their tender embraces' when the lights are re-lit. This
darkness prevents the narrator from doing more than obliquely alluding to
'the many pleasing incidents' which occurred, of course.[34] A wide range
of such devices were available to an author who wished to be suggestive
rather than explicit. Nevertheless, a recurring feature of indoor sexualized
locations is shade. Lovers are surrounded by 'a conscious Shade' provided
by fallen curtains at the moment they embrace, or sequestered in the shady
'recess' provided by a bed.[35] Though subject to different representational
techniques (complete darkness would have made for rather uninteresting
images), visual depictions display comparable elements. The women in
'The Peeper' (Illustration 14) were apparently without much light before they
were interrupted, while the light which floods into Araminta's room as Timante
opens the door suggests she had just been in darkness. (Illustration 15.) The
only light in 'The Three Gracelesses' seems to emanate from the man's
cello, but presumably originates from a fireplace to the left. (Illustration 16.)

[31] Brian Cowan, 'Reasonable Ecstasies: Shaftesbury and the Languages of Libertinism', *Journal
of British Studies* 37 (1998), pp. 111–38; Trumbach, 'Erotic Fantasy and Male Libertinism',
pp. 253–82.
[32] Wyngaard, 'Libertine Spaces', pp. 118, 113.   [33] 'The Marriage Morn', in *Hilaria*, p. 8.
[34] *Fruit-Shop*, vol. II, pp. 124, 130.
[35] 'Damon and Amoret', in *Consummation*, p. 24; 'Royal Assignation', in *Festival of Love*,
pp. 166–7.

The Peeper, or a stolen View of Lady C—'s Premises.

Illustration 14: *The Peeper, or a stolen View of Lady C's Premises.*
Inserted in *A Voyage to Lethe* (1741) BL: Cup.1001.c.4.

Illustration 15: Timante enters Araminta's bed-chamber. Frontispiece to *The Surprize* (1739).

Illustration 16:   *The Three Gracelesses*. Inserted in *A Voyage to Lethe*
(1741) BL: Cup.1001.c.4.

156   Reading Sex in the Eighteenth Century

Similarly, though quite distinct from de la Bretonne's open rural communities, the pastoral settings in English erotica place lovers beneath the shelter of a 'flow'ry lime' or near the 'purling brooks and shady groves' of a 'rural seat resort'.[36] Even the more formal gardens of France offer up suitable places, such as the labyrinth at Versailles.[37] Couples enjoy assignations surrounded by thick foliage 'in the willow's shade' 'beneath a weeping willow's shade' and 'beneath a shady tree'.[38] Indeed, readers are explicitly counselled to be 'secret lovers', and to seek out 'thick-embowering shades' when 'high-wrought rapture calls'.[39] As the repeated references to trees suggest, the enclosed outdoor space of a shaded sexualized location was most commonly provided by a grove.[40] The association of these shady locations with sexual activity was unmistakable. The 'sacred Grove' to which men and women go to consummate their desires in *A Description of the Temple of Venus* (1726) is distinguished from other parts of the landscape by the oaks which repel daylight.[41] Lovers seek out a 'solitary Grove' or long to be transported to a 'NAT'RAL-ARTIFICIAL grove' in order to enjoy each other.[42] Such locations are imagined to have a powerful effect on individuals. One female narrator entreats a man to 'do the feat' after spying him 'in a Grove': it was the 'time and place' which had aroused her, she explained.[43] The mere appearance of a grove through a window is considered a 'great Emolument to Love'.[44] Given such associations, it is not surprising that one narrator stumbles upon a man and woman on top of a haystack while in search of a shady grove, or that one young woman is depicted waiting hopefully in 'Venus' Grove', willing her lover to join her.[45] Furnishing 'secret shade', 'the close covert of a grove' was an ideal location for a tryst: it was 'By Nature form'd for scenes of Love'.[46]

If such locations were considered particularly suitable places for lovers' assignations, they were also seen as ideal metaphors for female bodies: women's bodies were moulded into secluded and shady places. In Swift's poem *The Lady's Dressing-Room* (1732), such bodies inspire disgust. At the centre of a

[36] 'The Adventure', in *Forty Select Poems*, p. 171; 'Mutual Love', p. 5; 'The Squire', p. 194; and 'The Return from Windsor Fair', p. 421. All in *Festival of Love*.
[37] *Genuine Memoirs of . . . Miss Maria Brown*, vol. I, p. 171.
[38] 'Mutual Love', p. 3; 'Roger and Molly', p. 148, both in *Festival of Love*; 'The Presumptuous Sinner', in *Bacchanalian Magazine*, p. 82.
[39] 'The Oeconomy of Love', in *Pleasures that Please on Reflection*, p. 20.
[40] Eighteenth-century definitions of 'grove' included 'a little wood', in Benjamin Martin, *Lingua Britannica Reformata; or, a New English Dictionary* (London, 1749); 'a little Wood: also a kind of mine', in Bailey, *Universal Etymological English Dictionary*; 'a walk covered by trees meeting above', in Johnson, *Dictionary*.
[41] *Description of the Temple of Venus*, p. 5.   [42] *Seventeen Hundred and Seventy-Seven*, p. 13.
[43] *Fifteen Plagues of a Maiden-Head*, p. 4.   [44] *Chinese Tale*, p. 17.
[45] 'Mutual Love', in *Bacchanalian Magazine*, p. 11; 'The Maid's Prayer', in [John Wilkes], *An Essay on Woman* (Aberdeen: Printed for James Hay, and sold by all the booksellers in town and country, 1788), p. 24.
[46] *Consummation*, p. 6; 'The Geranium', in *Pleasures that Please on Reflection*, p. 35.

scene of grimy filth is a chest into which the narrator tentatively reaches his hand. Likened to Pandora's box, the chest holds even greater ordure, and those terrible '*Secrets of the hoary Deep!*'.[47] Though sometimes prompting awe and fear, such depictions of female bodies were also sources of desire and pleasure in erotica. For the author of *The Secret History of Pandora's Box* (1742) Homer's 'cave of the nymphs' is the perfect allegory for 'the parts of the female sex'.[48] As a 'delicious enclosure' lying 'obscurely in a Cliff' with 'still some caves Incognita', or as an 'intricate and darksome Way', female genitalia resemble those places deemed suitable for erotic encounters.[49] In descriptions of female genitalia as a 'little snug retreat' set within 'a shady grove', or 'shaded soft' by 'a mossy grove', we can see the unmistakable echoes of sexualized locations.[50] Such are the associations of women's bodies and shady enclosure that the two entities literally melded into one. The 'dark recesses' and 'shady coverts' in one poem are indistinguishable as either women's bodies or locations.[51]

Women's genitalia are presented as grotto-like, as exemplified by the poem *Little Merlin's Cave* (1737).[52] This was a reprint of the poem *A Riddle: of a Paradoxical Character of an Hairy Monster* (c. 1725), which now contained a new introduction likening the female body to an actual grotto which had been constructed in the intervening period. This real Merlin's Cave was built by William Kent in 1735, in the royal garden of Queen Caroline. No longer surviving, it was apparently 'a veritable hybrid', combining grotesque rock work, six wax figures and various Gothic details, all set within a classical framework.[53] The interior depicted in Kent's original design bears little resemblance either to the description of the cave in the erotic poem, or to the image produced with the later edition of this poem.[54] But the exterior view of Merlin's Cave would have

---

[47] D—n S____t [Jonathan Swift], *The Lady's Dressing Room. A Poem*, 3rd edn. (Dublin, 1732), pp. 4, 5, 6. Swift's vivid evocation of this woman's space prompted a response from 'Miss W' – *The Gentleman's Study* – published in the same year. Miss W similarly drew an association between the nature of the space and the nature of the person to whom it belonged. See Miss W., 'The Gentleman's Study', in Roger Lonsdale (eds.), *Eighteenth-Century Women Poets* (Oxford: Oxford University Press, 1990), pp. 130, 134.

[48] *Secret History of Pandora's Box*, pp. 41, 44.

[49] *Fruit-Shop*, vol. 1, p. 22; *Little Merlin's Cave*, pp. 5, 6; *Chinese Tale*, p. 24.

[50] 'A Riddle', in *Festival of Love*, p. 149; 'Birth of the Rose', in *Pleasures that Please on Reflection*, p. 40.

[51] 'The Bridal Night', in *Pleasures that Please on Reflection*, p. 47.

[52] *Little Merlin's Cave*, esp. p. 3. In Martin, *Lingua Britannica Reformata*, grot or grotto means 'a vault, or cave'. In Bailey, *Universal Etymological English Dictionary*, grot or grotto is 'a cave or den'. In Johnson, *Dictionary*, grotto is defined as 'a cavern or cave made for coolness'.

[53] Naomi Miller, *Heavenly Caves: Reflections on the Garden Grotto* (London: Allen and Unwin, 1982), p. 84. Barbara Jones also mentions a 'Merlin's Cave'. See her *Follies and Grottoes*, 2nd edn. (1953; London: Constable, 1974), p. 150. This was probably one of the many imitations of the Merlin's Cave at Richmond. Another was in the garden at Merlin's Cave tavern, situated in the fields north of Clerkenwell. See Warwick Wroth, *The London Pleasure Gardens of the Eighteenth Century* (London: Macmillan, 1896), pp. 54–5.

[54] Plate 32, *The Designs of Mr. Inigo Jones and Mr. Wm. Kent* (London: John Vardy, 1744).

greeted the viewer with a concealed and darkened entrance, and it was this – and the shaded interior it suggested – which seemed irresistible to the eighteenth-century erotic imagination. Such associations gave erotic authors a rich source of suggestion and allusion. Contemporary readers of one eighteenth-century erotic poem could delight in the frisson of double meaning when the bathing Seymora reveals her wish to her lover, 'In my fair Fount you'd ever lye; / I'd cool you in my Grot'.[55]

As the image of the grotto indicates, eighteenth-century erotic authors were interested in cavernous depressions. This was in contrast to women's amorous writings of the seventeenth century in which landscapes served as relief maps and focused on altitude,[56] but it echoed an interest in depth which emerged in eighteenth-century writings on landscape and gardens.[57] There is some suggestion here of a theme which infuses much writing on gender and space: the masculine gaze which scans, maps and fixes a feminine object in an expression of power. However, as the discussion of indoor locations suggested, sexualized locations were not always landscapes to be mapped. Crucial scenes of erotic intimacy take place in carriages, for example. *The Rake of Taste* (1760) opens with a tryst in the '*Bath* machine', while the male narrator of *A Spy on Mother Midnight* 'scrap'd an Intimacy' with a woman in a stage.[58] Coaches are shady enclosures but are neither indoor nor outdoor. In the English material, distinctions of indoor/outdoor and urban/rural are displaced by the more important spatial quality of shady enclosure. Such encounters render the masculine experience less a visual and more a multi-sensual encounter. A man does not employ a mapping, unveiling, controlling, phallocentric gaze at these moments: he engages in total body submersion.

Threatened disclosure

As intimations to secrecy suggest, the shady enclosures of erotica give the impression of disguise and privacy. Rooms are conspicuously locked before any activity begins. 'Let's shut the Door, . . . and lock it', declares one female character before embarking on an encounter, while a man follows his lover into

---

[55] *Whim*, p. 11.
[56] James F. Gaines and Josephine A. Roberts, 'The Geography of Love in Seventeenth-Century Women's Fiction', in James Turner (ed.), *Sexuality and Gender in Early Modern Europe: Institutions, Texts, Images* (Cambridge: Cambridge University Press, 1993), pp. 290–3.
[57] Malcolm Andrews, *The Search for the Picturesque: Landscape Aesthetics and Tourism in Britain, 1760–1800* (Aldershot: Scolar Press, 1989), p. 61; John Dixon Hunt, *The Figure in the Landscape: Poetry, Painting, and Gardening during the Eighteenth Century* (Baltimore: Johns Hopkins University Press, 1976), pp. 228, 247. Also see chapter six for the medical and erotic aspects of this depth.
[58] *Rake of Taste*, p. 1; *Spy on Mother Midnight*, p. 9.

a chamber, from which he 'dismiss'd the Maid, and lock'd the Door, resolving to have no Interruption'.[59] When inside these closed rooms the activity of characters is often obscured by strategically placed items such as the screen. One young couple find refuge from the woman's mother by retiring behind 'a *large screen*', and another woman has sex with her lover behind a screen while her husband dozes on the adjacent sofa.[60] Yet this privacy is an illusion. Screens were fragile items, providing some coverage but not removing the frisson of risk. In this last example – a skit on criminal conversation and divorce cases – the maid witnesses the entire affair and subsequently reports it in court.[61] The thrill of movement between concealment and disclosure is an important characteristic of the erotic, and the threat (or promise) of disclosure is almost always present in this material.[62]

Many visual images include suggestions of observation. The portrait of the man on the wall in the frontispiece to *Kick Him Jenny* (1737) serves as a reminder that the couple are being watched through the keyhole. (Illustration 26.) The faces on the wall behind 'The Three Gracelesses' reinforce the obvious voyeurism of the two men. (Illustration 16.) Other faces intimate narrow escapes. In the curious scene depicted in Illustration 17, a smiling face – perhaps belonging to the lover of the woman whose husband has just entered the room – pokes out from beneath the woman's skirts. Interior scenes gave ample opportunity for furtive observation or sudden interruption. The apparently banal inclusion of doors in the visual images can be understood in this context. The couple from *Kick Him Jenny* in Illustration 26, the couple by the fire in Illustration 18 and the lovers in the two sofa scenes in Illustrations 19 and 20 and all have doors conspicuously placed behind them. Wyngaard comments that the sense of secrecy in the urban interior scenes in de la Bretonne was enhanced by the lack of doors or windows (despite the presence of doors in all four of the images she reproduces from his work).[63] Doors were important because, as in the scene from *The Surprize* (1739) (Illustration 15) and the engraving 'The

[59] *Kick Him Jenny*, p. 17; *Spy on Mother Midnight*, p. 31.
[60] Timothy Touchit [pseud.], *La Souricière. The Mouse-Trap. A Facetious and Sentimental Excursion through Part of Austrian Flanders and France. Being a Divertisement for Both Sexes* (London: For J. Parsons, Paternoster-Row, 1794), vol. I, p. 35; 'The Inseparable Pair', in *Festival of Love*, p. 311.
[61] Servants often spied on their masters and mistresses and gave evidence in actual legal divorce cases. See Lawrence Stone, *Road to Divorce: England, 1530–1987* (Oxford: Oxford University Press, 1990), pp. 220–30, 259.
[62] See, for example, Roland Barthes, *The Pleasure of the Text* (1973; Oxford: Blackwell, 1990), p. 9; David Freeberg, *The Power of Images: Studies in the History and Theory of Response* (Chicago: University of Chicago Press, 1989), p. 355; Mario Perniola, 'Between Clothing and Nudity', in M. Feher (ed.), *Fragments for a History of the Human Body: Part Two* (New York: Zone, 1989), p. 237.
[63] See Wyngaard, 'Libertine Spaces', p. 109.

Illustration 17:   Woman and child in suggestive scene. Inserted in *A Voyage to Lethe* (1741) BL: Cup.1001.c.4.

Illustration 18:   Armchair scene by the fire. Inserted in *A Voyage to Lethe* (1741) BL: Cup.1001.c.4.

Dog' (Illustration 2), they allow people to enter at crucial moments. Other architectural features served similar purposes. Superfluous drapes served to enhance 'the element of theatre' in eighteenth-century painting,[64] but in erotic images they imply disclosure. The drapery in the foreground of the two sofa scenes inserted in *A Voyage to Lethe* (1741) appears as if it has just been lifted to reveal the scene, or as if it might tumble down at any moment to obscure any future activity. (Illustrations 19 and 20.) Illustration 14 combined doors and drapes, but to no avail: their bodies obscured by the folds of heavy fabric, the two women are nonetheless seen by the man appearing through the door.

The full title of this engraving – 'The Peeper; Or a Stolen View of Lady C's Premises' – puns on the powerful association between women's bodies and architectural spaces. In linking architecture and bodies, erotic authors drew on a tradition in which the proportions of the classical orders of architecture were based on ideal-type human bodies, a tradition which experienced considerable popularity in the eighteenth century.[65] Rooted in scholarship fascinated by the ancient world, eighteenth-century building design revealed a strongly symbolic vision of the relationship between architecture and bodies. Echoing ancient culture, architects incorporated symbols of generation and fertility into their work, including both male and female reproductive organs. This 'sexual-symbolic thesis' was expressed in designs such as Sir John Soane's phallic design for a national monument.[66] In erotica, however, male bodies were not depicted as architectural constructions; it was women who were portrayed in this way. Imagined as rooms, women's bodies are reminiscent of the places where assignations are imagined to occur: a 'cell of Love' which echoed the confessional or nun's cell, for example.[67] Moreover, these spaces comprise conspicuous obstructive features which create a sense of disclosure. In *A Voyage to Lethe*, 'the Pillars of *Diana*' or thighs form 'the Entrance into the Gulf of Venus', while men in *The Whim!* (1782) have to negotiate the woman's 'snow-white thighs, That guard her Cyprian goal'.[68] If women present boundaries, then men have

---

[64] Charles Saumerez Smith, *Eighteenth-Century Decoration: Design and the Domestic Interior in England* (London: Weidenfeld and Nicolson, 1993), p. 170.

[65] Joseph Rykwert, *The Dancing Column: On Order in Architecture* (Cambridge, Mass.: MIT Press, 1996); Richard Varey, *Space and the Eighteenth-Century English Novel* (Cambridge: Cambridge University Press, 1990), p. 172; Borsay, 'Early Modern Urban Landscapes', p. 102. See also Philippa Tristram, *Living Space in Fact and Fiction* (London: Routledge, 1989), p. 259.

[66] Ponte, 'Architecture and Phallocentrism', pp. 274, 298. Ponte gives no source for the image of Soane's design which is reproduced on p. 300. It appears to be the design of 1816 for an unexecuted monument to commemorate Waterloo and Trafalgar. This is briefly mentioned in Dorothy Stroud's *The Architecture of Sir John Soane* (London: Studio, 1961), p. 165.

[67] 'Birth of the Rose', in *Pleasures that Please on Reflection*, p. 40. See also 'The Amours of the Gods', in Morris, *Festival of Anacreon*, p. 35.

[68] *Voyage to Lethe* (1741), p. 27; *Whim*, p. 5.

Illustration 19:   Sofa scene I. Inserted in *A Voyage to Lethe* (1741) BL:
Cup.1001.c.4.

Illustration 20:   Sofa scene II. Inserted in *A Voyage to Lethe* (1741) BL: Cup.1001.c.4.

to pass through those boundaries.[69] In pornography of the seventeenth and eighteenth centuries, sexual activities are described in similar terms, though comparatively devoid of allusion. A woman might be depicted being 'breached by this great weapon', as the man pushes through 'the defences', and his penis 'ploughs through all the obstacles in the cunny of a young virgin'.[70] In erotica, the violence is generally more implicit. As a man enters Merryland, he faces 'two Forts called LBA [labia] between which every one must necessarily pass'. 'The Fortifications are not very strong', the narrator explains, 'tho' they have *Curtains, Horn-works*, and *Ramparts*'. However, 'a little farther up the Country are two other Fortresses, called NMPH [nymphae]', and these, he cautions, 'have sometimes made a stout Resistance, against strong Attacks and skilful Engineers'.[71] Ultimately, though, these safeguards never prevented sex from taking place. Akin to the rooms in which sexual encounters took place, women's bodies might be 'shut and barricaded' by a 'door of bliss'.[72] But just as the locations promise the opportunity of disclosure, so the obstacles to women's bodies which male lovers have to negotiate are not insurmountable.

Such depictions were not thinly veiled allusions to intact hymens and women's virginity. While some references certainly allude to anatomy, these spatial metaphors were not simply mimetic representations of bodies. In early-modern legal narratives of rape, images of locked doors emphasized female vulnerability and the violation of women's boundaries.[73] In erotic writing, the apparent obstructions to feminine spaces convey the moral quality of modesty: an impediment which increased women's attractiveness and heightened men's desires. Modesty was an 'erotic double agent' deemed crucial to the continuation of heterosexual relationships in the eighteenth and nineteenth centuries; it could never be eradicated but was repeatedly rebuilt.[74] As enclosed spaces with permanent but ineffective barriers, female spaces allowed this process to be perpetually re-enacted in sexual encounters. Rather than interpreting grottoes and locked rooms simply as female genitalia, these spatial metaphors should

[69] Courtship advice to early-modern bachelors was couched in terms of warfare and attack. See David Cressy, *Birth, Marriage and Death: Ritual, Religion, and the Life-Cycle in Tudor and Stuart England* (1997; Oxford: Oxford University Press, 1999), p. 235.
[70] *School of Venus*, pp. 115, 116, 166.   [71] *New Description of Merryland*, pp. 15–16.
[72] 'The Oeconomy of Love', in *Pleasures that Please on Reflection*, p. 15. This characterization of rooms echoed the integration of the sexual and the spatial in eighteenth-century fiction. Samuel Richardson, for example, used the invasion of such spaces to represent the imminent invasion of women's bodies in both *Pamela* (1740–1) and *Clarissa* (1747–8). As one author has put it, 'For Richardson, the house or the room are virtually interchangeable with the body'. Tristram, *Living Space in Fact and Fiction*, pp. 239, 259.
[73] Garthine Walker, 'Rereading Rape and Sexual Violence in Early Modern England', *Gender and History* 10 (1998), p. 15.
[74] Ruth Bernard Yeazell, *Fictions of Modesty: Women and Courtship in the English Novel* (Chicago: University of Chicago Press, 1991), p. 22. See chapter seven for a more detailed discussion of modesty in erotica.

be seen as integrating the moral and the physical. Threatened disclosure in feminine spaces rendered feminine modesty concrete.

Soft opulence

Topographically and architecturally there was much convergence between sexualized locations and depictions of female bodies, yet both spaces and bodies have surfaces as well as structures. The concretization of moral qualities in the gendered spaces of erotica also emerged in the association between the textures of female bodies and sexualized locations. The interiors in which encounters occurred are sparsely furnished, in line with the fashionable eighteenth-century style, but opulent in materials. Beds naturally appear in the bed-chambers which were popular locations for sexual encounters in this genre, for instance the half-tester in the frontispiece to *Kick Him Jenny* (Illustration 26) and the luxurious bed in the frontispiece to *The Surprize* (Illustration 15). In written depictions, these lavishly furnished rooms feature extravagant beds with painted ceilings or beds secreted behind a curtain of 'the richest Genoa-velvet'.[75] Placed under generous canopies and in alcoves, a bed was transformed into a 'sweet Enclosure'.[76]

Such furnishings produced soft and velvety settings, and these are crucial attributes of the act of sex itself. A 'soft obscure retreat' is the perfect place in which to pursue 'soft deeds'.[77] Erotic encounters are themselves 'soft amusements'.[78] Significantly, softness was a gendered concept in the eighteenth century. Comments that bodies could be '*softened and enfeebled*' or that luxury threatened to 'soften and weaken both Men and Nations' illustrate that softness is used to indicate effeminacy.[79] Luxury affected the body, mind and soul, and softness implied emotional and moral as well as physical weakness. While a degree of receptive softness is not excluded from the bevy of admirable male characteristics, softness contrasts with the hard vigour deemed pre-eminently masculine. Indeed, erotica described women as 'the yielding soft and genial sex'.[80] The softness of erotic encounters is reflected in the spaces of female bodies which are 'soft within'.[81] Lined with sleek 'Red Sattin', luxurious 'Crimson Velvet, soft as th' Ermin's skin', or the sumptuous 'swan's soft plumage, and the ermine's down', these inviting spaces are much like the lush furnishings of bed-chambers.[82] Indeed, female bodies and sexualized locations offer the

---

[75] *Fruit-Shop*, vol. II, pp. 68–70; *Did You Ever See Such Damned Stuff?*, p. 91.

[76] *Description of the Temple of Venus*, p. 10.

[77] 'The Oeconomy of Love', in *Pleasures that Please on Reflection*, p. 20.

[78] *Seventeen Hundred and Seventy-Seven*, p. 13.

[79] *Of Luxury*, p. 25; *A Letter on the Nature and State of Curiosity* (London: J. Roberts, 1736), p. 6. See chapter one for a discussion of luxury and masculinity.

[80] *Fruit-Shop*, vol. II, p. 134.   [81] *Little Merlin's Cave*, p. 8.

[82] 'The Judgment Reversed, or Chloe Triumphant', in *Festival of Love*, p. 142; *Little Merlin's Cave*, p. 3; *A Riddle: Of a Paradoxical Character of an Hairy Monster*, p. 6.

very same tactile sensations; both display a softness which was regarded as a characteristic of sexual intercourse. The act of sex, sexualized locations and female spaces are thus conflated.

Repositories of pleasure

Women's bodies and the sexualized locations in erotica shared some key qualities: they were soft, shady enclosures which threatened disclosure. These powerful associations were further reinforced because the rooms in which sexual activity occurred would typically belong to the women involved. For example, the scenes of sex depicted in Illustrations 3 and 21 are situated in a woman's kitchen and laundry respectively. Narratives of entering a woman's room, particularly her bed-chamber, thus become narratives of heterosexual sex. In the poem 'Miss in her Teens', the recent sexual maturity of the thirteen-year-old Molly has provoked concern over the long-standing interest her fourteen-year-old cousin Dick displays in her. Fearing that a girl's room 'was a dang'rous place / For stratagem and ambuscade', Molly's mother keeps the key to her daughter's room hidden, forcing Dick to spy on Molly through the keyhole. He eventually manages to snatch the key, and when Molly next enters the room her efforts to bolt the door and obscure the keyhole are futile: he immediately flies out of his hiding place and the couple spend 'a pleasant afternoon' together.[83] Dick's cunning gained him entry to Molly's room, thus ensuring access to her body.

As Dick's furtive entry into Molly's room suggests, men are rarely invited into women's rooms by their owners. A range of techniques – disguise, connivance, force – are employed by men in order to gain access, and women ultimately exercise little control over who enters their rooms. For example, the man in *A Spy on Mother Midnight* cross-dresses to gain entry to his lover's room, in which they then have sex.[84] Just as men sometimes gain entry to women's spaces surreptitiously or by force, so the sexual encounters in erotica are frequently characterized by a lack of female consent or by varying degrees of violence. When Timante bounds into Araminta's room unannounced in *The Surprize* and administers a clyster, he invades both her space and her body.[85] (Illustration 15.) Another man's secret journey through the corridors of one woman's palace to her room not only concludes with a violent sexual encounter but mirrors

[83] 'Miss in her Teens', in *Festival of Love*, pp. 378, 380. See also 'The Inseparable Pair', in *Festival of Love*, p. 313; *Genuine Memoirs of . . . Miss Maria Brown*, vol. I, p. 117; 'The Nun. From Rabelais', in *Forty Select Poems*, p. 133.
[84] *Spy on Mother Midnight*, p. 31. See Robert A. Erickson, *Mother Midnight: Birth, Sex and Fate in Eighteenth-Century Fiction (Defoe, Richardson and Sterne)* (New York: AMS Press, 1986), pp. 23–8, on the popular fictional genre in which female gossips spoke frankly about sex.
[85] *Surprize*, pp. 7–9.

Illustration 21: *The Priest-ridden Washerwoman.* In *The Bacchanalian Magazine* (1793).

that sexual act.[86] Sexual intercourse is synonymous with entering the places belonging to women, often through the use of a degree of physical force.

In the language used to describe female bodies, women are rendered literally places of pleasure. The English term 'Merryland' – used to denote a female body – was supposedly translated into a pan-European notion of a feminine place of sexual pleasure: 'Frolich-landt' in German and 'Frolick-landt' in Dutch.[87] The continent of Merryland in the erotic *A New Description of Merryland* (1741) is an anonymous and generalized female body. In the comic play *The Fair Quaker* (1773) one man's exclamation – 'I am bound for merryland and wedlock harbour' – uses the term more specifically to refer to conjugal sexual pleasures.[88] In contrast, the single engraving *The Sailor's Adventure to the Streights of Merryland Or, An Evening View on Ludgate Hill* (1749) depicts prostitutes or 'Ladies of Game . . . of all sorts and sizes'. (Illustration 22.) The term Merryland could be used in a number of ways, but it always refers to a place of sexual pleasure which men visited. Similarly, in the erotic spoof *A Voyage to Lethe*, women are variously depicted as temples, landscapes, seascapes and ships or as guides to these places for the male narrator.[89] A series of sexual adventures are conveyed through the tale of a journey in which women are the mode of transport, the place travelled to, and the inhabitants of the destination.

---

[86] *Chinese Tale*, p. 17.   [87] *New Description of Merryland*, pp. 1–2.

[88] Charles Shadwell, *The Fair Quaker: or, The Humours of the Navy* (London: T. Lownds and T. Becket, 1773), p. 50.

[89] *Voyage to Lethe*, passim.

Illustration 22: J. Wake, *The Sailor's Adventure to the Streights of Merryland Or; An Evening View on Ludgate Hill*, engraved by John June (1749).

At the end of this particular book, however, the author drinks from the River Lethe and forgets his journey.[90] Not unlike Merryland or Lethe, the 'fruit-shop' refers both to female bodies and to a coffee house or brothel where 'the not yet depraved males of *English* generation' would go to initiate 'kindly intercourses' with women. But in order to proceed further than 'a kiss or a *feel*', a united couple must retire to either 'the lady's apartment, or some of the commodious places of reception.[91] To enjoy the later stages of a sexual liaison, men are conveyed to a woman's space. Indeed, when one woman writes to her lover complaining that he visits her 'only to go to bed here,' the man responds candidly from his home: 'This be the place of business, that the seat of pleasure'.[92] Women's spaces – both corporeal and architectural, whether prostitutes, lovers or wives – are literally repositories of pleasure.

These gendered spatial codes were employed in the construction of the garden of Sir Francis Dashwood (1708–81), who presided over the orgies of the notorious Hell-Fire Club. His West Wycombe garden, in a Buckinghamshire valley, was supposedly designed to represent a female body. It was complete with 'two little mounds, each surmounted by a bed of bright flowers' which shot streams of milky water into the air, and 'a triangle of dense shrubbery' from which gushed a stream of water.[93] The persistence of such associations makes it tempting to dismiss them as banal. Some of the features discussed above – such as the grotto – were of great vintage and continue to bear currency in our time.[94] This is largely to do with the physical body. As Paul Rodaway has claimed, geographical experience 'begins and ends with the body', and the constructions built by humans must surely reflect that in many complex ways, both indirect and direct.[95] As Eva Keuls comments on ancient Athens,

[T]he anatomical differences between men and women were *translated* into the shapes of their living spaces: women's reproductive organs are internal . . . Men's genitals on the other hand are conspicuous . . . *Analogously*, women spent their lives wrapped in veils, nameless, concealing their identity, and locked away in the dark recesses of closed-in

[90] Lethe is the river of Oblivion in classical mythology.   [91] *Fruit-Shop*, vol. II, pp. 134, 135.
[92] *Letters from the Inspector to a Lady, with the genuine answers* (London: For M. Cooper, at the Globe in Paternoster-Row, 1752), pp. 29, 28.
[93] Daniel P. Mannix, *The Hell Fire Club* (London: Four Square, 1961), p. 5. See also Jones, *Clubs of the Georgian Rakes*, pp. 99–100; McCormick, *Hell-Fire Club*, p. 120; and Burgo Partridge, *A History of Orgies*, 2nd edn. (1958; London: Spring Books, 1966), pp. 133–48. Also see Miller, *Heavenly Caves*, p. 79. I am grateful to Anna Clark for bringing this point to my attention.
[94] For some ancient erotic connotations of the grotto, see Miller, *Heavenly Caves*. Similarly, 'sexual connotations' were noted in the label for the sculpture *Grotto* (1995) by Tania Kovats, exhibited at the Hayward Gallery, London, 1996.
[95] Paul Rodaway, *Sensuous Geographies: Body, Sense and Place* (London: Routledge, 1994), p. 31. The rather simplistic diagram that Rodaway produces to illustrate the way in which 'the cultural filter' exists between the environment and perceived environment on the one hand and the person on the other, however, implies that it is not the body, but a whole host of factors which comprise the filter that mediates experience of the world (see ibid., p. 23).

homes. Men spent their lives in open areas, in the sunlit spaces of the Agora and other public domains.[96]

In this vision, which relies on what Elizabeth Grosz has described as 'a fundamental opposition between nature and culture', biology was mimicked in buildings and practice.[97] However, seeing bodies only as origins for constructions of space threatens to naturalize the body, and suggests that male and female bodies are understood in the same ways in different times and places. The places considered in this chapter are often distinctively eighteenth-century in character, though. Moreover, the distinction between representations of bodies and spaces was not absolute – the two were often indistinguishable. In eighteenth-century erotica, the originary status of the body is replaced with an isomorphism between the body and places. There was an '*interface*' between them, in which both locations and bodies consisted of collections of parts which formed different points of contact.[98] At work was a flexible process of mutual construction which involved many variables, and which enabled much variety and change.

And yet many of these feminine, erotic spaces were not unlike the 'dark recesses' associated with women's bodies in ancient Athens. Clearly, there are some aspects of bodies which have repeatedly inspired similar physical and imaginary constructions of space. These have been re-cast according to time and space, but there is a residual continuity rather than infinite and total invention. In his epic history of landscape metaphors, Simon Schama has dismissed the persistent association between moist caves or grottoes and female pudenda. The ubiquity of the image renders sustained analysis superfluous: 'it doesn't take a feverishly Freudian imagination', he writes, 'to see them as vaginal orifices in the face of the rock'.[99] There are elements of erotic culture which endure, but this only enhances their worth for historians, because the mundane is often that which is most deeply embedded in culture. To recognize spaces as vaginal orifices might be to restate a cliché. To recognize qualities of spaces as material renditions of feminized and sexualized moral states is to begin the process of deciphering a language which wielded considerable but subtle influence.

When John Dineley accused his wife of committing adultery with Sir Robert Jason in 1730, he enlisted the services of Henry and Esther Grove. Henry testified that he had observed Mary and Robert having sex under a tree, while Esther testified that she had seen the couple having sex in a field. At an appeal,

[96] Eva Keuls, *The Reign of the Phallus: Sexual Politics in Ancient Athens* (1985; Berkeley: University of California Press, 1993), p. 97 (emphasis added).

[97] Elizabeth Grosz, 'Bodies-Cities', in her *Space, Time, Perversion: Essays on the Politics of Bodies* (London: Routledge, 1995), p. 106.

[98] The notion of 'interface' is drawn from Grosz, ibid., p. 108. Emphasis in original.

[99] Simon Schama, *Landscape and Memory* (London: HarperCollins, 1995), pp. 367–74. Quote from p. 373.

it was admitted that the testimony was invented, and that Henry Grove had been paid by John Dineley to make the allegations.[100] Fields and the shade of a tree were two common places for sex to occur in erotica. Indeed, there appear to be similarities between many of the locations for sexual assignations noted in Lawrence Stone's accounts of marriage and those discussed here. Frequently, the meetings of couples from the middling sort, the gentry or the aristocracy allegedly occurred in the home of the woman, and often specifically in her bed-chamber or dressing room.[101] In addition, couples were reported as having had sex in a chaise or coach, in a bed surrounded by thick curtains or in a shielded garden.[102] Many of these encounters were illicit, and it is true that secluded and enclosed spots were ideal for secret assignations. Yet legal cases were not documentary evidence of where people had sex in the eighteenth century: they were 'semi-fictitious constructs' often built on the sands of 'brazen fabrication'.[103] In his discussion of *Dinely* versus *Dinely*, Lawrence Stone was puzzled by the locations chosen by Henry and Esther Grove, but when the evidence of erotica is brought into the historical frame the choice of location in such testimony is no longer incomprehensible. What emerges is a widely shared culture of sexualized locations and bodies. The erotic genre is no record of actual sexual behaviour in the eighteenth century, but it does reveal some of the cultural factors which worked to make such locations appear particularly appropriate for sexual encounters. Darkness, depth, enclosure and the threat (or promise) of disclosure were crucial attributes of both sexualized locations and female bodies. Soft, shaded and secluded settings such as grottoes, groves and rooms were portrayed as feminine sites of sexual action. Within this vision are secreted valuable understandings of gender and the act of sex.

Erotica reveals a powerful congruity between women and enclosed spaces at the level of the corporeal. At first glance this suggests a highly erotic charge to the historically powerful association between women and the 'private'. However, these feminine spaces are not entirely opposed to 'the world' in a simple public–private dichotomy: they are emphatically to be entered whenever others desired it and are perpetually busy with the action so crucial to the genre. Indeed, other work suggests that it was men's spaces – their studies or dressing rooms – which were subject to the most restricted access.[104] The butler in one elite late-eighteenth-century household described his master's study – not his

---

[100] Lawrence Stone, *Broken Lives: Separation and Divorce in England, 1660–1857* (Oxford: Oxford University Press, 1993), pp. 95–101.

[101] Ibid., pp. 119, 251, 272–3, and his *Uncertain Unions: Marriage in England, 1660–1753* (Oxford: Oxford University Press, 1992), p. 49.

[102] Stone, *Broken Lives*, pp. 120, 252, 95, 253.   [103] Ibid., pp. 7, 8.

[104] Colin Cunningham, An Italian House is My Lady: Some Aspects of the Definition of Women's Role in the Architecture of Robert Adam', in Perry and Rossington (eds.), *Femininity and Masculinity in Eighteenth-Century Art*, pp. 63–77.

mistress' bed-chamber – as 'the very sanctuary of my master's house'.[105] Yet the enclosed and secluded qualities of these feminine sexualized locations were important in distinguishing them from the new places of pleasure emerging throughout England. An erotic culture of enclosed space assumed a particular charge in a society where actual, lived space was undergoing rapid change. The idealized spaces in erotica are divested of many of the threats posed by urban commercial leisure, such as excessive display and luxurious consumption. Pleasure is safely ensconced in enclosed spaces where intricate codes of politeness are dropped and bristling sociability replaced by an easy intimacy comprised of an attractive mix of comfort and excitement.

Interpreted as consolation for transformations in lived urban space, the valorization of enclosed spaces of pleasure cautions that such changes produced a nostalgic, resistant 'underside', but ultimately this process serves to reify narratives of the modernity of eighteenth-century England. The feminization of sex and sexuality discussed here, however, unsettles other aspects of such narratives. The pivot of Laqueur's thesis of the birth of modern, opposite sexes is the reimagining of women as sexually passive. More recently, Laqueur's arguments have been integrated into a much broader model which posits the increasingly phallocentric nature of sex during the eighteenth century manifest in an 'obsession with the penis'.[106] Such arguments blend to create a story not only of women's marginalization, but also of a decline in women's sexual autonomy and sexual pleasure. The indivisible association between female bodies and sexualized locations in erotica contrasts markedly with this. Sexual differences located in bodies were certainly being depicted, but these were very different from – almost a reversal of – those commonly asserted. In erotica, women are thoroughly sexualized rather than desexualized, and sex itself is drenched in femininity rather than characterized by phallocentricism.

Men were submerged in an entirely female world when they embarked on sexual encounters. Indeed, sex is not simply regarded as an act, whether of reproduction, desire or violence; sex is a place for men to visit. Rendering the act of sex spatial means it can be contained and firmly situated. Imaginative or emotional mechanisms that allowed men to remain separate from sex and sexual pleasure were central to constructions of masculinity during this period: a concern to rescue reason from the murky waters of 'emotion and sensuality' lay at the heart of these constructions, and this may have become more pronounced during the eighteenth century.[107] For the male authors and readers of eighteenth-century erotica, sex is externalized as a thoroughly feminine space. A man can

---

[105] Stone, *Broken Lives*, p. 260. See also Wigley, 'Untitled', pp. 347–9.

[106] Hitchcock, 'Redefining Sex', p. 79 and passim. See my introduction for a more detailed discussion of these arguments.

[107] Quote from Fletcher, *Gender, Sex and Subordination*, p. 329. See also Tosh, 'Old Adam and the New Man', pp. 226–7.

easily extricate himself from sex: it could be a distant and far-off place and it could, as in *A Voyage to Lethe*, be forgotten. Either way, sex remains apart from masculine identities. This distance is an illusion, a ruse which enables men to experience and enjoy sex pleasures – both as characters in the texts and as readers of the texts. Nevertheless, it creates a world in which men decide whether to embark on sex. Economies of pleasure and imaginings of sex need to be separated, then, because while sex as phallocentric may be read as demoting female pleasure, rendering sex feminine did not make the women depicted in erotica sexually autonomous. Women do not control their own sexual spaces. Neither, however, do men. An approach to sexuality which resists locating *either* power and subordination *or* happy autonomy and equality can reveal the subtleties in past constructions of masculinity and femininity. The relationship of men to the spaces of sex is complex: they decide when to visit but they are not the proprietors. Feminine spaces are to be neither undermined nor conquered. Certainly violence is exercised, and vigorous masculinity championed. Yet force appears as a manifestation of a yearning to experience these spaces rather than a desire to destroy. The motivation was saturation not obliteration, and these feminine places were to remain intact and endure. But the assertion of force remained crucial to masculinity. While this chapter has discussed how women's bodies were depicted as spaces and female sexuality represented in structures, the following chapter shows how male bodies were portrayed in space and male sexuality conveyed through patterns of male movement associated with the quest for knowledge and the assertion of force.

6   Movement

Classic accounts of the history of the family chart the rise of companionate marriages in eighteenth-century households, characterized by new affective bonds and greater equality between spouses; more recent work in gender history suggests that violence became an increasingly less acceptable component of masculinity during this period. Certainly, in the eighteenth century, violence between men and women transgressed ideals of heterosexual harmony based on protective men and tender women. Nevertheless, women continued to suffer violence at the hands of men.[1] So deeply embedded were notions of male violence that, in her analysis of rape in early-modern England, Garthine Walker found that 'male force and female submission were culturally coded as erotically appealing'.[2] This coding was defined and perpetuated in erotic material. Having examined bodies as spaces in the previous chapter, this chapter focuses on bodies *in* space; it sets out to explore how gendered patterns of sexual behaviour were constituted by forms of movement. It demonstrates that while erotica disguised bodies through metaphor and concealed sexual activity with narrative devices, suggestiveness did not mean sex without power; in fact, stories of sexual intercourse were invariably stories of male force and female submission.

In depicting bodies in motion, eighteenth-century erotica was shaped by geographical knowledge and its modes of expression. These geographical modes

---

[1] For classic views of the rise of companionate and egalitarian marriage, see Stone, *Family, Sex and Marriage*; and Randolph Trumbach, *The Rise of the Egalitarian Family: Aristocratic Kinship and Domestic Relations in Eighteenth-Century England* (New York: Academic Press, 1978). On the containment of men's anger and physical aggression, see Robert B. Shoemaker, 'Reforming Male Manners: Public Insult and the Decline of Violence in London, 1660–1740', in Hitchcock and Cohen (eds.), *English Masculinities*, pp. 133–50, and his 'The Taming of the Duel: Masculinity, Honour and Ritual Violence in London, 1660–1800', *The Historical Journal* 45 (2002), pp. 525–45; Elizabeth Foyster, 'Boys will be Boys? Manhood and Aggression, 1660–1800', in Hitchcock and Cohen (eds.), *English Masculinities*, pp. 151–66. On ideals of harmony and the continued occurrence of domestic violence, see Margaret Hunt, 'Domesticity and Women's Independence in Eighteenth-Century London', *Gender and History* 4 (1992), pp. 10–33. On related issues, see Elizabeth Foyster, 'Creating a Veil of Silence? Politeness and Marital Violence in the English Household', *Transactions of the Royal Historical Society* 12 (2002), pp. 395–415.

[2] Walker, 'Rereading Rape', p. 16.

permeated widely in the literary culture of the period. For example, eighteenth-century fiction and travel literature were closely related. Fiction used the itinerary as a narrative form, and in much writing narrative was conceived 'as spatial design'.[3] Novelists even responded to famous voyages by writing their own travels.[4] This was also the age of the Grand Tour, and erotic writers echoed this aspect of elite male education in their claims that topography should yield both pleasure and improvement.[5] Indeed, the eighteenth century has been termed 'the age of gold for travellers, both real and imaginary'.[6] As a result, a raft of false travel guides and fictional accounts of new discoveries penned by armchair travellers appeared. Erotic authors mimicked these travel lies in many ways, for example by using prefaces which emphasized the truth and objectivity of the account.[7] Thomas Stretser's *A New Description of Merryland* (1741) was ostensibly written as a corrective to the work of 'modern Geographers', and to atlases, globes and modern histories which neglected to describe this country. But the author is keen to stress that he is only going to share with his readers information on the parts of the country that he has himself experienced, rather than 'amuse Mankind with the uncertain Guesses and fabulous Relations of idle Travellers'.[8] Stretser later criticizes this erotic work, and one of his first accusations is that the book is a travel lie:

The first Conception was owing to our Author's accidentally reading in Gordon's Geographical Grammer these Words, which Mr Gordon uses in speaking of Holland, viz. 'the Country lying very low, it's Soil is naturally wet and fenny'. Ha! said he, the same may be said of a **** as well as of Holland; this Whim having once entered his Noddle, he resolved to pursue the Hint, and try how far he could run the Parallel; his wise Head fancied here was a fine Scope to ridicule the Geographers, so he sets to scribbling.[9]

In satirizing such works, and in knowingly aping conventions of depicting women's bodies as land, erotic writers demonstrated both their wit and knowledge. They also 'ridiculed the Geographers', undermining contemporary Enlightened geographical practices by producing their own distinctive brand of travel lie. Men involved in erotic culture certainly played with notions of myth, truth and knowledge, blurring the distinction between empirical knowledge and imaginary knowledge so important to geographical exploration and to

[3] Varey, *Space and the Eighteenth-Century English Novel*, p. 4.
[4] Percy G. Adams, *Travelers and Travel Liars, 1660–1800* (1962; New York: Dover, 1980), p. 224.
[5] Chloe Chard, *Pleasure and Guilt on the Grand Tour: Travel Writing and Imaginative Geography, 1600–1830* (Manchester: Manchester University Press, 1999), pp. 22–6.
[6] Adams, *Travelers and Travel Liars*, p. 9. See also Matthew H. Edney, 'Reconsidering Enlightenment Geography and Map Making: Reconnaissance, Mapping, Archive', in Charles W. J. Withers and David N. Livingstone (eds.), *Geography and Enlightenment* (Chicago: University of Chicago Press, 1999), pp. 177–85.
[7] On this practice in the travel lie genre, see Adams, *Travelers and Travel Liars*, pp. 228–9.
[8] *New Description of Merryland*, pp. xi–xii, x.   [9] *Merryland Displayed*, p. 8.

the Enlightenment in general.[10] Indeed, 'geographical knowledge was an active part of Enlightenment knowledge', and geographical forms of expression were adopted in science and medicine.[11] Erotic authors were skilled at drawing on new knowledge and its practices, and here they reproduced ways of thinking about and representing space – particularly cartography – that embodied gendered inequalities of power.[12] In erotica, these forms of expression cast sexual differences into both spatial forms and relations in space. Michel de Certeau argued that the mapping mode was central to modern scientific knowledge, and to the power that such knowledge could wield. This stood in contrast to the itinerary or story mode, which was dominant in imaginative literature.[13] In the eighteenth century, however, the map/itinerary dichotomy does not correspond to science/literature. As Matthew Edney has argued, the 'linear route of the geographical traveller' emphasized by reconnaissance, and 'the systematic conceptualization and description of discrete areas across the earth's surface' entailed in mapping, are distinguishable but interdependent aspects of Enlightenment geographical knowledge.[14] In erotica, these approaches are combined: narrative leads smoothly to mapping with hardly a shift in register. This is manifest in descriptions of bodies in erotica: the movement of the male narrator progresses from a position above the stationary female body, across and then into the body. In this pattern, the implied movement of men in these descriptions thus transforms from a cartographic viewpoint into a position akin to a medical examination or geographical exploration. Employing this approach to female bodies through the adoption of geographical or spatial models of knowledge, the chapter argues, facilitated the representation of inequitable gender relations.

Patterns of description

In eighteenth-century erotica, female bodies are laid out for the reader in short descriptions which list distinct body parts in quick succession. In one poem,

> the girl was wond'rous fair,
> Black were her eyes, and brown her hair;
> Upon her cheeks sat blooming youth,

---

[10] John L. Allen, 'Lands of Myth, Waters of Wonder: The Place of the Imagination in the History of Geographical Exploration', in David Lowenthal and Martyn J. Bowden (eds.), *Geographies of the Mind: Essays in Historical Geography* (New York: Oxford University Press, 1976), pp. 42–53.

[11] Charles W. J. Withers and David N. Livingstone, 'Introduction: On Geography and Enlightenment', in Withers and Livingstone (eds.), *Geography and Enlightenment*, p. 13.

[12] See ibid., and Jeremy Black, 'Cartography as Power', in his *Maps and Politics* (London: Reaktion, 1997), pp. 11–28 for a useful summary.

[13] de Certeau, *Practice of Everyday Life*, pp. 199–21.

[14] Edney, 'Reconsidering Enlightenment Geography', p. 175. See also ibid., p. 190.

> And charming was her little mouth:
> Uncover'd was her lovely breast,
> That swell'd, as wanted to be prest.[15]

Though different descriptions stress different aspects of bodies, the manner in which they are listed here is typical of the erotic genre. Another woman is a collage of delightful parts:

> Her hair, that was as raven black,
> Hung o'er her shoulders and her back;
> Her breasts were like the driven snow,
> On which her nipples warmly glow;
> Her arm, her waist, her legs, her thighs,
> The Squire beheld with wond'ring eyes.[16]

To a lesser extent, male bodies are subject to the same form of description. Commendation is given to one man:

> With brawny legs and sturdy back,
> Well shap'd, broad-shouldered, young and tall.[17]

In the same collection of 1753, similar parts of a male body are highlighted:

> My limbs are brawny, nose is long,
> My shoulders broad, my back is strong.[18]

The narrator of *A Spy on Mother Midnight* (1748) is described by one woman in equivalent terms, as 'a rare well-made Man, . . . strong built and stout limb'd; . . . He has a hardy Complexion, a Pair of wanton Eyes, and a Nose! Ah! *Sukey*, such a Nose!'[19] Yet such descriptions differ noticeably from those of women. Male bodies lack the sheer range of body parts, the lucid details of brilliant colours, gentle contours, graceful shapes and sensuous textures. These depictions rarely display the vividness found in descriptions of female bodies, and underline size and strength alone. Most importantly, descriptions of male bodies spotlight very small areas of the body.

In contrast, descriptions of female bodies give some semblance of a whole woman through the quick-fire naming of body parts. Just as one erotic author favours the true taste of the 'regular orders of architecture' over the 'misshapen deformity' of the Gothic, so desirable bodies are harmonious composites of well-ordered parts.[20] *The Why and the Wherefore* (1765) tells a story of the birth of such regular bodies. Following a period when no discernible body parts

---

[15] 'The Chrystal Bottle', in *Forty Select Poems*, p. 10.
[16] 'The Squire', in *Festival of Love*, p. 231.   [17] 'The Ink Bottle', in *Forty Select Poems*, p. 47.
[18] 'The Filthy Beast', in *Forty Select Poems*, p. 124.
[19] *Spy on Mother Midnight*, p. 20. The mention of the nose was significant because connections were made between the size of the nose and that of the penis. See ibid., pp. 20–1, 29.
[20] *Fruit-Shop*, vol. I, p. ix.

could be identified, bodily elements first form into separate body parts, ready to enter into 'the composition of future human creatures'.[21] These distinct parts then bond, are 'assembled into distinct rudiments, or constituent members' and are then 'formed into perfect individuals by a regular contexture'.[22] The criterion of harmony is applied to female bodies exclusively. The narrator of *A Description of the Temple of Venus* (1726) describes in these terms a woman who visited him in a dream, explaining that although 'each distinct feature was not exactly regular . . . the whole was surprisingly beautiful'.[23] A second man describes his lover in a similar way: 'She has a lovely Shape, a majestick, but modest Air; a piercing Eye, that will soon look yielding: Features exactly suited to each other.'[24] One fictional female's description of herself at the age of fifteen is founded on similar exacting requirements:

> I was already above the middle stature, with a fair skin, clear sparkling black eyes, a well-shaped nose, pouting ruby lips, regular white teeth, and an agreeable dimple in my cheek; my hair was of a dark brown, which flowed in ringlets down a neck that was taper and well-shaped; an easy fall of the shoulders took off, in some degree, from that plumpness before, which is uncommon at my age; my shape was not remarkably slender, but proportioned to my body, and my legs and feet, which were particularly genteel, received grace from an easy unaffected air I was naturally possessed of; my hand and arm, already formed, were of the number of those which painters so attentively imitate.[25]

Moving from head to toe, women's bodies were described as agreeable and proportionate collections of separate parts. These short descriptions gave the male narrators and readers a view that enabled them to take in or glide across the whole female body.

There are other important differences between descriptions of male and female bodies. First, as in the last example, descriptions of female body parts transported the reader from the top of the body to the bottom. Second, and intimately tied to the first point, descriptions of female bodies often ended with a descent into the body. It was at this point that the architectural metaphors which envisaged bodies as collections of parts coalesced with topographical metaphors, which portrayed bodies being viewed, traversed and entered. The Picturesque mode transformed the way the landscape was described, thus changing the imaginative position of the author, artist, observer or reader. In some Picturesque visual and written culture, a high position is replaced by a low position, in which the spectator has the feeling of 'moving through rather than surveying' the landscape, and even of being submerged or 'enveloped'.[26] In

---

[21] *Why and the Wherefore*, p. 24.   [22] Ibid., p. 7.
[23] *Description of the Temple of Venus*, p. 36.
[24] Ibid., p. 39.   [25] *Genuine Memoirs of . . . Miss Maria Brown*, vol. I, pp. 63–4.
[26] Andrews, *Search for the Picturesque*, p. 61. See also Hunt, *Figure in the Landscape*, pp. 228, 247.

gardens this way of seeing and moving had an erotic component. A series of concealments and revelations teased the viewer, such that eighteenth-century gardens have been likened to a striptease.[27] A broader interest in moving through space was also reflected in fictional narratives.[28] The movement of the body of the author, narrator or reader in eighteenth-century erotica mirrored this Picturesque sense of moving through and being enveloped by the landscape.

The swift movement across the surface of and then into a body is clearest in those texts which employ an extended metaphor of land for the body. Male bodies are occasionally portrayed in terms of land. For example, one narrator locates the male genitals 'situate withal in a very pleasant and fertile Part of the Country, being a long Neck of Land, shaded by a Grove of Trees, and supported by a couple of Hills'.[29] But these descriptions do not conclude with a descent into the body. In contrast, in the poem *Consummation* (1741), Venus tempts Adonis by asking him to 'o'er all these various Charms unbounded rove',[30] before inviting him across and into her body:

> In these fair Locks, that o'er my Neck incline,
> Behold the Tendrils of the wanton Vine;
> In those soft Breasts you press, the Hills are seen,
> And the low Valley in the Space between;
> Thence see the Plain, the level Lawn extend,
> In sweet Declension see the Margin bend;
> There Ever-fruitful, pregnant with Delight,
> The Moss-grown Fountain courts the roving Sight.[31]

This 'roving sight' and the accompanying pattern of movement remained comprehensible in erotica at the close of the century, when a reader could be whisked across the woman's neck, breasts, waist, legs and arms, before resting in the darkened area of her genitalia.[32] In erotic descriptions of female bodies, the reader is invited to 'o'er her neck take nimble flight', or 'to range', and is given a reconnoitre of the body from above.[33] But this position is quickly transformed as the description skates over the body, traversing the surface in a horizontal movement. Ultimately, an entry into the body is made as the description shifts and gives the sense of moving down vertically.

Female bodies may not always have been described in this 'interiorizing' way. *Erotopolis. The Present State of Bettyland* (1684) begins with an account of the country of Bettyland – the female body – and its position, and soon plunges

[27] Pugh, *Garden-Nature-Language*, p. 109. Pugh is clearly inspired by Barthes' notion of the erotic. See Barthes, *Pleasure of the Text*.
[28] Cynthia Wall, *The Literary and Cultural Spaces of Restoration London* (Cambridge: Cambridge University Press, 1998), p. 215.
[29] *Voyage to Lethe*, p. 8.   [30] *Consummation*, p. 9.   [31] Ibid., pp. 8–9.
[32] 'The Bridal Night', in *Pleasures that Please on Reflection*, p. 47.
[33] Ibid., p. 47; 'Venus and Love', in *Bacchanalian Magazine*, p. 15.

the reader into a description of the soil.[34] Yet, while the author appears to have made a rapid descent into the female genitals, he repeatedly moves out from this position to take a more distanced view.[35] The journey across and into Bettyland is interrupted, then, but this oscillation between an aerial and an interior view is absent from the similar but later mid-eighteenth-century text *A New Description of Merryland* (1741). This book begins with an account 'OF THE NAME OF MERRYLAND AND WHENCE IT IS SO CALLED', followed by an aerial, cartographic description 'OF THE SITUATION OF MERRYLAND'. In this latter account, Merryland is placed within a 'continent', and the author reports its longitude and latitude.[36] The focus in *A New Description of Merryland* later transforms in the chapter 'OF THE AIR, SOIL, RIVERS, CANALS, &C', in which the reader learns of the lake 'VSCA' (vesica, meaning bladder) and the deep 'canal' (vagina) that runs through the middle of the land.[37] Crucially, it is in this chapter that the author describes the journey along the canal 'up to the Country', passing through the labia, the nymphae and the hymen.[38] The remaining chapters relay details of the inhabitants, the products and commodities, the rarities, the government and the religion of the land, before concluding with a lengthy description of penetrative sex couched in terms of the author's attempt to bring his boat to anchor in the harbour of Merryland.

This book begins with a cartographic approach – seeing the body as an area to be mapped – before moving through and into the body. Early in the text, the author reinforces this cartographic approach when he apologizes for not providing a map, claiming it would have been too expensive. He does, however, refer readers to an image in a book by 'Mr Moriceau', though he quickly confesses that the wax model invented by 'Sir R. M.' gives 'a better Idea of MERRYLAND than can possibly be done by the best Maps, or any written Description'.[39] This model of the female body was owned by the physician Richard Manningham, who gave lectures on midwifery and founded the first of London's lying-in hospitals in 1739.[40] The map, from Francis Mauriceau's treatise on female health and childbirth, was almost certainly one of the four engravings which depicted female torsos and pudenda splayed open and with each part carefully numbered. (Illustration 23.) The author of *A New Description of Merryland* later criticized Mauriceau for demonstrating 'but very little Skill in Anatomy in his description of these several Parts'. He denounces the medical 'Map of Merryland' as a 'baudy-Print' designed to entertain his readers, 'rather

---

[34] *Erotopolis. The Present State of Bettyland*, p. 3.
[35] For example, the pregnant woman's abdomen is described, and the 'very fair Prospect' that Bettyland displays is praised. See ibid., p. 14.
[36] *New Description of Merryland*, pp. 1, 3.   [37] Ibid., p. 11.   [38] Ibid., pp. 15–17.
[39] Ibid., p. 18. This was 'the curious Model or Machine' or '*Artificial Matrix*' used by the physician Richard Manningham. See *Merryland Displayed*, p. 36.
[40] Adrian Wilson, *The Making of Man-Midwifery: Childbirth in England, 1660–1770* (London: University College London Press, 1995), pp. 85, 114–16.

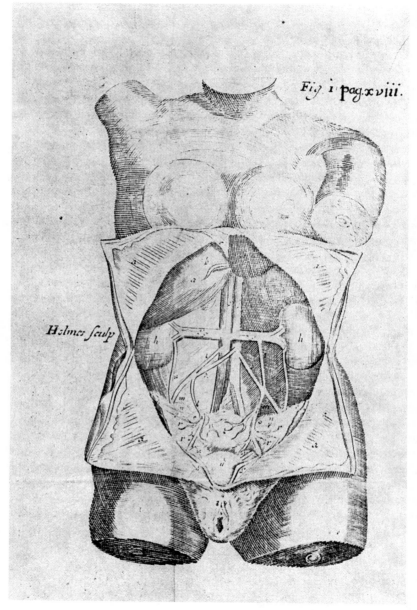

Illustration 23:   A female torso and reproductive organs. Francis Mauriceau's
The Diseases of Women with Child (1736).

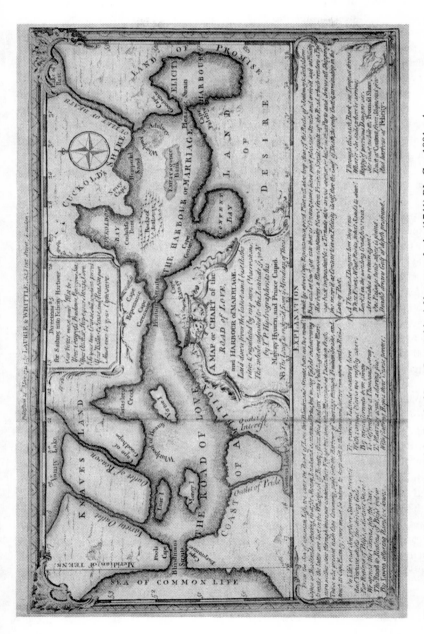

Illustration 24: *A Map or Chart of the Road of Love*. Inserted in *A Voyage to Lethe* (1741) BL: Cup.1001.c.4

than to give them any useful Instruction'.[41] But such 'maps' were well suited to this erotic book. Allowing the viewer to peer past the flesh, they give the impression of descending into the body. In addition, just as the author of *A New Description of Merryland* described the female body as land, so the medical writer Mauriceau also used this metaphor, denouncing other writers on female health as comparable to 'those *Geographers* who give us the Description of Countries they never saw, and (as they imagine) a perfect Account of them'.[42] Geographical metaphors for female bodies were used by erotic and medical writers alike; indeed, Mauriceau assured his readers that his book was not the medical equivalent of a travel lie. Such comments, and the description of his anatomical illustration as a map, highlight the links between geographical and medical approaches to the body.

The chapters of *A New Description of Merryland* are designed to take the reader above and into the female body. A very similar movement from an aerial to an interior view is described by 'Samuel Cock', the fictional sea-captain in *A Voyage to Lethe*. Approaching 'the Gulph of Venus', he enjoys a vantage point from which he 'commanded the charming Circumference of *Buttock-Land*'. He then travels further across 'a delightful Ivory Plain, which is terminated one way by two lovely rising Hills . . . and the other by a thick Grove of Trees, shading a Valley'. Moving up this valley, he reaches the place called '*Beth-Eden*' at its furthest end, and finally enters the gulf.[43] It is easy to see why a later bookseller or owner inserted a map into *A Voyage to Lethe*, called *A Map or Chart of the Road of Love, and Harbour of Marriage.* (Illustration 24.) The map is actually a representation of the Mediterranean designed to convey the perils and profits of courtship and marriage, and ostensibly to provide viewers with directions to reach 'Felicity Harbour'. Probably produced in the final decade of the eighteenth century, the date on this coloured engraving was erased and replaced with '1741' in hand, an act which reinforced the close relationship between the book and the map. Indeed, the map provides a visual reflection of the cartographic approach to the body that the narrator begins with, athough the locations mentioned do not correspond to those mentioned in the book. Thus, the movement from left to right across this map – from the 'Sea of common Life' to 'Felicity Harbour' – mirrors Sam's description of his journey across and into the woman's body.

Though the erotic book *The Fruit-Shop* (1765) was largely about male genitalia, its descriptions of female bodies switch between envisaging them as large areas of land to be viewed aerially or cartographically, and as smaller patches to travel through and into. In 'A description of the garden wherein the first fruit tree stood', the author proposes to proceed in the manner of 'strenuous naturalists'

---

[41] *Merryland Displayed*, pp. 35, 36.
[42] Mauriceau, *Diseases of Women with Child*, p. viii.   [43] *Voyage to Lethe* (1741), pp. 27–30.

by giving 'a geographical delineation of that chosen and happy spot'.[44] The book then charts the debates concerning which part of the world could make the claim that it experienced the fruit-shop (the male genitalia) first, describing female bodies as the continents of Asia, 'Africk', Europe and America, and conjuring images of maps once again.[45] Soon, however, the female body is transformed into a garden which, in the manner of eighteenth-century garden design, seduces and teases the viewer: 'the raptured mind was in a manner lost, while it enjoyed the sweet variety, and strayed through such windings of successive wonders'.[46]

In all these descriptions, erotic authors echoed landscape writing and garden design. They also mirrored the processes of cartography and exploration through which knowledge about the landscape was produced. In this way, they were part of a wider literary culture that drew on cartographic innovations in London after the Great Fire.[47] Moreover, erotic descriptions mimicked – and mocked – the 'new preoccupation with depth' which Ludmilla Jordanova has identified in the texts and practices of eighteenth-century science and medicine. According to this model of knowledge, information was 'based on looking deeply into and thereby intellectually mastering nature'. Gleaning knowledge from looking deep into the body, this model displayed a significant erotic dimension.[48] This is exploited in erotica. Scenes of inspection of female bodies in erotic material – which marry a descent into female bodies with the attainment of knowledge – are clearly sexualized encounters. A series of passages in *A Description of the Temple of Venus*, for example, recount the display and unveiling of groups of women of various nationalities in turn in front of the male narrator, and his assessments of each group.[49] This theme could also take the form of the Classical story of the Judgement of Paris, in which Paris chose the most beautiful of three goddesses. In 'The Rival Beauties' (1770), for example, a man likens himself to Paris, describing the way in which three women 'Display'd their charms before my critic eyes'.[50] At other times such events are conveyed through scientific metaphors. In *The Fruit-Shop*, for example, women are likened to comets which endure 'the prying power of our auxiliary glass tubes, telescopes, &c.'[51] Indeed, in *Did You Ever See Such Damned Stuff?* (1760), the King restrains his wife forcibly and inspects her naked body with a magnifying glass.[52]

[44] *Fruit-Shop*, vol. I, p. 19.   [45] Ibid., vol. I, p. 22.   [46] Ibid., vol. I, p. 42.

[47] Wall, *Literary and Cultural Spaces*, chapters three and four.

[48] Jordanova, *Sexual Visions*, pp. 57, 58. The erotic element of this model of knowledge is discussed by Jordanova at pp. 87–110.

[49] *Description of the Temple of Venus*, pp. 17–26.

[50] *Festival of Love*, p. 29. See also *Arbor Vitae*, p. 20, and *Forty Select Poems*, p. 31.

[51] *Fruit-Shop*, vol. I, p. 68. Other astronomical metaphors were used in *Whim*, p. 13; *Fifteen Plagues of a Maiden-Head*, p. 3; *Natural History of the Frutex Vulvaria* ([c. 1737]), p. 13.

[52] *Did You Ever See Such Damned Stuff?*, pp. 139–44.

Men were rarely surveyed in such ways. Two curious young women investigate their brother's genitals with a magnifying glass, but this evolves into the women's inspection of themselves. Indeed, one of them examines her sister's genitals following the familiar pattern of movement above, across and into the female body:

> The nice surveyor mov'd the glass,
> In curious search from place to place;
> First view'd the curious lawn above,
> Then all beneath the mossy grove;
> At last she fix'd her active sight
> On the sweet fountain of delight.[53]

As with anatomical practices, botanical and geographical investigation promised to yield knowledge: several curious botanists, the author of a book on the female plant writes, have long tried 'to *dive deep* into the *secret qualities* of this *unfathomable Shrub*'.[54] For the individual observing the examined body, knowledge is acquired through this pattern of movement. As the 'curious Enquirer' into the land of Lethe explains, being 'ambitious of transmitting Materials to Posterity for the Benefit of future Historians and Geographers', he has resolved 'to make it my Business this Voyage to dive into everything worth knowing'.[55] In the eighteenth century, the curious gaze indicated the power and possession of the observer; curiosity was also highly gendered, marking the 'cultural privilege of men', but the lustfulness of women.[56] Similarly, in erotica, certain ways of looking and describing are associated with the production of specialized knowledge and the expression of power in a range of intellectual endeavours, including writing about the landscape and garden design, geography, botany, science and medicine. These supposedly learned forms of inquiry are rendered prurient, though, gleaning specifically carnal knowledge through the experience of female bodies. Curiosity and 'prying power' are gendered and sexualized preoccupations.

Characters in space

Descriptions of female bodies allowed narrators and readers to explore and enter these bodies, whether as land, plant, sea or grotto. These descriptions

---

[53] 'The Magnifying Glass', in *Festival of Love*, pp. 354–6. A slightly different version of this poem had appeared earlier in Tim Merriman [pseud.], *The St. James's Miscellany, Or the Citizen's Amusement* (By T. Payne, at the Crown in Pater-Noster-Row, T. Ashley, in St Paul's Church-Yard, A. Dodd without Temple-Bar, E. Nutt at the Roy[al]-Exchange, and by the booksellers of London and Westminster, [c. 1730]), pp. 16–18.

[54] *Natural History of the Frutex Vulvaria* (1741), p. 11. The word is '*unfashionable*' in the c. 1737 edition, p. 11.

[55] *Voyage to Lethe* (1741), p. 74.

[56] Barbara M. Benedict, 'The "Curious Attitude" in Eighteenth-Century Britain: Observing and Owning', *Eighteenth-Century Life* 14 (1990), pp. 59–98. Quote at p. 86.

also rendered female bodies stationary objects of exploration, and the implied asymmetrical capacity for movement emerged again in depictions of liaisons between male and female characters. Of course, both female and male characters move in erotica. The technique of travel is often used in eighteenth-century literature to drive the plot, and some eighteenth-century erotic texts ostensibly written by prostitutes adopt a technique in which the plot moves along geographically as well as narratively. In such stories, the prostitute moves too. Yet this movement is linked to the woman's inappropriate sexual activity and agency. In the *Genuine Memoirs of the Celebrated Miss Maria Brown* (1766), Maria bemoans the fact that a man may be guilty of murder, but still held in esteem. In contrast, 'if [women] do but once deviate from the track delineated by custom on the chart of chastity . . . , if we attempt to pass one barrier without paying toll, or only mistake the intended barrier, we are arraigned at the bar of *honour*, and our *reputation* pronounced irreparable by a jury of *prudes* and *old maids!*'[57] Maria's outburst couches the restrictions placed upon women in spatial terms, and reveals the connection between women's curtailed movement and their appropriate sexuality. Indeed, it is Maria's movement which often produces regrettable repercussions. At the age of eleven, Maria leaves her home in England, to travel to a convent in a corrupt and degenerate France. It is during this trip that she is inspired to sexual thoughts upon hearing the story of a fellow female traveller. By the time she returns to England, the seeds of her downfall have already been sown, and she embarks on a series of meetings with men which prove to be disastrous for her. A second trip to France ultimately sees her descent into poverty and her meeting with the bawd who inaugurated her life as a prostitute.[58] In stories such as these, women's unrestricted movement has negative consequences.

It was in erotic portrayals of characters during assignations that these gendered codes of movement were most clearly displayed. The initial meeting of men and women is often told through a story of a chase. 'Saucy Jack' stops 'Miss Syres' along the 'flow'ry road' before laying her on the ground and having sex with her, while the man gazing at Kitty's window dreams of 'a painted, flow'ry mead' in which he can pursue and catch her.[59] Representing this pursuit metaphorically in *A Voyage to Lethe*, Samuel Cock describes how he 'sheer'd off in pursuit of a beautiful new Frigate', 'chased her several Weeks to no Purpose', and finally 'clapp'd her suddenly too in the Windward Passage'.[60] This chase continues and the woman escapes, but the language of hunting suggests the violence implicit in these chases. Penises are described 'in pursuit of

---

[57] *Genuine Memoirs of . . . Miss Maria Brown*, vol. I, pp. 146–7. See also ibid., vol. II, p. 225.

[58] Ibid, vol. I, pp. 29–30, 61–2, 192–8. Later, another woman is reported as going to plays, parks and gardens, but this – significantly – is a prelude to her descent into prostitution. See vol. I, pp. 211–12.

[59] 'Saucy Jack; or, the Bladish Adonis of Tottenham Court Road', in *Bacchanalian Magazine*, p. 61; 'A Soliloquy. Gazing at Kitty's Chamber Window', in *Festival of Love*, p. 288.

[60] *Voyage to Lethe* (1741), p. 72.

their Prey', and men as 'true-metal'd Hunters'.[61] *A Description of the Temple of Venus* concludes with a lengthy description of the narrator's pursuit of Themiris through a beautiful grove, passing a satyr chasing a nymph and Apollo chasing Diana, the goddess of hunting.[62] His exploration of this woman's body when he finally catches up with her perpetuates the theme:

> Is it possible for you to imagine where at last I found *Cupid*? He was seated on the lips of *Themiris*; I afterwards saw him in her Bosom; he flew down to her Feet, but I still found him out there; he hid himself beneath her Girdle, I follow'd him and shou'd never have given over the Pursuit, if *Themiris* dissolv'd in Tears, had not put an end to the Chase: He had now taken Refuge in her last Recess, 'tis so enchantingly delightful, that he is unable to leave it.[63]

The narrator followed Cupid over, around and into the woman's body, at which point he touches her (perhaps with his hand or penis) 'beneath her Girdle'. However, despite the man's use of persuasion and force, the pleasure of being 'deliciously Criminal' eludes him.[64]

Women were often caught and stopped prior to sex, then. In other encounters, women were shown waiting for men in an exposed and vulnerable state. Princess Tricolora is lying down waiting for the arrival of her new husband on the evening of their wedding, and to prepare for sex with Prince Discreet she 'placed herself on one of those long low chairs so pure and convenient for Pleasure to give Virtue a fall, and lay sprawling on her back'.[65] In *A Chinese Tale* (c. 1740), Cham-Yam reclines on a sofa to engage in the masturbation which will prompt the hidden man to rush towards her and transport her to the adjacent bed. Similarly, one woman in *The Prostitutes of Quality* (1757) is found by her lover in a 'languishing Posture, lying on a Couch, all undressed'.[66] The collection *Forty Select Poems* (1753) contains a series of encounters in which the man approaches an immobile woman. One woman is discovered by a 'youthful swain' lying on the grass with her petticoat and gown over her head, after which they have sex; another man finds a woman apparently asleep, clambers on to her bed, and 'began to downright sinning'; while a nun's pregnancy results from an encounter when 'father *Stiffrump*' enters her room as she lies naked on the bed.[67] Poems in the later collection *The Festival of Love* (1770) depict Palemon discovering Phyllira reclining on a couch, and Lubin approaching Lydia as she 'on a bank reclining lay'.[68] Sex usually began with a man approaching a stationary woman.

Such patterns contextualize Stretser's reference to Richard Manningham's wax models in *A New Description of Merryland*. Late-eighteenth-century wax

---

[61] *New Description of Merryland*, p. 31; *Spy on Mother Midnight*, p. 28.
[62] *Description of the Temple of Venus*, p. 60.   [63] Ibid., p. 61.   [64] Ibid., p. 62.
[65] *Did You Ever See Such Damned Stuff?*, pp. 71–4, 102.
[66] *Chinese Tale*, pp. 19, 25; *Prostitutes of Quality*, p. 170.
[67] 'The Raven', p. 185; 'The Chaplain', p. 45; 'The Nun', p. 133, all in *Forty Select Poems*.
[68] 'The Girdle of Venus', pp. 31–5; 'Epigram', p. 5, both in *Festival of Love*.

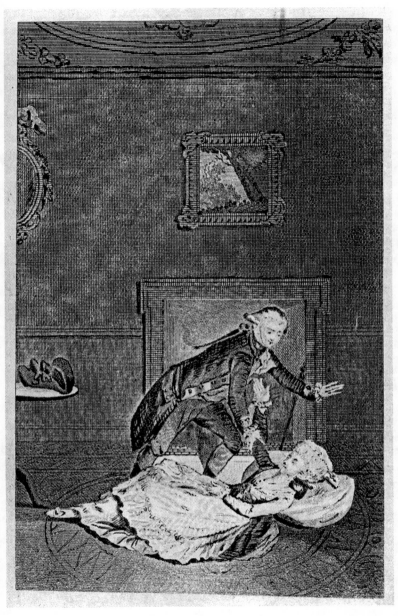

Illustration 25: *A Fine Subject on the Carpet*. Inserted in *A Voyage to Lethe* (1741) BL: Cup.1001.c.4.

anatomical models of female figures invariably reclined in 'passive, yet sexually inviting poses', in stark contrast to wax models of male bodies, which were 'upright muscle men'.[69] Three-dimensional medical representations of female bodies and erotic depictions traded in comparable ideas of potential gendered movement, and it is striking that many visual images in erotic books employ similar gendered codes of movement. In the frontispiece to *The Surprize* (1739), Timante bounds up the stairs and enters Araminta's room where she lies on the bed.[70] (Illustration 15.) In Illustration 17, a man has apparently entered the room to find the seated woman holding a child. His posture, together with his grimacing face, perhaps indicates violence, though the slight smiles on the faces of the woman and child suggest that this was not the intention, and that his outstretched arms are ready to embrace not attack. In *A Fine Subject on the Carpet*, the woman reclines on the floor, and her outstretched arm could indicate a request for help, or an invitation to the standing man to join her. (Illustration 25.)

In written depictions, the women portrayed waiting for men resemble not just wax models, but statuesque figures. In one episode in *The Fruit-Shop*, a woman retires to her house 'to be there in readiness for his reception', and is positioned so that she becomes the statuesque centrepiece to the marble artwork of the bed:

She was placed on a bed of the most elegant, as well as costly workmanship; all around it were fixed Cupids of Parian marble, each connected to the other by flowery wreaths. On Alexander's entering the apartment, she by a bound of affected emotion, so contrived matters that part of the bed-covering was thrown off, and he had so full a view of her well-formed limbs, &c. that he could no longer refrain.[71]

An almost indistinguishable scenario greets Anthony as he enters Cleopatra's room for the first time. Again surrounded by marble Cupids, this bed is also covered with a painted canopy depicting Mars and Venus. All is arranged so that, as Cleopatra undresses, the marble Cupids become animated, and the face of the painted Venus is 'suddenly vermillioned over with a blush of rivalship'.[72] In this performance, distinctions between the painted, sculpted and human figures are elided.

The texture of women's skin reinforces the sense of female bodies as cast figures. Their 'well-turn'd limbs' and 'iv'ry legs', their skin like 'marble' and their 'Soft-moulded legs! smooth-polished arms', are all reminiscent of carved statues.[73] Women's bodies were literally 'By nature form'd for soft

[69] Jordanova, *Sexual Visions*, pp. 44, 45.   [70] See *Surprize*, p. 7, for the description in the text.
[71] *Fruit-Shop*, vol. I, pp. 55–6.   [72] Ibid., vol. I, pp. 68–9.
[73] 'The Girdle of Venus Unbuckled', p. 31; 'The Judgment Reversed, or Chloe Triumphant', p. 142. Both in *Festival of Love*. 'The Bridal Night', in *Pleasures that Please on Reflection*, p. 47.

delight'.[74] To a degree, this is also true of representations of male bodies. In the poem 'Epistle', a woman strokes the penis or 'marble pillar', while the poem *An Elegy on the Lamented Death of the Electrical Eel* (1777) is a depiction of the male genitals as monument.[75] Yet these are objects to be revered and worshipped, not to be revealed, studied and explored as female statues were.[76] As Richard Cosway's (1742–1821) painting a *Group of Connoisseurs* (1771–5) suggests, the contemplation of statues of women was thought to bring gratification. (Illustration 5.) In this picture, six gentlemen discuss three sculptures of women. Two of the men are particularly fascinated by one of the naked statues. One man appears to stride towards the statue, eyes fixed on her naked buttocks, with his left hand raised as if to touch them and his right hand suggestively buried deep in his breeches. A second man is seated, legs astride, examining the statue through a looking-glass, with his left hand similarly thrust deep into the folds of his lap. Erotic depictions of female bodies as statues can be placed in this connoisseurial context.

This visual depiction of female statues highlights their immobility, in contrast to the active male viewers. Erotic depictions of women as statues capture something of this immobility. The colour of women's skin accentuated their statuesque quality. Venus displays 'delightful limbs exceeding the snow in whiteness; ivory, marble for their polished smoothness'.[77] Other women have breasts of 'spotless iv'ry white' or 'like the driven snow', and thighs 'the Colour of *Alabaster*'.[78] Whiteness was a mark of feminine beauty in visual art, and this whiteness of skin had racial implications which were very occasionally voiced in erotica.[79] However, the lack of discussion of cultural, ethnic or racial differences between women is striking. Primarily, the colour of women's skin was a sign of sexual – not racial – difference. It was also closely associated

---

[74] 'Miss and the Parson', in *Forty Select Poems*, p. 117. Also see 'The Chrystal Bottle', in *Forty Select Poems*, p. 10.

[75] 'Epistle', in *Festival of Love*, 85; *Elegy on the Lamented Death of the Electrical Eel*, see pp. 21–9 for the inscription. See also *Electrical Eel* (No publication details, [c. 1770]), p. 13, where the eel is referred to as 'this hieroglyphic rais'd on stone', perhaps alluding to Egyptian images of and monuments to the penis.

[76] Indeed, such viewings of male bodies were satirized in the eighteenth century, as for instance in Rowlandson's watercolour *Stowe Gardens*, in which a woman points her parasol at the lower abdomen of one of the male statues. Rowlandson's sketch is reproduced in Hunt, *Figure in the Landscape*, p. 198.

[77] *Fruit-Shop*, vol. II, p. 17. The descriptions of Venus may have been more likely to display such characteristics because Venus was known to many through statues. In addition, many sculptures of this period were lead figures painted white to simulate stone or marble. See Malcolm Baker, '"Squabby Cupids and Clumsy Graces": Garden Sculpture and Luxury in Eighteenth-Century England', *Oxford Art Journal* 18 (1995), p. 6.

[78] 'The Bridal Night', in *Pleasures that Please on Reflection*, p. 47; 'The Squire', in *Festival of Love*, p. 231; *Voyage to Lethe* (1741), p. 27.

[79] On whiteness and beauty, see Stewart, *Engraven Desire*, p. 15. On race in erotica see, for example, 'The Ink Bottle', in *Forty Select Poems*, pp. 46–50.

with the movement of their bodies: unlike men's bodies, women's bodies were
smooth, white and statuesque.

Force and violence

Women may have been still as sex commenced, but they did not remain so. Once
men had either stopped women or found women waiting, these men proceeded
to move the bodies of their female lovers around. Most encounters closely
resemble the experience wished for by one man:

> My arms! that shall, with eager haste,
> Encircle now your slender waist;
> Now round your neck be careless hung,
> And now o'er all your frame be slung:
> About your limbs my limbs will twine,
> And lay your glowing cheek to mine;
> Close to my broader, manlier chest,
> I'll press thy firm, proud-swelling breast;
> . . . .
> My murm'ring tongue shall speak my bliss,
> Shall court your yielding lips to kiss;
> Each kiss with thousands I'll repay,
> And almost suck your breath away;
> A thousand more you then shall give,
> And then a thousand more receive;
> In transport half dissolv'd we'll lie,
> Venting our wishes in a sigh![80]

The contrast between the perpetual movement of the man and the stationary
figure of the woman is striking. The woman is absolutely still apart from return-
ing kisses and being 'pressed' by her male lover. Samuel Johnson's dictionary
defines 'to press' as 'To squeeze; to crush . . . To constrain; to compel . . .
To enforce' and 'To act with compulsive violence, to urge; to distress'.[81] This
poem describes a form of forceful, even aggressive, movement.

Many erotic scenarios depict men coming across women whom they then
physically manoeuvre before having sex. Sometimes this act lacks violence:
one man who comes across a female friend in the woods 'gently laid' her on
the grass and has sex.[82] In other scenarios, the description of the sexual act
is brief and gives little away about its nature. One man's liaison with Sally
began as he 'stole into her room' and 'lay her on the bed', while another man
spies a woman and 'laid her down, amongst the dew'.[83] On most occasions,

---

[80] 'To Cynthia', in *Festival of Love*, p. 18.
[81] Johnson, *Dictionary*.   [82] 'The Apocrypha', in *Forty Select Poems*, p. 130.
[83] 'The Black Ey'd Maid', in *Bacchanalian Magazine*, p. 100; 'The Chrystal Bottle', in *Forty
Select Poems*, p. 12.

however, this act of manoeuvring women's bodies just prior to sex is described in terms which suggest a degree of force. Maria Brown's first lover follows her to her bed-chamber and, as Maria describes it, 'threw me upon the bed', while another virgin tells how a man 'flew into the room' and 'threw me down on the bed'.[84] In the poem 'Caelia Enjoy'd in Her Sleep', several key themes converged. The male narrator, whose previous attempts to have sex with Caelia have been scuppered by her 'stubborn will', whispers to the sleeping woman, and interprets her rising breast and the lack of 'rude Alarms' as the permission he had sought. He eagerly wins the 'Fort', noting her consent even though she is described as 'insensible and dead'.[85]

Philip Stewart has argued that the motif of the sleeping woman in eighteenth-century French erotica was '*in form* a symbolic rape', which revealed the contrivance that a woman would rather be 'taken' than 'give herself overtly'.[86] Descriptions of sexual activity in eighteenth-century English erotica certainly tend to erase the issue of female consent, because they assume female submission. In this way, they echo the testimony given in early-modern rape cases. Female submission was integral both to male denials of rape and to women's accusations of rape. Men claimed that women were willing and complicit. However, because women were expected to be modest and submissive, women in court were unable to claim that they had resisted *and* retain their reputation as modest. Women plaintiffs therefore claimed they had been forced to submit during rape, and in so doing echoed defendants' stories by stressing female complicity.[87] The roles of women in all sexual intercourse, whether consensual or not, were described as submissive. The only way women could describe acts of sexual assault without implicating their own consent, therefore, was to portray the sexual assault as an act of violence rather than of sex.[88] The language used in erotica was reminiscent of that used by female plaintiffs claiming that a rape had been perpetrated. In court, women might described how an assailant 'came into the bedroom [and] threw her down and attempted to be rude with her'; Walker claims that these victims could be portrayed as 'a mere rag doll', and such depictions were virtually indistinguishable from those in erotica.[89] However, while women in court used this language to differentiate acts of violence from acts of sex, in erotica a different process was at work. Erotic authors failed to distinguish between

---

[84] *Genuine Memoirs of . . . Miss Maria Brown*, vol. I, p. 117; 'The Maidenhead', in *Bacchanalian Magazine*, pp. 45–6.

[85] 'Caelia Enjoy'd in Her Sleep', in *St. James's Miscellany*, pp. 14–15.

[86] Stewart, *Engraven Desire*, p. 190. See pp. 175–233 for his lengthy discussion of this motif.

[87] Walker, 'Rereading Rape', p. 6.

[88] Ibid., p. 8; Anna Clark, *Women's Silence, Men's Violence: Sexual Assault in England, 1770–1845* (London: Pandora, 1987), p. 39.

[89] Ann Hobbs testifying in 1790, quoted in Clark, *Women's Silence*, p. 29; Walker, 'Rereading Rape', p. 12.

Illustration 26:   Sexual violence. Frontispiece of *Kick Him Jenny* (1737).

consensual and non-consensual sex; they also presented acts of violence as acts of sex.

Women are frequently depicted being physically coerced into sex in erotica, but while they might suffer aggression these women will ultimately feel pleasure. In one poem, for example, the woman is physically 'o'ercome' by her male lover, but she eventually 'yields' to his attentions.[90] Men are assured that women will not complain about rough treatment: 'Push as you will to give them pain, / They'll neither wince, nor yet complain'.[91] At other times, male aggression is presented as just. When Cham-Yam is 'fiercely seiz'd' regardless of her vociferous protestations in *A Chinese Tale*, the author simply draws the poem teasingly to a close.[92] Her treatment is a form of punishment for pondering aloud on 'The Charms of Woman, and her Pow'r' immediately before the attack.[93] These incidents, which might look like assaults to modern readers, are not distinguished from other types of sexual liaison. This becomes clear through a comparison of two poems apparently written by the same author, *Kick Him Nan* (1734) and *Kick Him Jenny* (1737). The frontispieces of these

---

[90] 'Mutual Love', in *Festival of Love*, p. 5.
[91] 'The Question Answered', in *Forty Select Poems*, p. 28.
[92] *Chinese Tale*, p. 25.   [93] Ibid., p. 20.

Illustration 27:   The wedding night. From title page of *Kick Him Nan* (1734).

poems (Illustrations 26 and 27) demonstrate the important similarities between
them. Though depicting on the one hand a servant's room and on the other the
chamber of an aristocrat, the interiors are virtually identical, apart from subtle
details such as the handle on the chamber pot, the style of candlestick, and
the use of a sword in *Kick Him Nan* and a walking stick in *Kick Him Jenny*.
There are also key similarities between the texts. Portraying a very violent
sexual encounter, *Kick Him Jenny* ends with the female servant's acquiescence
and her happy agreement to marriage, crowning the couple's 'Joys a-bed'.[94]
Set on the wedding night of a young aristocratic couple, *Kick Him Nan* depicts
a young virgin initially resisting her new husband – 'I dare not yield, and yet I
must' – though she ultimately 'struggled a Consent'.[95] Though part of the point
is to comment on the different sexual practices of different social groups, these
encounters shared a great deal. Here I want to draw attention to how the married
couple are envisaged performing the same kinds of sexual role as the unmar-
ried couple: the male overcoming or overpowering of any female resistance is
central to rapes and marital consummations alike. Female submission, either
freely given or coerced, was ultimately always present. Indeed, so ubiquitous

---

[94] *Kick Him Jenny*, p. 22.
[95] *Kick Him Nan: Or, a Poetical Description of a Wedding Night. By the Author of* Kick Him Jenny
(For T. Reynolds in the Strand, 1734), p. 6.

had descriptions of rapes of women become that one erotic author relishes the fact that the rape 'of a BOY is reserved a VIRGIN *Theme* for *mine*'.[96] The resulting poem was the only episode in eighteenth-century erotica for which the word 'rape' is used, and this was the rape of a man. There simply are no rapes of women in eighteenth-century erotica.

The patterns of movement revealed in geographical, medical and scientific modes of exploration were potent expressions of gendered power relations. In erotic narratives, male bodies are portrayed moving and acting in space, and certain patterns of male movement are associated with the quest for knowledge and the assertion of force. In metaphorical descriptions of sex, the movement of the male narrator/viewer progresses from a position above the stationary female body, across and then into the body. The implied movement of men in these descriptions thus transforms from a cartographic viewpoint into a position akin to a medical examination or geographical exploration. Notions of male movement and female immobility are again revealed in descriptions of men and women encountering one another prior to sex in which women are depicted waiting for men, and also in descriptions of men moving women around during sex. From explorations of stationary female bodies to encounters of some violence, the gendered patterns of movement which endorsed male movement and female immobility mutate into male force and female submission. Both in cases of implied movement in metaphorical descriptions and in depictions of male and female characters, male motion conveys knowledge, self-control and power. Indeed, there was a continuum of male violence, I would argue, that can be traced throughout these erotic encounters. According to Samuel Johnson, the word 'violence' might indicate 'Force; strength', 'An attack', 'Outrage; unjust force', 'Eagerness; vehemence', 'Injury; infringement', or 'Forcible defloration'.[97] In all of these senses, the word aptly conveys the treatment of women described in much eighteenth-century erotica. Civil politeness and happy domesticity apart, the erotic imaginary championed male sexual aggression against defenceless women.

For some eighteenth-century writers, the vulnerability of a woman to rape was part of her attractiveness to men, and the submission and weakness of women in erotic encounters was clearly compatible with wider expectations of modest femininity.[98] Correspondingly, the force and violence displayed by men during erotic encounters can be aligned with wider understandings of masculinity. There were anxieties in eighteenth-century England about the seduction of women by libertines, a practice regarded as 'not only ungenerous, unjust, unmanly, and cowardly, but even cruel to humanity'.[99] Yet behind warnings

---

[96] *Consummation*, p. ii.   [97] Johnson, *Dictionary*.
[98] Susan Staves, 'Fielding and the Comedy of Attempted Rape', in Beth Tobin (ed.), *History, Gender & Eighteenth-Century Literature* (Athens: University of Georgia Press, 1994), p. 102.
[99] *Lady's Magazine*, April 1775, p. 198.

given to women to resist and pleas made to men to control themselves lay powerful beliefs in men's aggressive sexual desires. 'Rape', Walker concludes, 'was easily depicted as an extreme expression of men's "lustfull Desires" and "pleasures".[100] Similarly, Anna Clark states that 'sexual violence committed by men on adult women tended to be seen as an extension of natural, everyday relations between the sexes'.[101] Strength and vigour were, as we saw in chapter four, crucial attributes of the celebrated male body, and male sexual violence could be seen as an expression of appropriate male vigour and authority. Some elite circles celebrated the 'heroic rapist', and men bragged about the sexual violence they had perpetrated against women. Actual men who had committed acts of sexual violence published their stories with the ostensible purpose of defending their reputations, but in a way which suggested a community of men who gained pleasure from reading such stories.[102] The valorization of male force in erotica can be positioned in the context of a similar readership of men, who found stories of rape and sexual violence supportive of dominant constructions of healthy masculinity and male sexuality. In fact, violence was an important expression of male passion. As one male narrator in erotica explained when his lover came to his room: 'Respect, and that Purity of Tenderness with which till now I had even regarded her, . . . was utterly erased; – the humble, the perfect Lover was extinct, and I was now all Man, resolute, desiring Man!' He was resolute and daring; she, we are told, offered 'the least Resistance'.[103] Such distinctions in the expression of sexual passion were important markers of sexual difference. By drawing on contemporary Enlightened knowledge, erotic authors expressed these differences through the associations and the navigations of space. The ability to move both oneself, and a female lover, was constitutive of a man's masculinity: during one encounter, a man's motion was initiated precisely 'to shew he was a man'.[104] The obverse – a woman who moved too much with her male lover – compromised masculinity.[105] Male movement, force and violence exemplified masculine vigour, while female recumbency, immobility and submission conveyed feminine vulnerability.

Patterns of male and female movement were embedded in and constitutive of inequitable gender relations. As one of Maria Brown's lovers announces as he flees the country, 'the *Geography of love* is a "nasty science"'.[106] Men were depicted breaking through the boundaries presented by female bodies and plunging deep into those bodies, moving towards women who were waiting, throwing those frozen women onto beds and engaging in sex while women remained absolutely still, if not unconscious. Such themes circulated in erotic

---

[100] Walker, 'Rereading Rape', p. 5.   [101] Clark, *Women's Silence*, p. 42.
[102] Ibid., pp. 34–5. See also p. 43.   [103] *Prostitutes of Quality*, p. 46.
[104] 'The Filthy Beast', in *Forty Select Poems*, p. 126.
[105] 'The Squire', in *Festival of Love*, p. 201.
[106] *Genuine Memoirs of . . . Miss Maria Brown*, vol. II, p. 174.

and court narratives, and they shaped how women and men articulated to themselves and to others intimate sexual experiences. The language used to describe non-consensual and consensual sex in erotica was certainly not a language used exclusively by men, therefore. In court, both female witnesses and male defendants conspired in the 'act of denying female agency'.[107] Moreover, female writers of eighteenth-century fiction also created scenarios of rape in which women felt pleasure; indeed rape has been described as 'the central paradigm for sexual experience' in their work. The frisson and romance of sexual violence in the fictional writings of women is undeniable. Yet female authors were careful to punish perpetrators and wrap these incidents in unequivocal moral comment.[108] While erotica traded in contemporary ideas about gender and sex, it was not an imprint of other genres; erotic stories of rape must be distinguished from the evidence of the courts and amatory fiction. Erotic fantasies of male sexual violence and female submission were free from both critical authorial comment and punishment by the judicial system. No one suffered lasting pain or distress in erotica; reluctance was always disingenuous, resistance inevitably yielded. In the end, everyone was willing and complicit in eighteenth-century erotica.

[107] Walker, 'Rereading Rape', p. 10.
[108] Quote from Bowers, 'Sex, Lies and Invisibility', pp. 52, 67. See my introduction for a discussion of rape scenes in women's 'amatory fiction'.

7   Pleasure

Roy Porter claimed that pleasure 'came into its own in the eighteenth century'.[1] Driving this elevation of pleasure were philosophical revisions of the role of the body in human nature, and its relationship to the soul and the mind. In scientific and religious writings from the mid-seventeenth century, the opposition between body and soul was denied.[2] The flesh had always been subordinate to the mind, but as the Enlightenment progressed naturalistic and materialist philosophy transformed the hierarchical mind-body pairing and thus enhanced the status of the corporeal.[3] Intimately linked to this transformation in the mind-body hierarchy was a new stress on the senses. This was particularly visible in the French philosophical tradition known as 'sensationism', which 'from the very experience of the body in seeing, hearing, smelling, tasting, and touching . . . led to the establishment of a new authority, the authority of experience'.[4] Concomitant with French sensationism was the work of British writers such as John Locke (1632–1704) and David Hume (1711–76), both of whom argued for the pre-eminence of sense-knowledge, challenging René Descartes' (1596–1650) assertion that intellectual judgement or reason alone was enough to support a

---

[1] Roy Porter, 'Enlightenment and Pleasure', in Roy Porter and Marie Mulvey Roberts (eds), *Pleasure in the Eighteenth Century* (Basingstoke: Macmillan, 1996), p. 1. See also Roy Porter, 'Material Pleasures in the Consumer Society', in Porter and Roberts (eds), *Pleasure in the Eighteenth Century*, p. 35. The libidinous view of the eighteenth century owes much to Lawrence Stone's account of a period of liberty lasting from around 1670 to 1770–90, which was sandwiched between the collapse of moral Puritanism and renewed moral reform. See his *Family, Sex and Marriage*, pp. 328–9, 422.

[2] Rosalie Osmond, *Mutual Accusation: Seventeenth-Century Body and Soul Dialogues in their Literary and Theological Context* (Toronto: University of Toronto Press, 1990), p. xiii. The soul–body dichotomy, which had been used in seventeenth-century poetry as an analogy of the relationship between husband and wife, was eroded. On the gendered nature of the soul–body pairing, see ibid., pp. 157–161.

[3] Roy Porter, 'Mixed Feelings: The Enlightenment and Sexuality in Eighteenth-Century Britain', in P.-G. Boucé (ed.), *Sexuality in Eighteenth-Century Britain* (Manchester: Manchester University Press, 1982), p. 5; G. S. Rousseau and Roy Porter, 'Introduction: Toward a Natural History of Mind and Body', in G. S. Rousseau (ed.), *The Languages of Psyche: Mind and Body in Enlightenment Thought* (Berkeley: University of California Press, 1990), p. 31.

[4] John C. O'Neal, *The Authority of Experience: Sensationist Theory in the French Enlightenment* (Pennsylvania: Pennsylvania State University Press, 1996), pp. 1–2.

belief in an individual's existence.[5] Changing ideas on the relative primacy of
body and mind and the pre-eminence of the senses were echoed in changing
attitudes towards sex: the Enlightenment exaltation of the body and its needs
could be easily aligned with a veritable unleashing of sexual desires. In France,
for example, it was philosophy, rather than libertine literature or medical texts,
which sparked a discourse on eroticism.[6] Certainly, echoing Lawrence Stone's
earlier claims about the impact of the Restoration, Roy Porter has claimed that
Enlightenment ideas about bodies furnished a prodigious 'hedonistic liberation
of the libido'.[7]

Alongside Porter's claim for the elevation of pleasure, though, stands
Laqueur's assertion about the desexualization of women. Thomas Laqueur
charts a 'revaluation of pleasure' which 'sacrificed the idea of women as inher-
ently passionate'.[8] Laqueur's argument rests on the idea that the eighteenth
century saw new ideas about the nature and primacy of human physicality, a
vision which produced the transition from a cultural 'gender' to the ontological,
physically based category of 'sex'.[9] Such changes were an integral component
of Enlightenment materialism. Both theses are depicted as products of new,
Enlightenment thinking; both reflect the momentous transformations in theories about bodies that apparently occurred during this period. But there is
an unresolved tension between the pictures of pleasure given by Laqueur and
Porter, and their implications for women.

The issue of gendered access to or experience of pleasure has been considered
by some historians of pornography in the context of materialist or sensationist
philosophy. Despite the apparently democratic elevation of pleasure in his later
work, Porter's examination of Enlightenment ideas in John Cleland's *Fanny
Hill, or Memoirs of a Woman of Pleasure* (1748–9) concluded that the sexual pleasures of the new materialist thinking applied largely to men.[10] This
revised Leo Braudy's earlier account of Cleland's book, which asserted that,
in the book's mechanistic materialist philosophy, 'Cleland through Fanny is
transmuted into the first feminist'.[11] But it is this view, which sees materialist
pornography as an important site of female agency, that dominates recent work
on eighteenth-century France. While acknowledging that the female narrators

---

[5] Ibid., p. 3. On the changing fortunes of the theories of the origins of knowledge, see Constance
Classen, *Worlds of Sense: Exploring the Senses in History and across Cultures* (London: Routledge, 1993), pp. 1–11; and Anthony Synnott, 'Puzzling over the Senses: From Plato to Marx',
in David Howes (ed.), *The Varieties of Sensory Experience: A Sourcebook in the Anthropology
of the Senses* (Toronto: University of Toronto Press, 1991), pp. 61–76.

[6] Michael Edmund Winston, 'From Literature to Medicine to Philosophy: Sexuality in Eighteenth-
Century France', unpublished PhD thesis, Emory University (1995).

[7] Porter, 'Mixed Feelings', p. 5. See Stone, *Family, Sex and Marriage*, p. 328.

[8] Laqueur, 'Orgasm, Generation', pp. 3, 35.

[9] Laqueur, *Making Sex*, p. 8.   [10] Porter, 'Mixed Feelings', p. 15.

[11] Leo Braudy, '*Fanny Hill* and Materialism', *Eighteenth-Century Studies* 4 (1970), p. 37.

in this material were often 'social victims and hence social inferiors', Margaret Jacob claims that these women gained power from their status as the new prophets of materialist philosophy. These women were 'not only irrepressibly participants, but also guides to the universe of the senses'.[12] Dorelies Kraakman has also argued that female characters gained agency from the 'sensationist' philosophy. Women were depicted as curious, knowledge-thirsty and active, using sense-perception as the route to sexual knowledge, and Kraakman hails this unequivocally as 'feminist'.[13] Materialist philosophy and an emphasis on the senses moulded pornography into a site of female sexual agency.

This chapter explores these issues in erotic culture. Though erotic authors referred to contemporary scientific, geographic, medical, scientific and historical works, they rarely drew directly from philosophical texts which explicitly discussed materialism or the senses.[14] Nevertheless, as described below, English erotic writers were aware of many debates which were manifestations of eighteenth-century materialism. Indeed, erotica was a genre very much concerned with sexual pleasure, and can be considered an integral part of this philosophically sustained, pleasure-seeking culture. Employing the framework of the five senses, I want to consider how pleasure and desire were discussed in the literature of eighteenth-century erotic cultures. What was deemed the cause of sexual desire? Through which senses was desire aroused? What type of sensual experiences were sanctioned? And how was gender implicated in these discussions?

Erotic authors elevated the physical experience of desire and sex; they also discussed the integral role that sense-experience played in the cause and effect of pleasure. Sex was portrayed as a literally sensual experience. As one man reports, 'we passed the Remainder of the Night in as much satisfaction as two Persons possess'd with a Passion (where the Senses only are call'd to counsel, and the Soul has no part) can find in the Enjoyment of each other'.[15] Indeed, the declaration of one of these erotic authors that 'we know nothing but by the medium of our sense' chimed with the contemporaneous proponents of 'materialism' and 'sensationism'.[16] As these comments suggest, the senses were not always differentiated. Much existing work on the senses is keen to stress that each sense has a distinct history.[17] Certainly, in common with Samuel Johnson

[12] Jacob, 'Materialist World of Pornography', pp. 164, 174.
[13] Kraakman, 'Reading Pornography Anew', p. 548.
[14] A notable exception was the use of Julien Offray de La Mettrie, *L'Homme-plante*, in *Man-Plant*. See chapters two and three above for a discussion of this erotic spoof.
[15] *Prostitutes of Quality*, pp. 47–8.   [16] *Fruit-Shop*, vol. I, p. 83.
[17] Historians have highlighted the declining importance of the sense of smell in the modern West, for example. See David Howes, 'Scent and Sensibility', *Culture, Medicine and Psychiatry* 13 (1989), pp. 81–9; Alain Corbin, *The Foul and the Fragrant: Odor and the French Social Imagination*, trans. by Miriam L. Kockan, Roy Porter and Christopher Prendergast (1982; Leamington: Berg, 1986); Classen, *Worlds of Sense*, pp. 15–36.

who listed 'sight; touch; hearing; smell; taste' in his definition of 'Sense', erotic authors discussed five different senses.[18] Yet descriptions of sense-perception often failed to separate senses from one another. For example, different senses were portrayed as having similar effects or yielding information of a comparable qualitative nature. Sometimes a range of senses was listed in a description of a body; at other times, general sensual pleasure was described.[19] On occasion, synaesthesia – where one sense-impression was produced by the stimulation of another sense – was also described. While taking each sense in turn, this chapter ultimately takes a more holistic approach. It argues that all the senses – even those on which erotic authors were apparently silent – collaborated to manufacture particular kinds of sexual liaisons and particular pleasures. Taste and smell operated in very limited ways to display some body parts and hide others, thus 'allowing' descriptions only of particular sexual acts. In contrast, sound, touch and sight showed process rather than parts, facilitating the transmission, feeling and arousal of sexual pleasure. A hierarchy of the senses was established, but each sense played a part in shaping a gendered economy of pleasure which conformed to the powerful heterosexual, masculinist vision which informed eighteenth-century erotica. There was no democracy of sexual pleasure in erotic material; and in cause, experience and effect, pleasures were gendered.

The causes of pleasure

Erotic authors debated where pleasure came from and how it was caused, and in these debates the impact of materialist philosophy on erotic authors is evident. When discussing the origin of desire, authors explicitly raised the mind-body pairing, debating whether desire was the product of stimulation by an external object such as an encounter with a lover, or was created internally, perhaps by the imagination or some pre-existing passion. Some authors, for example, are loath to wrench apart body and mind, and disrupt any simple dichotomy of mind versus matter. Desire in both sexes is produced by a combination of 'natures', 'inclinations' and 'strong temptations'.[20] Indeed, sex is 'the only perfect pleasure; because it employs, at one and the same time, the parts of the body, and the faculties of the soul'.[21] Authors playfully exploit opportunities for innuendo in drawing qualitative distinctions between the impact of external stimuli and that of the imagination. The narrator of *La Souricière* (1794) explains that 'The pleasures of the Imagination are capable of affording us great felicity', but his companion – a mature woman – replies, 'But *reality* generally goes *much further* in my opinion.'[22] Some authors may have appeared to elevate the

---

[18] Johnson, *Dictionary*.
[19] See, for example, *Why and the Wherefore*, pp. 34–5; *Prostitutes of Quality*, p. 211.
[20] 'The Fright', in *Forty Select Poems*, p. 1.   [21] *Secret History of Pandora's Box*, p. 53.
[22] *La Souricière*, pp. 29–30.

spiritual above the sensual, but such claims were disingenuous. The author of the preface to *A Description of the Temple of Venus* (1726) claims: 'The Design of this Poem is to prove, that our Happiness does not consist in those Pleasures that are administered to us by the Senses, but in the Sentiments of the Heart', only to add, 'nevertheless, our Felicity is never so perfect, as to be incapable of being ruffled by particular Accidents.'[23] However, there was ambivalence towards sexual desire which relied on the imagination rather than material stimuli.[24] In elevating 'actual' propellants of desire over and above 'imaginary' ones, male narrators and characters in particular stress the primacy of desire born of physical contact. In *The Surprize* (1739), for example, Araminta asks a man how he would behave if he found her naked and prostrate on her bed. He beseeches her to 'Shew me the *Thing itself*':

> For other Thoughts within us rise
> When Objects are before our Eyes,
> Than when Imagination brings
> Ideas only of the Things.[25]

While such a reply served as a mischievous ruse designed to encourage Araminta to undress, imaginative objects were presented as having a different impact from the 'real thing'. Ultimately, what stands out most forcefully is a championing of desire which is deeply physical in cause. Erotica favoured a materialist, physical approach to pleasure.

It is significant, then, that distinctions between desire caused by the imagination and desire caused by physical stimulus are often imagined to follow gendered lines. In the poem *A Chinese Tale* (c. 1740), a number of factors contribute to the final scene of masturbation by the woman Cham-Yam, including explicit paintings, books and the hot weather. Yet the factor which immediately precedes her disrobing is the power of her imagination: 'her Fancy prompts to see / The World's great *Primum Mobile*' [the penis].[26] In contrast to the man who watches Cham-Yam throughout her masturbation, and who rushes from his hiding place because 'the Scene' of her masturbating forced his 'Soul' to 'blaze', it is Cham-Yam's imagining of a man which arouses her passions.[27] In the comic *Did You Ever See Such Damned Stuff?* (1760), Princess Tricolora's thoughts of her lover have a similarly powerful effect on her body: 'And as that head of hers necessarily held correspondences with every part of her body; so on particular occasions, such as very tender thoughts indeed, there are constantly spirits sent express to the principal places'.[28] This is in stark contrast to

---

[23] *Description of the Temple of Venus*, p. ix.
[24] This ambivalence was shared by physicians. See Roy Porter, *'Barely Touching*: A Social Perspective on Mind and Body', in G. S. Rousseau (ed.), *The Languages of Psyche: Mind and Body in Enlightenment Thought* (Berkeley: University of California Press, 1990), p. 63.
[25] *Surprize*, p. 43.   [26] *Chinese Tale*, p. 22.   [27] Ibid., p. 24.
[28] *Did You Ever See Such Damned Stuff?*, p. 99.

the passion of the man who watches her earlier in the book, as she lay asleep, being tickled on her genitals by a glow-worm. In this instance, though the man has been 'meditating a discourse' of suggestive content, it is Tricolora who becomes the 'charming text' which makes him cry out in pleasure.[29] In erotic narratives, female desire born of imagination is acceptable, but a contrast is drawn between the women whose desires are aroused by thinking about men, and the men who react to the 'real' and tangible body before them.[30]

Indeed the form of desire held up for attack in many of these erotic books is an ethereal, incorporeal passion. In a genre peppered with satire, this passion is often criticized through religious allusion. The author of *The Fruit-Shop* (1765) debates the views of an advocate of the 'sterile system' in which sexual desire was kindled in the mind. He considers 'Whether a fire celestial being *conceived* and *kindled* in a *mind*, and on meeting with another similar, . . . is cosubstantiated [sic], and burns together in different breasts, till they expire in *ashes*, be strictly accurate'. Finally he explains that 'no female beauty hath ever made any impression on us, either through the eye or ear, whose effect was not felt to descend lower than the breast'.[31] This extract questions an incorporeal origin of desire through a reference to consubstantiation. This Protestant revision of the theology of the Eucharist asserted that the substance of the bread and the wine coexisted with the substance of Christ's Body and Blood after consecration. The erotic author uses this allusion to suggest that individuals' desire does not mingle in this way. Indeed, by questioning that a person's desire originated in the 'mind', and that it could burn with another's desire without contact, this author denies the power of intellectual or spiritual union, asserting the pre-eminence of physical experience. The author is particularly keen to stress the parts of the body in which sexual desire is felt, denying that desire strikes the heart, and asserting the intensity of physical, heterosexual and genital desire.

The religious-satirical component of eighteenth-century English erotica never approached the radical social critique of French pornographic material, but neither was this English material simply conservative and anti-Catholic.[32] Certainly, anti-Catholic feeling was revealed in the choice of sexualized locations, and an erotic text uses the insult of 'Popery' to refer to Catholicism.[33] But English erotica was anti-clerical, as the swipe against Protestant theology discussed above suggested. Many books used a religious analogy to ridicule certain forms of desire. Aroused while observing a beautiful woman in a church,

---

[29] Ibid., pp. 61, 62.
[30] See chapter one above for a discussion of the images of women reading erotic books that appeared in erotic narratives. These created a similar impression of women (but not men) responding to stimulants of the imagination.
[31] *Fruit-Shop*, vol. II, pp. 125, 126.   [32] As suggested by Hitchcock, *English Sexualities*, p. 19.
[33] See chapter five for anti-Catholic feeling revealed in sexualized locations; and *La Souricière*, p. 27, for a reference to 'Popery'.

the narrator of *A Spy on Mother Midnight* (1748) explains, 'I was in quite a different situation from the Apostle of the Gentiles, my Spirit and Flesh were both of a Mind'.[34] Here the author was distancing himself from St Paul, the man responsible for ushering in 'the new era of the Spirit' in Christianity, and emphasizing the flesh.[35] Indeed, as the erotic author goes on to explain, there was no merging of mind and body in this encounter, but an elevation of the latter: 'I had treated her in my own Mind as a Divinity, yet I was resolv'd to approach her as if made of Flesh and Bone, and should have been damnably vex'd to have found her Immaterial'.[36] What he initially finds, however, is a 'meer Prude': small comfort for a man who acknowledges his inability to 'assume the Habit of an aerial Being'.[37] The suspicion of an elevated, imaginative or spiritual passion in erotica is wrapped in allusions to religious faith, and this rejection of spiritual feelings became a crucial aspect of the genre's religious satire.

Taste and smell

While elevating sense-experience as the cause of pleasure, erotic authors gave some senses more attention than others. The senses of taste and smell in particular were discussed infrequently by erotic authors. In depictions of sexual activity, this absence served not to release the libido or enhance the sexual encounter, but severely to curtail experiential possibilities. While the metaphor of taste might be used to represent a woman's experience of penetration, 'Raptures of kissing we can . . . taste', and certainly open-mouthed kisses like the one enjoyed by the appropriately named Cherry, are enjoyed only rarely in this material.[38] Indeed, descriptions of mouths were opportunities for other senses to be invoked. Phrases such as 'strawberry nipples' and 'lips that wou'd challenge the cherry' emphasize the visual vibrancy of red, for example, as much as they do taste.[39] In another poem, a woman's lips are compared to a series of botanical and meteorological phenomena – 'the fresh rose-bud', 'the warm crimson of the blushing morn' and 'the gay blossoms of the summer thorn'. Though the lips display a 'ripen'd softness' and are indeed 'sweet', they are objects of aesthetic beauty, rather than of exceptional flavour.[40] Sight rather than taste governed the sensual experience of these lips.

---

[34] *Spy on Mother Midnight*, p. 3.
[35] F. L. Cross and E. A. Livingstone (eds.), *The Oxford Dictionary of the Christian Church*, 2nd edn. (1957; Oxford: Oxford University Press, 1974), p. 1048. St Paul laid the foundations for most Christian theology. The life of the Spirit begins at Baptism, which establishes the fellowship with the Holy Spirit.
[36] *Spy on Mother Midnight*, pp. 3–4.   [37] Ibid., pp. 4–5.
[38] 'The Geranium', in *Pleasures that Please on Reflection*, p. 38; 'Dick and Doll', p. 69, and 'The Squire', p. 195, both in *Festival of Love*.
[39] 'The Squire', in *Festival of Love*, p. 197; 'The Lover's Progress', in *Bacchanalian Magazine*, p. 78.
[40] 'Sonnet to Melissa's Lips', in *Festival of Love*, pp. 150–1.

Furthermore, it was exceptional for mouths to taste body parts other than mouths. Generally, the only parts of a body imbued with flavour were the genitals, and this was invariably disagreeable. In *A Voyage to Lethe* (1741), women's genitals are described as being 'water'd by a Rivulet somewhat of a brackish Taste'.[41] It is unclear whether this liquid emanates from the female body, or was male semen, but the liquid with a 'brackish taste' described in *The Fruit-Shop* is most certainly the latter.[42] In contrast to the many references to vaginal penetration, there are only scanty examples of oral sex,[43] and the material reveals a deep suspicion of oral sex in keeping with the emphasis on procreative sex. Some of the motivations behind this suspicion are suggested in *A Voyage to Lethe*. Sam Cock's imaginary voyage to Lethe takes in a visit to the 'Temple of Lust, dedicated to *Priapus*, a naked, misshapen Idol, bedecked with a Shrub called *Arbor Vitae*, to whom it is customary to offer another, called, *Frutex Vulvaria*.'[44] Worshippers are described in the act of fellatio, 'kissing and sucking the decorating Shrub with all the Marks of a furious Adoration'. Sam recoils from these rituals, and it is clear that the vitriolic criticism dealt to priapic worship in *A Voyage to Lethe* is driven partly by the author's associations between such worship and Catholicism, revealed when Sam explains that he does not take part in the ceremonies because he is 'a staunch Son of the Protestant Communion'. The author apparently regarded taking the Eucharist as a solely Catholic practice, and a despicable one.[45] Combining pagan ritual, Catholicism and oral sex, the author of *A Voyage to Lethe* perpetuated a long English tradition of linking despised sexual practices with belief systems regarded as dubious, particularly Catholicism.[46]

Discussions of the sense of smell likewise gave the impression of the curtailment of the range of sensations to be had in encounters with other bodies. Only rarely was there an olfactory dimension to sexual encounters, such as the 'Sweet smelt . . . hay on new-mown meads', or odour scattered by the wind.[47] When smells were ascribed to bodies, the odour was generally imagined to be

---

[41] *Voyage to Lethe* (1741), p. 28.   [42] *Fruit-Shop*, vol. I, p. 167.

[43] See, for example, 'The Girdle of Venus Unbuckled', in *Festival of Love*, p. 40; 'Jenny Sutton', in Morris, *Festival of Ancareon*, p. 39; *Why and the Wherefore*, p. 35.

[44] *Voyage to Lethe* (1741), p. 65.

[45] Ibid., p. 66. In the Catholic sacrament of Communion, the whole substance of the bread and wine had been converted into the whole substance of the Body and Blood of Christ, leaving only the appearance of bread and wine. This belief in transubstantiation was one of a number of theological difficulties Protestants had with 'Popery' at this time. See Colin Haydon, *Anti-Catholicism in Eighteenth-Century England, c. 1714–80* (Manchester: Manchester University Press, 1993), p. 5. However, not all references to the Eucharist were anti-Catholic. Communion weakened only gradually amongst Anglicans. See F. C. Mather, 'Georgian Churchmanship Reconsidered: Some Variations in Anglican Public Worship, 1714–1830', *Journal of Ecclesiastical History* 36 (1985), esp. pp. 265–75. Many thanks to Arthur Burns on this point.

[46] Hitchcock, *English Sexualities*, p. 61.

[47] 'Mutual Love', in *Bacchanalian Magazine*, p. 12; *Description of the Temple of Venus*, p. 2.

disagreeable. The nauseating smell of the first man with whom Maria Brown
has sex is in keeping with his distasteful character.[48] But it is the smell of female
bodies which received most attention. Suggesting a multi-sense experience, the
'astronomic observers' of the female genitalia in *The Fruit-Shop* are overcome
with 'rapturous ecstasy' when able 'to approach, smell it, or be plunged into
the middle of it!'.[49] The products of a woman's 'virgin bloom' might yield a
divine fragrance.[50] In one poem, the smell of a woman's genitals is an excuse
to have sex. A young man and woman observe a bull and cow having sex, and
the man explains that the bull knows when the cow is ready for sex when she
emits an odour. Not surprisingly, the woman responds with the declaration, 'Do
try if you can smell me?'. He lays her on the ground, kisses and touches her,
and 'Poor Sukey began to *stink*, / As bad, or worse, than ever.' The couple then
have sex.[51]

Yet such attitudes were unusual in a period in which the popular notion of
unveiling women to reveal an unsightly and odorous core was common. Female
genitals were thought to emit a particularly bad smell. Even the metaphor of
the flower could convey bad odour. 'Frutex Vulvaria' – as female bodies were
repeatedly termed – denoted displeasing odour.[52] A variety of vulvaria was also
known as 'stinking wild arach', and is described as smelling 'like the Sort of
Salt Fish call'd Old-Ling, or something like it'.[53] In one poem, this odour is
the excuse used by a tired man attempting to avoid sex with his voracious wife.
Despite her protestations that her vulva is 'fresh and sweet', after touching
her with his hand and smelling it he announces, 'Your marygold doth stink,
my dear'.[54] In *The Why and the Wherefore* (1765), this odour is regarded as a
punishment dealt by the men to the 'ugly flats' (unattractive vulvas): 'there has
always remained to them, probably from their fear and the filth and ordure in
which they had been rolled, such a rank smell as nothing afterwards could ever
purify'.[55] This smell of female genitals is therefore not only uninviting to men,
but is also an indication of women's ugliness and subjection.

There were two notable exceptions to the generally bad odour of bodies.
First, descriptions of male genitals favourably invoke a number of senses

---

[48] *Genuine Memoirs of . . . Miss Maria Brown*, vol. II, p. 19.   [49] *Fruit-Shop*, vol. I, p. 66.
[50] 'The Birth of the Rose', in *Pleasures that Please on Reflection*, p. 40.
[51] 'Love's Recipe for Stinking', in *Bacchanalian Magazine*, pp. 102–3.
[52] This term is used to describe the female genitals in *Wisdom Reveal'd*, p. 11, *Voyage to Lethe*
(1741), p. 65 and, of course, *Natural History of the Frutex Vulvaria* ([c. 1737]). Jonathan Swift's
poem *A Beautiful Young Nymph Going to Bed* (Dublin printed, London reprinted for J. Roberts,
1734) is a good example of the concern over women's interiors. Tobias Smollett revealed similar
anxieties about the aristocracy, suggesting that underneath their finery lurked dirty, loathsome
bodies. See Terence Bowers, 'Reconstituting the National Body in Smollett's *Travels through
Italy and France*', *Eighteenth-Century Life* 21 (1997), pp. 1–25.
[53] Bradley, *Dictionarium Botanicum*, vol. I. This same association between women's genitals and
fish can be found in a later poem. See 'Song', in *Festival of Love*, pp. 347–8.
[54] 'The Excuse', in *Forty Select Poems*, p. 169.   [55] *Why and the Wherefore*, p. 94.

simultaneously, including smell. The 'tree of life' in one book is one of the 'noblest kind for sight, smell, [and] taste', while the tree of life in another book breathes 'all its balmy Odours' (its semen) on the '*Frutex Vulvari*'.[56] Second, women's breath is frequently portrayed as having a pleasant smell. Their 'Balmy lips' will 'breathe perfume' like 'a gale / Passing o'er a fragrant vale', or 'balmy as the zephyr blows'.[57] In other words, while some body parts are almost erased by the workings of smell, women's lips and the semen and genitalia of men are foregrounded. Yet neither taste nor smell actually aroused the passions and rarely did they reflect that arousal. Rather, in contrast to the championing of all sense-experience implied by sensationism, taste and smell were deployed in a limited way and only a narrow range of sensual activities were sanctioned.

Sound

The sense of sound worked in starkly different ways to taste and smell, because the experience of sound was endowed with the potential 'to raise, to calm, or to vary the passions', including sexual passion.[58] During one orgiastic incident, 'the universal joy was still heightened to a higher pitch by the performance of a musical entertainment', and while Venus claimed to prefer 'the sense of feeling to that of hearing', Sol is depicted trying to woo her with 'the insinuating sounds of his lyre'.[59] If sound can arouse desire, then words can woo a lover. The narrator of *A Spy on Mother Midnight* attempts to seduce his beloved Maria with flattery and 'Catches and Love-Sonnets', before pandering to her apparent religiosity with 'Hymns and holy Stanzas'.[60] A correspondence between sight and hearing is transformed into synaesthesia when the effect on a woman looking at a man is compared to 'talk[ing] Bawdy in the Company of some raw inexperienced Country Virgin'.[61] As the discussion below explains, sound was akin to sight because it could itself arouse. Collaboration between sight and sound could be a mighty threat to appropriate sexuality. For example, the author of *A Description of the Temple of Venus* accounts for the lack of modesty amongst one people by recourse to their visual and aural experiences: their 'Eyes have accustom'd 'emselves to behold, and their Ears to listen, to the most offensive Things'.[62] There is no boundless surge of passionate noise in erotica, because while some sounds were clearly imagined to have a positive and vivifying effect on characters, others were believed to be detrimental to those who heard them.

---

[56] *Fruit-Shop*, vol. I, p. 75; *Wisdom Reveal'd*, p. 11.
[57] 'The Oeconomy of Love', in *Pleasures that Please on Reflection*, p. 14; 'To Lydia', p. 71; 'The Stray Nymph', p. 10; 'The Girdle of Venus Unbuckled', p. 31, all in *Festival of Love*.
[58] *Fruit-Shop*, vol. II, p. 114.   [59] Ibid., vol. II, pp. 54–5, 12.
[60] *Spy on Mother Midnight*, p. 5.   [61] *Teague-Root Display'd*, p. 20.
[62] *Description of the Temple of Venus*, p. 31.

Women were particularly vulnerable to those sounds which impelled the listener to engage in sex, and it was due to this susceptibility that one author advised virgins to 'shut their eyes and ears at nature's call'.[63] In the poem 'The Geranium', the point of vaginal penetration is marked by 'Nature' whispering in the ear of the woman, and by the woman's soft panting.[64] 'Listening to nature', it appears, was a euphemism for consenting to sex by falling silent. Silence in a woman therefore signalled the onset of vaginal penetration, highlighting the activity of male bodies and reflecting the power of that activity to produce women's consent. Indeed, sensible verbal language changed its form radically or ceased altogether when sex began. Moments of sex are fraught with 'fondly murm'ring sighs', sounds of 'soft'ning flatt'ry' and the 'tender murmurs' of a man which silence the woman's 'plaints' and 'sighs'.[65]

In the poem 'The Apocrypha' (1753), the woman remains mute even as her lover 'laid her charming legs aside', because she 'had no pow'r to chide'. Nevertheless, despite her obvious lack of agency, the narrator describes her as 'lovely and consenting'. To be sure, the man fails to speak too, but this is noted only after the event.[66] In 'The Presumptuous Sinner', Polly repulses the man's efforts, declaring, 'Oh, no – indeed, you shan't –'. Not only does he undermine these protestations by retorting that 'women's words are wind', but he 'hugg'd her till her breath grew short', effectively preventing her from making any further refusals.[67] These stories pictured female consent as submissive and unobstructive behaviour. As already discussed, rape was not clearly differentiated from other kinds of sex, and these accounts of women's virtual silence served to further blur the boundary between consensual and non-consensual sex.[68]

Female speech was often used to indicate sexual activity. Describing one encounter between a queen and a prince, the author of *Did You Ever See Such Damned Stuff?* writes: 'Talking was now out of the question: action took place of it . . . The Queen came to her speech again only in monosillables [sic]; and at length, she pronounced as clearly as her short breathing and sighs would give her leave of utterance, *Ah! Ah! Prince! – dear Prince!*'[69] A similar scenario takes place later, as the Prince Discreet attempts to seduce the Princess Tricolora. Unable to respond verbally to his advances, she simply lowers her eyes and blushes; and when the Prince asks how he should interpret her silence, she replies, 'Pray, . . . be quiet and have done'. There then ensues 'a tender debate, which was followed by a silence, interrupted, at length, by these words

[63] 'Epistle', in *Festival of Love*, p. 78.
[64] 'The Geranium', in *Pleasures that Please on Reflection*, p. 38.
[65] 'The Bridal Night', in *Pleasures that Please on Reflection*, pp. 41, 45, 47.
[66] 'The Apocrypha', in *Forty Select Poems*, p. 130.
[67] 'The Presumptuous Sinner', in *Bacchanalian Magazine*, p. 83.
[68] See chapter six above on rape in erotica.   [69] *Did You Ever See Such Damned Stuff?*, p. 18.

articulated in breaks – Dis-creet! I say, Dis-creet! . . . Dis – !'[70] These excla-
mations inform the reader that Discreet's attempts at seduction have been successful. Similarly, in the long poem *Kick Him Jenny* (1737), the onset of the
rape of Jenny is indicated by her speech, delivered in the same staccato style as
that of the Princess Tricolora. As penetration begins she cries out:

> For Heav'n's Sake, *Roger*, let me go;
> I do believe that you are – oh!
> That you are – oh! are oh? – are true –.[71]

Begging him to stop because she was about to vomit, Jenny manages to explain
that she will consent to be Roger's wife; her normal speech resumes only when
Roger ejaculates and sex ends. In these texts, the nature of female utterances
became the barometer of the sexual encounter. Indeed, in the metre of this
woman's dialogue the very rhythm of the male body was transmitted. Women's
speech did not convey delight felt by the woman, but the power of the man to
have a dramatic impact through the movement of his body.

Touch

Though sex was to some extent a collaborative sensual experience, a strict
hierarchy of senses was conveyed to the reader. And in the realm of the erotic
senses, touch was crowned the erotic sense *par excellence*. In one poem, the
woman's face provides the narrator with a beautiful vision, her breath with
delightful fragrance, her voice with angelic song and her mouth with heavenly
kisses; but only if the narrator is to 'the other sense employ' will he 'die with
pleasure'.[72] Part of the significance of touch lay in its apparent power to render
imaginary pleasure real. As one woman promises her male lover:

> No more shall Fancy's Scenes elude thy Touch,
> Thine are my Charms, or what Thou fancy'st such;
> . . . .
> And Thou shalt kindle at my Touch, and prove
> The dear, the blest *Reality* of Love.[73]

Both men and women are depicted experiencing each others' bodies through
this sense. The female 'cave' in *A Riddle* (c. 1725) is devoid of the capacity
for any sense other than touch, and the author reduces the female to a deaf
and dumb organ dedicated exclusively to judging the length and breadth of
male genitalia.[74] In *The Why and the Wherefore* (1765), the Chevalier Marino
instructs Signora Rosalba that bodies should be judged on the grounds of tactile

[70] Ibid., pp. 122–3.   [71] *Kick Him Jenny*, p. 20.   [72] 'Song', in *Festival of Love*, p. 235.
[73] 'Damon and Amoret', in *Consummation*, pp. 23–4.
[74] *A Riddle: Of a Paradoxical Character of an Hairy Monster*, p. 8.

sensation rather than appearance, reinforcing the idea that women should use touch to experience male bodies. Women's genitalia may not be pleasant to look at, he admits, but the 'disproportion of standard' of male genitalia means the latter display 'much more essential defects' in appearance. '[A]ny disappointment to the sight', however, is 'so fully compensated by the so much more sensual pleasures of the touch'.[75]

As indicated by the discussion of women's skin in chapter six, men also exercised touch in their experience of female bodies. Indeed, the cluster of books which discuss sex in terms of electricity envisage touch as the conductor of sexual passion for both men and women. In *Teague-Root Display'd* (1746), 'the Electrical Influence of the Female Root' on the male is mirrored in the way that '[t]he Female Root is the same way influenc'd by the Male'.[76] This symmetry is also observable in the two poems *The Electrical Eel; or, Gymnotus Electricus* (1770) and *The Torpedo* (1777), which claim the power of electricity for the male and female genitals respectively. In the latter, the female genitals are hailed as the ultimate source of electrical passion, while *The Electrical Eel* declares that the eel is the source of all electricity:

> What makes our first felicity,
> But his pure electricity,
> Divested of all fiction:
> Motion makes heat, and heat makes love,
> Creatures below, and things above,
> Are all produc'd by friction.

Removing any doubts about the precise nature of this friction, the author elaborated in a footnote, 'Friction, as defined by Dr Johnson, in his Dictionary, is the rubbing of two bodies together . . . [T]his friction I wish to be done in a morning'.[77]

In erotica, touch was a crucial way in which lovers experienced each other, and through which desire was aroused. But if desire was sparked by touch alone, then, as one author concedes, men and women might 'be made Electrical by Friction only, without the Intervention of each other' or by any number of inanimate or animate objects.[78] This was dangerous in a genre which promoted

---

[75] *Why and the Wherefore*, p. xii.   [76] *Teague-Root Display'd*, pp. 15, 16.

[77] *Electrical Eel: Or, Gymnotus Electricus* (No publication details, [c. 1770]), p. 11. The author was possibly eluding accusations of ignorance, by reproducing what he regarded as Newtonian views of electricity. John Freeke took issue with these views, claiming that to argue that electricity was caused by friction was like saying 'Water is caused by pumping.' See John Freeke, *An Essay to Shew the Cause of Electricity; And Why Some Things are Non-Electricable* (London: For W. Innys, in Pater-Noster Row, 1746), p. 8. Freeke was denounced as 'a pure Ignoramus' by Benjamin Martin in *A Supplement: Containing Remarks on a Rhapsody of Adventures of a Modern Knight Errant in Philosophy* (Bath: For the Author, and Mr Leake and Mr Frederick, 1746), p. 5

[78] *Teague-Root Display'd*, p. 17.

heterosexuality, and authors limited the damage threatened by this emphasis on touch in two ways. First, touch was never used in deciding upon a lover; the heterosexual nature of the relationship was always established first. Second, touch was used alongside other senses, particularly sight, to eliminate the likelihood of unwanted encounters. Men and women become animated with sexual desire when they are 'in View' of each other, and penetrative sex ensues if they 'advance to Contact'.[79] The caveat of sight guarded against the dangers of celebrating touch alone. One description of the first sexual experience of Adam and Eve after leaving Eden similarly links the senses of touch and sight: 'They rushed into each other's arms, and, to lose sight of all reproachful objects, they joined lips to lips, forehead to forehead, and confined the kind glancing of their eyes to themselves.' This combination of touch and sight is potent: 'Anon something fervid arose between them; and another thing courteously opened to receive it.'[80] Nevertheless, touch and sight were not of equal standing in manufacturing heterosexual encounters. To be sure, touch was crucial in depictions of heterosexual encounters: it was the key conduit through which sexual experience was acquired, and would often furnish bodies with the ultimate ecstasy. However, it built on established foundations of heterosexuality, presupposing the heterosexual nature of encounters. It did not, in other words, explain the cause of heterosexual desire, but demonstrated its peak.

Sight

It was the sense of sight which was endowed with the capacity to produce heterosexual relationships. In *The Fruit-Shop*, lovers are detected by the 'commissioned scouts' of the eyes. They search for the 'standard of *original beauty*' implanted in the mind of every man and woman, and it is the variability in the quality of people's sight which prevents everyone from desiring the same individual.[81] In a manner suggestive of the pervasive implicit violence towards women in this material, the author ominously explains that if this were not the case, 'if the same accomplished beauty were to strike all eyes alike', then she would lead 'a life in continual fear of acts of violation'.[82] Sight also provided lovers with tremendous pleasure. For the male explorer, for example, 'the very Sight of M E R R Y L A N D or any near approach to it, puts one in strange Raptures'.[83] Eyes were deemed so important to lovers because of their special sensitivity to desire. In an early text of 1707, a man asks his female companion, 'where does Love enter?', and she replies, '*Into the Eyes*'.[84] Eyes literally carried desire into the body.

---

[79] Ibid., p. 17.   [80] *Fruit-Shop*, vol. II, pp. 125–6.   [81] Ibid., vol. I, pp. 145, 144.
[82] Ibid., vol. I, p. 145.   [83] *New Description of Merryland*, p. 9.
[84] *Love's Catechism: Compiled by the Author of the* Recruiting Officer, *for the Use and Benefit of All Young Batchelors, Maids and Widows* (No publication details, 1707), p. 2.

Moreover, these organs allowed the exchange of desire, a process which used a well-developed language. The people of Merryland, for example, have little need for words, 'for they have the Art of communicating their Sentiments very plainly by their *Eyes and Actions*, so that mute Persons can (if I may be allowed the Expression) speak intelligibly by their Eyes'.[85] Such a language is put to use in courtship, particularly by women, whose 'animated glances' or 'enticing leer' suggest a readiness for sex.[86] In the poem *The Whim!* (1782), the myth of Diana the huntress, who shot Acteon and turned him into a stag as he watched her bathing, is transformed into the story of the bathing Seymora, who 'shot soft desire' at her lover with her eyes rather than her bow.[87] By contrast, the use of men's eyes to communicate desire is not always appropriate. One man entreats an allegedly female narrator to 'hear by begging Sight', but she simply rejects him as 'whining fool'.[88]

For women in particular, the conscious and deliberate use of this ocular language suggested not simply sexual responsiveness, but sexual proficiency. As the author of *The Fruit-Shop* explains, women's eyes achieve that 'twinkling brilliancy' when they are 'admitted into the secrets of coquetry'.[89] The forty-year-old woman in *La Souricière* displays her extensive knowledge of sex to the male narrator through her eyes: 'She knew, admirably well, how to use them to her best advantage, and was among the number of those generous creatures, who delight to inspire the *tender passions* . . . [S]he honoured me with her notice, and by ogles and sighs, endeavoured to *display her sensibilities*'.[90] Similarly, a prostitute engages in a comparable exercise with a young lawyer's clerk, and uses 'that visual tongue' to convey her wishes, 'without a word being spoke'.[91] Women were seemingly granted a degree of agency through their use of this language, but not all women were able to use it in the same way. The familiarity of these last two women with this ocular language – and by implication their sexual proficiency – is rendered convincing because of the first woman's age and the second's trade. The deliberate use of the eyes by these women was very different from the unconscious and involuntary visual communications made by most other women.

Indeed, generally the eyes of desirable women were unknowingly lascivious. Such unknowing eyes were clear and dark. These 'clear sparkling black eyes' indicate the person's inevitable and involuntary responsiveness.[92] Black eyes were a vital attribute of a beautiful woman, because the two qualities of

85 *New Description of Merryland*, p. 38.
86 *Fruit-Shop*, vol. I, p. 65; *Seventeen Hundred and Seventy-Seven*, p. 8.   87 *Whim*, p. 4.
88 *The Fifteen Pleasures of a Virgin. Written by the Suppos'd Author of the* Fifteen Plagues of a Maidenhead (No publication details, [c. 1707]), p. 8.
89 *Fruit-Shop*. vol. I, p. 65.   90 *La Souricière*, vol. I, pp. 21–2.
91 *Genuine Memoirs of . . . Miss Maria Brown*, vol. II, p. 112.
92 Ibid., vol. I, p. 63. See also *La Souricière*, vol. I, p. 34; *Prostitutes of Quality*, p. 36.

being 'black ey'd and wanton' were inextricably linked.[93] Men's eyes might
also indicate their lasciviousness, but such descriptions stressed men's activity
and physical force, often through the adjective 'vigorous'. One man, who displays 'great fervency' when engaging in 'Cyprian devotions', is described as
'a fine young fellow, robust and vigorous, with piercing eyes and an expressive
countenance'.[94] Another man, with a 'fine pair of black eyes' and 'capable of
a *rude* proceeding', makes 'vigorous impressions'.[95] In the cases of both men
and women, dark and sparkling eyes suggested a person who was particularly
lascivious. However, women's eyes in particular combined this lasciviousness
with passivity, and their eyes were deemed important objects of attraction.

Both male and female vision was to be restrained. Indeed, just as there were
limits placed on what a body could taste, smell, hear and touch, so sight was
to be regulated. Bright, sparkling eyes in women denoted sexual willingness,
and a familiarity with the ocular language of love suggested sexual reciprocity,
but too free a gaze was reprehensible. One author bemoans the situation in
which 'The daring eye may range with out controul', and women's vision
in particular 'lightens on the kindling view'.[96] Indeed, seeing too much of
a suggestive or improper nature damages women's eyes, the organs so vital
to their attractiveness. In the poem 'The Story of Pandora' (1741), Pandora
possesses the vital attribute of 'bright Eyes', which ensure her attractiveness
and perform their role in the language of courtship by emitting rays of light.
After opening the fateful box, however, her eyes lose their 'starry Fires', and are
lost in 'cloudy Mists'.[97] Pandora's eyes are ruined and they no longer indicate
responsive sexuality. This tale seems to recommend that women's vision is
curtailed not simply to avoid damage to their bodies, but in order that they
remain attractive to men.

As women's vision seemed to be regulated in order to ensure the continuation
of male desire, so the curtailment of men's vision served the same purpose. The
concern in both cases was for male pleasure. The woman most revered in *A
Description of the Temple of Venus* is she who seeks 'to elude the inchanted
Eye' of the man who watches.[98] Delaying tactics were widely recognized to
progress courtship in the eighteenth century. Dr Gregory counsels in his *Father's

[93] 'The Chrystal Bottle', in *Forty Select Poems*, p. 10; 'The Squire', in *Festival of Love*, p. 193.
[94] *Genuine Memoirs of . . . Miss Maria Brown*, vol. II, pp. 57, 55.
[95] *Did You Ever See Such Damned Stuff?*, p. 11. See chapter four above on the importance of vigour
in representations of male bodies.
[96] *Seventeen Hundred and Seventy-Seven*, p. 11.
[97] 'The Story of Pandora', in Philo-Brittanniae [pseud.], *The Potent Ally: Or, Succours from Merryland. With Three Essays in Praise of the Cloathing of that Country; and the Story of Pandora's
Box. To which is added . . . The Present State of Bettyland* ('Paris' [London]: Printed by direction
of the author, and sold by the booksellers of London and Westminster [Published by Edmund
Curll], 1741), pp. 24–5.
[98] *Description of the Temple of Venus*, p. 27.

Legacy to His Daughters (1774) that 'crosses and difficulties . . . and a state of suspense, are very great incitements to attachment, and are the food of love in both sexes'.[99] In this text, which was reprinted for a later audience in the *Lady's Magazine* of 1783, Gregory advises that '[a] fine woman shews her charms to most advantage when she seems most to conceal them'.[100] Of course, 'few things are much coveted, when they are easily procured'.[101] In erotica, the anticipation of things unseen was arousing, and the emphasis was exclusively on the delay instituted by women. Men's vision was manipulated by women in order to arouse and perpetuate male desire, rather than to protect men's attractiveness. While women received and transmitted desire in the ocular language of pleasure, the primary purpose of their eyes was to signal willingness and attractiveness. The involuntary appearance and behaviour of women's eyes indicated a perpetual receptivity and the inevitability of passive consent. This was not a vision of female agency or control, therefore. Whereas men's vision brought them pleasure (as observers) from looking at women, women's vision did not glean sexual pleasure for women; women's eyes were primarily either messengers or monitors.

In the collaborations between sight and touch, this inequitable economy of pleasure was further confirmed.[102] One of the most striking instances of how touch and sight were combined in erotica was when women were imagined handling male bodies. These encounters were vivid examples of how depictions of male bodies relied on the presence of fictional women. Male bodies were ostensibly revealed for the pleasure of women's vision. They exist 'to allure the ladies' ravished sight', and if looking at the male 'plant' gives women 'the thrill in every part', it was little surprise that a woman eagerly asks, 'L[or]d can't you let a Body see?'[103] Touching the male body gave women similar pleasure. Women feel 'the most sensible delight in *handling, exercising*' the penis, as '[t]his touch'd, alone the Heart can move'.[104] And again, women yearn to touch male genitals:

[99] Dr Gregory, *A Father's Legacy to His Daughters* (For W. Strahan, T. Cadell, in the Strand; and W. Creech, 1774), pp. 82–3.
[100] 'Extract from Dr. Gregory's Advice to his Daughters', *Lady's Magazine*, November 1783, p. 588.
[101] 'Men-Seducers. An Adventure at Cox's Museum', *Lady's Magazine*, June 1775, p. 319.
[102] Though Sander Gilman has privileged the role of touch in representations of sexuality, arguing that by the seventeenth and eighteenth centuries 'the image of touch seems to have become one with the heterosexual erotic', he recognizes how sight often worked in tandem with touch. See Sander L. Gilman, 'Touch, Sexuality and Disease', in W. F. Bynum and Roy Porter (eds.), *Medicine and the Five Senses* (Cambridge: Cambridge University Press, 1993), p. 213; Sander L. Gilman, *Inscribing the Other* (Lincoln: University of Nebraska Press, 1991), pp. 29–49. Condillac, a major theorist of sensationism, similarly prioritized sight and touch. See O'Neal, *Authority of Experience*, pp. 106–7.
[103] *Elegy on the Lamented Death of the Electrical Eel*, p. 8; *Mimosa*, p. 2; *Wisdom Reveal'd*, p. 23. See also chapter four above.
[104] *Mimosa*, p. iii; *Arbor Vitae*, p. 12.

> Where is there one – not longs to feel,
> The vigour of th' electric Eel,
> T' extract the fire by touch?[105]

In their ability to give delight, the two senses of sight and touch were often entwined. Women are expected to want to 'see, and touch the *plant*', to 'dare to see or feel', to 'turn their eyes, / And deign the thing to feel'.[106] Moreover, touching can arouse desire in a woman which will then emerge through her eyes: 'let one of the nicest Ladies take a Male-Root into her Hand, and she becomes instantly Electrical, and you may observe the quick and sudden Flashes of Electrical Fire dart from her Eyes'.[107] The desire felt by women on touching male bodies was imagined to exit from their eyes.

Indeed, women may have been mesmerized by looking at the penis, but male genitalia responded to the effects of that look. Penises grow 'more stiff, erect, and high' when treated to a look from the 'melting eye' of a woman, while 'a sly, bewitching glance' cast towards the 'tree of life' causes the 'very fruit . . . to dance'.[108] Male bodies also responded to women's touches. When 'under the Electrical Influence of the Female', the male teague-root becomes 'as stiff as a Poker', while the *arbor vitae* 'extends itself when it is so handled'.[109] Similarly, women are in 'raptures' over the Mimosa plant, but it is their efforts which 'rear this *plant* to an amazing height'.[110] The tree of life in *Wisdom Reveal'd* (c. 1732) will 'in a moment strangely *thrive*' at the touch of a Lady, and

> Grow twice as big, and twice as long,
> And more than twenty times as Strong.[111]

Lastly, in the poem 'The Geranium' (1789), the male plant will not rise for women's 'weak and vain' words, but only for women's sight and touch:

> Yet let the sun of thy bright eyes
> Shine but a moment, it shall rise!
> Let but the dew of thy soft hand
> Refresh the stem it straight shall stand![112]

In her discussion of the pornography of the late twentieth century, Susan Bordo argues that this material was constructed as a domain in which women were seen to legitimize men's bodies: 'Their validation – the transformation of embarrassed penis into proud phallus – is the point of the pornography'.[113] Such mechanisms appear to be at work in eighteenth-century erotica: it was the

[105] *Electrical Eel* ([c. 1770]), p. 19.
[106] *Mimosa*, p. 11; *Electrical Eel* ([c. 1770]), pp. 9, 26.   [107] *Teague-Root Display'd*, p. 18.
[108] *Mimosa*, p. 2; *Electrical Eel* ([c. 1770]), p. 3.
[109] *Teague-Root Display'd*, p. 15; *Arbor Vitae*, p. 4.
[110] *Mimosa*, p. iii.   [111] *Wisdom Reveal'd*, p. 12.
[112] 'The Geranium', in *Pleasures that Please on Reflection*, pp. 35–6.
[113] Bordo, 'Reading the Male Body', p. 275.

look and/or touch of women that constituted the catalyst for the transformation of penises into the state in which they were most admired. Just as women were established as the privileged viewers of male bodies (see chapter four), so through women's sight and touch the impetus for male desire was externalized. In this period, excessive desire in a man was thought to undermine his masculinity. Possible temptations were necessarily located outside the male body (in visual media such as statues, for example), and the charms of such temptations had to be repudiated. Surrender to such images was presented as having an effeminizing effect, which had to be resisted.[114] Showing male bodies in states of arousal risked appearing to relinquish this restraint and self-control. Thus, in erotica, the catalyst for male arousal was externalized, serving to exempt men from the responsibility for their own sexual desire, and safeguarding them from accusations of effeminacy.

While this appears to be an instance of the female agency discussed by Jacob and Kraakman in French pornography, the circulation of desire in the erotic economy of pleasure suggests otherwise. The process begun by the female look or touch on a male body was not reversed: men's looking at women's bodies did not produce dramatic signs of pleasure in those bodies, but merely excited the men. Women's looking at male bodies, on the other hand, was imagined literally to produce erections. The same asymmetry informed representations of touch. Female touching effected great changes in male genitalia and served ultimately to further bolster male pleasure. Yet there are very few descriptions of men bringing pleasure to women by touching female bodies. The texture of women's skin received comment, but ultimately this focused on the tactile pleasure received by men, rather than women. Women's bodies did not feel pleasure through the senses; rather they gave 'Rapture to the Touch'.[115]

Modesty and mutuality

I know but few, and I can boast as large a circle of acquaintance as most, who would not prefer a modest quaker, lapped up in small plaits, robed in plain attire, accompanied with the natural graces of simplicity, decency, and virgin coyness, though muffled like a pigeon, to one of our modern *fine ladies*, decked out for a birth-night ball, in the utmost splendor that can be conceived, with, perhaps, no other covering to the bosom than a solitaire, unattended with that most invaluable female virtue, MODESTY.[116]

[114] John Barrell, 'The Dangerous Goddess: Masculinity, Prestige and the Aesthetic in Early Eighteenth-Century Britain', in his *The Birth of Pandora and the Division of Knowledge* (Basingstoke: Macmillan, 1992), pp. 64, 66, 76; Breitenberg, *Anxious Masculinity*, p. 31.

[115] *Little Merlin's Cave*, p. 3. See also *A Riddle: Of a Paradoxical Character*, pp. 6, 8; 'The Judgment Reversed, or Chloe Triumphant', in *Festival of Love*, p. 142.

[116] 'Men-Seducers. An Adventure at Cox's Museum', *Lady's Magazine*, June 1775, p. 319.

The economy of pleasure in eighteenth-century erotica was based on a model of female sexuality as modest. The modest woman of eighteenth-century conduct literature and novels was situated between the distant, affected prude and the too liberal and knowing coquette: the modest woman was innocent of sexual knowledge and her own sexuality, but she was also responsive and would ultimately be co-operative in sex.[117] Crucially, modesty increased women's attractiveness and made men happy; women were thus advised that modesty was the key to capturing a man's heart.[118] On the one hand, modesty led to women's practices of concealment, and these practices were thought alluring and erotic. On the other hand, and in contrast to the prude whose affected aversion to men allowed them to feel unnoticed, the modest woman made it clear to men that their desire was returned.[119] But modesty was restraining as well as facilitative. Modest women did not display their sexuality in as open a manner as the coquette, and men were correspondingly limited by the concealments of modest women. Restraint of physical desire in both women and men was thus manufactured by female modesty.

Authentic modesty was difficult to identify, however. As writers in women's magazines worried that prostitutes used modesty to catch men, so the author of the erotic *Seventeen Hundred and Seventy-Seven* (1777) complained that prostitutes had adopted a 'modest air', and thus called for '[s]ome sign of trade' to distinguish them from modest women.[120] Conversely, the prostitute-narrator Maria Brown complains that 'modest' women have 'borrowed our gait, our air'.[121] The trait regarded as the indisputable marker of modesty was the female blush. Unlike the artificial colouring produced by cosmetics, the involuntary blush was a genuine marker of a woman's feelings, testament to her lack of pretence or manipulation, and representing her inevitable compliance.[122] This 'Characteristick of Womanhood', as one erotic author described it, appeared repeatedly in erotica.[123] In one poem in a collection of 1789, a young woman lies trembling, but her passionate longing for a man is signalled by 'Her cheeks perfus'd with decent red', which ensures that she is 'never more a maid to rise!'[124] Blushes were not only visible during the prelude, but could also be seen while sex was in progress. The narrator of *Kick Him Jenny* imagines that

---

[117] See Yeazell, *Fictions of Modesty*. Yeazell explains that, while the prude and the coquette were connected by an 'improper consciousness', the modest woman's virtue was increasingly imagined as 'something closer to a natural instinct than a conscious thought' (p. 53).

[118] 'On Modesty', *Lady's Magazine*, July 1773, p. 376; 'On Women', *Lady's Magazine*, January 1791, pp. 62–3.

[119] 'A Dissertation on Prudes', *Lady's Magazine*, June 1774, p. 309.

[120] 'On Women', *Lady's Magazine*, January 1791, p. 63; *Seventeen-Hundred and Seventy-Seven*, p. 14.

[121] *Genuine Memoirs of . . . Miss Maria Brown*, vol. II, p. 25.

[122] Yeazell, *Fictions of Modesty*, pp. 65–80.   [123] *Prostitutes of Quality*, p. 127.

[124] 'The Bridal Night', in *Pleasures that Please on Reflection*, p. 45. See also *Teague-Root Display'd*, p. 20.

he will see women's 'kindling Blushes rise' as he forcefully penetrates them.[125] The functions of the modest blush in erotica were similar to those of women's eyes: both were involuntary indicators of women's readiness and willingness for sex.

The modest blush was not simply a sign of women's willingness, but also a marker of their beauty. Dr Gregory advised his daughters that the blush is a girl's 'most powerful charm of beauty'.[126] Erotic authors certainly claimed that women became more attractive when displaying this vital characteristic. The blushing of one woman, combined with the lowering of her head and heaving of her breast, prompts the narrator of *The Rake of Taste* (1760) to cry out, 'Oh woman! lovely woman!'[127] The light dress of the princess in *Did You Ever See Such Damned Stuff?* is favourably described, 'but what rendered her more charming and more desirable was her confusion and blushes. On such an occasion, Modesty is ever a tributary to Voluptuousness.'[128] As one erotic author succinctly says of men, 'Resistance but inflames them more'.[129] But though modesty gave the impression of resistance, it indicated quite the opposite. Reflecting on one woman's self-congratulation at resisting sexual advances, one narrator comments, 'A woman really indifferent resists and scarce deigns to remember her resistance. A woman tenderly disposed, applauds herself for her refusals, and all in the act of applauding herself, recalls to mind the object; that object moves her, the melting mood ensues, and she concludes by surrendering. Generally speaking too much reflection upon resistance is a preparation for a defeat.'[130] The author of 'The Oeconomy of Love' counsels men to regard women's modest behaviour as an invitation to proceed with sex,

She perhaps,
Averse, will coldly chide, and half afraid,
Blushing, half pleas'd, the tumid wonder view
With neck retorted and oblique regard;
Nor quite her curious eye indulging, nor
Refraining quite. Perhaps when you attempt
To seek admission, toyful she resists
With shy reluctance; nathless you pursue
The soft attack [.][131]

In this model of female sexuality, excessive desire destroyed women's modesty. After being undressed and awoken by a man who then 'conquers' her, one woman's repeated entreaties to her lover to engage in sex transform her previously acceptable desires into 'usurping lust', which then ruins her body:

[125] *Kick Him Jenny*, p. 21.   [126] Gregory, *Father's Legacy*, pp. 26–7.
[127] *Rake of Taste*, p. 19.   [128] *Did You Ever See Such Damned Stuff?*, p. 71.
[129] 'The Boots', in *Forty Select Poems*, p. 189.
[130] *Did You Ever See Such Damned Stuff?*, pp. 111–12.
[131] 'The Oeconomy of Love', in *Pleasures that Please on Reflection*, pp. 14–15.

No more the rose's blush o'erspreads her face;
Lost is her charming form, and ev'ry grace.

By its close, the poem has become a warning against those 'lustful passions' which threaten to transgress the appropriate circumscription of women's physical desires.[132] Female bodies were those regarded as particularly prone to the dangers of excessive sexual desire, and this desire was often envisaged as an unwelcome intruder taking over the woman's body as she relinquished control of herself.[133] An excess of female desire did not simply pose a threat to women, however, but also to men's own pleasure. Lust eradicated women's modest blushes, and therefore their attractiveness and power to arouse men.

A mutuality of male and female desire was established through this theme of female modesty. A modest woman would respond to the attentions of her male lover with the correct consistency of chasteness and passion, her modestly blushing cheeks reflecting both 'half her inward flame' and her 'ingenuous shame'. This modest persona facilitated an encounter consisting of 'equal play' and 'equal bliss'.[134] Several sexual relationships were described using this language of equality. In a happy vision of a rural household, for example, a couple's equal labours are reflected in 'mutual fondness' and the way in which 'equally they lov'd'.[135] Yet just as men and women had distinct tasks in the household economy – in this case he took responsibility for the fields, she for the house and dairy – so the language of sexual equality clouded quite distinct and inequitable roles. Accounts which at the end characterized sexual encounters by 'equal' and 'mutual' desire might begin with descriptions of sexual violence. One woman – who explicitly refuses to engage in sex and who scratches and struggles during the encounter – is disarmed with the adverb 'modestly'.[136] Languages of modesty and mutuality in eighteenth-century erotica hid stark, gendered asymmetries in the economy of pleasure.

In eighteenth-century erotica, sex was in no way an unrestrained sensual experience. Taste and smell were imagined to play some role, but they served to curtail the options rather than to broaden them. Sounds assisted in the arousal of desire, women's voices marked the onset of sex, and touch provided supreme bliss, particularly for men. Sight was critical because it was imbued with the capacity to detect the opposite sex. Though it ultimately failed to explain the reason for heterosexual liaisons, the sense of sight allowed lovers to exchange desire, thereby facilitating the mutuality of the type of sex to

[132] 'The Girdle of Venus Unbuckled', in *Festival of Love*, pp. 40, 41, 42.
[133] See also 'The Mad Dog', in *Festival of Love*, p. 441; 'The Geranium', in *Pleasures that Please on Reflection*, p. 38.
[134] 'The Bridal Night', in *Pleasures that Please on Reflection*, p. 45.
[135] 'The Foolish Inquiry', in *Festival of Love*, p. 432.
[136] 'The Presumptuous Sinner', in *Bacchanalian Magazine*, pp. 82–3. Also see 'Saucy Jack; or, the Bladish Adonis of Tottenham Court Road', in *Bacchanalian Magazine*, pp. 61–2.

be championed. There was no jubilant celebration of the erotic potential of the senses in eighteenth-century erotica, therefore, and the senses were not allowed to range unfettered. Indeed, each sense was plied rigorously to mould the encounters and their participants according to a gendered and masculinist vision.

The women in erotica were not desexualized; they were crucial players in pleasurable encounters. Like the female characters in French pornography, these women experienced physical desire and pleasure through their senses. Yet the participation of these women in sensual experiences was governed by modesty: they were initially reticent about sex, but were permanently sexually responsive. These women displayed a passive sexuality, their sexual desire requiring only the smallest of words or the slightest of touches to be enlivened. Though physical stimulants of pleasure were elevated in erotica, women's perpetual responsiveness suggested a latent desire. In women's eyes especially, readers could observe an involuntary passion waiting to be triggered by the appropriate – male – stimulus. Once aroused, women's desire was an invitation to men, and women's pleasure was testament to men's own successful sexual activity.

Pleasure, and the degree to which people were 'sexualized' or 'desexualized', are spectres which have loomed large in historiography. In this chapter I have sought not simply to determine whether a capacity or propensity for sexual pleasure was present or absent in past representations of men or women, but to examine how pleasure itself was constructed, and to reconstruct the operation of gendered economies of pleasure. Women's bodies were invariably the monitor of the sexual encounters, gauging not only the onset and the nature of the activity, but also its force and rhythm. If women's modest sexual desire necessarily constructed men as active, the pleasure felt by female bodies worked to show the effectiveness of this activity. Ultimately, women's sensual experiences served to convey information about men, and their pleasure conferred vigorous heterosexuality upon male bodies. As a bawd counsels one of her 'working girls', a prostitute should 'attentively study her lover's temper, inclinations, and dispositions, so that she may form her own upon this pattern, and seem to see, speak, feel, only through his organs: such conduct is sure to rivet a man's affections'.[137]

---

[137] *Genuine Memoirs of . . . Miss Maria Brown*, vol. II, p. 163.

Conclusion

Erotica was firmly embedded in eighteenth-century culture. It was read by men in coffee houses, and by groups who mimicked new forms of association and fraternity. Authors, artists, readers and viewers drew on a considerable range of cultural resources in the production and consumption of erotica, including science, medicine, natural history, geography, botany, gardening design and landscape writing. Indeed, the texts and practices of erotic culture were knowingly founded on parasitic habits, and it was from this self-consciousness that much of the wit and satire of the writing sprung. The genre and its contexts were linked to others: erotica was related to pornography, but was also a close neighbour of romantic and amatory fiction, and it was read in settings associated with the respectability of the connoisseur and the abandon of the drunk. Nevertheless, there was a distinctive erotic mode of writing and gathering, one in which sexual pleasures were indulged in but restraint maintained. This mode, this culture, has its own history.

In this rich culture, sexual difference could be based on the role played by a man or woman in conception, but differences were also constituted by the way a body moved, the metaphorical associations a body carried or the way a person spoke or looked. Readers were presented with a variety of ways of understanding the relationship between male and female. Erotic authors spoke about how men's and women's bodies were both the same and different; they also exposed the construction of sexual differences as a process that could be disrupted. These discussions were satirical. Erotica played with attempts to fix sexual difference; it laughed at the absurdity of trying to decipher these complex and multifarious bodies. Yet this satire and this multiplicity was nevertheless forged in the context of a male-centred and heterosexual vision, in which hierarchical sex differences were ultimately ineradicable.

If we think about the way in which bodies are represented in eighteenth-century erotica as objects and spaces, or as things that moved or touched, we can see that women's bodies were thoroughly sexualized. Women's bodies were places where pleasure literally resided, but women lacked control over these spaces. Female pleasure as indicated by orgasm was not central to

222

these depictions, though even modest women displayed sexual desires and felt
sexual pleasure. Women's possession of sexual desire and their feeling of sexual
pleasure, however, did not mean they were autonomous agents, equal to men or
their partners in sex. It is true that men did not undermine female spaces, and
that male bodies could be soft and vulnerable, requiring women's nurturing and
restorative hands and eyes. But the people with power in erotic culture were men,
and one of the expressions of this was the way men were repeatedly distanced
from sex and desire. In aping the form of polite clubs, readers of erotica downplayed the sexual nature of the event of reading. In imagining the male plants in
erotica being enjoyed by female narrators, these readers allowed themselves to
view soft male bodies. In making sex a feminine place, men could disentangle
themselves from sex. In placing responsibility for male and female desire on a
modest model of female sexuality, erotic authors could keep masculinity and
sensuality clean apart. Of course, men read erotic texts, relishing the wit and
the sex; the disassociation of masculinity and sensuality was a textual ruse that
actually facilitated men's sexual pleasure. Yet it was a ruse that changed the
nature of erotic pleasure, making it acceptable to a model of refined masculinity.
It also created its own distinctively erotic pleasure gleaned from glimpses of
bodies and the suggestion of sexual action, made all the more seductive by the
proximity between sex and refinement. In English erotic culture, the bawdy,
raucous, libidinous elements of the eighteenth century collided with the refined
politeness for which the period is also renowned. Erotica applied the form of
refinement to the matter of sex.

Erotic cultures displayed considerable reflexivity with regard to other genres
and contemporary events, but authors did not churn out new books modelled on
established templates. Rather, these authors selected ideas strategically, combining the old and the new. Erotic authors made relentless but selective use
of other resources in a dynamic process of cultural exchange, in which they
selected only those ideas about bodies that served their own distinct, male-
centred and heterosexual motivations. Models of change developed in analyses
of economic and political spheres are ill-equipped to capture the processes
of negotiation and contestation integral to cultural change. Changes in understandings about sexual differences were often short-term rather than long-term,
insubstantial not transformative. Historians of gender working on earlier and
later periods are keen to speak of the 'constant and persistent', and the 'embed-
dedness and durability' of understandings of gender and gender relations.[1] And
key aspects of understandings of sexual difference endured in erotic material
throughout the eighteenth century, though depictions of male bodies were more
varied and changeable than those of female bodies. Cultural life comprised

[1] Gowing, *Domestic Dangers*, p. 29; Tosh, 'Old Adam and the New Man', p. 238.

varying currents of change and as a result there existed a range of modes of thinking about sex and sexual difference at any one moment.

Both sexes were depicted in erotic texts, but not everyone participated in erotic culture. Regardless of the emphasis placed on female bodies in erotic texts, it would be a mistake to claim that erotica constitutes 'material for the historian of sexuality, especially female sexuality'.[2] The contexts of this writing render it rich material for the historian of male sexuality and masculinity. Erotica was not a prescriptive genre; nor was it a mirror of the sexual behaviour of men. But these books – and the culture in which they were consumed – fastened positive qualities to male bodies. In this sense erotic culture was masculinist. Just as images within the texts validated particular male bodies, the very act of reading erotica was imagined to confirm men's learning and wit, and to reinforce their masculinity.

Which brand of masculinity did eighteenth-century erotica valorize? It would be inappropriate to situate erotica in the late-eighteenth-century underworld culture in which pornographers consorted with perpetrators of 'theft, pimping, rape, [and] blackmail'.[3] Nor should we align erotica with the libertine plebeian and artisanal manhood from the same period, forged through drinking and the singing of ribald songs in homosocial celebrations of bachelorhood, which prioritized 'excess rather than control'.[4] Such rakish dissipation was anathema to erotica. Rather, erotic culture grew out of an earlier, more elite manhood based on refinement. If erotica could be allied with anything libertine, then it was 'the refined and erudite libertinism of the early Enlightenment', which brandished a language of self-discipline rather than hedonism.[5] As erotic writing showed English men to be independent and self-possessed, so these texts promised sensual gratification of a kind that would safeguard masculine self-control. Erotic culture invited men to unite politeness and the libido, and it did so largely by combining the social and the sexual. Erotica championed the witty 'man of the world, . . . the *bon vivant*, the friend of the fair sex, the bottle and song', and these men felt intimate pleasures in communal gatherings.[6]

English erotica shared little of the 'freethinking and free living' libertinism that Robert Darnton claims fuelled the French Enlightenment works and pornographic books that played such a vital role in the revolution of 1789.[7] Nor did eighteenth-century erotic culture seem to contain much of the Wilkesite incarnation of British liberty and citizenship, or of the revolutionary-republican radicalism of late-eighteenth- and early-nineteenth-century London, whose ultras enjoyed practical and ideological links with

[2] Kraakman, 'Reading Pornography Anew', p. 547.   [3] McCalman, *Radical Underworld*, p. 2.
[4] Anna Clark, *The Struggle for the Breeches: Gender and the Making of the British Working Class* (London: Rivers Oram Press, 1995), p. 31.
[5] Cowan, 'Reasonable Ecstasies', p. 125.   [6] See chapter one above for original citation.
[7] Darnton, *Forbidden Best-Sellers*, p. 90.

pornography.[8] This erotic literature bore only faint echoes of the blatant political and philosophical radicalism that characterized both English and French pornography. Yet erotica was not without its politics. An historical approach – and in particular a cultural historical approach – holds the potential to 'break open the daily naturalism of what surrounds us'.[9] This book has sought to unpack the social and cultural meanings of depictions of male and female bodies. In doing so, it has argued that representations of male and female bodies were saturated with gendered economies of power and pleasure. Statements of sexual commensurability nevertheless imputed supremacy to male bodies. Blissful trysts displayed stark asymmetries of movement which were reliant on women's passive complicity and were barely distinguishable from rape. Behind proclamations of mutuality lurked imbalances in the arousal of desire and the manifestation of pleasure in bodies, such that women's bodies became ministering addenda to male satisfaction. Despite clear statements of sexual equivalence, despite the foregrounding of women's passions and despite the loving and tender descriptions of sexual acts, male power was endlessly shored up. Erotica may yield images of bodies that appear commonplace and banal, but the pleasures of eighteenth-century erotic culture – pleasures of the female body, of witty male sociability, of sex and of reading about sex – were no less political for their ubiquity.

[8] Clark, *Struggle for the Breeches*, p. 143; McCalman, *Radical Underworld*, pp. 207–19.
[9] Riley, *'Am I That Name?'*, p. 5.

Bibliography

only one × not used

MANUSCRIPTS

'Eros in Monachium or the Medmenham Garland Cull'd from the Franciscan Originals'
(c. 1760). Williams Andrews Clark Memorial Library, University of California Los
Angeles: MSS. E71M1 ca. 1760 Bound.

PRINTED PRIMARY SOURCES: NEWSPAPER AND PERIODICAL PUBLICATIONS

The Lady's Magazine
The Leeds Mercury
The Manchester Mercury
Sheffield Mercury
Town and Country Magazine

PRINTED PRIMARY SOURCES: OTHER WORKS

Place of publication is London unless otherwise stated.

A note on organization: unless the author is named on the title page, the erotic
items in this bibliography have been arranged alphabetically by title.

Adam's Tail; Or, the First Metamorphosis, 4th edn. (Printed for John Bell, near Exeter-
Exchange, in the Strand, 1774).
*The Adventures of a Cork-Screw, in which under the Pleasing Method of a Romance,
the Vices, Follies and Manners of the Present Age are Exhibited and Satirically
Delineated* (Dublin: For W. Whitestone, 1775).
[Helenus Scott], *The Adventures of a Rupee* (Dublin: Printed by W. Spotewood, for
Messrs Price, Whitestone, Walker, White, Beatty, Burton, E. Cross and Bryne,
1782).
Advice to the Officers of the British Army, 6th edn. (By W. Richardson, for G. Kearsley,
in Fleet-Street, 1783).
Arbor Vitae: Or, the Natural History of the Tree of Life (For E. Hill, in White-Fryers,
Fleet-Street, 1741).
'Arbor Vitae: Or, the Natural History of the Tree of Life', in Roger Pheuquewell [pseud.,
alias Thomas Stretser], *A New Description of Merryland. Containing a Topograph-
ical, Geographical, and Natural History of that Country*, 7th edn. (Bath: Printed
and sold by J. Leake there; and by E. Curll, at Pope's Head in Rose-Street, Covent-
Garden, 1741).

226

'The Arbor Vitae; Or, Tree of Life. A Poem', in *The Ladies Delight* (For W. James in the Strand, 1732).

Aristotle's Compleat Master-Piece. In Three Parts. Displaying the Secrets of Nature in the Generation of Man . . . To which is added, A Treasure of Health; Or, the Family Physician: Being Choice and Approved Remedies for all the Several Distempers incident to Humane Bodies, 11th edn. (Printed and sold by the Booksellers, [1725]).

Aristotle's Master-Piece: Or, the Secrets of Generation Displayed in all the Parts thereof (Printed and are to be sold at the Hand and Scepter near Temple-Bar, 1700).

[Astell, Mary], *A Serious Proposal to the Ladies, for the Advancement of their True and Greatest Interest. By a Lover of that Sex*, 2nd edn. (Printed for R. Wilkin, at the King's-Head in St Paul's Church-Yard, 1695).

The Bacchanalian Magazine and Cyprian Enchantress. Composed Principally of New and Convivial and Amorous Songs (For H. Lemoine, Bishopsgate Church-Yard, 1793).

Bailey, Nathaniel, *A Universal Etymological English Dictionary* (E. Bell, 1721).

Behn, Aphra, *The Works of Aphra Behn. Volume I: Poetry*, ed. Janet Todd (Columbus: Ohio State University Press, 1992).

Bingley, William, *Animal Biography; or, Authentic Anecdotes of the Lives, Manners, and Economy, of the Animal Creation*, 3 vols (1802; For Richard Phillips, No. 6, Bridge-Street, 1805).

Bradley, Richard, *The History of Succulent Plants* (For the Author, 1716).

A Philosophical Account of the Works of Nature (For W. Mears, at the Lamb, without Temple-Bar, 1721).

Dictionarium Botanicum; Or, a Botanical Dictionary for the Use of the Curious in Husbandry and Gardening, 2 vols. (For T. Woodward at the Half-Moon over-against St Dunstan's Church in Fleet-Street, and J. Peele at Locke's Head in Pater-Noster-Row, 1728).

[Hatchett, William], *A Chinese Tale. Written Originally by that Prior of China the Facetious Sou ma Quang, A Celebrated Mandarine of Letters; Under the Title of Chamyam Tcho Chang, or Chamyam with her Leg upon a Table . . . Inscribed to Thomas Dawson Esq; Cornet in Lieutenant-General Honeywood's Dragoons* (For J. Cooper in Fleet-Street; and sold by all the pamphlet-sellers of London and Westminster, [c. 1740]).

Cleland, John, *Fanny Hill, or Memoirs of a Woman of Pleasure*, ed. Peter Wagner (1748–9; Harmondsworth: Penguin, 1985).

Cole, Thomas, *Discourses on Luxury, Infidelity, and Enthusiasm* (For R. and J. Dodsley, in Pall-Mall, 1761).

Consummation: Or, the Rape of Adonis (For E. Curll, at Pope's Head, in Rose Street, Covent-Garden, 1741).

The Covent-Garden Magazine; Or, Amorous Repository: Calculated Solely for the Entertainment of the Polite World, and the Finishing of a Young Man's Education (G. Allen, 1773). [Only vol. II is extant.]

Cowper, William, *The Anatomy of Humane Bodies* (Oxford: Printed at the Theatre, for Sam. Smith and Benj. Walford, Printers to the Royal Society, at the Princes Arms in St Paul's Church Yard, 1698).

The Cuckold's Chronicle; Being Select Trials for Adultery, Incest, Imbecility, Ravishment, &c., 2 vols. (For H. Lemoine, Bishopsgate Church-Yard, 1793).

[Darwin, Erasmus], *The Botanic Garden; A Poem, in Two Parts. Part 1 containing The Economy of Vegetation. Part 2. The Loves of the Plants*, 2 vols. (For J. Johnson, St Paul's Church-Yard, 1791).

A Description of the Temple of Venus, at Cnidus (Printed and sold by Tho. Edlin, 1726).

The Designs of Mr. Inigo Jones and Mr. Wm. Kent (John Vardy, 1744).

Did You Ever See Such Damned Stuff? Or, So-Much-the-Better. A Story without Head or Tail, Wit or Humor. (For C. G. Seyffert, in Pall-Mall, 1760).

Directory, General and Commercial, of the Town & Borough of Leeds, for 1817 (Leeds: Printed by Edward Baines, at the Mercury-Office, 1817).

The Electrical Eel: Or, Gymnotus Electricus, and the Torpedo; A Poem (No publication details, [c. 1774]).

Adam Strong [pseud., James Perry?], *The Electrical Eel: Or, Gymnotus Electricus. Inscribed to the Honourable Members of the R***l S*****y* (No publication details, [c. 1770]).

Adam Strong [pseud., James Perry?], *Electrical Eel: Or, Gymnotus Electricus. Inscribed to the Honourable Members of the R***l S*****y* (For J. Bew in Paternoster-Row, 1777).

Lucretia Lovejoy, sister to Mr Adam Strong, author of the *Electrical Eel* [pseud.], *An Elegy on the Lamented Death of the Electrical Eel, or Gymnotus Electricus. With the Lapidary Inscription, as Placed on a Superb Erection, at the Expence of the Countess of H—, and Chevalier-Madame D'Eon de Beaumont* (For Fielding and Walker, No. 20 Pater-Noster-Row, 1777).

Emily De Varmont; Or Divorce Dictated by Necessity; to which are added the Amours of Father Sévin, 3 vols. (For G. Kearsley, no. 46, Fleet-Street, 1798).

[Charles Cotton], Ερωτοπολιζ *or Erotopolis. The Present State of Bettyland* (For Tho. Foy, at the White-Hart, over and against St Dunstan's Church in Fleet-Street, and at the Angel in Westminster-Hall, 1684).

[Charles Cotton], 'Erotopolis; Or, of the Situation of Bettyland', in [Philo-Brittanniae; pseud.], *The Potent Ally: Or, Succours from Merryland. With Three Essays in Praise of the Cloathing of that Country; and the Story of Pandora's Box. To which is added . . . The Present state of Bettyland*, 2nd edn. (Printed by direction of the author, and sold by the booksellers of London and Westminster, 'Paris', 1741).

Faustina: or the Roman Songstress, A Satyr, on the Luxury and Effeminacy of the Age (For J. Roberts, at the Oxford Arms, in Warwick Lane, [1726?]).

The Festival of Love; Or, a collection of Cytherean Poems, Procured and Selected by G—e P—e; and dedicated to his brother. Containing Elegant Translations from Anacreon, Sappho, Musaeus, Coluthus, Secundus, &c. and Innumerable Original Pieces never before Published, 6th edn. (For M. Smith, and by the editors permission, sold by the booksellers in Fleet-Street, Piccadilly, and Paternoster Row, [c. 1770]).

The Fifteen Comforts of Cuckoldom. Written by a Noted Cuckold in the New-Exchange in the Strand (No publication details, 1706).

The Fifteen Comforts of Matrimony: Or, A Looking-Glass for All Those who have Enter'd in that Holy and Comfortable State (No publication details, 1706).

Madam B—l [pseud.], *The Fifteen Plagues of a Maiden-Head* (By F. P. near Fleet-Street, 1707).

The Fifteen Pleasures of a Virgin. Written by the Suppos'd Author of The Fifteen Plagues of a Maidenhead (No publication details, [c. 1707]).

Forty Select Poems, on Several Occasions, by the Right Honourable The Earl of— (No publication details, [c. 1753]).

Freeke, John, *An Essay to Shew the Cause of Electricity; And Why Some Things are Non-Electricable* (For W. Innys, in Pater-Noster Row, 1746).

The French King's Wedding: Or, the Royal Frolick. Being a Pleasant Account of the Amorous Intrigues, Comical Courtship, Caterwauling and Surprizing Marriage Ceremonies of Lewis the XIVth with Madam Maintenon (By J. Smith, near Fleet-street, 1708).

The Fruit-Shop. A Tale, 2 vols. (For C. Moran, in Covent-Garden, 1765).

Miss W. [pseud.], 'The Gentleman's Study', in Roger Lonsdale (ed.), *Eighteenth-Century Women Poets* (Oxford: Oxford University Press, 1990).

Genuine Memoirs of the Celebrated Miss Maria Brown. Exhibiting the Life of a Courtezan in the Most Fashionable Scenes of Dissipation, 2 vols. (For I. Allcock, near St Paul's, 1766).

The Good and Bad Effects of Tea Consider'd (For John Wilkie, behind the Chapter-House, St Paul's Church-Yard, 1758).

Betsy Wemyss [pseud.], *Great News from Hell, Or the Devil foil'd by Bess Weatherby. In a letter from the Celebrated Miss Betsy Wemyss, the Little Squinting Venus, to the No Less Celebrated Miss Lucy C—r* (For J. Williams, on Ludgate-hill; and sold by J. Dixwell, in St Martin's Lane, near Charing-Cross, 1760).

Gregory, Dr, *A Father's Legacy to His Daughters* (For W. Strahan, T. Cadell, in the Strand; and W. Creech, 1774).

Hall, R., *Elements of Botany; Or, an Introduction to the Sexual System of Linnaeus. To which is added an English Botanical Dictionary* (By E. Hudson, Cross-Street, Hatton Garden; for Vernor and Hood in the Poultry; T. Hurst, Paternoster-Row, and R. Bent, Coventry-Street, Haymarket, 1802).

Harris's List of Covent Garden Ladies: Or Man of Pleasure's Kalendar, for the Year 1788 (For H. Ranger, at No. 9, Little Bridges-Street, near Drury-Lane Play-House, 1788).

Harris's List of Covent Garden Ladies: Or Man of Pleasure's Kalendar, for the Year 1789 (For H. Ranger, at No. 9, Little Bridges-Street, near Drury-Lane Play-House, 1789).

Harris's List of Covent Garden Ladies: Or Man of Pleasure's Kalendar, for the Year 1790 (For H. Ranger, at No. 9, Little Bridges-Street, near Drury-Lane Play-House, 1790).

Harris's List of Covent Garden Ladies: Or Man of Pleasure's Kalendar, for the Year 1793 (For H. Ranger, at No. 9, Little Bridges-Street, near Drury-Lane Play-House, 1793).

Hawkesworth, John, *An Account of the Voyages Undertaken by the Order of His Majesty for Making Discoveries in the Southern Hemisphere, and Successively Performed by Commodore Byron, Captain Wallis, Captain Carteret, and Captain Cook, in The Dolphin, the Swallow, and the Endeavour: Drawn up from the Journals which were Kept by the several Commanders, and from the Papers of Joseph Banks, Esq.*, 3 vols. (For W. Strahan and T. Cadell in the Strand, 1773).

Haywood, Eliza, *The Mercenary Lover: or, the Unfortunate Heiress* (1726), in *Selected Fiction and Drama of Eliza Haywood*, ed. Paula R. Backscheider (New York: Oxford University Press, 1999).

[Hewardine, or Hewerdine, William?], *Hilaria. The Festive Board* (Printed for the Author, 1798).

Horneck, Anthony, *Delight and Judgment: Or, a Prospect of the Great Day of Judgment, And its Power to Damp, and Imbitter Sensual Delights, Sports, and Recreations* (H. Hills Jun. for Mark Pardoe at the Sign of the Black Raven, over against Bedford House in the Strand, 1684).

Johnson, Samuel, *A Dictionary of the English Language*, 2nd edn., 2 vols. (By W. Strahan, 1755).

Kick Him Jenny; A Tale. To which is added The Female Contest, A Merry Tale, 11th edn. (For W. France near Leicest Fields, 1737).

Kick Him Nan: Or, a Poetical Description of a Wedding Night. By the Author of Kick Him Jenny (For T. Reynolds in the Strand, 1734).

The Ladies Delight. Containing . . . Ridotto al' Fresco. A Poem (For W. James in the Strand, 1732).

The Leeds Directory for 1809, Containing an Alphabetical List of the Merchants, Traders and Inhabitants in General (Leeds: Printed for the compiler, and for M. Robinson & Co. Booksellers, Commercial-Street, 1809).

A Letter on the Nature and State of Curiosity (J. Roberts, 1736).

Letters from the Inspector to a Lady, with the Genuine Answers (For M. Cooper, at the Globe in Paternoster-Row, 1752).

[Edward Ward], *Little Merlin's Cave. As it was Latel'y Discover'd by a Gentleman's Gardener, in Maidenhead-Thicket, to which is added, A Riddle: or a Paradoxical Character of an Hairy Monster, often found under Holland*, 4th edn. (For T. Read, in Dogwell-Court, White Fryers, 1737).

Love's Catechism: Compiled by the Author of the Recruiting Officer, for the Use and Benefit of All Young Batchelors, Maids and Widows (No publication details, 1707).

Luxury no Political Evil, but Demonstratively Proved to be Necessary to the Preservation and Prosperity of States (Sold by R. Baldwin, Paternoster-Row, [1780]).

MacKenzie, George, *The Moral History of Frugality. With its Opposite Vices, Covetousness, Niggardliness, Prodigality and Luxury* (Edinburgh, 1691).

Manley, Mary Delarivier, *Secret Memoirs and Manners of Several Persons of Quality, of Both Sexes. From the New Atalantis, an Island in the Mediteranean*, in Patricia Koster (ed.), *The Novels of Mary Delariviere Manley*, vol. I (1709; Gainesville, Fla.: Scholars' Facsimiles, 1971).

Secret Memoirs and Manners of Several Persons of Quality, of Both Sexes. From the New Atalantis, an Island in the Mediterranean, ed. Ros Ballaster (1709; Pickering and Chatto, 1991).

Vincent Miller [pseud.], *The Man-Plant: Or, a Scheme for Increasing and Improving the British Breed* (For M. Cooper, at the Globe in Pater-Noster-Row, 1752).

Martin, Benjamin, *A Supplement: Containing Remarks on a Rhapsody of Adventures of a Modern Knight Errant in Philosophy* (Bath: For the Author, and Mr Leake and Mr Frederick, 1746).

Lingua Britannica Reformata: or, a New English Dictionary (For J. Hodges, at the Looking-Glass, facing St Magnus' Church, London-Bridge; S. Austen, in Newgate-Street; J. Newbery, in St Paul's church-yard, in Little Britain; R. Raikes, at Gloucester; J. Leake and W. Frederick, at Bath; and B. Collins, at Salisbury, 1749).

Mauriceau, Francis, *The Diseases of Women with Child: As also the Best Means of Helping them in Natural and Unnatural Labours*, 7th edn., trans. Hugh Chamberlain (For T. Cox, at the Lamb, and J. Clarke, at the Bible, under the Royal Exchange in Cornhill, 1736).

[Thomas Stretser], *Merryland Displayed: Or, Plagiarism, Ignorance, and Impudence Detected. Being Observations upon a Pamphlet Intituled* A New Description of Merryland (Bath: Printed for the Author and sold by J. Leake; and the booksellers of London and Westminster, 1741).

Mettrie, Julien Offray de La, *L'Homme-plante* (Potsdam: Chretien Frederic Voss, 1748).

Milton, John, *Milton: Poetical Works*, ed. Douglas Bush (1966; Oxford: Oxford University Press, 1992).

[James Perry?], *Mimosa: Or, The Sensitive Plant. A Poem. Dedicated to Mr. Banks, and Addressed to Kitt Frederick, Dutchess of Queensbury Elect* (For W. Sandwich, near the Admiralty; and sold by all the booksellers within the Bills of Mortality, 1779).

Monsieur Thing's Origin: Or, Seignior D—o's Adventures in Britain (For R. Tomson, near Cheapside, 1722).

Montagu, Lady Mary Wortley, *Selected Letters*, ed. Isobel Grundy (Harmondsworth: Penguin, 1997).

Moore, John, *A View of Society and Manners in Italy*, 2 vols. (For W. Strahan; and T. Cadell, in the Strand, 1781).

Morris, Charles, *A Complete Collection of Songs*, 9th edn. (For James Ridgway, No. 1 York-Street, St James' Square, 1788).

The Festival of Ancareon: Being a Collection of Songs, 9th edn. (Printed for James Ridgway, opposite Sackville-Street, Piccadilly. Dublin: Reprinted for C. Jackson, no date [c. 1788]).

'The Natural History of the Arbor Vitae; Or, the Tree of Life, in Prose', in *The Ladies Delight* (For W. James in the Strand, 1732).

The Natural History of the Arbor Vitae: Or the Tree of Life; Versified and Explain'd (For J. Wilkinson, near Charing-Cross [Dublin?]; and sold by the booksellers of London and Westminster, [c. 1732]).

'The Natural History of the Arbor Vitae, or the Tree of Life', in *D—n Sw—t's Medley. Containing His Scheme for Making Religion and the Clergy Useful* (Dublin printed: London reprinted, and sold by all the booksellers in town and country, [c. 1749]).

Philogynes Clitorides [pseud., alias Thomas Stretser?], *The Natural History of the Frutex Vulvaria, or Flowering Shrub: As it is Collected from the Best Botanists both Ancient and Modern* (Publication details and date torn off, [c. 1737]).

[Thomas Stretser?], *The Natural History of the Frutex Vulvaria* (For E. Hill, in White-Fryers, Fleet-Street, 1741).

Pheuquewell, Roger [pseud., alias Thomas Stretser], *A New Description of Merryland. Containing a Topographical, Geographical, and Natural History of that Country,*

7th edn. (Bath: Printed and sold by J. Leake there; and by E. Curll, at Pope's Head in Rose-Street, Covent-Garden, 1741).

[John Armstrong], *The Oeconomy of Love: A Poetical Essay* (For T. Cooper, at the Globe in Pater-Noster-Row, 1736).

Of Luxury, More Particularly with respect to Apparel (For T. Green, over-against Falstaff's-Heed, near Charing-Cross, 1736).

[Charles Cotton], 'Of the Situation of Bettyland', in Philo-Brittanniae [pseud.], *The Potent Ally: Or, Succours from Merryland. With Three Essays in Praise of the Cloathing of that Country; and the Story of Pandora's Box. To which is added . . . The Present State of Bettyland* (Printed by direction of the author, and sold by the booksellers of London and Westminster, 'Paris', 1741).

The Old Serpent's Reply to the Electrical Eel (For M. Smith, and sold by the Booksellers near Temple-Bar, and in Pater-Noster Row, 1777).

On Rural Felicity; in an Epistle to a Friend (By J. Wilford, behind the Chapter-House, in St Paul's Church-Yard, 1733).

Ovid, *Publii Ovidoo Nasonis de Arte Amandi or, The Art of Love* (No publication details, [trans. Thomas Heywood, c. 1600]).

Ovid's Metamorphoses in Latin and English, Translated by the Most Eminent Hands, 2 vols. (Amsterdam: For Wetsteins and Smith, 1732).

Pepys, Samuel, *The Diary of Samuel Pepys*, ed. Robert Latham and William Matthews (Bell, 1976).

The Pleasures that Please on Reflection. Selected from the Album of Venus (For W. Holland, Garrick's Richard, No. 50, Oxford-Street, 1789).

The Polite Road to an Estate; Or, Fornication One Great Source of Wealth and Pleasure (For J. Coote, at the King's-Arms in Pater-Noster-Row, 1759).

Philo-Brittanniae [pseud.], *The Potent Ally: Or, Succours from Merryland. With Three Essays in Praise of the Cloathing of that Country; and the Story of Pandora's Box. To which is added . . . The Present State of Bettyland* ('Paris' [London]: Printed by direction of the author, and sold by the booksellers of London and Westminster [Published by Edmund Curll], 1741).

The Potent Ally: Or, Succours from Merryland. With Three Essays in Praise of the Cloathing of that Country; and the Story of Pandora's Box. To which is added The Present State of Bettyland, 2nd edn. ('Paris' [London]: Printed by direction of the Author and sold by the booksellers of London and Westminster, 1741).

The Practical Part of Love. Extracted out of the Extravagant and Lascivious Life of a Fair but Subtle Female (No publication details, 1660).

Pringle, Sir John, *A Discourse on the Torpedo Delivered at the Anniversary of the Royal Society, November 30, 1774* (For the Royal Society, 1775).

The Prostitutes of Quality; Or, Adultery a-la-mode. Being Authentic and Genuine Memoirs of Several Persons of the Highest Quality (For J. Cooke and J. Coote, opposite Devereux-Court, in the Strand, 1757).

The Rake of Taste, Or the Elegant Debauchee: A True Story (For P. Wicks, in Pater-Noster-Row, 1760).

Records of the Most Ancient and Puissant Order of the Beggar's Benison and Merryland, Anstruther (Anstruther: For private distribution, 1892).

A Riddle. In Answer to the Hairy Monster, by a Young Lady (No publication details, [Dublin?: 1725?]).

A Riddle: Of a Paradoxical Character of an Hairy Monster, Often found under Holland, 2nd edn. (Printed for A. Moore, near St. Paul's; and sold at most of the Pamphlet-Shops in London and Westminster, no date [c. 1725]).

Rochefoucauld, François de la, *A Frenchman in England: Being the* Mélange sur l'Angleterre *of François de la Rochefoucauld*, ed. Jean Marchand, trans. S. C. Roberts (1784; Cambridge: Cambridge University Press, 1933).

Tim Merriman [pseud.], *The St. James's Miscellany, Or the Citizen's Amusement* (By T. Payne, at the Crown in Pater-Noster-Row, T. Ashley, in St Paul's Church-Yard, A. Dodd without Temple-Bar, E. Nutt at the Roy[al]-Exchange, and by the booksellers of London and Westminster, [c. 1730]).

Santa-Maria; Or, The Mysterious Pregnancy. A Romance (For G. Kearsley, No. 46, Fleet-Street, 1797).

[Millot, Michel and L'Ange, Jean], *The School of Venus* (1655; trans. by Donald Thomas, London: Panther, 1972).

The Secret History of Pandora's Box (For T. Cooper in Pater-Noster-Row, 1742).

Seventeen Hundred and Seventy-Seven; Or, a Picture of the Manners and Character of the Age (For T. Evans, near York-Buildings, in the Strand, 1777).

Shadwell, Charles, *The Fair Quaker: or, The Humours of the Navy* (T. Lownds and T. Becket, 1773).

The Sixpenny Miscellany. Or, a Dissertation upon Pissing (Reprinted for A. Moore, near St Paul's, 1726).

Timothy Touchit [pseud.], *La Souricière. The Mouse-Trap. A Facetious and Sentimental Excursion through Part of Austria, Flanders and France. Being a Divertisement for Both Sexes*, 2 vols. (For J. Parsons, Paternoster-Row, 1794).

A Spy on Mother Midnight: Or, The Templar Metamorphos'd. Being a Lying-in Conversation. With a Curious Adventure. In a Letter from a Young Gentleman in the Country, to his Friend in the Town (For E. Penn, near St Paul's, 1748).

D—n S—t [Swift, Jonathan], *The Lady's Dressing Room. A Poem*, 3rd edn. (Dublin, 1732).

A Beautiful Young Nymph Going to Bed (Dublin printed, London reprinted for J. Roberts, 1734).

Supplement to the Historical Portion of the Records of the Most Ancient and Puissant Order of the Beggar's Benison and Merryland, Anstruther, *Being an Account of the Proceedings at the Meetings of the Society* (For private distribution, Anstruther, 1892).

The Surprize: Or, The Gentleman Turn'd Apothecary. A Tale Written Originally in French Prose; Afterwards Translated into Latin; and from thence now Versified in Hudibrastics (Printed and sold by the Booksellers of London and Westminster, 1739).

Paddy Strong-Cock [pseud.], *Teague-Root Display'd: Being Some Useful and Important Discoveries tending to Illustrate the Doctrine of Electricity, in a Letter from Paddy Strong-Cock, Fellow of Drury Lane, and Professor of Natural Philosophy in M. King's College, Covent-Garden, to W M W N, F. R. S. Author of a late Pamphlet on the Subject* (For W. Webb, near St Paul's, 1746).

Thistlewood, Thomas, *In Miserable Slavery: Thomas Thistlewood in Jamaica, 1750–86*, ed. Douglas Hall (Macmillan, 1989).

The Torpedo, A Poem to the Electrical Eel. Addressed to Mr. John Hunter, Surgeon: and Dedicated to The Right Honourable Lord Cholmondeley (Printed and sold by all the Booksellers in London and Westminster, 1777).

A True Account of the Aloe Americana or Africana . . . as also of Two Other Exotick Plants, call'd, The Cereus, or Torch-Thistle (For T. Warner, at the Black Boy in Pater-Noster-Row, and sold by H. Whitridge in Castle-Alley at the Royal Exchange; and Mr Cowell at Hoxton, 1729).

The Tryal of the Lady Allurea Luxury (For F. Noble, at his Circulating-Library in King-Street, Covent-Garden and J. Noble, at his Circulating-Library, in St Martin's Court, near Leicester-Square, 1757).

The Unsex'd Females: A Poem, Addressed to the Author of the Pursuits of Literature (For Cadell and Davies, 1798).

Vaillant, François Le, *Travels from the Cape of Good-Hope, into the Interior Parts of Africa*, 2 vols., trans. Elizabeth Helme (For William Lane, Leadenhall-Street, 1790)

Venus in the Cloister: Or, The Nun in her Smock ([Edmund Curll], 1725).

Vesalius, Andreae, *De Humani corporis fabrica Libri septum* (Basle: Ioannem Oporinum, 1555).

Captain Samuel Cock [pseud.], *A Voyage to Lethe; By Capt. Samuel Cock; Sometime Commander of the Good Ship the Charming Sally. Dedicated to the Right Worshipful Adam Cock, Esq; of Black-Mary's-Hole, Coney-Skin Merchant* (For J. Conybeare in Smock-Alley near Petticoat-Lane in Spittle Fields, 1741).

A Voyage to Lethe (For Mrs Laycock, at Mr Clevercock's [pseud.], in Smock-Alley, Glasgow, 1756).

Wallace, James, *Every Man his own Letter-Writer: Or, The New and Complete Art of Letter-Writing* (For J. Cooke, No. 17, Pater-Noster Row, 1780).

Watson, William, *Experiments and Observations tending to Illustrate the Nature and Properties of Electricity* (By Jacob Ilive, for the author, 1745).

Weeton, Ellen, *Miss Weeton's Journal of a Governess*, ed. Edward Hall (1939; Newton Abbot: David and Charles, 1969).

The Whim! Or, The Maid-Stone Bath. A Kentish Poetic (For J. Williams, in Paternoster-Row, 1782).

The Why and the Wherefore: Or, The Lady's Two Questions Resolved. Question the First; Why Men have not much to Boast of their Greatness, nor Women of their Beauty, in certain very Interesting Parts? . . . Question the Second. Wherefore is it that both Sexes are so Eternally Dear Lovers of that Same? Resolved in a Story intitled The Female Embassy (For J. Lamb, in the Strand, 1765).

[Wilkes, John], *An Essay on Woman* (Aberdeen: Printed for James Hay, and sold by all the booksellers in town and country, 1788).

Pego Borewell [pseud., alias John Wilkes], 'An Essay on Woman', in Adrian Hamilton, *The Infamous Essay on Woman: or, John Wilkes Seated between Vice and Virtue* (1788; André Deutsch, 1972).

Wilmot, John, Earl of Rochester, *The Works of the Right Honourable and the Late Earls of Rochester and Roscommon*, 2nd edn. (For Edmund Curll, at the Peacock with-out Temple-Bar, 1707).

The Works of John Wilmot, Earl of Rochester, ed. Harold Love (Oxford: Oxford University Press, 1999).

Wilson, George, *The Youth's Pocket-Companion: Or, Universal Preceptor*, 2nd edn. (For J. Coote, at the King's Arms, Pater-Noster-Row, 1749).

Wisdom Reveal'd: Or, The Tree of Life Discover'd and Describ'd. A Tale. To which is added The Crab-Tree; or, Sylvia Discover'd. By a Studious Enquirer into the Mysteries of Nature (For W. Shaw, and sold at all the Pamphlet-Shops in London and Westminster, [c. 1732]).

The Wit's Magazine (Harrison and Co., No. 18, Paternoster-Row, 1784).

PRINTED SECONDARY SOURCES

Place of publication is London unless otherwise stated.

Accati, Luisa, 'The Spirit of Fornication: Virtue of the Soul and Virtue of the Body in Friuli, 1600–1800', in E. Muir and G. Ruggiero (eds.), *Sex and Gender in Historical Perspective* (Baltimore: Johns Hopkins University Press, 1990), pp. 111–35.

Adams, Percy G., *Travelers and Travel Liars, 1660–1800* (1962; New York: Dover Publications, 1980).

Alaya, Flavia, 'Victorian Science and the "Genus" of Woman', *Journal of the History of Ideas* 38 (1977), pp. 261–80.

Allen, John L., 'Lands of Myth, Waters of Wonder: The Place of the Imagination in the History of Geographical Exploration', in David Lowenthal and Martyn J. Bowden (eds.), *Geographies of the Mind: Essays in Historical Geography* (New York: Oxford University Press, 1976), pp. 42–53.

Andrew, Donna, 'The Code of Honour and its Critics: The Opposition to Duelling in England, 1700–1850', *Social History* 5 (1980), pp. 409–34.

Andrews, Malcolm, *The Search for the Picturesque: Landscape Aesthetics and Tourism in Britain, 1760–1800* (Aldershot: Scolar Press, 1989).

Armbruster, Carol (ed.), *Publishing and Readership in Revolutionary France and America* (Westport, Conn.: Greenwood Press, 1993).

Armstrong, Nancy, *Desire and Domestic Fiction: A Political History of the Novel* (Oxford: Oxford University Press, 1987).

'The Pornographic Effect: A Response', *American Journal of Semiotics* 7 (1990), pp. 27–44.

Ashe, Geoffrey, *The Hell-Fire Clubs: A History of Anti-Morality* (1974; Stroud: Sutton, 2000).

Aubertin-Porter, Norma and Bennett, Alyx, *Oxford Coffee Houses, 1651–1800* (Oxford: Hampden, 1987).

Azouvi, François, 'Woman as a Model of Pathology in the Eighteenth Century', *Diogenes* 115 (1981), pp. 22–36.

Baker, Malcolm, 'Squabby Cupids and Clumsy Graces: Garden Sculpture and Luxury in Eighteenth-Century England', *Oxford Art Journal* 18 (1995), pp. 3–28.

Baker, T. H. (ed.), *Records of the Seasons, Prices of Agricultural Produce, and Phenomena Observed in the British Isles* (Simpkin, Marshall and Co., no date [c. 1888]).

Ballaster, Ros, *Seductive Forms: Women's Amatory Fiction from 1684 to 1740* (Oxford: Clarendon Press, 1992).

'Seizing the Means of Seduction: Fiction and Feminine Identity in Aphra Behn and Delarivier Manley', in Isobel Grundy and Susan Wiseman (eds.), *Women, Writing, History* (Batsford, 1992), pp. 93–108.

Barber, Charles, 'Reading the Garden in Byzantium: Nature and Sexuality', *Byzantine and Modern Greek Studies* 16 (1992), pp. 1–19.

Barker, Francis, *The Tremulous Private Body: Essays on Subjection* (1984; Ann Arbor: University of Michigan Press, 1995).

Barker, Hannah, 'Women, Work and the Industrial Revolution: Female Involvement in the English Printing Trades, c. 1700–1840', in Hannah Barker and Elaine Chalus (eds.), *Gender in Eighteenth-Century England: Roles, Representations and Responsibilities* (Longman, 1997), pp. 81–100.

Barker, Hannah and Chalus, Elaine (eds.), *Gender in Eighteenth-Century England: Roles, Representations and Responsibilities* (Longman, 1997).

Barrell, John, 'The Dangerous Goddess: Masculinity, Prestige and the Aesthetic in Early Eighteenth-Century Britain', in his *The Birth of Pandora and the Division of Knowledge* (Basingstoke: Macmillan, 1992), pp. 63–87.

Barry, Jonathan, 'Literacy and Literature in Popular Culture', in Tim Harris (ed.), *Popular Culture in England, c. 1500–1850* (Basingstoke: Macmillan, 1995), pp. 69–94.

Barthes, Roland, *The Pleasure of the Text* (1973; Oxford: Blackwell, 1990).

Bataille, Georges, *Eroticism* (1957; Marion Boyars, 1987).

Beard, Geoffrey, *The National Trust Book of the English House Interior* (1990; Harmondsworth: Penguin, 1991).

Belanger, Terry, 'Publishers and Writers in Eighteenth-Century England', in Isabel Rivers (ed.), *Books and their Readers in Eighteenth-Century England* (Leicester: Leicester University Press, 1982), pp. 5–25.

Belsey, Catherine, 'Reading Cultural History', in Tamsin Spargo (ed.), *Reading the Past: Literature and History* (Basingstoke: Palgrave, 2000).

Benedict, Barbara M., 'The "Curious Attitude" in Eighteenth-Century Britain: Observing and Owning', *Eighteenth-Century Life* 14 (1990), pp. 59–98.

Bennett, Judith, 'Feminism and History', *Gender and History* 1 (1989), pp. 251–72.

Berger, John, *Ways of Seeing* (BBC and Penguin, 1972).

Bergstrom, Carson, 'Purney, Pastoral and the Polymorphous Perverse', *British Journal for Eighteenth-Century Studies* 17 (1994), pp. 149–63.

Bermingham, Ann, 'The Aesthetics of Ignorance: The Accomplished Woman in the Culture of Connoisseurship', *Oxford Art Journal* 16 (1993), pp. 3–20.

Berry, Helen, '"Nice and Curious Questions": Coffee Houses and the Representation of Women in John Dunton's *Athenian Mercury*', *Seventeenth Century* 12 (1997), pp. 257–76.

'Rethinking Politeness in Eighteenth-Century England: Moll King's Coffee House and the Significance of Flash Talk', *Transactions of the Royal Historical Society* 6th series, 11 (2001), pp. 65–81.

Gender, Society and Print Culture in Late-Stuart England: The Cultural World of the Athenian Mercury (Aldershot: Ashgate, 2003).

Black, Jeremy, *Maps and Politics* (Reaktion, 1997).

Bold, Alan (ed.), *The Sexual Dimension in Literature* (Vision, 1982).

Bolla, Peter de, *The Discourse of the Sublime* (Oxford: Basil Blackwell, 1989).

Bordo, Susan, 'Reading the Male Body', in Laurence Goldstein (ed.), *The Male Body: Features, Destinies, Exposures* (Ann Arbor: University of Michigan Press, 1994), pp. 265–307.

Borsay, Peter, *The English Urban Renaissance: Culture and Society in the Provincial Town, 1660–1770* (Oxford: Oxford University Press, 1989).

'The English Urban Renaissance: The Development of Provincial Urban Culture, c.1680–1760', in his *The Eighteenth-Century Town: A Reader in English Urban History, 1688–1820* (Longman, 1990), pp. 159–87.

'Early Modern Urban Landscapes, 1540–1800', in Philip Waller (ed.), *The English Urban Landscape* (Oxford: Oxford University Press, 2000), pp. 99–124.

Boucé, Paul-Gabriel, 'The Secret Nexus: Sex and Literature in Eighteenth-Century Britain', in Alan Bold (ed.), *The Sexual Dimension in Literature* (Vision, 1982), pp. 70–89.

'Some Sexual Beliefs and Myths in Eighteenth-Century Britain', in Boucé (ed.), *Sexuality in Eighteenth-Century Britain* (Manchester: Manchester University Press, 1982), pp. 28–46.

'Chthonic and Pelagic Metaphorization in Eighteenth-Century English Erotica', in Robert Purks Maccubbin (ed.), *'Tis Nature's Fault: Unauthorized Sexuality during the Enlightenment* (Cambridge: Cambridge University Press, 1987), pp. 202–16.

Boucé, Paul-Gabriel (ed.), *Sexuality in Eighteenth-Century Britain* (Manchester: Manchester University Press, 1982).

Bourke, Joanna, *Dismembering the Male: Men's Bodies, Britain and the Great War* (Reaktion Books, 1996).

Bowers, Terence, 'Reconstituting the National Body in Smollett's *Travels through Italy and France*', *Eighteenth-Century Life* 21 (1997), pp. 1–25.

Bowers, Toni O'Shaughnessy, 'Sex, Lies and Invisibility: Amatory Fiction from the Restoration to Mid-Century', in John Richetti (ed.), *The Columbia History of the British Novel* (New York: Columbia University Press, 1994), pp. 50–72.

Braddick, Michael J., *State Formation in Early Modern England, c. 1550–1700* (Cambridge: Cambridge University Press, 2000).

Braddick, Michael J. and Walter, John, 'Grids of Power', in Braddick and Walter (eds.), *Negotiating Power in Early Modern Society: Order, Hierarchy, and Subordination in Britain and Ireland* (Cambridge: Cambridge University Press, 2001), pp. 1–42.

Braudy, Leo, '*Fanny Hill* and Materialism', *Eighteenth-Century Studies* 4 (1970), pp. 21–40.

Bray, Alan, 'To be a Man in Early Modern Society: The Curious Case of Michael Wigglesworth', *History Workshop Journal* 41 (1996), pp. 155–65.

'The Body of the Friend', in Tim Hitchcock and Michèle Cohen (eds.), *English Masculinities, 1600–1850* (Harlow: Longman, 1999), pp. 65–84.

Breitenberg, Mark, *Anxious Masculinity in Early Modern England* (Cambridge: Cambridge University Press, 1996).

Brewer, John, 'Reconstructing the Reader: Prescriptions, Texts and Strategies in Anna Larpent's Reading', in James Raven, Helen Small and Naomi Tadmor (eds.), *The Practice and Representation of Reading in England* (Cambridge: Cambridge University Press, 1996), pp. 226–45.

The Pleasures of the Imagination: English Culture in the Eighteenth Century (HarperCollins, 1997).

Brooks, Peter, *Body Work: Objects of Desire in Modern Narrative* (Cambridge, Mass.: Harvard University Press, 1993).

Brown, Kathleen, '"Changed . . . into the Fashion of Man": The Politics of Sexual Difference in a Seventeenth-Century Anglo-American Settlement', *Journal of the History of Sexuality* 6 (1995), pp. 171–93.

Brumble, H. David, *Classical Myths and Legends in the Middle Ages and Renaissance: A Dictionary of Allegorical Meanings* (Fitzroy Dearborn, 1998).

Buck, Anne, *Dress in Eighteenth-Century England* (Batsford, 1979).

Buckley, Thomas and Gottlieb, Alma (eds.), *Blood Magic: The Anthropology of Menstruation* (Berkeley: University of California Press, 1988).

Bullough, Vern L., 'Medieval Medical and Scientific Views of Women', *Viator* 4 (1973), pp. 485–501.

Burke, Peter, 'Overture: The New History, its Past and its Future', in Burke (ed.), *New Perspectives on Historical Writing* (Cambridge: Polity Press, 1991), pp. 1–24.

Burt, Richard and Archer, John Michael, *Enclosure Acts: Sexuality, Property and Culture in Early Modern England* (Ithaca, N.Y.: Cornell University Press, 1994).

Butler, Gerald, *Love and Reading: An Essay in Applied Psychoanalysis* (New York: Peter Lang, 1989).

Butler, Judith, *Gender Trouble: Feminism and the Subversion of Identity* (New York: Routledge, 1990).

Bodies That Matter: On the Discursive Limits of Sex (New York: Routledge, 1993).

Cannon, John (ed.), *The Oxford Companion to British History* (Oxford: Oxford University Press, 1997).

Carabelli, Giancarlo, *In the Image of Priapus* (Duckworth, 1996).

Carter, Philip, 'Men about Town: Representations of Foppery and Masculinity in Early Eighteenth-Century Urban Society', in Hannah Barker and Elaine Chalus (eds.), *Gender in Eighteenth-Century England: Roles, Representations and Responsibilities* (Harlow: Longman, 1997), pp. 31–57.

Men and the Emergence of Polite Society: Britain 1660–1800 (Harlow: Longman, 2001).

'Polite Persons: Character, Biography and the Gentleman', *Transactions of the Royal Historical Society* 12 (2002), pp. 333–54.

Castle, Terry, *Masquerade and Civilization: The Carnivalesque in Eighteenth-Century English Culture and Fiction* (Methuen, 1986).

Certeau, Michel de, *The Practice of Everyday Life*, trans. Steven Randall (1984; Berkeley: University of California Press, 1988).

Chard, Chloe, 'Effeminacy, Pleasure and the Classical Body', in Gill Perry and Michael Rossington (eds.), *Femininity and Masculinity in Eighteenth-Century Art and Culture* (Manchester: Manchester University Press, 1994), pp. 142–61.

Pleasure and Guilt on the Grand Tour: Travel Writing and Imaginative Geography, 1600–1830 (Manchester: Manchester University Press, 1999).

Chartier, Roger, 'Book Markets and Reading in France at the End of the Old Regime', in Carol Armbruster (ed.), *Publishing and Readership in Revolutionary France and America* (Westport, Conn.: Greenwood Press, 1993), pp. 117–36.

Clark, Alice, *Working Life of Women in the Seventeenth Century* (1919; Routledge, 1992).

Clark, Anna, *Women's Silence, Men's Violence: Sexual Assault in England, 1770–1845* (Pandora, 1987).

The Struggle for the Breeches: Gender and the Making of the British Working Class (Rivers Oram, 1995).

'Anne Lister's Construction of Lesbian Identity', *Journal of the History of Sexuality* 7 (1996), pp. 23–50.

Clark, J. C. D., *English Society, 1688–1832: Ideology, Social Structure and Political Practice during the Ancien Regime* (Cambridge: Cambridge University Press, 1985).

Clark, Peter, *British Clubs and Societies, 1500–1800: The Origins of an Associational World* (Oxford: Clarendon Press, 2000).

Classen, Constance, *Worlds of Sense: Exploring the Senses in History and across Cultures* (Routledge, 1993).

Cohen, Michèle, *Fashioning Masculinity: National Identity and Language in the Eighteenth Century* (Routledge, 1996).

'Manliness, Effeminacy and the French', in Tim Hitchcock and Michèle Cohen (eds.), *English Masculinities, 1660–1800* (Harlow: Longman, 1999), pp. 44–61.

Colley, Linda, *Britons: Forging the Nation, 1707–1838* (Pimlico, 1992).

Connell, R. W., *Masculinities* (Cambridge: Polity Press, 1995).

Conway, Alison, 'The Protestant Cause and a Protestant Whore: Aphra Behn's *Love-Letters*', *Eighteenth-Century Life* 25 (2001), pp. 1–19.

Copley, Stephen, 'Commerce, Conversation and Politeness in the Early Eighteenth-Century Periodical', *British Journal for Eighteenth-Century Studies* 18 (1995), pp. 63–79.

Corbin, Alain, *The Foul and the Fragrant: Odor and the French Social Imagination*, trans. Miriam L. Kockan, Roy Porter and Christopher Prendergast (1982; Leamington: Berg, 1986).

Corfield, Penelope J., *The Impact of English Towns, 1700–1800* (Oxford: Oxford University Press, 1982).

'History and the Challenge of Gender History', *Rethinking History* 1 (1997), pp. 241–58.

Cott, Nancy, 'Passionlessness: An Interpretation of Victorian Sexual Ideology, 1790–1850', *Signs* 4 (1978), pp. 219–36.

Cowan, Brian, 'Reasonable Ecstasies: Shaftesbury and the Languages of Libertinism', *Journal of British Studies* 37 (1998), pp. 111–38.

'What was Masculine about the Public Sphere? Gender and the Coffeehouse Milieu in Post-Restoration England', *History Workshop Journal* 51 (2001), pp. 127–57.

Crawford, Patricia, 'Attitudes to Menstruation in Seventeenth-Century England', *Past and Present* 91 (1981), pp. 47–73.

'Sexual Knowledge in England, 1500–1750', in Roy Porter and Mikulás Teich (eds.), *Sexual Knowledge, Sexual Science: The History of Attitudes to Sexuality* (Cambridge: Cambridge University Press, 1994), pp. 82–106.

Cressy, David, *Birth, Marriage and Death: Ritual, Religion, and the Life-Cycle in Tudor and Stuart England* (1997; Oxford: Oxford University Press, 1999).

Cross, F. L. and Livingstone, E. A. (eds.), *The Oxford Dictionary of the Christian Church*, 2nd edn. (1957; Oxford: Oxford University Press, 1974).

Crouch, Kimberly, 'The Public Life of Actresses: Prostitutes or Ladies?', in Hannah Barker and Elaine Chalus (eds.), *Gender in Eighteenth-Century England: Roles, Representations and Responsibilities* (Harlow: Longman, 1997), pp. 58–78.

Cruickshank, Dan and Wyld, Peter, *Georgian Town Houses and their Details* (1975; Butterworth Architecture, 1990).

Cunningham, Colin, '"An Italian House is my Lady": Some Aspects of the Definition of Women's Role in the Architecture of Robert Adams', in Gill Perry and Michael Rossington (eds.), *Femininity and Masculinity in Eighteenth-Century Art and Culture* (Manchester: Manchester University Press, 1994), pp. 63–77.

Darnton, Robert, 'Intellectual and Cultural History', in Michael Kammen (ed.), *The Past before US: Contemporary Historical Writing in the United States* (Ithaca, N.Y.: Cornell University Press, 1980), pp. 327–54.

'The Life Cycle of a Book: A Publishing History of D'Holbach's *Système de la Nature*', in Carol Armbruster (ed.), *Publishing and Readership in Revolutionary France and America* (Westport, Conn.: Greenwood Press, 1993), pp. 15–43.

The Corpus of Clandestine Literature in France, 1769–1789 (New York: Norton, 1995).

The Forbidden Best-Sellers of Pre-Revolutionary France (New York: Norton, 1995).

Davidoff, Leonore and Hall, Catherine, *Family Fortunes: Men and Women of the English Middle Class, 1780–1850* (Routledge, 1987).

Davis, Richard Beale, *A Colonial Southern Bookshelf: Reading in the Eighteenth Century* (Athens: University of Georgia Press, 1979).

Day, John C., *Coffee Houses and Book Clubs in Eighteenth- and Nineteenth-Century Northumberland* (Newcastle upon Tyne: John Day and Society of Antiquaries, 1995).

DeJean, Joan, 'The Politics of Pornography: *L'Ecole des Filles*', in Lynn Hunt (ed.), *The Invention of Pornography: Obscenity and the Origins of Modernity* (New York: Zone Books, 1994), pp. 109–23.

A Directory of Rare Book and Special Collections in the United Kingdom and Republic of Ireland (Library Association, 1985).

Donoghue, Emma, *Passions between Women: British Lesbian Culture, 1668–1801* (New York: HarperCollins, 1993).

duBois, Page, *Sowing the Body: Psychoanalysis and Ancient Representations of Women* (1988; Chicago: University of Chicago Press, 1991).

Duden, Barbara, *The Woman beneath the Skin: A Doctor's Patients in Eighteenth-Century Germany* (Cambridge, Mass.: Harvard University Press, 1991).

Edney, Matthew H., 'Reconsidering Enlightenment Geography and Map Making: Reconnaissance, Mapping, Archive', in Charles W. J. Withers and David N. Livingstone (eds.), *Geography and Enlightenment* (Chicago: University of Chicago Press, 1999), pp. 165–98.

Ellis, Markham, 'Coffee-Women, "The Spectator" and the public sphere in the early eighteenth century', in Elizabeth Eger, Charlotte Grant, Cliona o Gallchoir and Penny Warburton (eds.), *Women, Writing and the Public Sphere, 1700–1830* (Cambridge: Cambridge University Press, 2001), pp. 27–52.

Erickson, Robert A., *Mother Midnight: Birth, Sex and Fate in Eighteenth-Century Fiction (Defoe, Richardson and Sterne)* (New York: AMS Press, 1986).

Fabricant, Carole, 'Binding and Dressing Nature's Loose Tresses: The Ideology of Augustan Landscape Design', *Studies in Eighteenth-Century Culture* 8 (1979), pp. 109–35.

Feather, John, 'From Censorship to Copyright: Aspects of the Government's Role in the English Book Trade, 1695–1775', in Kenneth E. Carpenter (ed.), *Books and Society in History* (New York: Bowker, 1983), pp. 173–98.

A History of British Publishing (New York: Croom Helm, 1988).

Fee, Elizabeth, 'Science and the Woman Problem: Historical Perspectives', in M. S. Teitelbaum (ed.), *Sex Differences: Social and Biological Perspectives* (New York: Anchor Books, 1976), pp. 175–223.

Feher, M. (ed.), *Fragments for a History of the Human Body: Part One* (New York: Zone, 1989).

Fragments for a History of the Human Body: Part Two (New York: Zone, 1989).

Fragments for a History of the Human Body: Part Three (New York: Zone, 1989).

Fergus, Jan, 'Women Readers: A Case Study', in *Vivien Jones* (ed.), *Women and Literature in Britain, 1700–1800* (Cambridge: Cambridge University Press, 2000), pp. 155–76.

Findlen, Paula, 'Humanism, Politics and Pornography in Renaissance Italy', in Lynn Hunt (ed.), *The Invention of Pornography: Obscenity and the Origins of Modernity, 1500–1800* (New York: Zone Books, 1994), pp. 49–108.

Fish, Stanley, *Is There a Text in this Class? The Authority of Interpretive Communities* (Cambridge, Mass.: Harvard University Press, 1980).

Fissell, Mary, 'Gender and Generation: Representing Reproduction in Early Modern England', *Gender and History* 7 (1995), pp. 433–56.

Fletcher, Anthony, *Gender, Sex and Subordination in England 1500–1800* (New Haven: Yale University Press, 1995).

Flynn, Carol Houlihan, 'What Fanny Felt: The Pains of Compliance in *Memoirs of a Woman of Pleasure*', *Studies in the Novel* 19 (1987), pp. 284–95.

Foucault, Michel, *The History of Sexuality. Volume I: An Introduction* (1976; Allen Lane, 1979).

Foxon, David, *Libertine Literature in England, 1600–1745* (Shenval Press, 1964).

Foyster, Elizabeth, 'Boys will be Boys? Manhood and Aggression, 1660–1800', in Tim Hitchcock and Michèle Cohen (eds.), *English Masculinities, 1660–1800* (Harlow: Longman, 1999), pp. 151–66.

Manhood in Early Modern England: Honour, Sex and Marriage (Harlow: Longman, 1999).

'Creating a Veil of Silence? Politeness and Marital Violence in the English Household', *Transactions of the Royal Historical Society* 12 (2002), pp. 395–415.

Frantz, David O., *Festum Voluptatis: A Study of Renaissance Erotica* (Columbus: Ohio State University Press, 1989).

Frappier-Mazur, Lucienne, 'Truth and the Obscene Word in Eighteenth-Century French Pornography', in Lynn Hunt (ed.), *The Invention of Pornography: Obscenity and the Origins of Modernity, 1500–1800* (New York: Zone, 1993), pp. 203–21.

Freeberg, David, *The Power of Images: Studies in the History and Theory of Response* (Chicago: University of Chicago Press, 1989).

Freund, Elizabeth, *The Return of the Reader: Reader Response Criticism* (Methuen, 1987).

Gaines, James F. and Roberts, Josephine A., 'The Geography of Love in Seventeenth-Century Women's Fiction', in James Turner (ed.), *Sexuality and Gender in Early*

Modern Europe: Institutions, Texts, Images (Cambridge: Cambridge University Press, 1993), pp. 289–309.

Gallagher, Catherine, *Nobody's Story: The Vanishing Acts of Women Writers in the Marketplace, 1670–1820* (Oxford: Clarendon, 1994).

Geertz, Clifford, *The Interpretation of Cultures: Selected Essays* (1973; London: Fontana, 1993).

George, Margaret, 'From "Goodwife" to "Mistress": The Transformation of the Female in Bourgeois Culture', *Science and Society* 37 (1973), pp. 152–77.

Gilman, Sander L., *Difference and Pathology: Stereotypes of Sexuality, Race, and Madness* (Ithaca, N.Y.: Cornell University Press, 1985).

Inscribing the Other (Lincoln: University of Nebraska Press, 1991).

'Touch, Sexuality and Disease', in W. F. Bynum and Roy Porter (eds.), *Medicine and the Five Senses* (Cambridge: Cambridge University Press, 1993), pp. 198–224.

Goldstein, Laurence (ed.), *The Male Body: Features, Destinies, Exposures* (Ann Arbor: University of Michigan Press, 1994).

Gould, Stephen Jay, *The Flamingo's Smile: Reflections in Natural History* (New York: Norton, 1985).

Goulemot, Jean-Marie, *Forbidden Texts: Erotic Literature and its Readers in Eighteenth-Century France*, trans. James Simpson (1991; Cambridge: Polity Press, 1994).

Gowing, Laura, *Domestic Dangers: Women, Words, and Sex in Early Modern London* (Oxford: Clarendon Press, 1996).

Common Bodies: Women, Touch and Power in Seventeenth-Century England (New Haven: Yale University Press, 2003).

Greene, Richard, *Mary Leapor: A Study in Eighteenth-Century Women's Poetry* (Oxford: Clarendon Press, 1993).

Griffin, Susan, *Pornography and Silence: Culture's Revenge against Nature* (Women's Press, 1982).

Grimal, Pierre, *Dictionary of Classical Mythology*, trans. A. R. Maxwell-Hyslop (Oxford: Blackwell, 1986).

Grosz, Elizabeth, 'Bodies-Cities', in her *Space, Time, Perversion: Essays on the Politics of Bodies* (Routledge, 1995).

Haliczer, Stephen, *Sexuality in the Confessional: A Sacrament Profaned* (Oxford: Oxford University Press, 1996).

Hall, Lesley A., *Hidden Anxieties: Male Sexuality 1900–1950* (Cambridge: Polity Press, 1991).

Hamilton, Adrian, *The Infamous Essay on Woman: Or, John Wilkes Seated between Vice and Virtue* (André Deutsch, 1972).

Harvey, Karen, '"The Majesty of the Masculine Form": Multiplicity and Male Bodies in Eighteenth-Century Erotica', in Tim Hitchcock and Michèle Cohen (eds.), *English Masculinities, 1660–1800* (Harlow: Longman, 1999), pp. 193–214.

'The Century of Sex? Gender, Bodies and Sexuality in the Long Eighteenth Century', *The Historical Journal* 45 (2002), pp. 899–916.

Haskell, Francis, 'The Baron d'Hancarville: An Adventurer and Art Historian in Eighteenth-Century Europe', in *Past and Present in Art and Taste: Selected Essays* (New Haven: Yale University Press, 1988), pp. 30–45.

Hay, Douglas and Rogers, Nicholas, *Eighteenth-Century English Society* (Oxford: Oxford University Press, 1997).

Haydon, Colin, *Anti-Catholicism in Eighteenth-Century England, c. 1714–80* (Manchester: Manchester University Press, 1993).

Hegeman, Susan, 'Imagining Totality: Rhetorics of and versus Culture', *Common Knowledge* 6 (1997), pp. 51–72.

Héritier-Augé, Françoise, 'Semen and Blood: Some Ancient Theories Concerning their Genesis and Relationship', in M. Feher (ed.), *Fragments for a History of the Human Body: Part Three* (New York: Zone, 1989), pp. 158–75.

'Older Women, Stout-Hearted Women, Women of Substance', in M. Feher (ed.), *Fragments for a History of the Human Body: Part Three* (New York: Zone, 1989), pp. 280–99.

Hill, Bridget, *Women, Work and Sexual Politics in the Eighteenth Century* (1989; Montreal: McGill-Queen's University Press, 1994).

Hitchcock, Tim, 'Redefining Sex in Eighteenth-Century England', *History Workshop Journal* 41 (1996), pp. 73–90.

English Sexualities, 1700–1800 (Basingstoke: Macmillan, 1997).

'Sociability and Misogyny in the Life of John Cannon, 1684–1743', in Tim Hitchcock and Michèle Cohen (eds.), *English Masculinities, 1660–1800* (Harlow: Longman, 1999), pp. 25–43.

Hitchcock, Tim and Cohen, Michèle (eds.), *English Masculinities, 1660–1800* (Harlow: Longman, 1999).

Hodnett, Edward, *Image and Text: Studies in the Illustration of English Literature* (Scolar Press, 1982).

Holub, Robert C., *Reception Theory: A Critical Introduction* (Methuen, 1984).

Hope, Valerie, *My Lord Mayor: Eight Hundred Years of London's Mayoralty* (Weidenfeld and Nicolson, 1989).

Howes, David, 'Scent and Sensibility', *Culture, Medicine and Psychiatry* 13 (1989), pp. 81–9.

Hudson, Nicholas, 'From "Nation" to "Race": The Origin of Racial Classification in Eighteenth-Century Thought', *Eighteenth-Century Studies* 29 (1996), pp. 247–64.

Hult, David F., *Self-Fulfilling Prophecies: Readership and Authority in the First Roman de la Rose* (Cambridge: Cambridge University Press, 1986).

Hunt, John Dixon, *The Figure in the Landscape: Poetry, Painting, and Gardening during the Eighteenth Century* (Baltimore: Johns Hopkins University Press, 1976).

Hunt, Lynn (ed.), *The New Cultural History* (Berkeley: University of California Press, 1989).

The Invention of Pornography: Obscenity and the Origins of Modernity, 1500–1800 (New York: Zone Books, 1993).

Hunt, Margaret, 'Hawkers, Bawlers, and Mercuries: Women in the London Press in the Early Enlightenment', in Margaret Hunt, Margaret Jacob, Phyllis Mack and Ruth Perry (eds.), *Women and the Enlightenment* (New York: Haworth Press, 1984), pp. 41–68.

'Domesticity and Women's Independence in Eighteenth-Century London', *Gender and History* 4 (1992), pp. 10–33.

Hutton, Patrick H., 'The History of Mentalities: The New Map of Cultural History', *History and Theory* 20 (1981), pp. 237–59.

Hyde, Melissa, 'Confounding Conventions: Gender Ambiguity and François Boucher's Painted Pastorals', *Eighteenth-Century Studies* 30 (1996), pp. 25–57.

Iser, Wolfgang, *The Implied Reader: Patterns of Communication in Prose Fiction from Bunyan to Beckett* (Baltimore: Johns Hopkins University Press, 1974).

　Prospecting: From Reader Response to Literary Anthropology (1989; Baltimore: Johns Hopkins University Press, 1993).

Jacob, Margaret C., *The Radical Enlightenment: Pantheists, Freemasons and Republicans* (Allen and Unwin, 1981).

　'The Materialist World of Pornography', in Lynn Hunt (ed.), *The Invention of Pornography: Obscenity and the Origins of Modernity, 1500–1800* (New York: Zone Books, 1993), pp. 157–202.

Jacquart, D. and Thomasset, C., *Sexuality and Medicine in the Middle Ages* (Cambridge: Polity Press, 1988).

Jameson, Eric, *The Natural History of Quackery* (Michael Joseph, 1961).

Jardine, N., Secord, J. A. and Spary, E. C., (eds.), *Cultures of Natural History* (Cambridge: Cambridge University Press, 1996).

Jenner, Mark S. R. and Taithe, Bertrand O., 'The Historiographical Body', in R. Cooter and J. Pickstone (eds.), *Medicine in the Twentieth Century* (Amsterdam: Harwood Academic, 2000), pp. 187–200.

Johns, Adrian, 'The Physiology of Reading in Restoration England', in James Raven, Helen Small and Naomi Tadmor (eds.), *The Practice and Representation of Reading in England* (Cambridge: Cambridge University Press, 1996), pp. 138–61.

Jones, Barbara, *Follies and Grottoes*, 2nd edn. (1953; Constable, 1974).

Jones, Louis C., *The Clubs of the Georgian Rakes* (New York: Columbia University Press, 1942).

Jones, Vivien, 'The Seductions of Conduct: Pleasure and Conduct Literature', in Roy Porter and Marie Mulvey Roberts (eds.), *Pleasure in the Eighteenth Century* (Basingstoke: Macmillan, 1996), pp. 108–32.

Jones, Vivien (ed.), *Women and Literature in Britain, 1700–1800* (Cambridge: Cambridge University Press, 2000).

Jordanova, Ludmilla, *Languages of Nature: Critical Essays on Science and Literature* (Free Association Books, 1986).

　Sexual Visions: Images of Gender in Science and Medicine between the Eighteenth and Nineteenth Centuries (Harvester Wheatsheaf, 1989).

Kappeler, Susanne, *The Pornography of Representation* (Cambridge: Polity Press, 1986).

Kates, Gary, 'The Transgendered World of the Chevalier/Chevalière d'Eon', *Journal of Modern History* 67 (1995), pp. 558–94.

Kearney, P. J., *The Private Case: An Annotated Bibliography of the Private Case Erotica Collection in the British (Museum) Library* (Jay Landesman, 1981).

　A History of Erotic Literature (Macmillan, 1982).

Kelly, V. and von Müche, D. E. (eds.), *Body and Text in the Eighteenth Century* (Stanford: Stanford University Press, 1994).

Kendrick, Walter, *The Secret Museum: Pornography in Modern Culture* (New York: Viking, 1987).

Keuls, Eva, *The Reign of the Phallus: Sexual Politics in Ancient Athens* (1985; Berkeley: University of California Press, 1993).

King, Helen, 'Sowing the Field: Greek and Roman Sexology', in Roy Porter and Mikulás Teich (eds.), *Sexual Knowledge, Sexual Science: The History of Attitudes to Sexuality* (Cambridge: Cambridge University Press, 1994), pp. 29–46.

Klein, Lawrence, 'The Third Earl of Shaftesbury and the Progress of Politeness', *Eighteenth-Century Studies* 18 (1984–5), pp. 186–214.

'Gender, Conversation and the Public Sphere in Early Eighteenth-Century England', in Judith Still and Michael Worton (eds.), *Textuality and Sexuality: Reading Theories and Practices* (Manchester: Manchester University Press, 1993), pp. 100–15.

'Gender and the Public/Private Distinction in the Eighteenth Century: Some Questions about Evidence and Analytical Procedure', *Eighteenth-Century Studies* 29 (1995), pp. 97–109.

'Politeness and the Interpretation of the British Eighteenth Century', *The Historical Journal* 45 (2002), pp. 869–98.

Knauft, Bruce M., 'Bodily Images in Melanesia: Cultural Substances and Natural Metaphors', in M. Feher (ed.), *Fragments for a History of the Human Body: Part Three* (New York: Zone, 1989), pp. 198–279.

Koerner, Lisbet, 'Carl Linnaeus in his Place and Time', in N. Jardine, J. A. Secord and E. C. Spary (eds.), *Cultures of Natural History* (Cambridge: Cambridge University Press, 1996), pp. 145–62.

Kraakman, Dorelies, 'Reading Pornography Anew: A Critical History of Sexual Knowledge for Girls in French Erotic Fiction, 1750–1840', *Journal of the History of Sexuality* 4 (1994), pp. 517–48.

Langford, Paul, *A Polite and Commercial People: England, 1727–1783* (Oxford: Oxford University Press, 1989).

Laqueur, Thomas, 'Orgasm, Generation, and the Politics of Reproductive Biology', *Representations* 14 (1986), pp. 1–41.

Making Sex: Body and Gender from the Greeks to Freud (Cambridge, Mass.: Harvard University Press, 1990).

Lefebvre, Henri, *The Production of Space*, trans. Donald Nicholson-Smith (1974; Oxford: Blackwell, 1991).

Lemay, H. R., 'Anthonius Guinerius and Medieval Gynecology', in J. Kirshner and S. F. Wemple (eds.), *Women of the Medieval World* (Oxford: Blackwell, 1985), pp. 317–36.

Lew, Joseph W., 'Lady Mary's Portable Seraglio', *Eighteenth-Century Studies* 24 (1991), pp. 432–50.

Liliequist, Jonas, 'Peasants against Nature: Crossing the Boundaries between Man and Animal in Seventeenth- and Eighteenth-Century Sweden', *Journal of the History of Sexuality* 3 (1991), pp. 393–423.

Lillywhite, Bryant, *London Coffee Houses: A Reference Book of Coffee Houses of the Seventeenth, Eighteenth and Nineteenth Centuries* (Allen and Unwin, 1963).

Littlewood, A. R., 'Romantic Paradises: The Role of the Garden in the Byzantine Romance', *Byzantine and Modern Greek Studies* 5 (1979), pp. 95–114.

Lloyd, Genevieve, *The Man of Reason: 'Male' and 'Female' in Western Philosophy* (Methuen, 1984).

Loth, David, *The Erotic in Literature: A Historical Survey of Pornography as Delightful as it is Indiscreet* (New York: Messner, 1961).

Love, Harold, *Scribal Publication in Seventeenth-Century England* (Oxford: Clarendon Press, 1993).

'Refining Rochester: Private Texts and Public Readers', *Harvard Library Bulletin* 7 (1996), pp. 40–9.

Lovell, Terry, 'Subjective Powers: Consumption, the Reading Public and Domestic Woman in Early Eighteenth-Century England', in John Brewer and Ann Bermingham (eds.), *The Consumption of Culture, 1600–1800: Image, Object, Text* (Routledge, 1995), pp. 23–41.

Mannix, Daniel P., *The Hell Fire Club* (Four Square, 1961).

Martensen, Robert, 'The Transformation of Eve: Women's Bodies, Medicine and Culture in Early Modern England', in Roy Porter and Mikulás Teich (eds.), *Sexual Knowledge, Sexual Science: The History of Attitudes to Sexuality* (Cambridge: Cambridge University Press, 1994), pp. 107–33.

Massey, Doreen, *Space, Place and Gender* (Cambridge: Polity Press, 1994).

Mather, F. C., 'Georgian Churchmanship Reconsidered: Some Variations in Anglican Public Worship, 1714–1830', *Journal of Ecclesiastical History* 36 (1985), pp. 255–83.

Maxted, Ian, *The London Book Trades, 1775–1800: A Preliminary Checklist of Members* (Folkestone: Dawson, 1977).

The London Book Trades, 1735–1775: A Checklist of Members in Trade Directories and in Musgrave's 'Obituary' (Exeter: Exeter Working Papers in British Book Trade History, University of Exeter, 1983).

McCalman, Iain, *Radical Underworld: Prophets, Revolutionaries and Pornographers in London, 1795–1840* (Cambridge: Cambridge University Press, 1988).

McCorison, Marcus A., 'Some Eighteenth-Century American Book Collectors, their Collections and their Legacies', in Carol Armbruster (ed.), *Publishing and Readership in Revolutionary France and America* (Westport, Conn.: Greenwood Press, 1993), pp. 191–204.

McCormick, Donald, *The Hell-Fire Club: The Story of the Amorous Knights of Wycombe* (Jarrolds, 1958).

McDowell, Paula, *The Women of Grub Street: Press, Politics, and Gender in the London Literary Marketplace, 1678–1730* (Oxford: Clarendon Press, 1998).

'Women and the Business of Print', in Vivien Jones (ed.), *Women and Literature in Britain, 1700–1800* (Cambridge: Cambridge University Press, 2000), pp. 135–54.

McKendrick, Neil, Brewer, John and Plumb, J. H. *The Birth of a Consumer Society: The Commercialisation of Eighteenth-Century England* (Europa, 1982).

McKeon, Michael, 'Historicizing Patriarchy: The Emergence of Gender Difference in England, 1660–1760', *Eighteenth-Century Studies* 28 (1995), pp. 295–322.

McLaren, Angus, 'The Pleasures of Procreation: Traditional and Biomedical Theories of Conception', in W. F. Bynum and Roy Porter (eds.), *William Hunter and the Eighteenth-Century Medical World* (Cambridge: Cambridge University Press, 1985), pp. 323–41.

McNay, Lois, *Foucault and Feminism: Power, Gender and the Self* (Cambridge: Polity Press, 1992).

McRae, Andrew, *God Speed the Plough: The Representation of Agrarian England, 1500–1660* (Cambridge: Cambridge University Press, 1996).

Mendelson, Sara and Crawford, Patricia, *Women in Early Modern England, 1550–1720* (Oxford: Clarendon Press, 1998).

Merchant, Carolyn, *The Death of Nature: Women, Ecology, and the Scientific Revolution* (Wildwood House, 1982).

Michaelson, Patricia Howell, 'Women in the Reading Circle', *Eighteenth-Century Life* 13 (1990), pp. 59–69.

Miller, Naomi, *Heavenly Caves: Reflections on the Garden Grotto* (Allen and Unwin, 1982).

Montgomery, Robert L., *Terms of Response: Language and Audience in Seventeenth-and Eighteenth-Century Theory* (Philadelphia: Pennsylvania State University Press, 1992).

Moulton, Ian Frederick, *Before Pornography: Erotic Writing in Early Modern England* (Oxford: Oxford University Press, 2000).

Mudge, Bradford K., *The Whore's Story: Women, Pornography, and the British Novel, 1684–1830* (Oxford: Oxford University Press, 2000).

Nead, Lynda, 'The Female Nude: Pornography, Art and Sexuality', *Signs* 15 (1990), pp. 323–35.

Nenadic, Stena, 'English Towns in the Creative Imagination', in Philip Waller (ed.), *The English Urban Landscape* (Oxford: Oxford University Press, 2000), pp. 316–41.

Newman, Louise M., 'Critical Theory and the History of Women', *Journal of Women's History* 2 (1991), pp. 58–68.

Niedermeier, Michael, '"Strolling under Palm Trees": Gardens – Love – Sexuality', *Journal of Garden History* 17 (1997), pp. 186–207.

Norberg, Kathryn, 'The Libertine Whore: Prostitution in French Pornography from Margot to Juliette', in Lynn Hunt (ed.), *The Invention of Pornography: Obscenity and the Origins of Modernity, 1500–1800* (New York: Zone Books, 1994), pp. 225–52.

Nussbaum, Felicity, *Torrid Zones: Maternity, Sexuality, and Empire in Eighteenth-Century English Narratives* (Baltimore: Johns Hopkins University Press, 1995).

O'Connell, Sheila, *The Popular Print in England* (London: British Museum Press, 1999).

O'Connor, Eugene Michael, *Symbolum Salacitatis: A Study of the God Priapus as a Literary Character* (Frankfurt am Main: Peter Lang, 1989).

Ogborn, Miles, *Spaces of Modernity: London's Geographies, 1680–1780* (New York: Guilford Press, 1998).

O'Neal, John C., *The Authority of Experience: Sensationist Theory in the French Enlightenment* (Philadelphia: Pennsylvania State University Press, 1996).

Orr, Bridget, 'Whore's Rhetoric and the Maps of Love: Constructing the Feminine in Restoration Erotica', in Clare Brant and Diane Purkiss (eds.), *Women, Texts and Histories, 1575–1760* (Routledge, 1992), pp. 195–216.

Osmond, Rosalie, *Mutual Accusation: Seventeenth-Century Body and Soul Dialogues in their Literary and Theological Context* (Toronto: University of Toronto Press, 1990).

Partridge, Burgo, *A History of Orgies*, 2nd edn. (1958; Spring Books, 1966).

Paster, Gail Kern, *The Body Embarrassed: Drama and the Disciplines of Shame in Early Modern England* (Ithaca, N.Y.: Cornell University Press, 1993).

Peakman, Julie, 'Medicine, the Body and the Botanical Metaphor in Erotica', in Kurt Bayertz and Roy Porter (eds.), *From Physico-Theology to Bio-Technology: Essays in the Social and Cultural History of Biosciences: A Festschrift for Mikuláš Teich* (Amsterdam: Clio Medica, 1998), pp. 197–223.

Mighty Lewd Books: The Development of Pornography in Eighteenth-Century England (Basingstoke: Palgrave, 2003).

Pearson, Jacqueline, *Women's Reading in Britain, 1750–1835: A Dangerous Recreation* (Cambridge: Cambridge University Press, 1999).

Perniola, Mario, 'Between Clothing and Nudity', in M. Feher (ed.), *Fragments for a History of the Human Body: Part Two* (New York: Zone Books, 1989), pp. 236–65.

Perry, Gill and Rossington, Michael (eds.), *Femininity and Masculinity in Eighteenth-Century Art and Culture* (Manchester: Manchester University Press, 1994).

Perry, Ruth, *Women, Letters and the Novel* (New York: AMS Press, 1980).

'Colonising the Breast: Sexuality and Maternity in Eighteenth-Century England', in John C. Fout (ed.), *Forbidden History: The State, Society, and the Regulation of Sexuality in Modern Europe* (Chicago: University of Chicago Press, 1992), pp. 107–37.

Pinchbeck, Ivy, *Women Workers and the Industrial Revolution, 1750–1850* (1930; Virago, 1981).

Pincus, Steve, '"Coffee Politicians Does Create": Coffeehouses and Restoration Political Culture', *Journal of Modern History* 67 (1995), pp. 807–34.

Plomer, Henry R., *A Dictionary of the Printers and Booksellers ... in England, Scotland and Ireland from 1668 to 1725* (Oxford: Oxford University Press, 1922).

Plomer, Henry R., Bushell, G. H. and Dix, E. R. McC., *A Dictionary of the Printers and Booksellers ... in England, Scotland and Ireland from 1726 to 1775* (Oxford: Oxford University Press, 1932).

Ponte, Alexander, 'Architecture and Phallocentrism in Richard Payne Knight's Theory', in Beatrix Colomina (ed.), *Sexuality and Space* (New York: Princeton Architectural Press, 1992), pp. 272–305.

Porter, Roy, *English Society in the Eighteenth Century* (Harmondsworth: Penguin, 1982).

'Mixed Feelings: The Enlightenment and Sexuality in Eighteenth-Century Britain', in Paul-Gabriel Boucé (ed.), *Sexuality in Eighteenth-Century Britain* (Manchester: Manchester University Press, 1982), pp. 1–27.

'"The Secrets of Generation Display'd": Aristotle's *Master-piece*', in Robert Purks Maccubbin (ed.), *'Tis Nature's Fault: Unauthorized Sexuality during the Enlightenment* (Cambridge: Cambridge University Press, 1987), pp. 1–21.

'*Barely Touching*: A Social Perspective on Mind and Body', in G. S. Rousseau (ed.), *The Languages of Psyche: Mind and Body in Enlightenment Thought* (Berkeley: University of California Press, 1990), pp. 45–80.

'The Literature of Sexual Advice before 1800', in Roy Porter and Mikulás Teich (eds.), *Sexual Knowledge, Sexual Science: The History of Attitudes to Sexuality* (Cambridge: Cambridge University Press, 1994), pp. 134–57.

'Enlightenment and Pleasure', in Roy Porter and Marie Mulvey Roberts (eds.), *Pleasure in the Eighteenth Century* (Basingstoke: Macmillan, 1996), pp. 1–18.

'Material Pleasures in the Consumer Society', in Roy Porter and Marie Mulvey Roberts (eds.), *Pleasure in the Eighteenth Century* (Basingstoke: Macmillan, 1996), pp. 19–35.

'Reading is Bad for Your Health', *History Today* 48 (1998), pp. 11–16.

Porter, Roy and Hall, Lesley, *The Facts of Life: The Creation of Sexual Knowledge in Britain, 1650–1950* (New Haven: Yale University Press, 1995).

Porter, Roy and Teich, Mikulás (eds.), *Sexual Knowledge, Sexual Science: The History of Attitudes to Sexuality* (Cambridge: Cambridge University Press, 1994).

Post, John D., *Food Shortage, Climatic Variability, and Epidemic Disease in Preindustrial Europe: The Mortality Peak in the Early 1740s* (Ithaca, N.Y.: Cornell University Press, 1985).

Potts, Alex, *Flesh and the Ideal: Winckelmann and the Origins of Art History* (New Haven: Yale University Press, 1994).

Pugh, Simon, *Garden-Nature-Language* (Manchester: Manchester University Press, 1988).

Radway, Janice A., *Reading the Romance: Women, Patriarchy, and Popular Literature* (1984; Verso, 1987).

Rainbolt, Martha, 'Their Ancient Claim: Sappho and Seventeenth- and Eighteenth-Century British Women's Poetry', *The Seventeenth Century* 12 (1997), pp. 111–34.

Ranum, Orest, 'The Refuges of Intimacy', in Roger Chartier (ed.), *A History of Private Life. Vol. III: Passions of the Renaissance*, trans. Arthur Goldhammer (Cambridge, Mass.: The Belknap Press of Harvard University Press, 1989), pp. 207–31.

Raven, James, 'Memorializing a London Bookscape: The Mapping and Reading of Paternoster Row and St Paul's Churchyard, 1695–1814', in R. C. Alston (ed.), *Order and Connexion. Studies in Bibliography and Book History: Selected Papers from the Munby Seminar, Cambridge, July 1994* (Cambridge: Brewer, 1997), pp. 175–200.

'New Reading Histories, Print Culture and the Identification of Change: The Case of Eighteenth-Century England', *Social History* 23 (1998), pp. 268–87.

'Historical Introduction: The Novel Comes of Age', in James Raven and Antonia Forster with the assistance of Stephen Bending (eds.), *The English Novel 1770–1829: A Bibliographical Survey of Prose Fiction Published in the British Isles. Volume I: 1770–1799*, general editors: Peter Garside, James Raven and Rainer Schöwerling (Oxford: Oxford University Press, 2000), pp. 15–121.

'The Book Trades', in Isabel Rivers (ed.), *Books and their Readers in Eighteenth-Century England: New Essays* (Leicester University Press, 2001), pp. 1–34.

Raven, James, Small, Helen and Tadmor, Naomi (eds.), *The Practice and Representation of Reading in England* (Cambridge: Cambridge University Press, 1996).

Richter, Simon, 'Wet-Nursing, Onanism, and the Breast in Eighteenth-Century Germany', *Journal of the History of Sexuality* 7 (1996), pp. 1–22.

Riley, Denise, *'Am I That Name?': Feminism and the Category of 'Women' in History* (Basingstoke: Macmillan, 1988).

Rivers, Isabel (ed.), *Books and their Readers in Eighteenth-Century England* (Leicester: Leicester University Press, 1982).

Robertson, Elizabeth, 'Medieval Medical Views of Women and Female Sexuality in the *Ancrene Wisse* and Julian of Norwich's *Showings*', in L. Lomperis and S. Stanbury (eds.), *Feminist Approaches to the Body in Medieval Literature* (Philadelphia: University of Pennsylvania Press, 1993), pp. 142–67.

Roche, Daniel, 'Printing, Books and Revolution', in Carol Armbruster (ed.), *Publishing and Readership in Revolutionary France and America* (Westport, Conn.: Greenwood Press, 1993), pp. 1–14.

Rodaway, Paul, *Sensuous Geographies: Body, Sense and Place* (Routledge, 1994).

Roe, Shirley A., *Matter, Life, and Generation: Eighteenth-Century Embryology and the Haller-Wolff Debate* (Cambridge: Cambridge University Press, 1981).

Roper, Lyndal, *Oedipus and the Devil: Witchcraft, Sexuality and Religion in Early Modern Europe* (Routledge, 1994), pp. 1–34.

Rose, Gillian, *Feminism and Geography: The Limits of Geographical Knowledge* (Cambridge: Polity Press, 1993).

Rousseau, G. S., 'The Pursuit of Homosexuality in the Eighteenth Century: "Utterly Confused Category" and/or Rich Repository', *Eighteenth-Century Life* 9 (1985), pp. 132–68.

'The Sorrows of Priapus', in his *Perilous Enlightenment: Pre- and Post-Modern Discourses. Sexual, Historical* (Manchester: Manchester University Press, 1991), pp. 65–108.

Review of Peter Wagner's *Erotica and the Enlightenment, Eighteenth-Century Fiction* 4 (1991–2), pp. 175–8.

Rousseau, G. S. and Porter, Roy, 'Introduction: Toward a Natural History of Mind and Body', in G. S. Rousseau (ed.), *The Languages of Psyche: Mind and Body in Enlightenment Thought* (Berkeley: University of California Press, 1990), pp. 3–44.

Rousseau, G. S. and Porter, Roy (eds.), *Sexual Underworlds of the Enlightenment* (Manchester: Manchester University Press, 1987).

Roworth, Wendy Wassyng, 'Anatomy is Destiny: Regarding the Body in the Art of Angelica Kauffman', in Gill Perry and Michael Rossington (eds.), *Femininity and Masculinity in Eighteenth-Century Art and Culture* (Manchester: Manchester University Press, 1994), pp. 41–62.

Runge, Laura L., 'Beauty and Gallantry: A Model of Polite Conversation Revisited', *Eighteenth-Century Life* 25 (2001), pp. 43–63.

Russett, Cynthia, *Sexual Science: The Victorian Construction of Womanhood* (Cambridge, Mass.: Harvard University Press, 1989).

Rykwert, Joseph, *The Dancing Column: On Order in Architecture* (Cambridge: Mass.: MIT Press, 1996).

Sainsbury, John, 'Wilkes and Libertinism', *Studies in Eighteenth-Century Culture* 26 (1998), pp. 151–74.

Schama, Simon, *Landscape and Memory* (HarperCollins, 1995).

Schiebinger, Londa, 'Skeletons in the Closet: The First Illustrations of the Female Skeleton in Eighteenth-Century Anatomy', in C. Gallagher and T. Laqueur (eds.), *The Making of the Modern Body: Sexuality and Society in the Nineteenth Century* (Berkeley: University of California Press, 1987), pp. 42–82.

The Mind Has No Sex? Women in the Origins of Modern Science (Cambridge, Mass.: Harvard University Press, 1989).

'The Anatomy of Difference: Race and Sex in Eighteenth-Century Science', *Eighteenth-Century Studies* 23 (1989–90), pp. 387–405.

Nature's Body: Gender in the Making of Modern Science (Boston: Beacon Press, 1993).

'Mammals, Primatology and Sexology', in Roy Porter and Mikuláš Teich (eds.), *Sexual Knowledge, Sexual Science: The History of Attitudes to Sexuality* (Cambridge: Cambridge University Press, 1994), pp. 184–209.

'Gender and Natural History', in N. Jardine, J. A. Secord and E. C. Spary (eds.), *Cultures of Natural History* (Cambridge: Cambridge University Press, 1996), pp. 163–77.

Scott, Joan Wallach, *Gender and the Politics of History* (New York: Columbia University Press, 1988).

Schneller, Beverly, 'Using Newspaper Advertisements to Study the Book Trade: A Year in the Life of Mary Cooper', in O. M. Brack (ed.), *Writers, Books, and Trade: An Eighteenth-Century English Miscellany for William B. Todd* (New York: AMS Press, 1994), pp. 123–43.

Sedgwick, Romney, *The History of Parliament: The House of Commons, 1715–1754*, 2 vols. (History of Parliament Trust, 1970), vol. II.

Senelick, Laurence, 'Mollies or Men of Mode? Sodomy and the Eighteenth-Century London Stage', *Journal of the History of Sexuality* 1 (1990), pp. 33–67.

Sharpe, Kevin, *Reading Revolutions: The Politics of Reading in Early Modern England* (New Haven: Yale University Press, 2000).

Shepard, Alexandra, 'Manhood, Credit and Patriarchy in Early Modern England', *Past and Present* 167 (2000), pp. 75–106.

Meanings of Manhood in Early Modern England (Oxford: Oxford University Press, 2003).

Sherman, William, *John Dee: The Politics of Reading and Writing in the English Renaissance* (Amherst: University of Massachusetts Press, 1995).

Shevelow, Kathryn, *Women and Print Culture: The Construction of Femininity in the Early Periodical* (Routledge, 1989).

Shoemaker, Robert B., *Gender in English Society, 1650–1850: The Emergence of Separate Spheres?* (Longman, 1998).

'Reforming Male Manners: Public Insult and the Decline of Violence in London, 1660–1740', in Tim Hitchcock and Michèle Cohen (eds.), *English Masculinities, 1660–1800* (Harlow: Longman, 1999), pp. 133–50.

'The Taming of the Duel: Masculinity, Honour and Ritual Violence in London, 1660–1800', *The Historical Journal* 45 (2002), pp. 525–45.

Silverman, Kaja, *Male Subjectivity at the Margins* (New York: Routledge, 1992).

Smart, Carol, *Feminism and the Power of the Law* (Routledge, 1989).

Smith, Charles Saumerez, *Eighteenth-Century Decoration: Design and the Domestic Interior in England* (Weidenfeld and Nicolson, 1993).

Smith, Nigel, *Literature and Revolution in England, 1640–1660* (New Haven: Yale University Press, 1994).

Snell, Keith, 'Agricultural Seasonal Unemployment, the Standard of Living, and Women's Work in the South and East, 1690–1860', *Economic History Review* 2nd series, 34 (1981), pp. 407–37.

Solkin, David H., *Painting for Money: The Visual Arts and the Public Sphere in Eighteenth-Century England* (New Haven: Yale University Press, 1992).

Spufford, Margaret, *Small Books and Pleasant Histories: Popular Fiction and its Readership in Seventeenth-Century England* (Cambridge: Cambridge University Press, 1981).

Staves, Susan, 'The Man of Mode and the Secrets of Genteel Identity', *Studies in Eighteenth-Century Culture* 19 (1989), pp. 117–28.

Married Women's Separate Property in England, 1660–1833 (Cambridge, Mass.: Harvard University Press, 1990).

'Fielding and the Comedy of Attempted Rape', in Beth Fowkes Tobin (ed.), *History, Gender & Eighteenth-Century Literature* (Athens: University of Georgia Press, 1994), pp. 86–112.

Stephan, Nancy Leys, 'Race, Gender, Science and Citizenship', *Gender and History* 10 (1998), pp. 26–52.

Stephen, Leslie (ed.), *Dictionary of National Biography* (Smith, 1885–1903).

Stevenson, David, *The Beggar's Benison: Sex Clubs of Enlightenment Scotland and their Rituals* (East Linton: Tuckwell Press, 2001).

Stewart, Philip, *Engraven Desire: Eros, Image and Text in the French Eighteenth Century* (Durham, N.C.: Duke University Press, 1992).

Stone, Lawrence, *The Family, Sex and Marriage in England, 1500–1800* (Weidenfeld and Nicolson, 1977).

Road to Divorce: England, 1530–1987 (Oxford: Oxford University Press, 1990).

'Libertine Sexuality in Post-Restoration England: Group Sex and Flagellation among the Middling Sort in Norwich in 1706–07', *Journal of the History of Sexuality* 2 (1992), pp. 511–26.

Uncertain Unions: Marriage in England, 1660–1753 (Oxford: Oxford University Press, 1992).

Broken Lives: Separation and Divorce in England, 1660–1857 (Oxford: Oxford University Press, 1993).

Stott, Rebecca, 'The Dark Continent: Africa as Female Body in Haggard's Adventure Fiction', *Feminist Review* 32 (1989), pp. 69–89.

Stroud, Dorothy, *The Architecture of Sir John Soane* (Studio, 1961).

Sturges, Robert S., *Medieval Interpretation: Models of Reading in Literary Narrative, 1100–1500* (Carbondale: Southern Illinois University Press, 1991).

Synnott, Anthony, 'Puzzling over the Senses: From Plato to Marx', in David Howes (ed.), *The Varieties of Sensory Experience: A Sourcebook in the Anthropology of the Senses* (Toronto: University of Toronto Press, 1991), pp. 61–76.

Tadmor, Naomi, '"In the Even My Wife Read to Me": Women, Reading and Household Life in the Eighteenth Century', in James Raven, Helen Small and Naomi Tadmor (eds.), *The Practice and Representation of Reading in England* (Cambridge: Cambridge University Press, 1996), pp. 162–74.

Taylor, Anne, *Bacchus in Romantic England: Writers and Drink, 1780–1830* (Basingstoke: Macmillan, 1999).

Thacker, Andrew, 'Foucault and the Writing of History', in Moya Lloyd and Andrew Thacker (eds.), *The Impact of Michel Foucault on the Social Sciences and the Humanities* (Basingstoke: Macmillan, 1997), pp. 29–52.

Thaddeus, Janice Farrar, 'Mary Delany, Model to the Age', in Beth Fowkes Tobin (ed.), *History, Gender & Eighteenth-Century Literature* (Athens: University of Georgia Press, 1994), pp. 113–40.

Theweleit, Klaus, *Male Fantasies. Volume I: Women, Floods, Bodies, History*, trans. Stephen Conway (1977; Cambridge: Polity Press, 1987).

Thirsk, Joan (ed.), *The Agrarian History of England and Wales* (Cambridge: Cambridge University Press, 1985), vol. V (II).

Thomas, Donald, *A Long Time Burning: The History of Literary Censorship in England* (Routledge, 1969).

Thomas, Keith, 'The Double Standard', *Journal of the History of Ideas* 20 (1959), pp. 195–216.

Thompson, Roger, *Unfit for Modest Ears: A Study of Pornographic, Obscene and Bawdy Works Written or Published in England in the Second Half of the Seventeenth Century* (Macmillan, 1979).

Thompson, W. and Annetts, J., *Soft-Core: A Content Analysis of Legally Available Pornography in Great Britain 1968–90 and the Implications of Aggression Research* (W. Thompson, 1990).

Thornton, Peter, *Authentic Decor: The Domestic Interior, 1620–1920* (Weidenfeld and Nicolson, 1984).

Timbs, John, *Club Life of London, with Anecdotes of the Clubs, Coffee-Houses and Taverns of the Metropolis during the 17th, 18th, and 19th Centuries*, 2 vols. (Richard Bentley, 1866).

Tosh, John, 'What Should Historians do with Masculinity? Reflections on Nineteenth-Century Britain', *History Workshop Journal* 33 (1994), pp. 179–202.

'The Old Adam and the New Man: Emerging Themes in the History of English Masculinities', in Tim Hitchcock and Michèle Cohen (eds.), *English Masculinities, 1660–1800* (Harlow: Longman, 1999), pp. 217–38.

Treadwell, Michael, 'London Trade Publishers 1675–1750', *Library* 6th series, 5 (1982), pp. 99–134.

'1695–1995: Some Tercentenary Thoughts on the Freedoms of the Press', *Harvard Library Bulletin* 7 (1996), pp. 3–19.

Tristram, Philippa, *Living Space in Fact and Fiction* (Routledge, 1989).

Trumbach, Randolph, *The Rise of the Egalitarian Family: Aristocratic Kinship and Domestic Relations in Eighteenth-Century England* (New York: Academic Press, 1978).

'Modern Prostitution and Gender in *Fanny Hill*: Libertine and Domesticated Fantasy', in G. S. Rousseau and Roy Porter (eds.), *Sexual Underworlds of the Enlightenment* (Manchester: Manchester University Press, 1987), pp. 67–85.

'The Birth of the Queen: Sodomy and the Emergence of Gender Equality in Modern Culture, 1660–1750', in M. B. Duberman, M. Vicinus and G. Chauncey (eds.), *Hidden from History: Reclaiming the Gay and Lesbian Past* (Penguin, 1989), pp. 129–40.

'Sex, Gender, and Sexual Identity in Modern Culture: Male Sodomy and Female Prostitution in Enlightenment London', *Journal of the History of Sexuality* 2 (1991), pp. 186–203.

'Erotic Fantasy and Male Libertinism in Enlightenment England', in Lynn Hunt (ed.), *The Invention of Pornography: Obscenity and the Origins of Modernity, 1500–1800* (New York: Zone Books, 1993), pp. 253–82.

Sex and the Gender Revolution. Volume I: Heterosexuality and the Third Gender in Enlightenment London (Chicago: University of Chicago Press, 1998).

Turner, Cheryl, *Living by the Pen: Women Writers in the Eighteenth Century* (Routledge, 1992).

Turner, David, '"Nothing is so Secret but Shall Be Revealed": The Scandalous Life of Robert Foulkes', in Tim Hitchcock and Michèle Cohen (eds.), *English Masculinities, 1660–1800* (Harlow: Longman, 1999), pp. 169–92.

Fashioning Adultery: Gender, Sex and Civility in England, 1660–1740 (Cambridge: Cambridge University Press, 2002).

Turner, James G. (ed.), *Sexuality and Gender in Early Modern Europe: Institutions, Texts, Images* (Cambridge: Cambridge University Press, 1993).

Varey, Richard, *Space and the Eighteenth-Century English Novel* (Cambridge: Cambridge University Press, 1990).

Vickery, Amanda, 'Golden Age to Separate Spheres? A Review of the Categories and Chronology of English Women's History', *The Historical Journal* 36 (1993), pp. 383–414.

‘Women and the World of Goods: A Lancashire Consumer and her Possessions', in John Brewer and Roy Porter (eds.), *Consumption and the World of Goods* (Routledge, 1993), pp. 274–301.

The Gentleman's Daughter: Women's Lives in Georgian England (New Haven: Yale University Press, 1998).

Wagner, Peter, 'The Discourse on Sex – or Sex as Discourse: Eighteenth-Century Medical and Paramedical Erotica', in G. S. Rousseau and Roy Porter (eds.), *Sexual Underworlds of the Enlightenment* (Manchester: Manchester University Press, 1987), pp. 46–68.

Eros Revived: Erotica of the Enlightenment in England and France (Secker and Warburg, 1988).

‘Anticatholic Erotica in Eighteenth-Century England', in Wagner (ed.), *Erotica and the Enlightenment* (Frankfurt: Peter Lang, 1991), pp. 166–209.

Wagner, Peter (ed.), *Erotica and the Enlightenment* (Frankfurt: Peter Lang, 1991).

Walker, Garthine, 'Rereading Rape and Sexual Violence in Early Modern England', *Gender and History* 10 (1998), pp. 1–25.

Wall, Cynthia, *The Literary and Cultural Spaces of Restoration London* (Cambridge: Cambridge University Press, 1998).

Walsh, Linda, '"Arms to be Kissed a Thousand Times": Reservations about Lust in Diderot's Art Criticism', in Gill Perry and Michael Rossington (eds.), *Femininity and Masculinity in Eighteenth-Century Art and Culture* (Manchester: Manchester University Press, 1994), pp. 162–83.

Weatherill, Lorna, *Consumer Behaviour and Material Culture in Britain, 1660–1760* (Routledge, 1988).

Weil, Rachel, 'Sometimes a Sceptre is Only a Sceptre: Pornography and Politics in Restoration England', in Lynn Hunt (ed.), *The Invention of Pornography: Obscenity and the Origins of Modernity* (New York: Zone Books, 1994), pp. 125–53.

Weisser, Susan Ostrov, *A 'Craving Vacancy': Women and Sexual Love in the British Novel, 1740–1880* (New York: New York University Press, 1997).

Wigley, Mark, 'Untitled: The Housing of Gender', in Beatrix Colomina (ed.), *Sexuality and Space* (New York: Princeton Architectural Press, 1992), pp. 326–89.

Williams, Carolyn D., *Pope, Homer and Manliness: Some Aspects of Eighteenth-Century Classical Learning* (Routledge, 1993).

Wilson, Adrian, *The Making of Man-Midwifery: Childbirth in England, 1660–1770* (University College London Press, 1995).

Wilson, Colin, 'Literature and Pornography', in Alan Bold (ed.), *The Sexual Dimension in Literature* (Vision, 1982), pp. 202–19.

Wilson, Penelope, 'Classical Poetry and the Eighteenth-Century Reader', in Isabel Rivers (ed.), *Books and their Readers in Eighteenth-Century England* (Leicester: Leicester University Press, 1982), pp. 69–96.

Withers, Charles W. J. and Livingstone, David N. (eds.), *Geography and Enlightenment* (Chicago: University of Chicago Press, 1999).

Wrightson, Keith, 'Estates, Degrees and Sorts: Changing Perceptions of Society in Tudor and Stuart England', in Penelope Corfield (ed.), *Language, History and Class* (Oxford: Basil Blackwell, 1991), pp. 30–52.

Wroth, Warwick, *The London Pleasure Gardens of the Eighteenth Century* (Macmillan, 1896).

Wyngaard, Amy, 'Libertine Spaces: Anonymous Crowds, Secret Chambers, and Urban Corruption in Rétif de la Bretonne', *Eighteenth-Century Life* 22 (1998), pp. 104–22.

Yeazell, Ruth Bernard, *Fictions of Modesty: Women and Courtship in the English Novel* (Chicago: University of Chicago Press, 1991).

UNPUBLISHED THESES

McGowan, Antony J., 'The Sublime Machine: Conceptions of Masculine Beauty, 1750–1850', PhD thesis, Open University (1996).

Moulton, Ian Frederick, 'Before Pornography: Explicitly Erotic Writing in Early Modern England', PhD thesis, Columbia University (1995).

Winston, Michael Edmund, 'From Literature to Medicine to Philosophy: Sexuality in Eighteenth-Century France', PhD thesis, Emory University (1995).

Index

abortion, 121
Adam's Tail, 129
adultery, 171
Adventures of a Corkscrew, 140
Adventures of a Rupee, 61
advertisements, 54–5
age, 138–9, 149–50
agriculture, 3, 111–13
amatory fiction, 29–33, 59, 198
America, 143
Annales, 7
Anstruther, Scotland, 63
Arbor Vitae, 39, 43, 83, 89–94, 129, 138
Aristotelian medicine, 81–9
Aristotle's Masterpiece, 16–18, 23, 97
Armstrong, John
    'The Oeconomy of Love', 44, 76, 140, 144, 219
Armstrong, John Warnford, 61
Astell, Mary, 46, 116
Athenian Mercury, 63

Bacchanalian Magazine, The, 52, 56, 133
Ballaster, Ros, 29
Barrell, John, 71
Barry, Jonathan, 39
bedchambers, 167–8, 172
beds, 166, 190
Beef-steak society, 61
Beggar's Benison, 63–6, 69, 71, 74, 96
Behn, Aphra, 29, 137
Belsey, Catherine, 2
Bergstrom, Carson, 149
Bermingham, Anne, 71
Berry, Helen, 62, 75
Bold, Alan, 21
Bordo, Susan, 125, 216
Boswell, James, 74
botany, 3, 22–3, 51, 53, 55, 57, 82–5, 89–94, 112–16, 121, 135–7, 141, 186; *see also* Bradley, Richard
Boucher, François, 150

Bradley, Richard, 93, 136
Braudy, Leo, 200
breastfeeding, 118
breasts, 94–5, 113, 117–19
Breitenberg, Mark, 123, 125
Bretonne, Rétif de la, 151, 152
Brewer, John, 40
Burke, Peter, 7
Butler, Gerald, 45
Butler, Judith, 9, 98

Cannon, John, 46
Carter, Phillip, 11, 74
cartography, 177, 181–5
Catholicism, *see* Roman Catholicism
censorship, 3, 19, 36–8, 41
Certeau, Michel de, 177
change, 6–8, 10–12, 74–5, 79–80, 88, 101, 122–3, 125, 171, 223–4
Chartier, Roger, 38
Chinese Tale, A, 16, 23, 27–8, 48, 131, 188, 203
Clark, Anna, 197
Classics, 55–8, 68, 71, 113, 114, 118
Cleland, John, 19, 24, 26, 28, 48, 54, 131, 200
clitoris, 110, 112
clothing, 23
clubs, 61–2; *see also* Beggar's Benison; Medmenham Monks
coffee houses, 11, 61–3, 71
    and gender, 62–3
Cohen, Michèle, 75
Cole, Thomas
Comerford, James, 61
Compleat Sett of the Charts of the Coasts of Merryland, A, 37
conception, 81–9, 112, 122, 134
condoms, 109
consent, 167, 192–4, 209, 215; *see also* rape
Consummation: Or, The Rape of Adonis, 23, 143, 180
contraception, 121

conversation, 71
Cook, James, 139
Cooper, Mary, 42–3
Cooper, Thomas, 42
Cosway, Richard, 69, 191
Cotton, Charles
    Erotopolis, 22, 43, 103–5, 110, 111,
        180
Crewe, Emma, 49
cross-dressing, 99
cultural history, 2–3, 7
curiosity, 186
Curll, Edmund, 13, 19, 37

D'Eon, Chevalier, 99, 129
Darnton, Robert, 25, 61, 224
Dashwood, Sir Francis, 66, 68, 170; *see also*
    Hell-Fire club
Defoe, Daniel, 19
DeJean, Joan, 21
demography, 139, 142–5
Descartes, René, 199
Description of the Temple of Venus, A, 27, 98,
    99, 156, 179, 188, 203, 208, 214
Did You Ever See Such Damned Stuff?, 48,
    185, 203, 209, 219
dildo, 25, 134, 149
Dineley, John, 171
diseases of Women with Child, The, see
    Mauriceau, Francis
domesticity, 4, 10–11, 103, 117, 196
drinking, 28, 36, 52, 64–5, 73–5
Dublin, 71
Duden, Barbara, 81

effeminacy, 60, 79, 98, 166
Electrical Eel, The, 44, 124, 211
electricity, 22, 87, 211
*Elegy on the Lamented Death of the Electrical
    Eel, An*, 130, 132, 191
England, 132
Enlightenment, 1, 3, 124, 199–201
erotic culture, 1–4, 13, 18–19, 35–77, 88–9,
    222–3
    and politeness, 75–6
erotica, 1–2, 8, 12–33
    books, 38–76
    definition, 20
    producers of, 42–4
Erotopolis. The Present State of Bettyland, see
    Cotton, Charles
eyes, 212–15

Fair Quaker, The, 168
Fanny Hill, see Cleland, John

Fergus, Jan, 49
fertility, 97, 111–20, 133–9, 141; *see also*
    conception; pregnancy
Festival of Love, The, 39, 44, 54, 62, 188
Fifteen Comforts of Cuckoldom, The, 51
Fifteen Comforts of Matrimony, The, 50
Fifteen Plagues of a Maiden-Head, The, 37
Findlen, Paula, 21
Fish, Stanley, 55
Fissell, Mary, 79
flagellation, 138
Fletcher, Anthony, 74, 79
Forty Select Poems, 188
Foucault, Michel, 8–9
Foyster, Elizabeth, 11
France, French, 41, 58, 92, 114, 133, 140–2,
    150, 156, 187, 199, 200
    French writing, 21, 25–7, 35, 45, 47, 57,
        148, 152, 204, 217; *see also L'Ecole des
        Filles*
Frappier-Mazur, Lucienne, 21
Freemasonry, 66
Fruit-Shop, The, 50, 52, 86, 95, 98, 114, 133,
    139, 143, 144, 150, 152, 184–5, 190, 204,
    206, 207, 212, 213
Frutex Vulvaria, 43, 82, 83, 88–91, 112,
    119–21, 141–2, 207
Fuseli, Henry, 49

Galenic medicine, 78, 81–2, 84, 86, 88, 90,
    117
gardens, 111, 114, 128, 147, 170, 172, 180,
    185; *see also* pastoral
Geertz, Clifford, 2
gender history, 6–10
genital structure, 89–94
*Genuine Memoirs of the Celebrated Miss
    Maria Brown, The*, 28, 48, 96, 140,
    187
geography, 3, 64–5, 106, 132–3, 147, 175–7
Goulemot, Jean-Marie, 26, 45–6, 59
Gowing, Laura, 80
Graham, James, 58
Grand Tour, 176
Great News from Hell, 109, 114
Greek, *see* Classics
Gregory, Dr, *Father's Legacy to His
    Daughters*, 214, 219
Grosz, Elizabeth, 171
grottoes, 157–8, 165, 171
Grove, Henry and Esther, 171

hair
    beards, 95–6, 99
    pubic hair, 96–7

Hall, Lesley, 125
Hamilton, William, 69
Harris' List of Covent Garden Ladies, 37
Harvey, William, 83
Haywood, Eliza, 29, 31
Hell-Fire club, 66–8, 74, 170
    Limerick Hell-Fire club, 71–3
Héritier-Augé, Françoise, 120
heterosexuality, 65, 81, 89, 91, 94, 98–100,
    121, 129, 139, 141, 145, 211–12
Hilaria, 52, 94, 108
Hitchcock, Tim, 66, 79, 80
Hogarth, William, 71
homoeroticism, 65
homosexuality, 211; *see also* lesbianism
homosociability, 36, 61–76, 145
Hook, Captain, 47
Hottentot Venus, 59, 97
Hudson, Nicholas, 78
Hume, David, 199
humour, 33, 51–2, 55–6, 59, 66–7, 127, 130,
    176, 222
humours, *see* Galenic medicine
Hunt, Lynn, 19–21
Hunt, Margaret, 42
Hunter, John, 87

imagination, 202–5, 210
impotence, 137–8
intertextuality, 3–4, 53, 55–6, 198
Ireland, 132
Iser, Wolfgang, 45
Italy, Italian, 114, 128, 132, 140

Jacob, Margaret, 201, 217
Jason, Sir Robert, 171
Johnson, Samuel, 58, 100, 192–4, 201,
    211
Jones, Vivien, 46
Jordanova, Ludmilla, 185

Kauffman, Angelica, 128
Kent, England, 132
Kent, William, 157
Keuls, Eva, 170
Kick Him Jenny, 159, 166, 194–5, 210,
    218
Kick Him Nan, 194–5
kissing, 205, 210
Kit-Kat club, 62, 71
Knight, Richard Payne, 69
Kraakman, Dorelies, 201, 217

L'Ecole des Filles, 26–7, 76
L'homme plante, *see* Mettrie, Offray de la

Lady's Dressing Room, The, 156
Lady's Magazine, The, *see* women's
    magazines
Langford, Paul, 1
Laqueur, Thomas, 5–7, 78–82, 84, 89, 125,
    173, 200
Larpent, Anna, 57
Latin, *see* Classics
Leapor, Mary, 56
Lefebvre, Henri, 151
lesbianism, 98
Licensing Act (1695), 36
Limerick, 71; *see also* Hell-Fire club
Linnaeus, Carl, 22, 113
Lister, Anne, 9, 56
literacy, 39
Little Merlin's Cave, 51, 88, 91–2, 106, 110,
    116, 157
Locke, John, 199
London Stationers' Company, 37
London, 41
love, 29, 137
luxury, 59–60, 68, 150, 166

Manchester, England, 63
Manley, Mary Delarivier, 19, 29–31
Manningham, Richard, 181, 188
Man-Plant, The, 43, 83, 110, 113, 118,
    142–4
Martensen, Robert, 89
masculinity, 10–12, 36, 73–7, 122–3, 125–7,
    145, 173–4, 196–7, 217, 224; *see also*
    restraint
Masonry, *see* Freemasonry
masturbation, 16, 25, 46, 52, 65, 144,
    203
materialism, 199–203
maternalization, *see* motherhood
Mauriceau, Francis
    The Diseases of Women with Child, 83, 84,
    181–4
McDowell, Paula, 42, 43
medicine, 177, 181–5, 188–190; *see also*
    science
Medmenham Monks, *see* Hell-Fire club
Memoirs of a Woman of Pleasure, *see* Cleland,
    John
men
    male bodies, 7, 178, 180, 207, 210–11,
    215–17
    see also reading: and men; penis
menstruation, 81, 119–20
Mercenary Lover, The, *see* Haywood, Eliza
Merchant, Carolyn, 102
Merlin's cave, 157, 158

Merryland Displayed, see Stretser, Thomas
Merryland, 2, 64, 91, 168; *see also* Stretser,
    Thomas
metaphor, 22–4, 106, 124, 184
Mettrie, Offray de la
    L'homme plante, 84
midwifery, 59, 134, 181
Miller, Phillip, 22
Milton, John
    Paradise Lost, 150
Mimosa; or, the Sensitive Plant, 44, 129, 130,
    135
modernity, 1, 146–7, 173
modesty, 59, 97, 150, 165, 196, 217–20
Montagu, Lady Mary Wortley, 56, 58
Moore, John, 128
morality, 30–2, 59–60, 68
Morris, Charles, 43, 62, 143
motherhood, 103, 118–19, 122; *see also*
    breastfeeding; breasts
Mudge, Bradford, 18, 19

narrative, 26–8, 32
nation, nationhood, 126, 127, 139–45
nature, 95, 98, 102, 131, 171, 209
New Atalantis, The, see Manley, Mary
    Delarivier
New Description of Merryland, A, see Stretser,
    Thomas
novels, 18–19, 30, 45, 46, 49, 55, 176, 218;
    see also Richardson, Samuel

'The Oeconomy of Love', *see* Armstrong,
    John
Old Serpent's Reply to the Electrical Eel, The,
    130, 132, 134
Omaih, 139
One Hundred and Seventy-Seven, 139
one-sex model of sexual difference, 5–6,
    10, 78–102, 105; *see also* Laqueur,
    Thomas
oral sex, 206
orgasm
    female, 81–2, 88, 102, 111
    see also conception
Orr, Bridget, 103
ovaries, 84
ovid, 16–18, 31, 47, 124

Parsons, Humphrey, 73
passionless woman, 4, 10, 49, 102, 104; *see*
    also sexual desire: women
pastoral, 111, 149–51
patriarchy, 10, 21, 88–9, 126–7, 225; *see also*
    power

penis, 94–5, 99–100, 108, 112, 118, 173, 178;
    see also genital structure
Pepys, Samuel, 45, 76
Perry, James, 44
picturesque, 179–80
Pleasures that Please on Reflection, The,
    62
Polite Road to an Estate, The, 112
politeness, 1, 10–11, 62, 71, 74, 196, 223; *see*
    also refinement
politics, 6–7, 146, 224–5
population, *see* demography
pornography, 13, 18–29, 35–6, 45–6, 54,
    62, 124, 131, 146, 148, 165, 200, 216,
    225
Porter, Roy, 1, 199
Potent Ally, The, 73
power, 146, 196, 224–5
pregnancy, 120–1
print culture, 3, 13–19
privacy, 151, 158–9, 172
    and reading, 45, 46, 49–50, 66–7
Prostitutes of Quality, The, 54, 55, 110, 133,
    188
prostitutes, prostitution, 36, 55, 64, 66,
    104–5, 109, 168, 187, 213, 218, 221
psychoanalysis, 125–6, 150
publicity
    and reading, 46–7, 61–2, 64, 66–7, 76

Queen Caroline, 157

race, 78–9, 95–6, 139–41, 144, 191
Rake of Taste, The, 140, 157, 158, 219
Ranum, Orest, 151
rape, 21, 30–1, 133, 146, 165, 192–7, 209; *see*
    also sexual violence
Raven, James, 36, 39
reading
    erotica 3, 9–10, 13, 18–19, 30, 35–77
    and men, 54–8, 61–77
    and women, 46–50, 54, 56–9, 76–7
    see also literacy; privacy; publicity
refinement, 36
religion, 55, 64, 67–8, 86, 129–30, 148–9,
    199, 204–5; *see also* Roman
    Catholicism
restraint, 1–2, 33, 36, 59–60, 65–6, 68,
    214–15, 218, 222
Richardson, Samuel, 19, 28–9, 48, 165
Richter, Simon, 118
Riddle, A, 39, 157, 210
Roach, James, 37
Rochester, Earl of (John Wilmot), 16–18, 27,
    31, 55, 137

Rodaway, Paul, 170
Roman Catholicism, 204
Rowlandson, Thomas, 191
Royal Society, 87

Sade, Marquis de, 25
Saussure, Cesar de, 62
Schama, Simon, 171
Schiebinger, Londa, 78
science, 3, 53, 55, 79, 82–9, 101, 124,
    147, 177, 185; see also
    Enlightenment
Scotland, 165; see also Anstruther,
    Scotland
Secret History of Pandora's Box, The, 42, 61,
    110, 157
seduction, 31–2, 47–8
self-control, see restraint
semen, 81, 121, 134, 206, 208
sensationism, 199, 208
senses, 199–217
separate spheres, 4, 79, 102–3, 147, 172
Seventeen Hundred and Seventy-Seven, 23,
    218
sexual desire, 98–100, 201–21
    men, 197
    women, 4, 46–50, 76, 102–11, 118–19,
        121–2, 173–4, 213–14, 221
    see also orgasm
sexual difference, 3–7, 10, 114, 116–17, 120,
    122, 125, 197, 222
sexual freedom, 1
sexual pleasure, 59–60, 81–2, 167–70, 222–3;
    see also orgasm
sexual violence, 9, 20–1, 150, 165, 167–8,
    174, 192–8, 209–10, 212, 220; see also
    rape
Shoemaker, Robert B., 79
sight, 208, 212–17
smell, 206–8
Soane, Sir John, 162
Society of Dilettanti, 68–71, 73
sodomy, 79, 94–5, 121, 140
Solkin, David, 71
sound, 208–10
Souricière, La, 202, 213
Spain, 132, 142, 148
Spectator, The, 58
Spufford, Margaret, 49
Spy on Mother Midnight, A, 25–6, 50, 99, 144,
    149, 158, 205, 208
Stewart, Phillip, 18, 26, 193
Stone, Lawrence, 61, 126, 172, 199
Stretser, Thomas

A New Description of Merryland, 22, 37,
    43, 48, 50–3, 57, 64, 65, 91, 103–6, 108,
    110, 112, 117, 119, 120, 122, 124, 168,
    176, 181–4, 188, 213
Merryland Displayed, 48, 53, 124
see also Merryland
Surprize, The, 52, 159, 166, 167, 190,
    203

taste, 205–6
Tatler, 58
tea, 48
Teague-Root Display'd, 22, 100, 131, 132,
    211
Thérèse Philosophe, 25
Thistlewood, Thomas, 76
Thomas, Donald, 36
Thornton, Bonnel, 62
Torpedo, The, 108, 211
touch, 210–12, 215–16
Towneley, Charles, 69
travel writing, 3, 53, 55, 57, 59, 64–5, 106,
    128, 176, 187; see also cartography
two-sex model of sexual difference, 5–6, 10,
    78–102, 146, 173, 200; see also Laqueur,
    Thomas

Unsex'd Females, The, 49
uterus, 112, 113, 117, 122

venereal disease, 109
Venus in the Cloister, 37
Vesalius, 89
vigour, 132–3, 174, 197, 214
violence, 175; see also rape; sexual
    violence
Voyage to Lethe, A, 13, 24, 50, 52, 61,
    133, 140, 162, 168, 174, 184, 187,
    206
vulva, 99–100

Wagner, Peter, 12, 19–21, 25, 43
Walker, Garthine, 146–7, 193, 197
Walpole, Horace, 68
war, 126, 141–3
Ward, Edward, 43
Watson, William, 22
Wellington, Duke of, 128
Wemyss, Betsy, see Great News from Hell
Whim!, The, 132, 162, 213
Why and the Wherefore, The, 99–100,
    108, 119, 131, 133, 143, 178, 207,
    210
widows, 130

Wilberforce, William, 38
Wilkes, John, 23, 67
Wilmot, John, *see* Rochester, Earl of
Wilson, Colin, 21
Wisdom Reveal'd, 88, 89, 93, 124, 129, 132,
    134, 136, 137, 216
Wit's Magazine, The, 15
women, 4–6
    and agency, 49, 102, 121–2, 173, 200–1,
    215, 217

female bodies, 7, 65, 125, 128, 131–3, 135,
    156–8, 162–71, 177–86, 206–7, 210–11
    see also amatory fiction; domesticity;
    erotica: producers of; passionless woman;
    reading: and women; sexual desire:
    women
women's history, 6–10
women's magazines, 31–3
Worsdale, James, 71
Wyngaard, Amy, 151

Do you think her theses changed greatly a some pt?

Masculinity + homosexual - when was this present.

~~Should Hand~~ R. Sex has been criticized

by some for not addressing

John Wilkes work in erotica ↔ but dealing w/ him in social club setting.

book too textual / internal

- weakness - more social club discussion

more social club b/c book too textual/internal

- not taking on Wilkes?

9 780521 055727